D1523234

WITHDRAWN

Character and Personality in the Novels of William Faulkner

For Rósa

Character and Personality in the Novels of William Faulkner

A Study in Psychostylistics

Ineke Bockting

University Press of America Inc.
Lanham • New York • London

Copyright © 1995 by
University Press of America,® Inc.
4720 Boston Way
Lanham, Maryland 20706

3 Henrietta Street
London, WC2E 8LU England

Library of Congress Cataloging-in-Publication Data

Bockting, Ineke
Character and personality in the novels of William Faulkner : a study in
psychostylistics / Ineke Bockting
p.   cm.
Includes bibliographical references (p.   ) and index.
1. Faulkner, William, 1897-1962–Knowledge–Psychology.   2. Characters
and characteristics in literature.   3. Faulkner, William, 1897-1962–
Characters.   4. Personality in literature.   5. Psychology in literature.
I. Title.
PS3511.A86Z633   1995
813'.52–dc20   94-45344 CIP

ISBN 0-8191-9849-8 (cloth: alk paper)

Contents

Preface

The work before you is not a study of William Faulkner, the author, or of his home town of Oxford, Mississippi. Rather, I have focused here on the 'people' that Faulkner created in his four major psychological novels: *The Sound and the Fury* (1929); *As I Lay Dying* (1930); *Light in August* (1932) and *Absalom, Absalom!* (1936). I have tried not to write *about* these 'people,' either as literary characters or as human beings, but to let them come alive in their own time, through their own texts. The term *psychostylistics* in my title testifies to the fact that this has involved a coming together and at times an actual 'intertwining' of the textual approaches of stylistics and psychoanalysis. This is also not a systematic study, therefore, of stylistics or psychoanalysis, as I have used from both fields only that which could illuminate, or problematize, Faulkner's art. I have generally avoided taking a stand against other scholars where this would have led me away from the characters, but I have made use of previous criticism where this could sharpen the points I was trying to make. I hope I have illustrated, in any case, that critical practice with regard to characterization can benefit from an interdisciplinary approach.

In the first chapter of my work, I propose a way of looking at the literary character that is faithful both to its realness and its constructedness. In the next chapters, I give an inside view of the textual process of characterization, as this takes place in some of Faulkner's most memorable 'people.' Starting point is the individual's own endeavors to create and sustain a 'self' through his text. As it turns out, however, Faulkner gave his 'people' less and less text of their own; that is, while Benjy Compson is still characterized completely through his own text, Charles Bon, on the other end of the spectrum, has virtually no text of his own. In other words, the text of the self becomes more and more openly a text created by the other—the family, society, history—in the course of the novels that my study includes. My own perspective, meanwhile, is that of the outsider, who looks at the Yoknapatawpha county and the larger South with curiosity, compassion and admiration. Faulkner considered such an outside perspective important, as his introduction of Shrevlin McCannon as speaker in *Absalom, Absalom!* indicates. It cannot, however, avoid conveying something about the observer herself as well as about the observed.

Even though this is not a study, then, of Faulkner himself, or of his home town, the times I was able to spend in Oxford have been of great value to me. Visiting the places that Faulkner frequented, whether it be the Oxford square, Taylor's grocery, or Sardis

Lake, taught me to understand his characters better. Walking the road that comes into Oxford from Alabama, I could visualize the smoke stack that Lena Grove in *Light in August* saw when she first reached the town. The journey of the Bundrens in *As I Lay Dying* came alive for me when James York showed me the place where a relative of his was buried in the back yard because the flooded river prevented the family from reaching the cemetery. I treasure all the stories that the people of Oxford shared with me. To mention only a few: Miss Bessie Sumners' memories of the first-grade school-teacher she and Faulkner shared; Aston Holley's remembrance of his friendship with Faulkner's stepson Malcolm; Howard Duvall's recollection of Faulkner's dismay when he hesitantly asked him to sign his copy of *Intruder in the Dust*; and Charles Nelson's wonderful story of the time when Faulkner put one dollar's worth of gas in his father's tank to repay him for driving him to the place where he had to give a speech, and even giving the speech for him.

Much of the actual work on this book was done at the University of Mississippi at Oxford. I thank Donald Kartiganer and Bill Ferris for discussing Faulkner and the South with me, and for their interest in my work. I want to extend my gratitude also to Larry McCay for providing lodgings for me at the Alumni House on campus for extended periods, and to the nice people working for him, as well as to Square Books for a wonderful place to read and write. I was fortunate to be able to work at other universities as well. My appreciation goes to the Freie Universität of Berlin, Germany, for a grant to do research at the John F. Kennedy-Institut; to the Alderman Library of the University of Virginia at Charlottesville, and to the Center for Faulkner Studies at Southeast Missouri State University at Cape Girardeau, for opening their files for me. I am especially grateful to Robert Hamblin of Cape Girardeau for his encouragement. I also thank Lee Jenkins, Jay Martin, Norman Holland, Bernard Paris and Bertram Wyatt-Brown, who showed an interest in my work, discussed it with me or read parts of it.

Closer to home I must express my gratitude to my colleagues, some of them former teachers, John Neubauer, Gene Moore, Rob Kroes, Joost Baneke, Peter Verdonk, Frederike van der Leek, Marijke Rudnik and Paul Werth, all of whom read the manuscript more than once, as well as to Ton Hoenselaars, Dineke Ten Hoorn Boer, Jan Willem Bomhof and Hans Bockting.

Closer still, my thanks go to my two sons, Efraïm and Herre Trujillo, who found me pretty preoccupied at times, to my daughter-in-law Helga Laufey Finnbogadóttir, and, of course, to Ad, who has been through all the stages with me.

1

The Literary Character:
Between Life and Linguistic Sign

any character that you write takes charge of his own behavior. You can't make him do things once he comes alive

William Faulkner reminded his audience again and again, in talks and interviews, that to him his characters were *real*: 'flesh-and-blood people that will stand up and cast a shadow' (Gwynn and Blotner 1959:47), and he spoke of them as 'people that I have known all my life in the country I was born in' (Fant and Ashley 1964:96f.). Faulkner believed in the self-sufficiency and independence of the character. As he put it: 'there is always a point in the book where the characters themselves rise up and take charge and finish the job' (Meriwether and Millgate 1980:244). To him this extended even beyond the actual work: 'when the book is finished, that character is not done, he still is going on at some new devilment that sooner or later I will find out about and write about' (Gwynn and Blotner 1959:78).

Other writers have expressed a similar belief in the self-determination of the literary character. T.S. Eliot, for instance, stressed the powers of the character when he explained that 'a bit of the author may be the germ of a character, but that, too, a certain character may call out latent potentialities in the author' (Gordon 1988:28). E.M. Forster pointed to the necessary balance of powers between the author and his character: 'The characters arrive when evoked, but full of the spirit of mutiny. For they have these numerous parallels with people like ourselves, they try to live their own lives and are consequently often engaged in treason against the main scheme of the book. They "run away," they "get out of hand";... if they are given complete freedom they kick the book to pieces, and if they are kept too sternly in check they revenge themselves by dying' (1988:72).

The literary theorist William Harvey focused explicitly on the *personality* of the literary character.[1] As he put it: the author 'must accept his characters as asserting their human individuality and uniqueness in the face of all ideology (including his own limited point of view)' (1965:25). Ilham Dilman, in the same spirit, argued that the

---

1 Literary theory is hampered by a confusion between *character* as the imaginary 'person' of the novel and *character* as his or her psychological make-up or disposition. To avoid this confusion, I will speak of the former as the (literary) character and the latter as his or her personality. In psychiatry and psychology personality has traditionally been understood as the more consciously presented foreground, superficial mannerism, or social mask (the form), and character as the more unconscious background, or core (the content). This question recalls the distinction by Freud between form as the ego's socially conditioned reworking and content as related to the id (1900; 1908). However, since both form and content are to a certain extent socially determined, the question is where the one ends and the other begins. 'Modern ego psychology,' Gilbert Rose writes, 'sees both id and ego developing out of an undifferentiated matrix rather than ego arising from id... It is no longer tenable to relate id only to content and ego only to form' (1986:9).

author must consider the character's personality and ask himself questions such as: Would this character perform this action that I want him to perform?; Would he be able to bear the grief that I must make him suffer?[2] Faulkner himself suggested that the character ought to have enough personality to shape his own fate, leaving the author 'to trot along behind him with a paper and pencil trying to keep up long enough to put down what he says and does' (Fant and Ashley 1964:111). At the same time, of course, he knew, as we do, that characters are not physical beings but creations of words. In fact, Faulkner's characters are creations of words that are not at all mimetic of real life but highly rhetorical and literary.

Theorists have addressed this artistic feat: the creation of the character *between life and linguistic sign*. Their approaches set out to specify in how far or to what degree the character in fiction resembles the physical and psychological reality of human beings, and can therefore be understood by extending our knowledge of real people. James Phelan (1989), for instance, distinguishes the mimetic, thematic and synthetic components of character in fiction. His work consists of an exploration and discussion of how these different components are interrelated: the synthetic is necessarily always present, but can be more or less foregrounded; the mimetic and thematic can be more or less developed. My discussion shall, in a sense, take the opposite direction, and explore how, or to what extent, the real person and the literary person are both 'like texts.' Although the physical body of a human being is a concrete object of reality that can be touched, seen and heard, personality, in real life as well as in fiction, is a cognitive construction[3] that is theory-dependent.[4] It is the similarity in the ways we understand personality in fiction and in real life, by 'reading texts,' that makes the literary character so much like the real person.

The present study, then, consists of an exploration of literary characters through what they have most clearly in common with real persons: their personalities. It seems that only if a literary personality is a 'possible personality,' that is, only if it is a 'well-formed text,' constructed along the same principles that are believed to be operative in real life, will it give the impression of an authentic 'flesh-and-blood' person such as Faulkner set out to create. The importance of the psychological authenticity of the literary character has been stressed, for instance, by Simon Lesser. As Lesser puts it: while the reader usually 'accepts, and even seems to welcome, departures from the literal facts about experience, he insists that the most airy fantasy, no less than a naturalistic novel, have some valid reference to psychological realities' (1957:193). The question is of course: what are these 'psychological realities'? I argue that in contrast to characters in the earlier 'realist' tradition, in the modern(istic) characters of Faulkner's psychological novels *The Sound and the Fury*, *As I Lay Dying*, *Light in August* and *Absalom, Absalom!* the complexity, the layeredness, the fluidity, and the paradoxical

---

2 Considering Dostoyevsky's *The Idiot*, Dilman points out that 'in his notebooks we find Dostoyevsky asking whether or not Aglaya is the "idiot's" mistress.' As he put it: 'Dostoyevsky feels that once the writing of the novel is on its way and has got off the ground it is not up to him whether or not Aglaya will be the Prince's mistress. He is asking: Can she be? Would she have him? And is he, "the poor knight," man enough to have her?' (1984:112).

3 I use the term *cognitive*, here, in its modern meaning, which includes all the relevant emotive elements (cf. *The Fontana Dictionary of Modern Thought*).

4 For an overview of personality constructs, see Hampson 1982.

qualities of identity itself have become a 'psychological reality.' Faulkner's modernist dismissal of surface appearances in favor of deeper psychological realities—'the human heart in conflict with itself' (Fant and Ashley 1964:51)—forms a clear link with the Freudian personality construct.

Focusing on behavior and the energy behind it, my study will present a pragmatic approach to personality. Both the real person *and* the literary person, I argue, characterize themselves by how they structure their worlds, or in other words, by how they create their own place within a social structure. The question of what personality *is*, which psychology has not been able to answer in a satisfying way, can thus be recast pragmatically as the question of what personality *does* in the world. Philosophically, the question concerning the essence of personality thus becomes: what happens in us, with us and through us on account of our personalities? In real life as well as in fiction, personality presents itself as a text: a *narrative* with its repetitions, its conflicts, its cause-effect relations and its temporal progression.

The Freudian Connection

Faulkner's biographer Joseph Blotner has reported one of Faulkner's childhood memories: 'I ran away to a doctor in the family and I browsed through his books. I learned plenty from them. I was interested in the brain. I learned that it had parts—a section for speech, for touch, and so on' (1984:34). Later, as Mick Gidley has argued, Faulkner had access to Freud's early theories in some of the books that his 'friend and mentor,' Phil Stone, ordered in 1922 'with Faulkner "in mind"' (1971:79). These included James Harvey Robinson's *The Mind in the Making*; Havelock Ellis's *Little Essays of Love and Virtue*; and Louis Berman's *The Glands Regulating Personality*. James Watson in addition mentions Sigmund Freud, Sir James Frazer's *The Golden Bough*, and Ellis's *Studies in the Psychology of Sex* (1992:27f.; cf. Snell 1991:141f.). As Susan Snell puts it in her biography of Phil Stone: 'Whatever else such selections indicate, these inferences appear sound: if there were now a conscious decision by the two men [Faulkner and Stone] that Faulkner write fiction, they planned to go about it scientifically. The human heart must be dissected for character motivation, hence the new psychology books' (1991:141).

But Faulkner was of course no neurologist, psychiatrist or psychologist. He told interviewers: 'What little of psychology I know the characters I have invented and playing poker have taught me. Freud I'm not familiar with' (Gwynn & Blotner 1959: 268). Even so, Carvel Collins wrote: 'Members of the New Orleans group [with whom Faulkner and Sherwood Anderson associated] have told me that they were fascinated by Freudian theory in those days and that their talk was full of it, as one might expect' (1954:36; cf. Blotner 1984:147). Faulkner's unfinished novel *Elmer*, on which he worked in Paris in 1925, includes what Joseph Blotner calls 'passages heavy with Freudian imagery,' and some critics consider these so 'heavy' that they speak of parody. Faulkner's early novel *Mosquitoes* (1927) features two characters who, while discussing the personality of a third, mention Freud and Havelock Ellis, which led John Irwin to observe: 'if the author of the novel was not familiar with Freud, his characters certainly were' (1980:5). Faulkner himself agreed that everybody talked about Freud when he lived in New Orleans, but again added: 'I have never read him. Neither did

Shakespeare. I doubt if Melville did either, and I'm sure Moby Dick didn't' (Meriwether and Millgate 1980:251). All playfulness aside, Faulkner seems to be saying here that the real expert on personality does not need a Freud to tell him what he knows intuitively already. Perhaps these ostentatious negations also signal a certain fear of the loss of control over his material.

The connection between Freud and Faulkner, in any case, is a multifaceted one. Faulkner, after all, had what Lee Jenkins has called an 'intuitive perception of the depth and character of mental aberration and the various modes of mental functioning—as they appear in his characters' (1981:148). Freud, on the other hand, had an intuitive perception of what made a good story. As Jeffrey Berman writes: 'Freud could not recite a case history without transforming it into a story.' In addition he remains, 'like a novelist,' 'interested in character for its own sake' (1987:277f.). In an interview with the Italian author Giovanni Papini, in 1934, Freud said: 'I am a scientist by necessity, and not by vocation. I am really by nature an artist... My oldest and strongest desire would be to write real novels, and I possess a mine of first-hand materials which would make the fortune of a hundred novelists. But I am afraid now it would be too late' (Ruitenbeck 1973:99f.; quoted in Martin 1988:212f.). Freud strongly believed in the links between psychoanalysis and literature. In his essay 'Delusions and Dreams in Jensen's *Gradiva*' (1907), he concludes: the 'creative writer cannot evade the psychiatrist nor the psychiatrist the creative writer, and the poetic treatment of a psychiatric theme can turn out to be correct without any sacrifice of its beauty' (quoted in Berman 1987:30).

The Freudian Personality Construct

The classical Freudian personality construct is a layered one, comprising the subconstructs of the *id*,[5] the *super-ego* and *ego-ideal*,[6] and the mediating functions of the *ego* (Freud 1923;1932), all of which are to a large extent unconscious.[7] To the mediating *ego-functions* belong regulations of motor functions and affect; the cognitive function of *reality testing*, that is, the ability to distinguish between reality and imagination; and the regulation, harmonization and integration of impulses of the id and

---

5 This is Freud's term 'das Es'; the impersonal and neuter pronoun stresses the universality of the instinctual drives.

6 Super-ego and ego-ideal develop through the introjection of parental attitudes. Freud himself does not differentiate clearly between the punishment-directed super-ego and the reward-directed ego-ideal. This distinction is important to some neo-freudians, such as Karen Horney.

7 There exists, of course, the well-known distinction between *unconscious processes*, which can never reach consciousness, or only by means of special techniques (hypnosis), and *pre- (or sub)conscious processes*, which might come to the surface of consciousness, but have not (yet). As Lawrence Kubie (1961), whose terminology follows Freud's distinctions, argues, the preconscious serves the condensation, intuition and conservation of information so that it is accessible when needed. It is the seat of creativity. Creativity is blocked when preconscious material is repressed instead of being allowed to flow. As Bruce Kawin explains it, both the unconscious and the conscious are rigid. The conscious is determined by social custom, the unconscious by childhood traumata we all acquire (beginning with the trauma of birth). The preconscious, however, is 'free'; it can make the 'imaginative leap' of creativity (1972:14). I shall, in this work, assume the distinction between the unconscious and the preconscious. However, a distinction between what may become conscious and what will never is often difficult to make. I shall at times try to make the distinction if it seems important; Faulkner himself sometimes does (cf. *Absalom, Absalom!* 117). At other times, I shall use the term *unconscious* in the neutral sense of not-conscious.

the super-ego. A discussion of these regulating, harmonizing and integrating functions entails a dynamic, conflict-determined perspective on personality. Many so-called defense mechanisms, studied more exhaustively by Anna Freud (1937), play a role in the continuous process of mediating between id and super-ego.[8] These defense mechanisms can be seen to belong to different stages of development; projection, denial, and undoing, for instance, are mechanisms belonging to early stages of development—in grown-ups, they entail a regression to a pre-reality testing stage of development—while intellectualizing is a later one and does not imply such far-reaching regression. Quentin Compson in *The Sound and the Fury* and Darl Bundren in *As I Lay Dying*, as we shall see, first use rationalization as a defense mechanism, shifting to more primitive ones as their mental states deteriorate.

Personality, in this dynamic view, is determined by the strength of the instinctual drives, their developmental level, and possible disturbances in their development[9]; by the effectiveness of the reality-testing functions of the ego; by the severity of the super-ego, and by the success of specific defense mechanisms—mature, immature, neurotic, or a mixture of these—which teaches an individual to make use of them habitually (cf. Kaplan and Sadock 1988:142). Neurotic symptoms, as Freud argued, 'are based on the one hand on the demands of the libidinal instincts and on the other hand on those made by the ego by way of reaction to them' (Anna Freud ed. 1986:306).[10] Freudian theory thus links personality with the adaptive patterns with which an individual satisfies 'instinctual forces' as well as the demands of physical and social reality, and these pat-

---

8 Summarizing the discussion since the 1930s, Kaplan and Sadock mention as 'mature defenses': (i) altruism: 'the vicarious but constructive and instinctually gratifying service to others'; (ii) anticipation: 'the realistic anticipation of or planning for future inner discomfort'; (iii) asceticism: 'the elimination of directly pleasurable affects attributable to an experience,' whereby 'gratification is derived from the renunciation'; (iv) humor: 'the overt expression of feelings without personal discomfort or immobilization and without unpleasant effect on others'; (v) sublimation: 'the gratification of an impulse whose goal is retained, but whose aim or object is changed from a socially objectionable one to a socially valued one'; and (vi) suppression: a 'conscious act of controlling and inhibiting an unacceptable impulse, emotion, or idea.' More immature or neurotic defenses include (i) repression: 'a mechanism in which unacceptable mental contents are banished or kept out of consciousness'; (ii) denial: 'a mechanism in which the existence of unpleasant realities is disavowed'; (iii) displacement: 'a mechanism by which the emotional component of an unacceptable idea or object is transferred to a more acceptable one; (iv) dissociation: 'a mechanism involving the segregation of any group of mental or behavioral processes from the rest of the person's psychic activity'; (v) introjection: 'the internalization of characteristics of the object with the goal of establishing closeness to and constant presence of the object'; (vi) intellectualizing: 'a mechanism in which reasoning or logic is used in an attempt to avoid confrontation with an objectionable impulse and thus defends against anxiety'; (vii) projection: a 'mechanism in which a person attributes to another those generally unconscious ideas, thoughts, feelings, and impulses that are in himself undesirable or unacceptable'; (viii) isolation: 'a mechanism involving the separation of an idea or memory from its attached feeling tone,' and (ix) undoing: 'a mechanism by which a person symbolically acts out in reverse something unacceptable that has already been done or against which the ego must defend itself' (1988:144; 312).

9 Freud basically distinguishes the following developmental levels of the id: (i) the 'oral stage,' in which drives are directed towards the need to suck, swallow and chew; (ii) the 'anal stage,' in which drives center around the eliminatory functions of the digestive tract, and (iii) the 'phallic stage' in which the sexual organs become the center of drives. Traumatic experiences of different kinds may cause disturbances in development, leading to so-called fixations on a certain level of development, and predisposing the individual towards regression to defense mechanisms belonging to this level.

10 Instincts are defined by Freud (1905) as 'the physical representative of an endosomatic, continuously flowing source of stimulation, as contrasted with a "stimulus," which is set up by *single* excitations coming from *without*.' The instinct thus lies 'on the frontier between the mental and the physical' (Anna Freud ed. 1986:310).

terns appear as 'styles of defense and directly observable behavior' (Kaplan and Sadock 1988:142ff.).

Classical Freudian theory has been of great importance to literary theorists. Marthe Robert, for instance, has argued that all art, including the novel, originates in what Freud has called 'the family romance of the neurotic.'[11] Briefly, the idea is that the psychological development of the young individual knows different stages. During the first stage the infant believes itself to be the constant focus of its caretakers' attention. Eventually it discovers that this is not the case. In order to deal with the insecurity that this discovery causes, the child invents a story in which it is a foundling; that is, it discovers that the caretakers who pretended to be its parents are not the real ones, because these would never have forced it to take second place. In this way the child can distance itself from its caretakers while at the same time remaining the focus of attention of some mystical set of parents in the imagination. During the second stage of development, the child, 'evicted' from its 'infantile paradise by the knowledge of sexual difference' (Robert 1980:204), starts to distinguish between its mother and its father. Because its dealings with mother are so intimate, it now constructs its story in such a way that its mother is the real parent and the unsatisfactory male character that its mother lives with is not. The real father comes to be seen as a substitute one and the fictive one becomes real. This newly acquired 'real' but absent father can now become the child's hero, while the available one is pushed outside the family circle. The child is no longer a 'foundling' but a 'bastard.' The availability of the mother, in the meantime, makes it impossible to idealize her. The child has now entered the Oedipal phase. From a 'pre-Oedipal narcissus' it has become a 'narcissistic Oedipus.'

Fantasy novels and realistic novels, Robert has argued, exemplify two different stages in this psychological development of humans. The author of the realistic novel regresses, through his art, to the position of the 'narcissistic Oedipus.' This is the phase in which some reality testing has become possible: the individual at least tries to relate to reality, or to use Robert's words: he learns 'to see the world as it is and to take an *interest* in what is going on' (1980:81). The author of the fantasy novel, on the other hand, regresses further back, to the position of the 'pre-Oedipal narcissus.' This is the pre-reality testing period, in which defense mechanisms such as projection, denial and undoing are active, allowing the author to make his own reality, irrespective of the real. Of course, many fictional works do not fall exclusively into one category—fantasy or realism—but are mixtures of the two. The most successful novel, Robert argues, would be one 'where *a purely literary combination of elements* achieves the near-impossible feat of making it simultaneously for and against reality, completely on "the other side" and entirely here' (1980:45f. note 23).

Classical Freudian theory has been important for Faulkner scholars as well. John T. Irwin (1980), for instance, bases his discussion of Faulkner's psychological novels on the Oedipus complex and its relation to the problem of incest, which figures so prominently in Faulkner's work. However, although the approach can, for instance, throw light on the rivalry between Henry Sutpen and Charles Bon in *Absalom, Absalom!*, or the agony of Quentin Compson in *The Sound and the Fury* and in *Absalom,*

---

11 Later Freud stated that the mental configurations of the family romance are not limited to the neurotic, but are part of the normal psychological development of humans.

Absalom!, it cannot do much to illuminate Benjy Compson's extreme and persistent attachment to his sister Caddy in *The Sound and the Fury*. One may, however, supplement Irwin's classical Freudian approach by neo-freudian and post-freudian insights.

The Post-Freudian Construct

For Freud, the basis of personality is the id with its instinctual drives, eventually to be controled by the developing ego. Although post-freudians share many of the basics of classical Freudian theory, they are much more interested in the ego, which they believe goes beyond the basic mediating functions of Freud. As they see it, the ego does not arise out of a need for the id to be tempered, but exists from birth as a distinct force with its own separate drives. Ego drives, as specified for instance by Erik H. Erikson, are ultimately directed towards autonomy. To reach this goal the first developmental task is to gain a basic trust in the environment. Only if this developmental phase has been completed with reasonable success can the individual ego develop itself in the direction of this autonomy.

The emphasis on the pre-Oedipal phase of ego-development, as found especially in the work of Melanie Klein, brings to light the early development of the personality, the importance of which Freud saw but was unable to analyze satisfactorily.[12] Freud's 'instinct theory,' with its emphasis on rivalry with the father, which finds its resolution through introjection, is supplemented here by 'object-theory,' focusing on elementary feelings of love and hate towards the mother's breast.[13] The primary 'ego-task' of the newborn is a resolution of this ambivalence. Klein has distinguished two phases or positions: the 'paranoid-schizoid position,' in which the infant must work through its fear and suspicion of the breast, and the 'depressive position,' in which it learns to accept that the breast it loves and the breast it hates are in fact one and the same. This latter phase is characterized, she argues, by feelings of guilt and shame and linked to this the need to make repairs for the destructive feelings towards the breast, and finally towards the mother as a person. When the child can perceive the mother as integrated person, it is also able to perceive her relationship with the father. At the start of the Oedipal period of development, according to Klein, the child is confronted for the first time with the intimate relation between the parents, and its exclusion from this relationship. It is the primitive figure of the *fusion of the parents* (Klein 1975:79) that one finds in the monologues of both Quentin Compson and Darl Bundren.

Frances Tustin's work with autists has shown the importance of the developmental tasks of the early paranoid-schizoid phase. Autism, she believes, is the result of a failure to incorporate the 'good breast' and deny the 'bad breast,' which are necessary manoevres during the time in which the primitive defense mechanism of splitting is active. This developmental task, she argues, has to be accomplished before the child can enter the depressive phase. A failure to introject 'the good breast,' or 'the good

12 Duytschaever argues that Freud did see the importance of the early developmental period, but believed that it was too soon to focus his theory towards it as long as the Oedipal phase had not been studied completely (1990:87).
13 Freud (1905), incidentally, did recognize the importance of the mother's breast as a love-object; as he put it: 'There are... good reasons why a child sucking at his mother's breast has become the prototype of every relation of love. The finding of an object is in fact a refinding of it' (Anna Freud ed. 1986:357).

mother,' leads to the typical withdrawal of autists and their concentration on self-engendered sensory experience through rocking, head banging, twirling and clutching of 'autistic objects' (Tustin 1986:102ff.).

Julia Kristeva (1986) has brought the pre-Oedipal personality development into the realm of discourse. Her 'semiotic' refers to a discourse of mother and child, which is based on childbirth and breast-feeding, and which is fragmented and impulsive. Such discourse focuses especially on skin contact, smell, taste, posture and gazing. As Elizabeth Fivaz Depeursinge has shown, for instance, the discourse between infant and caretaker can only be successful if the infant's gaze is embedded within the gaze of this caretaker,[14] and if this gaze itself is again embedded within the 'tactile/kinesthetic contact' of holding, posturing and supporting that this caretaker offers (1991:103).

As we shall see, post-freudian theories can do much more to illuminate Benjy Compson's ritual behavior in *The Sound and the Fury* than classical Freudian theory. They can also throw light on the origins of Darl Bundren's mental illness in *As I Lay Dying*, and on Joe Christmas's violence in *Light in August*. They cannot, however, adequately deal with the complexity of Christmas's interpersonal relations or, for that matter, with those of Jason Compson in *The Sound and the Fury*. These relations can be better understood within the neo-freudian theories.

The Neo-Freudian Construct

While both the Freudian and the post-freudian theories possess an *intra*personal orientation, neo-freudian theories tend towards a more *inter*personal orientation, stressing more specifically the importance of the family and the society at large for personality development. Karen Horney, for instance, isolates a drive towards self-fulfillment in the world, which all individuals naturally possess. In her analyses of patients, friends, literary characters and herself, however, she discovered defensive strategies that impair and obstruct this drive. These defensive strategies can explain the mismatch between an individual's goals and his actions in the world.

Like the Kleinean approach, the Horneyan approach stresses the quality of the early relationship between parent and child. Any disturbance in this relationship, Horney argues, will cause a certain measure of anxiety in the child. There may be a great many unfavorable conditions for the development of the child, but when summarized, Horney believes, these 'all boil down to the fact that the people in the environment are too wrapped up in their own neuroses to be able to love the child' (1956:221). As a consequence, it 'does not develop a feeling of belonging, of "we," but instead a profound insecurity and vague apprehensiveness' (1956:221). To conquer this anxiety, it learns to use specific strategies, or neurotic solutions, which tend to be reinforced through experiences.

Horney distinguishes three major types of neurotic solutions: firstly, the compliant defense of the self-effacing personality, in which the child opts to meet every expectation of the environment, bringing with it the development of a set of values such as goodness, sympathy, love, generosity, humility, and a distaste for ambition, egoism, callousness etc. (the latter, however, are nevertheless secretly admired because they re-

14 Duytschaever speaks of the gleam in the mother's eye (1990:93), thereby emphasizing the necessary quality of this encounter.

present strength); secondly, the aggressive defense of the arrogant-vindictive personality, which is characterized by efficiency, resourcefulness, mastery, perfectionism, narcissism and arrogance; and thirdly, the retreating defense of the detached personality, with its love of independence, its worship of freedom and its hypersensitivity to influence of any kind.[15] An individual who uses this last defense, Horney writes, will 'react with anxiety to physical pressure from clothing, closed in spaces, long term obligations, the inexorability of time and the laws of cause and effect' (1950:191ff.), something we shall see in *As I Lay Dying* in the personality of Jewel Bundren, and in *Light in August* in the personality of Joe Christmas.

In this body of theory, the construct *personality* entails a 'direction of development' rather than a fixed type (Horney 1950:191). Such a 'direction of development' is determined both by the individual's goals and by the defensive solution to deprivation that he uses, with experiences in the outside world playing an important role. As Bernard Paris puts it: 'Although Horney, like Freud, sees psychological problems as originating in early childhood, she does not see the adult as simply repeating earlier patterns, and she does not explain his behavior through analogies with childhood experience. Once the child begins to adopt defensive strategies, his particular system develops under the influence of external factors, which encourage some strategies and discourage others, and of internal necessities, whereby each defensive move requires others in order to maintain its viability' (1991:324). Personality concerns one moment in a personal life history, and can be understood as 'the present constellation of defenses' (Paris 1991:324).

In his work on Thackeray, Stendhal, George Eliot, Dostoevsky, and Conrad, Paris explores the appropriateness of Horney's approach for the study of fiction. As he puts it: 'Though her psychology (like any other) is far from providing a complete picture of human nature, Karen Horney deals astutely with the same patterns of intra-psychic and interpersonal behavior that form the matter (and often the structure) of a good many novels and plays' (1974:xf.). Horney's approach, because it takes into account all the experiences of an individual and not only those of infancy, can throw light on the origin and the development, as well as the paradoxes of various forms of 'anti-social' behavior as shown for instance by Joe Christmas in *Light in August* and Jason Compson in *The Sound and the Fury*.

The emphasis of the neo-freudian Gregory Bateson on the family relations of the young child, finally, has produced explanations of schizophrenic and schizoid behavioral patterns. Bateson proposes an etiology of schizophrenia that is based on deviant learning processes. As he puts it: 'learning occurs always in some context which has formal characteristics... this structured context also occurs within a wider context—a metacontext if you will—and... this sequence of contexts is an open, and conceivably infinite, series' (1972:245). Problems arise for an individual in a learning situation if there is an incongruence or conflict between context and metacontext, that

---

15 The different defense mechanisms always conceal their opposite tendencies, which are also present on a deeper level. The detached personality, for instance, also contains a hidden aggressive trend.

is, if learning must take place in a wider context that punishes this same learning.[16]

In such a paradoxical situation, an individual can never perform properly; he must either be right in the immediate context and violate the conditions of the wider context, or he must succeed in the wider context and fail in the narrow context. For this kind of situation the term *double bind* was coined, as 'a situation in which no matter what a person does, he "can't win"' (1972:201). It will become clear that the double bind, as a metaphor of the communicative tangle in which certain vulnerable individuals may find themselves, can make a real contribution towards an understanding of Quentin Compson's suicide in *The Sound and the Fury*.

Narrative Approaches

The various Freudian personality constructs, as elaborated above, are capable of bringing to the fore and illuminating the layeredness, complexity and conflictual nature of personality in Faulkner's texts. More recently, psychoanalysts such as Roy Schafer and Donald Spence have especially stressed the narrative nature of psychoanalysis. As Jerome Bruner has argued, psychoanalysts 'began inquiring whether the object of analysis was not so much archaeologically to reconstruct a life as it was to help the patient construct a more contradiction-free and generative narrative of it' (1982:9). To help the individual 'construct a narrative discourse whose syntax and rhetoric are more plausible, more convincing, more adequate to give an account of the story of the past than those that are originally presented, in symptomatic form' became the aim of psychoanalysis (Brooks 1987:10). Spence himself speaks of constructing 'a narrative account that provides a coherent picture of the events in question' (1986:180).

Psychoanalytic treatment takes the shape of a dialogue, in which the personality of the analysand shows itself by degrees, and as a process (cf. Baneke 1991:7). This emphasizes both the role of the speaker/writer and of the listener/reader. Joost Baneke mentions with respect to this the Thematic Apperception Test (TAT), a well-known projection test (Murray 1943; Bellak 1986), which analyzes and classifies personality, for diagnostic reasons, by way of the stories that a person tells about certain standardized pictures, for the most part showing human figures.[17] The following aspects of the story can for instance be studied: Is there a central character in the story with whom the person tested identifies?; What are the typical actions, emotions, motives, defense mechanisms etc. of this central character?; Which situational influences play an important role in the story?; What is the story's plotline?'; 'How do the different aspects above relate to each other?: Which stylistic characteristics pervade throughout the

---

16 In a more recent study, Luc Ciompi argues with regard to schizophrenia: 'An example of psychosocial disturbances is severely discontinuous, contradictory, and confusing interpersonal experiences and environmental stimuli (i.e. information in the broadest sense) which will impede the build-up of coherent programmes of behaviour,' resulting in: 'a decreased capacity to deal adequately with complex emotional and/or cognitive situations, and an increased sensitivity for stress' (1989:16).

17 Test-reports on personality also have the form of narratives. One well-known example is the Minnesota Multiphasic Personality Inventory (MMPI), which was developed in the 40s and is, according to Jay Martin, still the most widely used personality profile today (1988:104). Making use of more than 500 questions that individuals must answer, it works on the basis of scales and test patterns, which produce a narrative report that foregrounds attributes such as 'energetic,' 'easily bored,' 'impulsive,' 'risk-taking,' 'ego-centric,' 'demanding of others,' 'intelligent,' 'thoughtful,' and so on. In such 'narratives' of personality, behavioral patterns are concentrated and condensed, as they are in fictions.

different stories that an individual tells? (Baneke 1991:9). Stylistic characteristics pervading throughout different stories can be seen to convey identity themes, allowing one to grasp what Norman Holland has called 'an unchanging essence, a "personality"' permeating 'the millions of ego choices that constitute the visible human... ever changing and different, yet ever continuous with what went before' (1975:815).

'Psychological narrative,' Joost Baneke writes, is determined by 'the double structure of manifest and hidden content, of the obvious and the occult, of actual events and possible future or past events, of temporality and timelessness' (1992:8). Different authors have explored the connections between certain personality-classifications and the narrative structures of stories. Ernest Keen, for instance, has discussed 'how the paranoid person narratizes his life' (1986:176), taking as a starting-point the three polarities that form the structure of experience: temporality, morality, and sociality, or in other words: past and future, good and evil, and self and other. Paranoid stories, Keen argues, mediate these polarities in a characteristic way. Firstly, the 'newness' of the future is something that cannot be allowed. Instead the future has to remain dominated by 'the expectation, the already formulated emplotment which assimilates everything to its preexisting terms.' Thus, Keen points out, 'the possibility of a future in the usual sense does not exist' (1986:177).

On the issue of good and evil, Keen argues, the paranoid narrative places evil in the world outside, 'pressing in on' the goodness in the self (1986:179). The locating of good in the self and evil in the world outside explains the cataclysmic nature of the paranoid narrative; the succumbing of this self cannot but cause the world to come to an end. The paranoid narrative forms a clear contrast with the depressive narrative, which locates evil inside the self. This contrast is clear when we compare Jason Compson's paranoid narrative in *The Sound and the Fury* to his brother Quentin's depressive one, although in Quentin's story, as we shall see, one finds some evidence of a depressive-paranoid delusion, which seems to combine the two by positing the evil inside the self as the cause of evil and suffering out there in the world.

The third aspect of the paranoid narrative concerns the relationship between self and other that it inscribes. Essential to the paranoid life story is a very specific kind of loneliness, which is not, however, lamented as a deprivation. Instead, Keen argues, the narrative constantly 'affirms it, asserts it, even creates it and defends it' (1986:181). Trying to stay away from evil, the paranoid narrative posits above all its refusal to share, intermingle, or even border on other stories. We shall see how Jason Compson in *The Sound and the Fury* constantly needs to deconstruct the stories of others in order to guard his own sense of self. By refusing influence of any kind, the paranoid narrative denies the vital completion of self through others, but it also denies the other a self. 'What is at stake here,' Keen writes, 'is not just learning something; what is at stake is letting the other be other, which makes it possible for him or her to be a self, and letting that otherness matter for me, which forces me to create, and continually recreate, myself' (1986:183).

The relation between personality and narrative illustrated in the approaches above will form the starting-point of my exploration of characterization in William Faulkner's psychological novels: *The Sound and the Fury, As I Lay Dying, Light in August*, and *Absalom, Absalom!* This relation can be formulated in terms of the concept of *mind-style* coined by the linguist Roger Fowler.

On Mind-Style

Roger Fowler has coined the term *mind-style* to refer to 'any distinctive linguistic presentation of an individual mental self' (1977:103). He defines this 'distinctive linguistic presentation' elsewhere in terms of 'consistent structural options, agreeing in cutting the presented world to one pattern or another' (1977:76), and in terms of 'consistent stylistic choices' that signify 'particular, distinctive, orderings of experience'; 'consistent linguistic choices which build up a continuous, pervasive, representation of the world' (1986:9; 150ff.). Mind-style, then, is concerned with the expression in language of the conceptualization of 'reality' in a particular mind. Such a definition begs the question of what 'reality' in fact *is*—or in the context of this study, the question of what kinds of 'realities' Faulkner's texts create.

The Concept of Reality

Whatever the physical world is like, our organs of perception are 'tuned' in such a way that our conceptualization of it can only be partial. In his discussion of the specific human skill of reading, the neurobiologist William Calvin gives the following example of the censoring capacities of the mental apparatus:

There are some nerve cells in the rear of the human brain that become specialists in recognizing vertical lines, and others in horizontal lines... together to identify a 'T.'... Frogs weren't interested in the difference between 'T' and 'I,' but they were sure interested in moving black spots on light backgrounds—such as an insect to eat.
(1986:159)

As this example suggests, frogs and humans do not live in the same reality. In other words, frogs, although they possess sharp vision, do not seem to perceive humans visually at all. As far as vision is concerned we do not exist for them; we are not part of their reality. Different species, because of their different sense organs, which censor and organize things in the physical world in different ways, live in different realities.

Members of the same species, however, because of the large amount of mental framework they share (since this evolved especially for their survival *as a species*, not as individuals) *do* live in a shared reality to a large extent (cf. van der Leek 1989:30ff.). It is important to remember that this sharing of reality applies to the human species as well. But, as Douglas Hofstadter puts it:

We simply take what is common to all of us so much for granted that it is hard to see how much we have in common with other people. It takes the conscious effort of imagining how much—or how little—we have in common with other types of entities, such as stones, cars, restaurants, ants, and so forth, to make evident the large amount of overlap that we have with randomly chosen people. What we notice about another person immediately is not the standard overlap, because that is taken for granted as soon as we recognize the humanity of the other person; rather, we look beyond the standard overlap and generally find some major differences, as well as some unexpected, additional overlap.
(1980:376)

Faulkner believed that this universally human reality also involves feelings and basic needs. As he put it: 'the problems of the human heart... have nothing to do with what race you belong to' (Fant and Ashley 1964:52); 'man, whether he's black or white or red or yellow still suffers the same anguishes, he has the same aspirations, his follies are the same follies, his triumphs are the same triumphs' (Gwynn and Blotner 1959). It is against this background, in fact, that the tragedy of his characters takes its shape.

In his work, basic human emotions such as happiness and grief and the appreciation of beauty reveal this basic human uniformity, even if his characters often have difficulty realizing that this is so. In *Intruder in the Dust*, for instance, young Charles Mallison learns the implications of this common humanity as he contemplates the feelings of Lucas, 'an old nigger who had just happened to outlive his old nigger wife' (161):

He was grieving. You dont have to not be a nigger in order to grieve
(25)

Understanding Lucas's emotions makes Charles understand Lucas's basic humanity.[18] The deputy in Faulkner's story 'Pantaloon in Black' in *Go Down Moses*, however, seems beyond learning when he says: 'But when it comes to the normal human feelings and sentiments of human beings, they [blacks] might just as well be a damn herd of wild buffaloes' (122).

The universality of basic emotions has been emphasized from other fields of art as well. Leonard Bernstein, the famous musical director and composer, argues:

Hunger. Impatience. Certainly the deepest universals we all share are emotions, or affects; we all have the same capacity for passion, fear, anticipation, aggression. We all display the same physiological manifestations of affect; our eyebrows go up with anticipation; our hearts pound with passion; and fear affects us universally with goose flesh.
(1976:15)

In his lecture series about the universality of music, Bernstein explains his view that music all over the world is based on the same musical tones, which naturally sound together when a string, or another free-moving element such as a column of air, is vibrating: the 'harmonic series,' of which the first five notes, beginning with the tonic, or ground note, form 'humanity's favorite pentatonic scale,' known from 'all corners of the earth, as from Scotland, or from China, or from Africa, and from American Indian cultures, from East Indian cultures, from Central and South America, Australia, Finland' (1976:29). As he puts it: 'All music—whether folk, pop, symphonic, modal, tonal, atonal, polytonal, microtonal, well-tempered or ill-tempered, music from the distant past or the imminent future—all of it has a common origin in the universal phenomenon of the harmonic series' (1976:33).

In music, as in literature, the notion of ambiguity is very important, for instance, when it remains uncertain which note *is* the tonic. Simply speaking, Bernstein argues, music is based on creating tension within a fixed system, the harmonic series; the higher the tension, the greater the relief, the feeling of happiness and of beauty when

---

18 In *Paris Trout* by Pete Dexter one finds the opposite revelation, as the young black girl Rosie Sayers sees a white woman cry: 'Rosie had never seen a white person cry before—none except the little ones—and it surprised her that they had those feelings too' (1989:8).

the tonic is finally reached. A piece ending on the seventh note, therefore, will instill a sense of suspension—of grief—because it came so close to being resolved. One hears this and can be affected by it without having any knowledge of scales at all. The phenomenon is very beautifully conveyed in Carson McCullers' *The Member of the Wedding*:

> Frankie stood waiting for the night. And just at that moment a horn began
> to play. Somewhere in the town, not far away, a horn began a blues tune...
> Then, without warning, the thing happened that at first Frankie could not
> believe. Just at the time when the tune should be laid, the music finished,
> the horn broke off. All of a sudden the horn stopped playing. For a moment
> Frankie could not take it in, she felt so lost... But the music did not come
> again. The tune was left broken, unfinished.
> (1987:54f.)

I am not arguing that this *biological reality*, as I shall call it, is the 'real world out there'; I am only arguing that it is a universally human structuring of the reality that we must assume is out there but that we can never fully know. We share it with all members of our species simply *because* we are co-members. It constitutes the largest, most essential, part of human reality, and it forms the basis on which our social reality is built.

If biological reality, then, is created by nature, *social reality*, on the other hand, is created by humans through social interaction. In contrast to biological reality, which is pre-cultural and thus pre-dialogic, social reality is by nature dialogic; that is, it has involved, somewhere along the line, a negotiation between speech partners. As Russell Jacoby has argued: 'If the social reality is ultimately derived from individuals, it is not immediately; rather, it has a drift, a momentum, a weight of its own... The content of the social laws is not nature but *second nature*: coagulated history. They are manmade, but they also make men; they are dialectic, at once subject and object, neither totally one or the other' (1973:65). Social reality, thus, encompasses rather stable conceptualizations and laws, which have been negotiated before and are now shared by relatively large groups of people. Institutions like schools, prisons, mental hospitals, marriage and dinner parties; games like chess, football and flirting or teasing; and works of art such as fictions, drama, ballet, sculptures, and clothing, all are examples of such representations. Many instances of social reality embody also aspects of biological reality (think of flirting and of clothing), because they also satisfy biological needs.

While many representations of social reality are the property of large groups, others are shared by much smaller groups, even by only two people; and many of these have to be negotiated by the individual himself through the power of the 'fragile thread' (*Absalom, Absalom!* 313) of language. I shall call such representations *interpersonal reality*, to distinguish this fleeting form of reality from independently existing, or imposed, social reality. Even though, as human beings, we share our basic mental framework and a certain social heritage, our different positions—both mental and physical—in the world will decide which facets of it will be included automatically in our mental representations of it. Faulkner has thematized this issue in many of his novels. Lucas Beauchamp in *Intruder in the Dust*, for instance, cannot 'see' himself as a common slave because he is a direct descendent of the white patriarch. Thus he refuses 'to mean mister to anybody even when he says it' (58). This idiosyncratic viewpoint nearly costs him his life.

All humans have a sense of reality that is private, or 'deviant.' However, this de
viance must never go beyond certain limits. The psychoanalyst Lawrence Frank has
pointed out that 'different cultures tolerate varying degrees of deviation from the
socially sanctioned patterns of conduct.' As he puts it: 'when the individual's private
world deviates too far from the official culture we speak of mental disorders; when the
individual's overt conduct transgresses the culturally defined inviolabilities, or conflicts
with cultural requirements, we speak of delinquency and criminality'(1938:625; quoted
in Blos 1941:9). Thus, avoiding too much deviance is a social necessity. Being able to
create and sustain a sense of reality, and to share it with others to a large enough extent, is also a biological necessity. Faulkner's novels, as we shall see, explore especially the effects of being unable to create or sustain a sense of reality, or of having a
sense of reality that cannot be shared with others. The former may lead to despair
(Quentin Compson; Darl Bundren; Joe Christmas), the latter to the forceful imposition
of that reality on others (Benjy Compson; Jason Compson; Joanna Burden).

Style and the Mental Self

Mind-style, as we have seen, is the conception of reality as it is conveyed by the individual, including past and present worlds, as well as the various 'possible worlds' of
anticipation, expectation, desire, dream, hope and fear. Thus it necessarily combines
aspects of biological, social, interpersonal and private reality in a personal combination. Roger Fowler himself makes a distinction between conscious and not-
conscious stylistic choices when he discusses two separate ways of conveying this
conception of reality, which are 'clearly identifiable in specific areas of linguistic
structure.' Firstly, as he points out, 'a narrator or a character may directly indicate his
or her judgements and beliefs, by the use of a variety of *modal* structures'; secondly,
'other parts of language, indirectly but nevertheless convincingly, may be *symptomatic*
of world-view' (1986:131f.). Mind-style is not in the first place a matter of the
conscious message of a speaker; rather, it forms the background of his messages. In
other words, it is a matter of personal 'ideology.'

An individual's mental self, in this view, shows itself in his 'consistent stylistic
choices': his *style*. As M.A.K. Halliday has argued, 'style is a manifestation of the individual' (1971:343). Henk Hillenaar defines style as a battle between the code and the
desires of body and imagination; style here represents a refusal of the individual to con-
form completely to his society and culture. As Hillenaar puts it, style is a declaration
of individuality (1990:6). Scholars in different fields have recognized the relation
between style and the manifestation of individuality, focusing on the linguistic features
favored by the individual. In the field of lexis one may think, for instance, of linguistic
choices with a difference in connotation, register, generality, abstractness, affective
content or mood, and of newly-coined words, which Faulkner's characters often use;
but one may also think of the phonological and morphological elements that these
lexical choices consist of and the syntactic patterns that employ them. Let us examine
some aspects that are especially important in understanding Faulkner's characters.

Phonology concerns the different sounds (vowels and consonants) that make up lexical
items, as well as concurrent paraverbal aspects such as pitch, intonation, volume,

tempo, rhythm and stress, together called tone of voice. In Faulkner's texts, different phonological choices are occasionally depicted graphologically, as are hesitations and pauses.[19] *Morphology* is concerned with the internal structure of the various lexical items that an individual uses. Many of Faulkner's characters convey highly ambiguous mental representations through unusual morphological choices, for instance: 'not-people,' 'unbelief,' and 'undefeat' (Quentin Compson), 'no-wind' and 'no-sound' (Darl Bundren), or 'not-fish' and 'not-blood' (Vardaman Bundren).

Lexicalization in itself gives an indication of the kinds of concepts for which the speaker has a name. In Fowler's words: 'the lexis of a person... can be regarded as mapping the conceptual repertoire of the person' (1986:151). This 'conceptual repertoire' categorizes objects—concrete and abstract—in the world around a certain prototype or typical member. The more closely an object resembles this prototype, John Taylor (1989) argues, the more central is its membership; the less closely it resembles the prototype, the less central it is, until it seems to fall out of the category into a neighboring one.[20] Membership of a category, then, is graded, while the categories themselves have fuzzy boundaries and a certain measure of overlap. The lexical categories in themselves form prototype categories such as *noun, adjective, adverb,* and *verb.* The same applies to phonological, morphological, and syntactic categories, such as *tonic, genitive, tense,* and *transitive.* Past tense, for instance, has as its central meaning reference to past time. More marginal is its 'counterfactuality' (as in the sentence *I wish I could),* and its 'pragmatic softening' (as in *I wanted to ask you*) (cf. Taylor 1989:153). The traditional categories of pragmatics such as *deictic, speech-act* and *inference* may be considered prototype categories with graded membership and fuzzy boundaries as well.

From studies of the cognitive development in children it has become clear that the central meaning of a category is learned earliest. During the child's early cognitive development the past tense, for instance, is used only for 'punctual events,' that is, for events that do not extend over time, such as those conveyed by the verbs *drop, break, crash* and *hit,* and of those only the ones that involve 'a highly salient change in state—usually a change for the worse—for one of their participants' (Taylor 1989:243). The prototype meaning of past tense, then, is not simply 'pastness' but more specifically, 'completion in the immediate past of a punctual event, the consequences of which are perceptually salient at the moment of speaking' (Taylor 1989:243).

Categories are extended from their central meanings through metonymy and metaphor. Metonymic extension typically involves the establishing of connections in meaning between entities that are contiguous in space or time, that is, those that exhibit spatial or temporal closeness; metaphoric extension typically involves the same for entities that are contiguous in affect, that is, those that exhibit emotional closeness. From these definitions it should be clear that the categories of metonymy and metaphor are themselves prototype categories with fuzzy, overlapping boundaries. It is in these

---

19 In Fernando Poyatos's words: 'the nonactivities of silence and stillness respectively' (1983:11).
20 Taylor discusses, for instance, how such objects as cups, bowls and vases are organized into categories, each containing a prototype member that possesses the optimum measurement (width-depth ratio) for the category. With an increase in width-depth ratio, he argues, the cup becomes a bowl; with a decrease in width-depth ratio, the cup becomes a vase.

fuzzy areas of overlap that most of the conceptual differences between people occur.

That categories possess graded membership and fuzzy boundaries becomes clear if one considers the meaning of so-called 'hedges.' Hedges are defined as 'resources of a language which enable a speaker to express degree of category membership' (Taylor 1989:76). They are metalinguistic devices, in that they comment on the linguistic choices of the language user himself. Examples include the sentence adjunct *strictly speaking* which 'tightens up a category,' or pulls it together, by giving full status to a marginal member. Nearly the same function is performed by *technically speaking*. In a negative context, *strictly speaking* may distinguish between non-members that are closer to and those that are more distant from the category.[21] *Loosely speaking*, on the other hand, reorganizes a category through the exclusion of central members. Another example is formed by the conjunction *in that*, which introduces into a given category an entity that does not possess certain essential attributes.[22] Hedges point to the speaker's awareness of shared categories of conceptualization, and thereby establish the presence of a speech partner. 'When they are used to indicate degree of fit between experience and known category,' Keith Kernan argues, hedges not only involve 'the cognitive operations necessary to measure that fit but also an understanding or appreciation on the part of the speaker of what might be reasonably assumed to be in the mind of the hearer... The use of hedges... involves an awareness of mutual knowledge' (1990:220).

Although categories are usually labeled, nameless categories also exist (cf. Sperber and Wilson 1986:92f.). This may be a general lack existing in the speech community; we simply do not have terms, for instance, to name all the different classes of our olfactory sensations. It may, however, also be a personal 'deviation.' The result will be what Fowler has called: 'the noticeable suppression of a term, or the substitution of a noticeably complex expression for what... would be a simple term,' or 'underlexicalization' (1986:152). We shall see this underlexicalization clearly in the next chapter on *The Sound and the Fury*, in Benjy Compson's text. Related 'deviations' include what Fowler calls 'overlexicalization': 'the availability, or the use, of a profusion of terms for an object or concept' (1986:154); and 'undergeneralization' and 'overgeneralization': 'variation in generality or abstractness of terms' (1986:152). Lexical choices that are related in meaning, finally, create 'lexical sets' (cf. Verdonk 1988:25), or 'semantic fields,' which may indicate personal areas of experience and interest. Like pure repetitions, they may indicate involvement or obsession.

These variations or deviations may be a matter of conscious choice or they may point to a certain degree of unripeness of the mental apparatus, as in Benjy Compson in *The Sound and the Fury*. They may form symptoms of the operations of the unconscious, and show the workings of certain defense mechanisms, such as denial and rationalization, which aim at avoiding 'dangerous' conceptualizations, as we shall see in the texts of Quentin Compson in *The Sound and the Fury* and Darl Bundren in *As*

---

21 Taylor gives the following examples: 'Strictly speaking, a bat is not a bird'; 'Strictly speaking, a TV set is not a bird.' That the first sentence is acceptable when the second is not proves that a bat is closer to the category *bird* than a TV.

22 Taylor quotes Herrmann's (1975) example: 'He killed Alice in that he did nothing to keep her alive' (1989:78).

I Lay Dying. It is necessary, in this respect, both to listen to what is said and to what is *not* said. Baneke asks some questions about one of his patients that are relevant also to Faulkner's characters, for instance to Quentin Compson in *The Sound and the Fury*: 'Why does the patient first talk about parents, and later only about father? Where is the mother, for example, in his story? Those questions are aroused by the revelations in this story: not only revelations of what is said, but also of what is nót said' (1992:4).

Within the field of *syntax*, transitivity patterns are of prime importance. By transitivity is meant the relation between subject and object in the sentence, as expressed by the verb. This relation can be material (as in *Rósa drinks her milk*); mental (as in *Rósa loves her milk*) and relational (as in *To Rósa milk means security*). Verbs that must express a relationship to an object are called *transitives* (for instance the verb *delight*); verbs that cannot express such a relationship are called *intransitives* (for instance the verb *die*), while some verbs can either be transitive or intransitive (for instance the verb *eat*). The transitive construction, as Taylor has pointed out, derives from early two-word constructions, such as an agent-action combination. The earliest transitive sentences that are produced by a child—the prototypical ones—involve 'two, and only two, participants, a salient, punctual event initiated by one of the participants, resulting in a perceptible consequence for the other participant' (1989:244). Prototype extension of transitive constructions concerns the occurrence of non-human, abstract, metonymic and metaphoric participants; of non-punctual events; and of non-perceptible consequences (as in the sentences *This car holds three*; *This suggestion entails a rejection* and *This restaurant does not allow smoking*). Immature or deviant transitivity patterns, as we shall see, play an important role in the characterization of Benjy Compson in *The Sound and the Fury*.

Transitivity, in M.A.K. Halliday's words, is 'the cornerstone of the semantic organization of experience... man's interpretation of his experience of the world, his understanding of its processes and of his own participation in them' (1971:359; cf. Fowler 1986:156). This means, among other things, that one can study the kinds of roles that an individual habitually inscribes for himself in the language he uses, for instance that of passive experiencer of an internal or an external process, or that of agent of such processes (cf. Hurst 1987). One can then explore whether these processes characteristically involve other people or objects. The choice between using an active or a passive construction (to put either the agent or the experiencer in subject position) is of importance here as well. The ability to use passives, Taylor has explained, occurs relatively late in the cognitive development of the child, long after it is able to use even the non-central transitivity patterns (1989:245), because of the child's natural—egocentric—tendency to see itself as the acting center of the world. The active construction always remains the more usual—or unmarked—form. More generally, language normally keeps its ego-centric organization throughout life.

Deixis, in particular, shows this ego-centric organization of language. The individual organizes the self at first through the proper name (cf. De Levita 1965:173) and soon through the pronoun *I*. Thus he inscribes in language a personal position in the world that is not only physical but social and psychological as well. This allows him also to relate other objects and phenomena to this personal position. In other words: an individual normally relates everything to himself in an ego-centric way, so that it is *his* spatial and temporal location, *his* social rank, and *his* communication role that must be considered the center to which all things are relative. This relativity is readily accessible, as it is linguistically encoded by means of *deictic expressions*: coded links between language and the world that is evoked. The specific point to which the deictic terms are anchored—the zero-point of the speech event or the 'deictic center' (Levinson 1983:664)—is normally the position of the language user.

One may distinguish between personal deixis, spatial deixis, temporal deixis and social deixis. Personal deixis is concerned with the roles of speech-partners, and is encoded in language through personal pronouns. First-person pronouns position the speaker in the speech situation, while second-person pronouns posit the presence of an addressee. As Henry Widdowson puts it: 'The first and second person pronouns ("I" and "you") identify participants and provide the necessary terminals so to speak, whereby people are connected in communicative interaction.' 'They co-exist,' he continues, 'in the same plane of involvement. Thus they are, in principle, interchangeable in the turn-taking of talk: the second person is a potential first person, and each presupposes the existence of the other' (1993:35). Both are in the first place terms of address. Third-person pronouns, on the other hand, are terms of reference rather than of address. They refer to a third party that may or may not be present.[23] 'When people are referred to in third person terms,' Widdowson argues, 'they are distanced, put at a remove from involvement' (1993:35). Pronouns, then, when they are used deictically, cast individuals in their roles of outsider or insider with regard to a certain language event.

Spatial deixis specifies the location of entities in space relative to the deictic center. The most straightforward deictic terms are the demonstratives *this* and *that* and the adverbials *here* and *there*, which locate an entity close to the deictic center (*this* and *here*) or further away from the deictic center (*that* and *there*). Some motion verbs, such as *go* and *come*, have built-in deictic aspects. *Go* stipulates a movement away from the deictic center (as in the sentence *Susan has finally gone home*), but *come* is more complicated, as it may stipulate a movement towards the deictic center (as in *The mail has finally come*); towards an addressee (as in *John doesn't mind coming to get you*); or towards the home-base of either (as in *You shouldn't have come all the way to my house; I could've come to yours*).

Temporal deixis specifies the position of an event in time relative to the position in time of the language event. This occurs first of all through tense, which is the most pervasive deictic, since it is to be found in virtually every sentence. Tense, as Lyons puts it, 'grammaticalizes the relationship which holds between the time of the situation that is being described and the temporal zero-point of the deictic context' (1977:678). Simply speaking, present tense posits the simultaneity of event and utterance; past tense the anteriority of the event, and future tense its posteriority.[24] Under the assumption of 'deictic simultaneity' (Lyons 1977:685), adverbials of time, such as *now* or *at this*

---

23 Whereas the third-person plural *they* excludes addressee, the first-person and second-person plurals are more complex: *we* can be in- or exclusive of addressee, while *you* may include addressee and audience or addressee only.

24 See Werth (1981) for an overview of the full range of the temporal possibilities of tense.

moment; *earlier* or *recently*, and *soon* or *presently* refer to a position in time that is simultaneous with, before, and after the language event respectively.

Spatial and temporal deixis are closely related. *This*, *that* and *there*, for instance, are able to indicate location as well as time (*That is my train!* versus *That is my departure time!*). These deictic terms may also indicate emotional stance. By his use of the deictic *this*, for instance, a speaker may not only evoke spatial or temporal proximity, but also emotional nearness. Lyons calls this 'empathetic deixis' (1977:677). The most prototypical usage of the adverbial, however, remains the spatial one. If the language user is in motion, moreover, dimensions of time can be expressed in terms of location and the other way around (as in *I started feeling hungry 100 miles ago; if we don't find a place to eat within 10 minutes from here I am going to faint*).

Social deixis, finally, specifies the social rank of a referent in relation to the deictic center. The best-known social deictics are perhaps kinship terms, such as *father*, *mother*, *brother* and *sister*. Others are *boss*, *teacher*, *pupil* and so on. It is through social deixis, especially, that discourse encodes power-relations. These can be symmetrical or asymmetrical. For instance, if one of the speech partners uses a first name to address the other while the other uses title and last name, the power relation is inscribed as asymmetrical, and if both use first name, or last name and title, the power relation is inscribed as symmetrical (cf. Fillmore 1971:78ff.).

Although language normally has an ego-centric orientation, it is very well possible for a speaker to assume the viewpoint of someone else. 'Taking the other fellow's point of view' (Fillmore 1971:44) is not a rare phenomenon at all, since 'people are able to imagine themselves seeing the world through the eyes of others as well as from their own point of view' (Chafe 1976:52), or as Douglas Hofstadter has put it: 'I can fire up my subsystem for a good friend and virtually feel myself in his shoes, running through thoughts which he might have, activating symbols in sequences which reflect his thinking patterns more accurately than my own' (1980:386). However, in order for the personal voice to stay anchored to the position of the speaker—and in order for the self to remain organized—viewpoint shifts must always be limited to a few linguistic items, or else be 'marked' by attributive clauses and other devices. If viewpoint shifts involve deictic elements, one can speak of 'deictic projection' (Lyons 1977:579).

Viewpoint shift on a limited scale occurs for instance when, in speaking to a child, a proper name is used instead of a pronoun, as Caddy Compson in *The Sound and the Fury* does when talking to her brother Benjy: 'What are you trying to tell Caddy' (7). Since young children find it difficult to take the other's point of view, the speaker, in such a case, takes the child's point of view and uses the term that the child itself would have used. Mr. Compson in *Absalom, Absalom!* frequently performs deictic projection, when he takes the point of view of his son Quentin by speaking of 'your grandfather' and 'your grandmother' instead of 'my father' and 'my mother.' The social deictic here (*grandfather*; *grandmother*) shows the deictic projection while the personal deictic (*your*) remains anchored to the position of the speaker, Mr. Compson.

Spatial and temporal deixis can also encode deictic projection. This happens when *this*, *here* and *now* are used rather than *that*, *there* and *then*: a forward shift of adverbials of time and place. Mr. Compson, in *Absalom, Absalom!*, uses this form of deictic projection in times of heightened emotional investment, for instance in 'yes, she was weeping now!' (69). Narrated monologue (free indirect discourse) is a specifically literary form of limited deictic projection, which features what Dorrit Cohn calls the 'transformation of figural thought-language into the narrative language of third-person fiction' (1983:100). One finds the same forward shift of adverbials of time and place here, but person pronouns and tense remain firmly anchored to the position of the speaker.

In all of the instances above, deictic projection is limited, some deictics always remaining anchored to the position of the speaker. If deictic projection is more extensive, however, the utterance must be anchored to the position of the speaker through the attributive devices and constructions of quoted monologue. Here we are concerned with the traditional attributive verbs that present the different forms of saying and thinking, which introduce direct quotations, as well as with such graphological signs as quotation marks and the colon.

As we shall see, deviations in deictic projection and anchoring in Faulkner's characters often point to developmental and emotional problems. While Benjy Compson in *The Sound and the Fury*, for instance, is unable to perform deictic projection, his brother Quentin is unable to keep his deictic projection anchored, thereby losing the stability of the self, and his brother Jason neurotically repeats his anchoring again and again, afraid to mingle his views with others.

Attributive constructions play a large role in viewpoint shifts, whether they are accomplished through deictic projection (as in quoted monologue) or not (as in psychonarration). In the latter instance, we are concerned both with the type of the attributive clause, showing the various mental activity verbs of psychonarration such as *know*, *believe*, *hope*, *remember*, *wonder*, *conclude*, *regret*, and with the form of the attribution itself.

Generally speaking, the attributive verbs here indicate the specific mental activity of an experiencer (the one whose point of view is expressed), but may also give information as to the truth-value that the speaker assigns to the attribution. For example, with his choice of the attributing verbs *know* and *understand* (as in *The boy knew he was going to die soon*), an attributor normally indicates agreement (it is 'true,' according to the attributor, that the boy will die soon)[25]; with a verb like *imagine* (as in *The boy imagined he was going to die soon*) the attributor indicates disagreement (the boy's thought that he will die soon, according to the attributor, is a false one), while verbs like *think* or *believe* (as in *The boy thought he was going to die soon*) create a neutral context in which to reflect the experiencer's mental activity (the attributor refrains from expressing his views on the truth of the attribution).[26] That the specific choice of a speaker's attributive verb may have great consequences will become clear in my discussion of Joe Christmas's personality in Chapter 4.

With regard to the form of the attribution itself, one can distinguish the 'small-

---

25 Compare the oddity of a sentence such as *He knew he was going to die soon but he was wrong* with the redundancy of a sentence such as *He knew he was going to die soon and he was right*. This indicates that consent is part of the inherent meaning of *know*.

26 Thus, *He believed he was going to die soon and he was right* and *He believed he was going to die soon but he was wrong* are both possible.

clause,' the 'to-infinitive,' the 'how-clause,' and the 'that-clause.' The term *small-clause*, in Frederike van der Leek's definition, refers to a complement of a mental activity verb, which may, but need not be, verbal. If the complement is verbal, it is a small-clause only if the verb is non-finite and not accompanied by the infinitive marker *to*. Such a construction, van der Leek (1992) argues, is non-epistemic, in that it makes no reference to a truth-judgment of the experiencer; instead it simply signals the experience as such. A beautiful example of the small-clause is found in Henry James's short story 'The Beast in the Jungle' (1983:327-383):

> He saw the Jungle of his life and saw the lurking Beast; then, while he looked, perceived it, as by a stir of the air, rise, huge and hideous, for the leap that was to settle him.

In the clause 'he... perceived it... rise,' the observer identifies completely with the experience of the matrix subject 'he.' This, in fact, is an example of what Dorrit Cohn has called 'consonant psycho-narration,' in which the observer, without passing judgment, 'yields to the figural thoughts and feelings' of the experiencer (1983:31), which in this case clearly amount to a hallucination.[27] That the construction does not normally allow for a judgment by an attributor is clear from the oddness of the following sentences: *He knew the Beast rise*; *He imagined the Beast rise.*

Because the small-clause conveys situations as experienced rather than epistemically (in terms of what is considered true of the world), the construction is especially suitable for depicting states of altered consciousness, such as dreams, hallucinations, depersonalization and mental deficiency, when truth-judgment is avoided, impaired, disturbed or impossible.[28] Faulkner's novels, with their concentration on deviant states of mind, contain many examples of this form of attribution, for instance the external narrator's accounts of Joe Christmas's depersonalized behavior in *Light in August*:

> He heard his voice say... and he watched his hand swing
> (261)

The construction is found throughout Benjy's Compson's text in *The Sound and the Fury*; in Quentin Compson's text in *The Sound and the Fury* when his psychosis has overtaken him; and in Vardaman Bundren's text in *As I Lay Dying* when he is overwhelmed by anger at his mother's death.

Another instructive example of the small-clause construction is from James Joyce's 'A Painful Case' in *Dubliners*:

> He felt his moral nature falling to pieces.
> (107)

Again, the attributor refrains from expressing what the matrix subject ('he') believes to be true of the world, or his (the attributor's) own judgment to this effect. Instead, he renders in his own words what he, through identification, assumes this experiencer to be feeling. The attributor might, however, have expressed some form of epistemic

---

27 See James Phelan's interesting discussion of the story and the meaning of this hallucination (1989:61ff.).
28 An example that conveys the special atmosphere of a dream through its many small-clauses is found in William Gass's 'The Pederson Kid': 'I dreamed coming in from the barn and finding his back to me in the kitchen and wrestling with him and pulling him down and beating the stocking cap off his head with the barrel of the gun. I dreamed coming in from the barn still blinking with the light and seeing him there and picking up the shovel and taking him on.'

evaluation of the experiencer by using, instead of the small-clause, a to-infinitive, a how-clause, or a that-clause.

If Joyce's narrator had used a to-infinitive, the sentence would have read: *He felt his moral nature to be falling to pieces*. With such a construction, the attributor would have signaled the experiencer's epistemic evaluation of his situation based solely on his experience as such. Virtually the same effect is reached by the how-clause: *He felt how his moral nature was falling to pieces*, except for the greater distance between the viewpoint of the attributor and that of the experiencer, as evoked through the past tense of the verb phrase *was falling*. The epistemic evaluation of the experiencer allows for a judgment by the speaker: *He knew his moral nature to be falling to pieces* (he was right); *He imagined his moral nature to be falling to pieces* (he was wrong). Finally, by using a that-clause, the attributor would have indicated that the experiencer reached a conclusion on his experience, based not only on this experience but also on independently existing knowledge available to him. In this case Joyce's narrator would have made the following utterance: *He felt that his moral nature was falling to pieces*. Now the experiencer's conclusion—*My moral nature is falling to pieces*—is expressed and not just the experience that gave rise to it.[29] With his choice of attributive verb, the attributor may add a judgment on this conclusion: *He knew that his moral nature was falling to pieces* (he was right); *He imagined that his moral nature was falling to pieces* (he was wrong).

As we can see in these examples, the verb *feel* gradually changes its meaning from perception verb to cognition verb—showing, incidentally, how these classifications are again prototype categories—when moving from the small-clause via the to-infinitive and the how-clause to the that-clause. In other words, the perception aspect of the activity decreases in favor of the cognition aspect. The order in which the various forms of attribution have been discussed also shows an increasing distance between attributor and attributee. Narratologically speaking, these forms of psychonarration are gradually more distant, or 'dissonant' (Cohn's term), as they are mediated by an attributor who, to use Cohn's words, 'even as he focuses intently on an individual psyche, remains emphatically [more] distanced from the consciousness he narrates' (1983:26). If attributor and attributee are one, the attributor attributes attitudes to himself, either in the present or in the past: *I feel/felt my moral nature falling to pieces*; *I feel/felt how my moral nature is/was falling to pieces*; *I feel/felt my moral nature to be falling to pieces*; *I feel/felt that my moral nature is/was falling to pieces*. Here an increasing 'splitting,' as if into two personae takes place: an 'observing self' and an 'experiencing self.'

The various forms of attributive constructions discussed above concern the attributor's assumptions about the mental activity of the attributee. That each attribution can easily be complemented by the adjunct *obviously* shows that the attributor will normally base his attribution on observable behavior, verbal or nonverbal:

He obviously saw the Beast rise (because he moved back suddenly).

He obviously felt his moral nature to be falling to pieces (because he started to cry).

---

29   This is why the attributive verb *conclude* can only be used in the that-clause construction: *He concluded that his moral nature was falling to pieces* is possible, but not *He concluded his moral nature to be falling to pieces* or *He concluded his moral nature falling to pieces*.

She obviously remembered how the soup tasted bad (because she shud-
dered).
She obviously concluded that she would be safe (because she said she was
going to take a nap).

Normally speaking, the attribution of mental activity concerns, implicitly or explicitly, the observation of behavior and the assigning of cause-effect relations to this behavior. This assigning of cause-effect relations to observed behavior occurs automatically and often unconsciously. What this tells about the attributor rather than about the attributee forms the subject of 'attribution research.'

Attribution research, in social psychology, concerns itself with the processes that inter-vene between the observation of human behavior and the assignment of cause-effect relations to this behavior. It 'examines the layman's analysis of behavioral causation for the purpose of how this analysis effects his own behavior' (Jones 1967:x; cf. Kelley and Michela 1980; Kassin and Baron 1985). As Berkowitz explains it, 'the individual wants to know the cause of the actions or feelings that interest him because he thinks this knowledge will help him cope with the situations facing him. He presumably believes he can deal with people more effectively if he understands why they behave as they do or, for that matter, why he himself acts or feels in a certain way' (1980:94). Harold Kelley has argued more generally that 'the common person's understanding of a particular event is based on the perceived location of that event within a temporally ordered network of interconnected causes and effects' (1980:343). Researchers have stressed, however, that these cause-effect relations should not be considered in a strictly scientific sense, but as a perceived, subjective causal structure consisting of connections both stable and unstable, proximal and distal, past and present, actual and potential, and simple and complex.

Faulkner's novel *As I Lay Dying*, especially, foregrounds observation, which lies at the heart of all attribution. In this novel, eyes are of the utmost importance. The characters, all members of a close-knit group of isolated Mississippi farmers, watch each other constantly: 'meeting one another's eye and making like they hadn't touched' (81); looking 'at one another with long probing looks, looks that plunge unimpeded through one another's eyes and into the ultimate secret place' (128). Large parts of Faulkner's *Absalom, Absalom!*, on the other hand, foreground imagination, thematizing the assignment of cause-effect relations to imagined behavior. Throughout the text, the different narrators ponder the 'why?' of this imagined behavior. Time and again, the different speakers of *Absalom, Absalom!* pronounce statements—suggestions, hopes, fears, desires and expectations—that conjure not only human behavior but also the pos-sible reasons behind this behavior. Characterization through attribution, then, is one of Faulkner's stylistic hallmarks.

Various other stylistic features play a role in evoking a particular language user's position in the world and his understanding of, and attitudes towards, its events, processes, participants and circumstances. Thematization, for instance, concerns a speaker's 'choice of what to put first' as a reflection of 'what is uppermost in his mind' (Verdonk 1988:51). Modals reflect the degree of necessity, certainty and commitment that a speaker feels with regard to the world evoked. Causal connectors convey the speaker's need to provide explanations, justifications, evidence and motivations for his mental representations. Negation, as William Labov puts it, 'expresses the defeat of an expectation that something would happen' (1972:380f.). Negation and negative prefixes, then, may convey a contrast between the situation as conceptualized by the speaker and an expected situation. With regard to questions, Labov argues: 'If we consider the compelling character of all questions... it is clear that all requests, even the most mitigated, are to be heard against an unrealized possibility of negative consequences if they are not answered' (1972:384f.). Progressives typically characterize a situation as incomplete, unstable or unfinished (cf. Goldsmith and Woisetschlaeger 1982). They focus on non-structural or phenomenological qualities and thus on incidental observation and immediate experience. Non-progressives, on the other hand, tend to stress relative stability, completeness or a finished state. They focus on structural qualities and thus on repeated observation: on knowledge. Progressive tense, then, creates an expectation of change with regard to an existing worldview, while non-progressives create an expectation of permanence.

Finally, I shall devote special attention to the appended groups—'post-positioned non-finite relative clauses' (cf. Toolan 1990:96)—that occur frequently in the texts of some of Faulkner's characters. Appended groups, or 'quasi-clauses,' Irena Kaluza writes, are 'single words or constructions always placed after the simple clause,' sharing 'the presence of a punctuation mark (usually a comma, sometimes a colon, semicolon or even a full stop) to separate them from the preceding simple clause' (1967:26). They cover so-called prepositional constructions, nominative absolute free adjuncts, absolute free adjuncts and continuative subclauses. Kaluza shows how these appended groups may have no recognizable internal structure (as in 'I could feel water beyond twilight, smell'), but usually they possess at least some internal patterning, which shows their adjectival nature ('the grass was ankle deep, myriad'); their adverbial nature ('the sunlight slanted into it, sparse and eager'); or their verbal nature ('she looked at me, serene and secret and chewing'). Due to their position at the end of sentences, their incompleteness and their lack of internal structure, appended groups often evoke a certain measure of ambiguity. This is especially so if they are combined into series. Thus, as Kaluza points out, in texts that contain many appended groups, 'there is a finely graded scale of diminishing clarity of articulation... suggesting the fluidity of the mental content conveyed: from some degree of clarity where reason interprets experience to the dim and blurred impressions experienced in a dream-like state of mind' (1967:67).

Many other aspects of style might have been discussed here. My purpose, however, was to introduce some of those that are of special importance to characterization in Faulkner's texts. We are concerned here with what Fowler has called 'a small set of presumably universal categories which characterize different kinds of events and process, different types of participants in these events, and the varying circumstances of place and time within which events occur' (1986:156). Such properties of language show, or reflect, how the human mind structures reality; they reflect the cognitive properties of the human mind. The specific use that is made of these patterns by an individual in specific situational contexts, together with the habitual deviations from them, constitutes the mental self as reflected in language, or *mind-style*.

My study of *Psychostylistics*, then, examines the values of an approach to the literary character that combines findings of mainstream psychiatry and psychology with those of literary stylistics, especially mind-style. In the following chapters I shall explore how some of the major characters in *The Sound and the Fury, As I Lay Dying, Light in August* and *Absalom, Absalom!* evoke their mental selves by creating, through their narration, the worlds in which they live, including past and future worlds as they impinge on the reality of the present. But let us close this chapter with a brief discussion of the ways in which the characters' realities can be understood by the reader.

The Importance of the Frame

For the character inside fiction, as for the reader outside of it, concepts acquire meaning through their inclusion as central or more marginal members into prototype categories. These prototype categories possess built-in representations of physical and social laws as well as links with other prototype categories. Such connections between categories present 'natural' thinking patterns that originate from experience in the world and that have been called 'default options' (Hofstadter 1980:352). Default options are organized into *frames*, connecting objects, attributes and state verbs, and *scripts*, connecting objects, attributes and action verbs. Frames and scripts, then, reflect prototype instances of scenes and events respectively, which include the characteristics of people commonly found in them as well as forms of behavior normally associated with being in them (cf. Cantor *et al.* 1982; Tversky and Hemenway 1983).

The Frame in Literature

Literary works usually evoke fictional scenes and events that stay completely within a universally human biological reality. This is why when, in a story, a solid object is in a particular place, another solid object cannot be in the same place at the same time. The story need not specify that this second object is in a different place; the reader can infer this from prototype knowledge of the physical world.[30] As Douglas Hofstadter has put this: 'When the story has been completely told, you have built up quite an elaborate mental model of a scene, and in this model all the objects obey physical law' (1980:362). However, although such physical default options are normally binding, stories may cancel them; the connections they prescribe must then be overruled explicitly by presenting states that cannot exist or events that cannot take place, such as 'two cars approaching each other and then passing right through each other' (Hofstadter 1980:362).

Culture provides its own default options, its own frames and scripts, but they are much less binding. If for instance dinner is served, it may be inferred that there will be bowls of soup on the table. Culture, however, has many more options than physical reality; this because it is not given by nature but is actually developed through interaction between subjects within a specific group. Food may consist of different items; it may be served in different ways and different places. There is nothing natural in its being on a table, in the sense that it is natural for water to flow downhill. Culture,

---

30 Children from the age of six months onwards already know that one object cannot move through the space occupied by another object (cf. Baillargeon *et al.* 1985).

much more than physical reality, demands from an individual that he choose between alternative frames and scripts, or keep in mind several at the same time (ambiguity).[31] In literature, as well as in daily life, such indeterminacy can easily lead to different inferences among different people. When an author introduces a dinner into his story, a reader who is hungry may visualize soup, salad, main course and dessert; another may envision a much simpler meal or some 'junk food'; while a third may not 'see' any specific item at all. Perhaps this is not important for the story. However, if an author does not want readers to have so much inferential freedom to follow their own default options in this way, he must make his intentions clear and invite the choosing of more detailed frames.

Menakhem Perry defines the frame for literature as a 'system of hypotheses' that can 'create maximal relevancy among the various data of the text—which can motivate their "co-presence" in the text according to models derived from "reality"' (1979:43). In Perry's theory, each hypothesis forms a sort of label that can answer questions such as: What is happening?; What is the state of affairs?; What is the situation?; What are the motives?; What is the purpose?; What is the speaker's position? As Perry makes clear, these processes of choosing frames and of determining word meanings are simultaneous; one cannot first choose the frame, nor can one first decide on meaning. On the one hand, the frame selected is the one that can best accommodate the linguistic items in the text; on the other hand, the frame chosen will determine the specific meanings of its words. The word *heart*, for instance, can fit into a physical as well as into many cultural frames; it can be the subject of jokes, word-games, irony, metonymy and metaphor. Reading is a matter of 'guessing frames (from "sign-posts" and conventions) and selecting the one that works in the best way possible' (Perry 1979:44).

'The selection of any particular frame leads *ipso facto*,' Perry argues, 'to supplying information (filling gaps) which has no direct verbal basis in the text.' 'A comparison between that which a reader understands without any difficulty from a text and that which has explicit bases in this text,' he adds, 'may startle anyone who is unaware of the phenomenon of supplying material "under the aegis" of the frames. Most of what the reader infers from the text... is the reader's own gap-filling' (1979:45). The frame that the reader chooses is most valuable if it can accommodate as many items of the text as possible, including frames that were chosen previously and are still operative at the moment. At any given point in the text, the preferred frame will connect all the elements present in the closest way, 'allowing them the least degree of "freedom"' (1979:45). In general, a frame that also creates some order among elements is preferable to one that does not do so, and especially the relationship of causality is a strong link. However, as the choosing of frames is instantaneous and unconscious, the most conventional frame available at a certain moment, because it is easiest and fastest to grasp, will tend to be the preferred one.

A reader does not embark on the project of choosing frames after he has finished a chapter, a page, or a paragraph. Psychological experiments have proven that this happens already in a text of only a few words. As soon as more than one linguistic item has been encountered, the reader starts to arrange, relate and link them, as well as fill

31   In Jerome Bruner's words' 'culture itself comprises an ambiguous text that is constantly in need of interpretation by those who participate in it' (1986:122).

gaps and even anticipate. Readers, Perry argues, will always try to hold on to a frame that they have chosen as long as possible; that is, they will actively try and fit new material into the existing frame by looking for relations with material already present: relations of metonymy, synecdoche or analogy. Thus, readers will tend to consider new information as extending, specifying, including, paralleling, or contrasting with old information.[32] But any sequence not only influences the stretch of discourse that follows it, it is also the outcome of what went before.

Readers will not give up their hypotheses as soon as they are unable to include new material. As long as there is insufficient material to justify choosing a different frame, they will hold on to the former and leave the decision to change 'pending.' There is always a tension, then, between the new material pulling one way and the chosen frame pulling the other way. Thus, there is always a certain measure of '"backward" action,' as the reader must draw on frames that went before, 'go back and re-think the grounds for having constructed them,' for the purpose of expanding the frame so that old material can find additional utilization, or for the purpose of retrospective transformation so that new material can be included without contradiction (Perry 1979:59).

Only if this becomes impossible will the reader cancel a frame and replace it with another. Such cancellation may have different causes. Firstly, new material may contradict old material, so that it is necessary to cancel the chosen frame 'after the fact' as having been wrong from the start. Often this is the author's intention; he has been deliberately misleading. Secondly, new material may not contradict old material, directly or indirectly, but it may appear that this new material allows for a tighter organization in a different frame of new and previous information. Thirdly, new material may not cancel the old frame 'after the fact' but it may require the choosing of a new frame to replace and succeed the old one. The substitution of frames, whether by cancelling or replacement, Perry argues, does not happen instantly; the old frame becomes gradually more difficult to use, a new frame seems to present itself as a possibility, and may 'by degrees—when the "revolution" is inevitable' end up 'displacing the old one.' Seen in this light, part of the text will often exist 'simultaneously "between two frames"' (1979:61).

Conclusion

I have argued that humans, because of the similarities in their physical nature and the continuity of their patterns of social behavior—including language and literary conventions—share, to a certain degree, a common conception of reality. This pre-existing, or imposed, reality makes it possible for the individual to anticipate events by relying on frames and scripts as organized sets of expectations. I have made it clear that such frames and scripts, consisting of assumptions that stipulate how things will probably unfold in the future, can be the only basis of our readings of fiction. Frames,

32 Perry illustrates 'the phenomenon of adaptation to previous material' with an experiment conducted by Howes and Osgood (1954): 'The participants were given lists of 4 disconnected words and asked to associate about *the last one only*. It was found that despite the request to ignore the preceding words, the resultant associations were determined by these words as well. Thus, for instance, the word "dark" in the sequence "devil—fearful—sinister—dark" raised the association of "hell" more frequently than a neutral series, where "dark" was preceded by three numbers or three nonsense words' (1979:51).

although implicit and taken for granted, provide the very foundation of fiction, or as Hofstadter puts it: 'you can create artificial universes, in which there can happen non-real events with any amount of detail that you care to imbue them with. But the class symbols themselves, from which all of this richness springs, are deeply grounded in reality' (1980:362). From such 'class symbols,' prototype representations, or frames the story 'takes off.' In the words of Bruner, the story forms 'an instantiation of models we carry in our own minds' (1986:7).

Because of a reader's tendency to fall back on frames that exist with regard to his own world, the storyworld remains apart from the actual world only as long as, and to the extent that, this is explicitly given in the text. Fictions, then, and the personalities created by them, are read as variations on, extensions of, and deviations from the appropriate frames, or as Perry puts it: 'The frame serves as a guiding norm in the encounter with the text, as a negative defining principle, so that deviation from it becomes perceptible and requires motivation by another frame or principle' (1979:37).

Only if one appreciates the existence of a large shared physical and social reality and the importance of the frames, including literary ones, that organize this reality, can one understand the magic of human imagination, which is constantly active to infer a 'possible world' beyond the literary text. As regards the character's personality, these inferences are based on a sense, shared by author and reader, of what human nature *is*, or, as Marvin Minsky puts it:

> Isn't it remarkable that words can portray human individuals? You might
> suppose this should be impossible, considering how much there is to say.
> Then what permits a writer to depict such seemingly real personalities? It is
> because we all agree on so many things that are left unsaid. For example,
> we assume that all the characters are possessed of what we call 'common-
> sense knowledge,' and we also agree on many generalities about what we
> call 'human nature.'
> (1988:53)

Changing frames, in a joint effort of reader and writer, constantly create new implications, causing the gradual 'fleshing-out' of a character beyond what is explicitly presented in the text, and making him into a 'possible person,' a person who might have been.

2
Mind-Style in *The Sound and the Fury*

*There is no past present or future. Using tenses to
divide time is like making chalk marks on water*
(Janet Frame)

In Chapter 1, I have argued that by studying *mind-style*, the 'consistent stylistic choices of a speaker,' one can understand this particular individual's conceptualization of reality as a text: his or her worldview or, psychologically speaking, the organizing of experience that fills his or her individual need for order. The brothers Benjy, Quentin and Jason Compson from *The Sound and the Fury* are very suitable subjects for the study of mind-style. One would expect that as siblings they share their fictional reality to a very large extent and, indeed, their stories abound with shared events. Circumstances, however, have forced them to create unusual worlds for themselves, worlds that deviate from one another in such a way that they seem far apart yet tangled through mutual needs. The worlds of Benjy, Quentin, and Jason Compson, as they are conveyed through their stylistic choices, are deviant; as fictional 'persons' they are disturbed or impaired. Mind-style, however, only shows this indirectly, because it focuses not so much on the impaired functions as on what is left, that is, on how the impaired person presents himself as a fellow human being, or as Ivy McKenzie puts it: as a 'single organism, the human subject, striving to preserve its identity in adverse circumstances' (quoted in Sacks 1986:4). Faulkner intuitively understood such 'attempts... at restitution, at reconstructing a world reduced to complete chaos' (Sacks 1986:4). Construction, not deconstruction, is a feat here.

My analyses of the mind-styles of the Compson brothers concern what McKenzie has called 'the study of *an organised chaos*... reorganised on an unstable basis' (quoted in Sacks 1986:4). It is this 'organised chaos' that constitutes the worlds of Benjy, of Quentin and of Jason, just as 'organised chaos' constitutes the worlds of us all.[33] However, the Compson children unfortunately had to construct their worlds on a very 'unstable base,' one that would not sustain the two most sensitive ones and turned the

---

33 That the human brain organizes 'chaos,' no matter how adverse the circumstances under which it must do so, has been shown experimentally, for instance with co-called 'split brain' patients: people in whom the connection between the two hemispheres of the brain, the corpus callosum, is not functioning properly. An example is given by Smith Churchland. In this experiment two pictures are flashed to a split brain patient, one to his left hemisphere and one to his right. When the patient is asked to pick out matching objects, his two hands pick out different things. The subject will confabulate why he did so, producing one unified story; in other words, he does *not* produce two stories, such as: one half of my body wants... and the other half wants..., even if he is fully aware of his condition and of the purpose of the test. This is the case, Smith Churchland argues, because it is the brain's special task to create unity (1986:174ff.). Language, I argue, is a special tool to accomplish this task.

third into what Faulkner himself called 'the most vicious character… I ever thought of' (Meriwether & Millgate 1980:146).

Benjy Compson

I tried to say, but they went on

When one reads the first section in *The Sound and the Fury* (pp. 3-85) dated April seventh, 1928 for the first time, the world that is created will be difficult to understand; several readings, as well as clues from other sections, may be needed to make sense of it. What is immediately clear, however, when one reads the first two pages of the text up to the italics, which seem to form a kind of unity, is its limited lexical repertoire. The nouns in this part of the text are all concrete, pointing to things that can be seen:

12x fence
5x flag (and 3x the pronoun 'it')
4x grass and tree(s)
3x flower and pastures
2x shadow(s)
1x table, bird and garden

Abstract concepts—*space* and *void*—are also presented as concrete forms:

Through the fence, between the curling flower spaces, I could see them hitting.

We came to the broken place and went through it.

These descriptions possess a poetic beauty and freshness that is also found when a complex phrase is substituted for a simple concrete noun: 'Luster was hunting in the grass by the flower tree'; 'Luster came away from the flower tree' (3).

The lexical set that is formed by these linguistic choices is clearly one of nature, in which a few man-made objects play a role: the pastures and the garden, which are still part of the natural world, and the table, the flag and the fence. The word *fence*, with twelve occurrences in two pages, seems especially to point to a personal area of interest. The verbs that present human activities and states are extremely general: *hit*, *was*, *held*, *took*, *put* and the only verb of attribution *said*. Other verbs are more specific, but still elementary, such as *came*, *went*, *stopped* and *looked*. By contrast, the verbs that describe the activities of objects and animals are more complex:

Then there was a bird slanting and tilting on it.

The flag flapped on the bright grass and the trees.

Benjy's Mind-Style

The impression that is created in this first piece of text is that of a subject who is preoccupied with a limited number of concrete objects, most of them from nature: a 'person' with a very small vocabulary, like a young child busy discovering the world. Underlexicalization and overgeneralization with regard to nouns and verbs suggest that category formation and extension are still in a primitive stage of development. As Leonard Small has pointed out with regard to the cognitive development of children: 'the earliest stage of the development of thought [is] one in which a child projects himself into objects, which he thus animates… A subsequent stage is the development of concrete thinking; the final stage is abstract or categorical thinking' (1980:166). The speaker here seems to be in the second stage of cognitive development, working on establishing his place amongst the objects around him, and repeating again and again the names of the concrete objects that he already knows.

To come to such a conclusion with regard to the cognitive development of the speaker of this part of *The Sound and the Fury*, the reader must be guided by an understanding of the text's communicative intentions. One must not expect a 'realistic' representation of speech. Faulkner uses language iconically, suggesting through the appropriate stylistic choices the personality of this subject. It is Faulkner's great achievement that, as Leech and Short put it, 'the illusion is... created that we are "overhearing"' a 'rudimentary ordering' of 'direct sensory impressions' (1985:207). Yet, to understand this ordering, the reader can only rely on frames and scripts —including, of course, literary ones—that organize real-world experience: frames that will extend the reader's knowledge beyond what is actually there in the text. As soon as this happens, Benjy, as a 'possible person,' can 'stand on his feet and begin to move.'

The Baby Frame

The impression that Benjy is at a stage between baby and young child is strengthened by the syntax of the passage. Most of the sentences that are used are simple and short; a majority consist of necessary elements only. If they are complex, they usually show parataxis, for instance: 'They took the flag out, and they were hitting. Then they put the flag back and they went to the table, and he hit and the other hit.' Benjy's language, thus, seems structured by 'chronological iconicity,' presenting experiences in chronological order, and signaling that in his conception there is little or no indication of 'the relationship between events, or of their relative importance' (Leech and Short 1985:219).

Among the few cases where Benjy uses hypotaxis, once an adverbial clause of simultaneity is used: 'I looked through the fence while Luster was hunting in the grass.' As John Taylor (1989) has explained, temporal connectors, such as *while*, are the more central ones in the prototype category. A child is able to use them at an earlier age than causal connectors, which are not found here at all, suggesting that Benjy has not yet reached this developmental stage. The other cases of subordination both concern a small-clause:

I could see them hitting.
I... watched them going away.

The small-clause typically conveys only one point of view: that of an observer who moves in closely and identifies with the matrix subject (the individual whose experience is presented). In first-person narration this means that the observer-speaker 'steps into the shoes' of his experiencing self and simply (re)lives his experience without passing judgment on it. By refraining from positing an epistemic evaluation on the part of the experiencer, the small-clause, then, is one of the techniques with which an author can depict the mental immaturity of the young child.

The other types of appended clauses that accompany mental activity verbs, the to-infinitive, the how-clause and the that-clause are never used. As I have argued in Chapter 1, they signal a certain truth-judgment on the part of the experiencer with regard to his experience.[34] Such clauses, in first-person narration, present a doubling of consciousness—a split between observing self and experiencing self—of which Benjy seems not yet capable. Benjy conveys, through the exclusive use of the small-clause, his experience 'raw,' that is, without 'intellectual mediation' (Mellard 1970:234), presenting himself as an individual who is not yet able to think *about* himself or his experience.

The sentence containing the small-clause that was mentioned above—'I could see them hitting'—suggests at the same time that Benjy has not completely mastered the adult use of transitivity. The transitive construction, as we have seen, is a verbal construction that expresses the syntactic relation between subject and object. It develops out of early two-word combinations such as those frequently used by Benjy: 'he hit and the other hit.' By using the transitive verb *hit* as an intransitive verb, the text suggests that Benjy is still largely in a pre-transitive stage of development. Only if he himself is the subject of his sentences, and if the mental activity is visual, can Benjy use a transitive verb: 'I could see them'; 'I watched them.'

This finding can also explain the curious fact that Faulkner chooses not to connect Benjy's reporting sentences with his quotations:[35]

'Listen at you, now.' Luster said.

'Come on.' Luster said.

'Shut up that moaning.' Luster said.

'Wait a minute.' Luster said.

The fact that Benjy has not quite mastered even the most prototypical of transitive constructions makes it impossible for him to connect the words of others, which he repeats, with the physical activity of their speaking. Thus, he presents again, as with the verb *hit*, a transitive verb (*said*) as if it were intransitive. Notice, incidentally, the perfect parallelism of these constructions, which can be compared to the construction '"Here, caddie." He hit,' showing exactly the same structure. (Here Benjy does not even present the act of saying at all, giving a quotation and describing an action in two separate sentences). It seems, then, that to him the verb *said* is not a verb of attribution at all but a simple intransitive action verb like *hit*. Both activities have their effects, and affect him somehow as well, but Benjy does not know exactly how or why. His text suggests, through the virtual absence of transitive constructions, that Benjy does not completely understand the relations between objects, and between objects and their actions; his world is one of separate entities, actions and events without connections of, for instance, responsibility, participation, authority, incentive, submission, or cause and effect.

The development in the young child of the ability to use transitive constructions, even the less central forms, always predates the use of passives by a long stretch (Taylor 1989:245). Thus it is no wonder that no passive constructions are found in Benjy's text. Negation, which demands the creation of an alternative world of broken

---

34 Examples of the to-infinitive and the how-clause would have been *I could see them to be hitting*; and *I could see how they were hitting*. An example of the that-clause would have been: *I could see that they were hitting*.

35 In the earliest manuscripts we do not yet find this characteristic, stressing the deliberate nature of the deviation.

expectation; and requests, which evoke a world of negative consequences if they remain unanswered (Labov 1972:380f.; 384f.), are not found here either. Benjy, it seems, cannot visualize such things. Root modals and counterfactual verbs, such as those of obligation and desire, are also not found. Like negations and questions, they require the possibility of conceptualizing an alternative world.

A significant characteristic of Benjy's text is the abundant use of progressives. These suggest less the temporal aspect of the activity presented than the phenomenological aspects of its subjects. By using progressives in such large quantities, Benjy's text presents him as having no abstract comprehension of objects, actions or events as completed totalities or finished states. It is clear that he cannot extend his understanding of an action beyond what he can see. When Benjy does use a perfect, he does so only in its most prototypical sense: for a salient, punctual event in the near past. Benjy's text also contains a profusion of deictics. We shall first look at his pronouns here. It has been noted that Benjy's forms of reference are unusual. As Fowler puts it: 'he uses *personal pronouns* in an odd way—"them... they... They... they... they... he... the other..."'—without identifying who he is referring to and without varying the words he uses to refer to them' (1986:134). The many third-person pronouns do not in themselves strike one as particularly childlike, however. Such 'non-referential implicitness of the pronoun system,' as Dorrit Cohn calls it, together with the story's beginning '*in mediam mentem*,' is one of the most striking features of the autonomous monologue (1983:221). Pronouns are normally used when a speaker can assume that a listener is able to identify the referent and, since speaker and listener are one in an autonomous monologue, this is always the case.

It is, in fact, more curious that Benjy uses the name of his companion Luster so many times, and hardly ever refers to him with the aid of a pronoun. It seems as if the sound of his companion's name has some magical quality for Benjy. The ritualistic effect of this is compounded by the perfect parallelism of the reporting sentences that was mentioned before. As a contrast to the use of the proper name, the pronouns in the text may convey a lack of emotional investment in unimportant objects or individuals. It is this aspect, the utter concentration on one companion or caretaker, that helps to create the childlike impression of Benjy's mind-style. The mystical personification of important objects may also be mentioned in this connection:

I went back along the fence to where the flag was.
We went along the fence and came to the garden fence, where our shadows were.

Described in this way, these privileged objects—the flag and the shadows—seem to have chosen their positions close to another important object—the fence—on their own account. Apart from his third-person pronouns, Benjy's text contains many instances of the first-person pronoun *I*, indicating that he has at least a primitive sense of self:

I could see them hitting.
I went along the fence.
I went along the fence.
I looked through the fence
I held to the fence and [I] watched them going away.
I went back along the fence
I held to the fence.

In sentences that contain first-person pronouns, Mary Jane Hurst has argued, a character 'places himself in role structures suitable and unique to his personality and behavior' (1987:71). But the only role that Benjy ascribes to himself is that of agent of a simple, stereotypical action; his sense of self, then, seems developed only as far as simple instantaneous actions that are constantly repeated are concerned.

Through the use of his pronoun *I*, Benjy is able to present his own position in the world as a deictic center. Deictic projection, however, is impossible for him, because this would involve putting another individual in the deictic centre and presenting the situation from the spatial, temporal, social and psychological position of this individual. This would naturally involve the creation of an alternative world, something that seems impossible for Benjy. To perform deictic projection, the individual must have what has been called a 'theory of mind,' that is, he must possess the ability to know 'that other people know, want, feel, or believe things,' and that these things may be different from what he himself knows, wants, feels and believes (Baron-Cohen *et al.* 1985:38; cf. Frye and Moore 1991). Very young children are not yet capable of this. This finding also suggests why Benjy cannot use transitivity unless he himself is the subject of his sentence.

In this part of Benjy's text there are no instances of deictic projection. As we have seen, his attributive verbs generally do not really function as attributive verbs but only as simple action verbs. In addition, Benjy's use of the pronoun *we*, which may show an ability to perform deictic projection if it entails the active knowledge that what is in the other's mind matches up with what is in one's own mind, concerns only place and direction, a path followed together:

we went along the fence
we stopped
We went along the fence and [we] came to the garden fence
We came to the broken place and [we] went through it.

As these clauses show, the shared activities of Benjy and Luster all possess the same stereotypical characteristics. If one considers all the instances of first-person pronouns, it becomes clear that Benjy does not really perform any independent actions except for the action of seeing. For all other actions he needs the company of Luster or the guidance and stability of an inanimate object—the fence—or both.[36]

Adverbial deictics are also present in the first two pages of Benjy's text. These include those of time such as *then*, which is always used to refer to the very next thing that happens, and those of place and direction, such as *through*, *between*, *towards*, *along*, *away from* and *across*. But all of them are used in a crude way; they 'do not add up,' as Fowler puts it, 'to a comprehensible picture of the positions and movements of... himself, and Luster' (1986:134). Benjy's orientation in time and space is not completely absent, as some critics have argued, but it certainly seems precarious. All in all we can say upon reading the first two pages of Benjy's text that the mind-style

---

36 Critics have pointed to Benjy's frequent usage of the term *fence*, and have linked it to the theme of restriction. Without denying that this theme is important for the novel, it must be noted that the object, here, seems to have the function of providing support: the stability that he still needs more than freedom in his phase of development. A hole is thus called 'broken place,' indicating that he views it as an imperfection rather than an opportunity to escape restriction.

with which Faulkner artistically creates Benjy as a 'possible person' prompts the reader to rely on a frame of world-knowledge by which Benjy is characterized as a young child: a baby busy establishing the physical reality in which he has to find a place as an entity separate from the objects around him. Thus he is creating the basis of the social reality that will make him a member of the family in which he lives.

Reframing and Extending

One will be surprised to read, then, in the words of Luster, that this day is, in fact, Benjy's thirty-third birthday:

'Listen at you, now.' Luster said. 'Aint you something, thirty three years old, going on that way. After I done went all the way to town to buy you that cake.'
(3)

If you dont hush up, mammy aint going to have no birthday for you. If you dont hush, you know what I going to do. I going to eat that cake all up. Eat them candles, too. Eat all them thirty three candles.
(4)

It is obvious that the baby frame mentioned must present problems. But, as Menakhem Perry (1979:59f.) has argued, readers do not discard a constructed frame as soon as one new element in a story seems to contradict it. They will, instead, try to fit new material in, if at all possible, by considering it as somehow paralleling, including, or contrasting with old material, and by extending it in a certain direction. Thus, one might perhaps consider Luster's words to be ironical, or Benjy to be misquoting him. Still, a tension is created, causing some 'backward action': some rethinking of the grounds for having chosen the frame in the first place (Perry 1979:58). The end of this opening section, then, will certainly leave the reader with a considerable amount of confusion. At this point a sudden transition seems to occur to a different situation.

Although in this next section, starting with the italics on page 4, many elements of the situation seem the same, the weather certainly is much colder, and a different companion—Caddy—is introduced. Here no quotation marks at all are found, and the distancing of attributive clause and quotation, which was so obvious in the first section, is also absent:

Uncle Maury said to not let anybody see us, so we better stoop over, Caddy said
(4).

Close reading will reveal that this transition was brought about by Luster's remark: 'Cant you never crawl through here without snagging on that nail' (4), which brings back a memory of a similar experience at an earlier time. The events of April 7, then, seem to spark off chains of memory extending back into Benjy's past.

While Benjy's text presents the happenings of April 7 in perfect chronology, and although the memories themselves are chronological as well, suggesting that he actually relives them, these transitions give the text as a whole its characteristic 'psychological sequencing.' The textual order here reflects 'the order in which impressions occur in the mind' (Leech and Short 1985:236). It shows how impressions 'simply "fall upon the mind"... through selection without reference to the will or to commonplace logic' and reveal 'a person's mind' (Apter 1979:74). I shall not follow all these transitions throughout the text, since this has been done satisfactorily before (cf. Volpe 1964). I shall instead follow the baby frame forward during the day of April seventh, 1928, as well as back into the past, to show what kinds of conclusions can be drawn in this way concerning the characterization of Benjy Compson.

The linguistic choices that prompted the election of the baby frame continue past the first section into Benjy's memories of earlier times, but so do the problems concerning this frame. Many times Benjy is called a baby:

> Mother took my face in her hands and then she held me against her. 'My poor baby.' she said.
> (9)
> You're not a poor baby. Are you. Are you. You've got your Caddy. Haven't you got your Caddy.
> (9f.)

But Benjy's clothing, for instance, does not suggest a baby: 'Are you going to take that baby out without his overshoes' (9). His posture obviously is that of a grown man: 'You calling that thing a baby... A man big as T.P.' (10). Eventually, in different memories, Benjy's exact age is given:

> 'Come on, now.' Dilsey said. 'You too big to sleep with folks. You a big boy now. Thirteen years old. Big enough to sleep by yourself'
> (49)
> 'Well, I dont want him carried, then.' Mother said. 'A five year old child.'
> (72)

By this time it has, of course, also become clear that Benjy has far too many memories to be a young child. These memories, moreover, concern his siblings, who are clearly growing up, and several generations of caretakers. Sooner or later a conclusion must be reached that Benjy is, in fact, both a baby and a grown man: a grown-up man with the mind of a baby, or a baby with the body of a grown-up man.

Faulkner himself called Benjy 'an idiot,' and he described his interest in Benjy in the following way: 'I became interested in the relationship of the idiot to the world that he was in but would never be able to cope with and just where could he get the tenderness, the help, to shield him in his innocence.' He defined this innocence as: innocence 'in the sense that God had stricken him blind at birth, that is, mindless at birth, there was nothing he could ever do about it' (Meriwether and Millgate 1980:146). Benjy's brother Jason calls him 'that damn looney' (13), and his companion Luster calls him 'deef and dumb,' a 'born looney' (56).[37] He knows that *'folks dont like to look at a looney'* because *'taint no luck in it'* (22), and he threatens: 'They going to send you to Jackson, where you belong. Mr Jason say so. Where you can hold the bars all day long with the rest of the looneys and slobber. How you like that' (62).

The Psychostylistics of Mental Retardation

The impression that the text creates through specific stylistic choices attributed to Benjy is that Benjy suffers from mental retardation, such as may derive from incomplete

---

37 This does not necessarily mean that he is deaf and dumb as critics have argued. There is evidence to assume that Benjy cannot speak; he does, however, seem to be able to hear.

growth, impairment, or lack of integration of brain cells (cf. Small 1980:209).[38] Frame knowledge of retardation can thus help the reader to 'flesh out' the character. Benjy's impairments have disrupted the normal establishment of the categories of physical reality, and thus also provided a faulty basis on which to build his social reality. He perceives the world in a deviant way, at least for his age, and he has no understanding of the society in which he lives.

Much of Benjy's text consists of quotations from others. Curiously, in these quotations Benjy takes over all the colloquialisms that these others use and that never occur in his own text. Benjy, it seems, understands the words of others only on the level of sounds. His quoting is therefore better called 'echoing' or 'echolalia.' Leech and Short dismiss the importance of these echoes in their discussion of mind-style (1985:204). The simple fact, however, that Benjy echoes others so much is an indication of his mental deficiency (cf. Small 1980:333; Smith Churchland 1986:186; Kaplan and Sadock 1988:557). What is more, Benjy cannot remember everything he has ever heard, so that his echoing presumes unconscious selection of those utterances that have somehow moved him, and therefore show his mind-style as well. It is significant, for instance, that Benjy remembers the many times he is told to 'hush.' He seems to perceive and remember, somehow, that he is never encouraged to express himself. We can say, then, that these echoes of other people's words, as indications of the things that have moved Benjy, form part of *his* world. Still, Benjy is not really 'mindless' in the literal sense; some qualities of his mind are intact or even enhanced. As the psychiatrist Oliver Sacks has said of his patients:

> What is this quality of mind, this disposition, which characterises the
> simple, and gives them their poignant innocence, transparency,
> completeness and dignity...? If we are to use a simple word here, it would
> have to be 'concreteness'—their world is vivid, intense, detailed, yet
> simple, precisely because it *is* concrete: neither complicated, diluted, nor
> unified, by abstraction.
> (1986:164)

No matter how far back into memory it goes, Benjy's text is made up of concrete nouns, presenting the things that he can see, hear, smell, and feel. In this case, 'sensations and basic responses are all we have' (Minter 1979:381).

The lexical sets that can be identified in Benjy's text show how fond he is of nature. The pasture, the trees, the flowers, the bright grass, the farm animals, the

---

38 Benjy shows many characteristics of autism as well. As Kaplan and Sadock argue, autistic disorder is characterized by specific behavioral abnormalities. These include: no awareness of the feelings of others, no comfort seeking with others in time of distress, no imitation play, no social play, no verbal, paraverbal or nonverbal communication, echolalia, attachments to unusual objects—'autistic objects'—which are clutched rather than touched and tasted, as normal children do (cf. Tustin 1986), and extreme distress over change in the environment, with unreasonable insistence on following routines. Autists may 'selectively ignore spoken language directed at them, and so they are often thought to be deaf' (Kaplan and Sadock 1988:559). Kaplan and Sadock argue that the main differentiating features between autistic disorder and mental retardation, which may but need not occur together, is that the mentally retarded relate to others in accordance with their mental age, whereas autists do not (1988:559). 'Unlike both normal and mentally retarded children,' Rosenbaum and Sonne write, 'autistic children show signs of having very serious language-learning difficulties,' especially in the area of deixis (1986:52; cf. Kaplan and Sadock 1988:557). See for a discussion of Benjy Compson's autism Sara McLaughlin 1987.

smooth shapes of the fire and the branch sustain him and bring him peace. The branch, especially, is on his mind very often; many pages contain the word as often as five times. As James Mellard suggests: 'The branch is the source and symbol of what are probably the best memories of Benjy's life... there is nothing but void in his memory before the branch episode, so in a real way the branch becomes the origin of life for him as water is the origin of life itself' (1970:236). In a similar way, the mirror, which is mentioned again and again in the scene in which Benjy's name is changed, seems to stand for his urge to 'frame' the situation: his need for stability, and his longing for his own place amongst the members of his family. We can also see this desire to belong from his use of the pronoun *we*:

We could hear the roof and the fire, and a snuffling outside the door.
We could hear them.
We could hear the fire and the roof.
(77,78,78)

While it is not at all so certain that 'we' could hear all this, Benjy, showing again his lack of a 'theory of mind,' cannot conceptualize the situation in another way.

Benjy's lexical choices, as we have seen, present his world in terms of concrete objects among which he can feel at home. But, as Oliver Sacks has noticed in his patients: 'The concrete is readily imbued with feeling and meaning—more readily, perhaps, than any abstract conception. It readily moves into the aesthetic, the dramatic, the comic, the symbolic, the whole wide deep world of art and spirit' (1986:166). Benjy's underlexicalization, Fowler argues, 'does not simplify, but attempts to analyse a complicated geometrical concept'; it does not seem a 'laborious struggle to a concept for which there might be a simple word which Benjy does not know, but the creation of a perception which Benjy has and which is unusual (a strangely shaped space edged by the shapes of the flowers)' (1986:153).

Benjy's perceptions are extraordinarily sensitive, making large demands on his limited vocabulary. Therefore, while he has fewer words at his command than a 'normal' person, he, in fact, needs more of them. What is conveyed, then, is not so much the distorted world or the impaired brain of Benjy, but an alternative world of poetic beauty. Adjectives are very important in this respect; they are simple and sensory, repeated again and again, but their effect is extraordinary: 'We ran up the steps and out of the bright cold, into the dark cold' (7). In addition, Benjy uses beautiful similes, which work especially to connect the person he loves with the aspects of nature that he understands and to which he feels close: 'Her hair was like fire, and little points of fire were in her eyes... She smelled like trees' (82).

As is usual in small children, Benjy shows signs of the assimilation of perceptual functions; this means that the activation of one perceptual scheme overflows into another (cf. van Ree 1975). Because a baby learns by assimilating seeing with other perceptual functions, it will try to listen to, touch, smell, and, especially, taste what it sees. While normal children eventually learn to differentiate between things that can be seen, heard, smelt, etc., Benjy has never learned to categorize his experience in this way. Instead, he has cultivated and perfected this childlike synaesthesia. The text presents this aptly through small-clauses, which convey that Benjy is able to:

smell the bright cold.
smell the clothes flapping

hear the roof.
hear it getting night
(6,15,71,82)
Very often, Benjy's mind-style shows personification of inanimate objects, thus conveying the magical world of the young child:
The spoon came up and I ate
The bowl went away.
The room went away... the room came back
The candles went away.
Her rings jumped on Caddy's back.
The cushion went away.
(29,29,50,65,71,73)
Elements from nature seem to have the same magical powers:
The ditch came up out of the buzzing grass.
The tree quit thrashing.
The moonlight came down the cellar stairs.
the moonlight jumped away
The grass was buzzing in the moonlight where my shadow walked on the grass.
The flowers came back.
the fire went away.
(40,44,45,45,53,63,66)
as well as parts of the human body:
She gave me a flower and her hand went away.
My voice went louder then and my hand tried to go back to my mouth
(11,68)

As many of these examples show, Benjy is especially sensitive to the disappearing of objects; it seems that he feels extremely helpless, unable to do anything about it but cry. Only very seldom does he conceptualize his own initiative of going away:
Benjy, Caddy said, Benjy. She put her arms around me again, but I went
away.
(46)
'Benjy.' Caddy said. She came again, but I went away.
(47)
Benjy, who feels very hurt here because Caddy does not 'smell like trees' any more after having used perfume, conceives of an unusually self-sufficient action. Still, the parallelism of his text suggests that it is an instinctive reaction rather than a conscious decision.

Benjy cannot easily distinguish himself from others. In the following beautiful example, the pronoun *we* shows how much he feels one with his beloved sister: 'Caddy stopped and lifted me. We staggered.' Benjy, naturally, does not stagger, being carried by his sister, but it is clear that he has not quite reached the developmental stage where he can conceptualize himself as a separate human being. He also seems detached from his own experiences, for instance that of pain: 'I put my hand out to where the fire had been... My hand jerked back and I put it in my mouth and Dilsey caught me' (67).

While underlexicalization by itself would make it difficult enough for Benjy to find the words to reflect on his physical sensations, an additional difficulty is that he does not understand these sensations to be located inside himself. Dizziness, for instance, is attributed to the world around him:

The ground kept sloping up... Quentin held my arm and we went towards the barn. Then the barn wasn't there and we had to wait until it came back. I didn't see it come back. It came behind us and Quentin set me down in the trough where the cows ate. I held on to it. It was going away too, and I held to it. (23f.)

Notice here, also, the use of the pronoun *we*. Once more it is clear that Benjy has no 'theory of mind'; in his innocence he assumes that he shares his world with Quentin and believes that Quentin also has to wait until the barn comes back.

Just as Benjy has problems acknowledging his physical sensations, he is often unaware of his emotions. Their expression shows itself through the reactions of others, which Benjy repeats without comment: 'I held to the fence and watched them going away. "Listen at you, now." Luster said. "Aint you something, thirty three years old, going on that way"' (3). If Benjy does not always acknowledge or understand his own feelings, neither does he understand those of others very well, even if they influence him emotionally: 'Mother put her handkerchief under her veil. "Stop it, Mother." Jason said. "Do you want to get that damn looney to bawling in the middle of the square"' (13). Benjy sees his mother's behavior, and apparently tends to react to it, but he does not know what it means.

Sometimes, however, it seems that Benjy is able to remember his own expression of grief at an earlier time, especially when Caddy was still there:

'I'll run away and never come back.' Caddy said. I began to cry. (21)

I wasn't crying, but I couldn't stop. I wasn't crying, but the ground wasn't still, and then I was crying. (23)

I cried louder and pulled at Caddy's dress. 'Go away, Charlie.' Caddy said. Charlie came and put his hands on Caddy and I cried more. I cried loud. (54)

Notice the uncharacteristic negations: 'I wasn't crying'; 'I couldn't stop.' In these sections there is at times even a trace of self-reflection to be observed in Benjy's text: 'It was hot inside me, and I began again. I was crying now, and something was happening inside me' (25). One of these moments of greater awareness concerns the experience at the branch, which marks the 'birth' of Benjy's story. Here his syntax is more advanced as well: 'Caddy turned around and said "Hush." So I hushed... "Hush now." she said. "I'm not going to run away." So I hushed' (21). Benjy's text reveals here, through the causal connector *so*, an elementary understanding of cause and effect. Even if it concerns only the familiar sequence of his sister's voice and his consequent feeling of peace, he understands that it is *her* voice that causes him to become quiet. On April 7 Benjy seems to have lost this ability to understand simple causality, together with the sister who made it happen.

Remembering this extraordinary day of the branch experience, Benjy is even able to give a summary of the discussions of his companions instead of a simple echoing of their words. This requires considerable 'intellectual mediation,' and has been over-looked by critics who argue that Benjy is incapable of reflection:

> When Quentin came back Versh stopped and hollered that he was going to tell. Caddy told him that if he wouldn't tell, they'd let him come back. So Versh said he wouldn't, and they let him.
> (21)
> Jason said he wasn't afraid of snakes and Caddy said he was but she wasn't and Versh said they both were and Caddy said to be quiet, like Father said.
> (42f.)

Since the branch scene is Benjy's earliest memory, and he could express himself in a more sophisticated way then, we must conclude that his intellectual abilities have actually deteriorated through the years. Since the passages in italics, in which Benjy turns most deeply into his memories and actually relives his emotions, also show these characteristics of his early mind-style, more complex processes must take place in his mind than can usually be identified at the surface.

We have seen that Benjy does not understand other people's emotions. He also does not understand their words, even though he repeats them. The golf term *caddie*, for instance, is unknown to him, but the sound is nevertheless meaningful because it is the same as the name of his sister: *Caddy*. For this reason, the golf term *tee* is changed into the more familiar sound *table*, which apparently does have some meaning for Benjy: 'He went to the table. "Fore caddie." he said. He hit' (61). In the context of the golf game, the sound of Caddy's name always comes up in association with the act of hitting, which can only add to the sorrow Benjy feels when he is confronted, again and again, with the great void caused by her leaving home. Luster, in a cruel mood, takes advantage of this and tells Benjy: 'You want something to beller about. All right, then. Caddy... Caddy. Beller now. Caddy' (63). Clearly, Benjy does not understand that he misinterprets the words of others, and he does not know that others misinterpret him. Although it is hearing the word *caddie* that makes him cry, he simply repeats Luster's words without comment:

> The man said 'Caddie' up the hill... 'What he moaning about now.' 'Lawd knows.' Luster said. 'He just starts like that. He been at it all morning. Cause it his birthday, I reckon.'
> (18f.)

Underlexicalization with respect to verbs that present human activities and states, as we already saw, leads to overgeneralization. Underlexicalization, in this case, is not a capacity to generalize out of experience.[39] Benjy seems able to conceptualize only

---

39 Young children initially overextend their categories. This is why they, for instance, will use the word *doggie* for all furry animals, or the word *daddy* for all men. This overextension, however, does not involve the broadening out of adult categories, but rather seems to evolve from their own, incomplete or incorrect, prototypes. Taylor discusses the example of a child who first used the word *clock* for 'an unfamiliar picture of a cuckoo clock,' which became its prototypical clock. Subsequently, it extended the category in different directions to include different clocks, watches, pictures of watches, meters, dials, timers, radios, telephones and bracelets, until it finally limited the category to the adult one, including clocks and watches (1989:254f.). The process of category extension is an automatic and highly productive process, which finds

a very few human activities, and he categorizes those he does know in an idiosyncratic way, very much like a young child. His use of the verb *have* provides an example: 'Luster had some spools and he and Quentin fought and Quentin had the spools' (34). The activities of non-human agents, however, are conveyed much more vividly, suggesting that Benjy understands them better, feels closer to them, or is more intensely moved by them:

the flowers rasped and rattled against us.
the pigs were grunting and snuffling.
The cows came jumping out of the barn.
(4,5,23)

This tendency, in fact, runs counter to what is usually found in young children, who first learn to conceptualize the activities of human behavers.[40] Benjy's idiosyncratic use of prepositions, on the other hand, does bring to mind the cognitive development of young children, whose play reflects the salience of 'in relations' (Taylor 1989:251):[41]

He lay there, laughing into the grass.
T.P. fell up the hill, into the moonlight
Then he fell into the flowers
the water ran into the table.
(43f.,45,45,81)

Benjy and the Family

It is clear that Faulkner characterizes Benjy as forever a child, who needs peace, order and security. Such desires, according to Mellard, 'are best fulfilled in a child's world dominated by strong, compassionate parental figures, either actual or surrogate' (1970:245). Benjy's father tries to provide Benjy with the love and understanding he needs, and he certainly succeeds to some extent. As Benjy's mind-style shows, he sees his father *in light*, suggesting the quality of his love for him:

'Oh.' Father said. Light fell down the steps, on him... He stooped and took me up, and the light came tumbling down the steps on me too
(27)
There was a light at the top of the stairs. Father was there
(70)

But Mr. Compson is also an alcoholic, 'who toys with the emotions and needs of his children' (Minter 1979:383), and who tries to pass on 'the traditions which he himself lacked the strength to uphold' (Volpe 1964:105).

Moreover, Benjy's mother shows severe narcissistic and hypochondriac behavior.

its curbing and channeling through social interaction. Mentally handicapped children may reach this state abnormally late or not at all, while schizophrenics, who experience a breakdown of already established adult conceptual processes, seem to regress to a typical child-like overinclusiveness and fuzziness of categories (cf. Laffal 1979:20ff.; van Ree 1974:120ff.).

40 The disinterest in human activities in favor of non-human ones is, in fact, one of the diagnostic criteria of autism.

41 As Taylor explains, experiments show that 'below age three (by which time they seem to have worked out the different meanings of *in*, *on*, and *under*) children have very clear ideas about where objects "belong".' They invariably put one object inside another, irrespective of instructions, and if this is not possible, they put it on top (1989:251).

She lies in bed, a cloth folded over her head, crying: 'He'll wake up at daybreak, and I simply cannot bear another day like today' (71). To her, Benjy is 'a judgment' on herself (5) and she changes his name because she cannot stand to have an idiot named after her brother. She is unable to give Benjy any real love, and he feels the effects of her paradoxical behavior:

> Mother took my face in her hands and then she held me against her. 'My
> poor baby.' she said. She let me go.
> (9)
> 'Bring him here.' Mother said... 'No, no. Not in my lap. Let him stand
> up.' 'If you'll hold him, he'll stop.' Caddy said. 'Hush.' she said.
> (72)

His mother's fussing over Benjy's health is in fact purely egocentric: '"Are you going to take that baby out without his overshoes." Mother said. "Do you want to make him sick, with the house full of company"'(9).

Although Benjy echoes all of this, he, of course, does not understand it. But lack of love is part of his world, and he must turn elsewhere for the fulfillment of his needs. Benjy, sensitive as he is, feels 'the vacancies his parents' inadequacies have created in his life' (Minter 1979:380), and has learned to depend on his sister Caddy completely:

> 'Hush, Mother.' Caddy said. 'You go up stairs and lay down, so you can
> be sick...' She led me to the fire and I looked at the bright, smooth shapes.
> (73f.)

On April 7, 1928, when Caddy has long left home, the lost sister or, as Faulkner called her, 'that doomed little girl... trying to hold that crumbling household together' (Blotner 1984:211), still has to provide all the love and the security that is missing in his mother's behavior.

Benjy is unable to forget Caddy, because for him there is no difference between actual experience and memory. His mind registers no distinction between the present and the past, but unremittingly recalls an 'exact replica of the incident' (Vickery 1954:1022). As Faulkner expressed it: 'To that idiot, time was not a continuation, it was an instant, there was no yesterday and no tomorrow, it all is this moment, it all is [now] to him' (Meriwether & Millgate 1980:147). Benjy needs only some small provocation to start behaving as if what he remembers is happening all over again. Very often the remembrance of his sister Caddy's smell forms the transition between different memories in which she offered love and security. What she gave him was a baby's world, in which warmth and a familiar smell are all that is needed:

> *'Hush.' Caddy said. 'I'm coming.' I hushed and Dilsey turned back the*
> *spread and Caddy got in between the spread and the blanket... 'Now.' she*
> *said. 'Here I am.'... She snuggled her head beside mine on the pillow...*
> *The room went black.* Caddy smelled like trees.
> (51)

The remembrance of the sound of Caddy's name has an incantatory function for Benjy:

> *Then I saw Caddy, with flowers in her hair, and a long veil like shining*
> *wind. Caddy Caddy* 'Hush.' T.P. said. 'They going to hear you. Get down
> quick.' He pulled me. Caddy. I clawed my hands against the wall Caddy...
> He pulled me on. Caddy
> (45)

The Tragic World of Benjy Compson

Benjy's isolation, after Caddy's departure, arises from his inability to understand verbal communication. This was clear already on the first pages of his section, from the fact that he does not connect the words of speakers with their physical activity of speaking. That Benjy desperately wants to communicate, however, is made explicit in one of the most moving passages of the text,[42] where he tries in vain to communicate something of himself to the girls passing by his fence, showing his tragedy in a world of words:

I tried to say, but they went on, and I went along the fence, trying to say, and they went faster. Then they were running and I came to the corner of the fence and I couldn't go any further, and I held to the fence, looking after them and trying to say.
(59)

But Benjy's ability to perceive simple actions he can understand to be communicative acts is clear from his observation of a cow's activity: 'The cow stood in the lot, chewing at us' (40). Just as the cow, in Benjy's conception, uses the physical activity of its chewing as a communicative act, so Benjy uses his physical activity of 'saying' as a communicative act. Benjy does not see the difference because he does not understand that one must say *something* to communicate, he does not know that the verb *say* is necessarily transitive. In other words, Benjy is unaware that while the physical activity of 'trying to say' creates meaning in a perceiver, it is the act of saying *something* that communicates.[43]

Only his sister Caddy, when she was still living with Benjy, understood his manner of 'saying.' Only she would try and grasp the meanings he wanted to communicate: '"Did you come to meet Caddy." she said, rubbing my hands. "What is it. What are you trying to tell Caddy"' (7). Only she was willing to share his world, a world of purity and natural things; and only she ever used the pronouns *we* and *ourselves* to Benjy, answering his need for togetherness: '"We dont like perfume ourselves." Caddy said. *She smelled like trees*' (49). But Caddy is gone, and Benjy's memories never receive the 'coloring' of a normal memory. Because their emotional weight is not diminished with time, all his memories retain the whole impact of the actual experience. Every time he hears Caddy's name, every time he holds on to the fence through which she used to come towards him, Benjy remembers her in an equally vivid way. And every time he cries for her, or for the feeling that she would give him:

You cant do no good looking through the gate, T.P. said. Miss Caddy done gone long ways away. Done got married and left you. You cant do no good, holding to the gate and crying. She cant hear you.... Ain't nothing going to quiet him, T.P. said. He think if he down to the gate, Miss Caddy come back. Nonsense, Mother said.
(58f.)

Benjy cannot get over his feelings of loss. In his primitive mind-style, habit, form and ritual play important roles. This is why, when riding the buggy, he must pass the

---

42 This would speak against 'diagnosing' Benjy as an autist, as McLaughlin (1987) has done.
43 Tragically, Benjy's meaning is completely misunderstood. His 'trying to say' is interpreted as sexual harassment, and as a result Benjy is castrated.

monument on the square of Jefferson on the right each time, because only then does his world have the proper configuration:

the bright shapes went smooth and steady on both sides, the shadows of them flowing across Queenie's back. They went on like the bright tops of wheels. Then those on one side stopped at the tall white post where the soldier was. But on the other side they went on smooth and steady, but a little slower.
(12)
The shapes flowed on. The ones on the other side began again, bright and fast and smooth, like when Caddy says we are going to sleep.
(13)

Benjy can only understand the world on this primitive level of familiar smells, shapes and rhythms. His personality does not ask for change; he is the first victim of a world that has lost its stability, its direction, its traditions. As Faulkner once expressed it: 'He recognized tenderness and love though he could not have named them, and it was the threat to tenderness and love that caused him to bellow when he felt the change in Caddy' (Meriwether & Millgate 1980:246).

Quentin Compson

if I'd just had a mother so I could say Mother Mother.
By the time the reader reaches Quentin's story (pp. 86-205), dated June second, 1910, much information has already been conveyed about the Compson family and about the person of Quentin. This makes the beginning of the second section of the novel very different from the beginning of the first. Part of Quentin's characterization has already taken place through Benjy's conceptualizations of Quentin's behavior. Benjy must, however, be considered unreliable where it concerns his understanding of the worlds of others because his mind is underdeveloped. As Faulkner explained: 'He cannot distinguish between what was last year and what will be tomorrow, he doesn't know whether he dreamed it, or saw it' (Meriwether & Millgate 1980:147f.). Yet his sensitivity and his honesty—he has no ability to plot his story for any personal purpose—tempt the reader into carrying the frame that organizes Benjy's linguistic choices over into Quentin's story.

Although Quentin does not play the all-important role in Benjy's life that his sister Caddy does, Benjy presents his behavior on several occasions, and also echoes his verbalizations in scenes that are essential to Benjy himself. The earliest instance of this is the branch experience: the 'primal scene' of the brothers,[44] where Quentin forbids Versh to unbutton Caddy's dress:

'Unbutton it, Versh,' she said.
'Dont you do it, Versh.' Quentin said.
'Taint none of my dress.' Versh said.
'You unbutton it, Versh.' Caddy said. 'Or I'll tell Dilsey what you did

---

44 As Irving Howe puts it, 'In the water-splashing incident to which Benjy so persistently returns, the behavior of the Compson children is an innocent anticipation of their destinies; each shows himself as he will later become' (1962:160).

yesterday.' So Versh unbuttoned it.
'You just take your dress off.' Quentin said. Caddy took her dress off and threw it on the bank. Then she didn't have on anything but her bodice and drawers, and Quentin slapped her and she slipped and fell down in the water...
'Now I guess you're satisfied.' Quentin said. 'We'll both get whipped now.'
'I don't care.' Caddy said. 'I'll run away.'
'Yes you will.' Quentin said.
'I'll run away and never come back.' Caddy said.
(20f.)
Later that night Quentin is crying, and in bed he turns his face to the wall. Just as the wet little sister who 'smelled like trees' is forever Benjy's 'primal image,' so Caddy's 'muddy drawers,' which were caused by Quentin because it was *he* who made her fall, will be Quentin's.

Benjy's text mentions Quentin in the name-changing scene, where Quentin tells his father of his fight to defend Caddy's honor; and in the wedding scene, where he brings his brother something warm to drink and supports him when he is sick. Also, Benjy's text focuses on a situation where their father has been drinking and speaks to Quentin—or in front of Quentin to their mother—in a cynical, nihilistic way: 'Bad health is the primary reason for all life. Created by disease, within putrefaction, into decay. Versh... Take the decanter and fill it' (50). Benjy's primitive echoing of their father's words provides an early indication of Quentin's relation to his father, in which discussion is constantly sought yet essentially fruitless.

Quentin's story, like Benjy's, contains passages in italics, the first one occurring at the end of the second page in both stories. Since the reader is likely to pause momentarily at such a transition and consider the stretch just read as some kind of unity, I shall, as in Benjy's case, concentrate on these first two pages (pp. 86,87) and comment on the understanding of Quentin as a 'possible person,' that is, on the provisional frame constituting his personality that the reader may have chosen to rely on by this time.

Quentin's Mind-Style

The first sentence of Quentin's text offers a poetic personification of the shadow that is very similar to something Benjy's text might have presented: 'the shadow of the sash appeared on the curtain.' In Benjy's magical mind-style, important objects such as shadows, are personified, and move in a self-reliant way, as in: 'my shadow walked on the grass' (53). Even though Benjy might also have used a specific verb like *appeared* to establish the activity of such an important magical object, it is more likely that he would have used the more general verb *came*, which he always uses for this type of activity.

Having become accustomed to the limitations of Benjy's language, its simplicity and its concreteness, one is confronted with an abrupt change in style in this section. Quentin's language is full of abstract terms: *time, hope, desire, experience, needs, folly, despair, victory, illusion, mind, habit.* Close reading will reveal, however, that these terms are almost all his father's words, repeated by Quentin and presented without quotation marks. These words seem to be internalized by Quentin in a way that is similar to Benjy's passages in italics, where he does not use quotation marks. Compare Benjy's narration with Quentin's:

> *I could hear the roof. Father leaned forward and looked at Quentin. Hello, he said.*
> (77)
> when Father gave it to me he said I give you the mausoleum of all hope and desire... Because no battle is ever won he said.
> (86)

As we can see, Benjy's text still shows some punctuation marks, the period and the comma, while Quentin's text uses no graphological signs at all to indicate a separation of viewpoints. There are long passages in which Quentin performs deictic projection, using the deictics his father would use, in which *I* refers to Father and *you* to himself.

We must conclude from these passages, which make up almost half of the first two pages of the story, that the borders between Quentin's own self and his father have become very thin. In these pages we find 'Father said' or 'he said' without formal punctuation four times, to which can be added an instance when the thought seems to be Quentin's, but when 'Father said that' is added just in time, as an afterthought. At one point Quentin's thoughts are 'like Father said'; at another Quentin is 'thinking what he [Father] said.' All these things 'Father said' are cynical and nihilistic in nature: 'Father said that constant speculation regarding the position of mechanical hands on an arbitrary dial which is a symptom of mind-function. Excrement Father said like sweating.' One must not automatically assume, however, that Mr. Compson always spoke in such a nihilistic way, even if Benjy 'quotes' the same sort of utterances. A listener always selects, consciously or unconsciously, what to remember and what to repeat. It is Quentin's 'choice,' just as it is Benjy's, to remember these specific words out of all the things his father must have said throughout the years. This 'choice,'· together with the way in which Quentin presents it, forms part of Quentin's own mind-style and of *his* conception of reality.

Most of Quentin's linguistic choices are concerned with time:

> it was between seven and eight oclock
> I was in time again, hearing the watch.
> remember time
> forget it now and then for a moment
> trying to conquer it.
> listening to it [the watch].
> Hearing it
> listens to a watch or a clock.
> a second of ticking
> the long diminishing parade of time
> to tell almost to the minute
> a minute clicking of little wheels.
> to wonder what time it was.
> the position of mechanical hands on an arbitrary dial

In contrast to Benjy's underlexicalization, these examples show the profusion of terms and phrases that Quentin has at his command to talk about the concept of time. It is clear that he wants to escape the effects of time: 'I got up and went to the dresser and slid my hand along it and touched the watch and turned it face-down and went back to bed. But the shadow of the sash was still there and I had learned to tell almost to the minute, so I'd have to turn my back to it.' Notice that the repeated parataxis gives this passage a certain mechanical quality, which is also present in Benjy's section. Quentin's syntax shows a sense of simultaneity that has an oppressive, inescapable quality: 'When the shadow of the sash appeared... [then] it was between seven and eight oclock and then I was in time again, hearing the watch.'

In contrast to Benjy's simple report-like discourse, Quentin's text is full of self-evaluations, attached as appended groups to the main clauses. Irena Kaluza has studied such appended groups as a pervasive characteristic of Quentin's text. Due to their position at the end of the sentence, their incompleteness and their lack of internal structure, appended groups often create and express a certain ambiguity, especially when they are combined into series. They concern sentiments that occur to Quentin while certain events are taking place, as well as the actions that reveal these sentiments and the mental activity that evaluates them.[45] All are reported as events in their own right: 'But the shadow of the sash was still there and I had learned to tell almost to the minute, so I'd have to turn my back to it, feeling the eyes animals used to have in the back of their heads when it was on top, itching.' Through the explicative clause 'so I'd have to turn my back to it,' the text conveys Quentin's need to give compelling, logical reasons for his actions.

The adverbial clause of simultaneity 'feeling the eyes animals used to have in the back of their heads when it was on top, itching' is especially revealing. It may be seen to possess a second appended clause in the form of the small-clause: 'itching,' in which the speaker, Quentin, 'steps into the shoes' of the experiencers, the animals. The clause may, however, also be considered a second adverbial clause of simultaneity: 'I'd have to turn my back to it, [while] feeling... [while] itching.' In one case, the animals are itching, in the other case it is Quentin who is itching. The ambiguous construction suggests that on an unconscious level Quentin identifies himself with these animals. Notice, in connection with this, also his confusion of singular and plural; one may wonder, once more, what or who exactly is 'itching.'

In Quentin's text, then, there exists, as Kaluza points out, 'a finely graded scale of diminishing clarity of articulation,' 'suggesting the fluidity of the mental content conveyed: from some degree of clarity where reason interprets experience to the dim and blurred impressions experienced in a dream-like state of mind.' 'Since the constructions with at least a medium degree of ambiguity are definitely preponderant,' Kaluza argues, 'Quentin's mental experience as conveyed by the appended groups comes out mostly as fragmentary, disconnected, blurred' (1967:67). These appended clauses disrupt the course of events, so that the action is suspended in an evaluative stance that adds to the sense of oppression.

The many negatives, futures and modals also move 'away from the line of narrative

---

45 Benjy also reveals his sentiments, quotes others who convey his own sentiments, and reports on his actions that reveal these sentiments. But because he is unaware of doing so we cannot consider his discourse evaluative.

events,' this time 'to consider unrealized possibilities' (Labov 1972:387). In contrast to Benjy, who presents observed worlds, remembered worlds, and dreamed worlds with the same degree of reality—he cannot construct an alternative world as an abstract possibility—Quentin's text presents many different alternative worlds:

not that you may remember
that you might forget
I dont suppose
You dont have to.
You can be oblivious
you will regret.
If it had been
Thinking it would be
Why shouldn't it?

Quentin's negations concern several allusions to a sister and seem to compare his own situation with that of someone else; someone, perhaps, upon whom Quentin looks as an example but whose life is easier than his on account of having no sister:

the good Saint Francis that said Little Sister Death, that never had a sister.
That Christ... That had no sister.

Questions and imperatives also lead beyond the sequence of narrative events, and delay the action, by demanding or requesting action ('Wonder. Go on and wonder'), or information ('Why shouldn't it?'). Quentin's progressives in addition suspend the actions as unfinished states, and, where they are used in series, concentrate them by bringing them together in a single time span. Quentin's usage of progressives does not, as in Benjy's case, indicate that he cannot understand an action as a totality, but it does indicate that he cannot conceptualize their termination, conveying an oppressive sense of actions that cannot stop.

Like Benjy's, Quentin's text features the use of the personal pronoun *I* and its related form *me* in a substantial number of clauses;

1 I was in time again
2 when Father gave it to me
3 I lay listening to it.
4 I dont suppose
5 I heard
6 I got up and went to the dresser and slid my hand along it and touched
    the watch and turned it face-down and went back to bed.
7 I had learned
8 I'd have to turn
9 I knew
10 I couldn't see it
11 I began to wonder
12 I saying
13 I could have looked... thinking

In one instance Quentin places himself in the role of an agent of a series of simple actions (*6*). Notice the circularity of these actions: out of bed to do something and into bed again. In one case Quentin is the agent of an action/process (*12*), and once he is the beneficiary of an action (*2*). In all other cases Quentin shows himself as the experiencer of a process. Only once is this process located outside Quentin himself (*1*), but it is this process, never-ending time, that Quentin wants to escape. In all other cases the verb refers to an internal process. This process may be perceptual in its first orientation (*3,5*), or basically cognitive (*4,7,8,9,10,11,13*), but it never concerns affect. The perceptual processes are exclusively the result of auditory stimuli; they again concern the experience of time and thus have a negative connotation here. Of the cognitive processes two create a negative state (*4,10*), one an obligation (*8*), one an uncertainty (*11*), and one an unrealized possibility (*13*). It is clear, then, that Quentin's mental processes are by and large self-directed and negative.

Naturally, one should also examine the clauses in which Quentin performs deictic projection and voices his father's views. Our attention should be with the pronoun *you*:

1 I give you the mausoleum of all hope and desire
2 you will use it
3 I give it to you
4 you may remember
5 you might forget it
6 the idle habits you acquire
7 you will regret.

The discourse is of a prescriptive nature. As Quentin sees it, his father stipulates his only action (*2*). When Quentin is the beneficiary of an action, the received entity is a negative one: 'the mausoleum of all hope and desire' (*1,3*) and 'idle habits' (*6*). In all other instances Quentin's text conveys how his father places him in the same role in which he places himself: namely in that of an experiencer of an internal process that defines an unrealized situation, or a negative as well as unrealized one, but never a positive or a realized one. Turning this observation around, we could also say that Quentin obediently and loyally accepts the roles to which his father has assigned him.

Depression

By the time the reader has reached the first passage in italics, a provisional frame will have presented itself that can organize the different aspects of Quentin's mind-style: the serious, withdrawn little boy of the branch scene, in Benjy's text, has grown into a serious, withdrawn, and even depressed young man. In addition, it seems that Quentin has remained curiously dependent on his father's views. His abstract thinking contains virtually nothing but his father's words, incorporated almost seamlessly into his own text; and the roles that Quentin adopts seem to be those his father considers appropriate for him. Quentin's sensory impressions are all concerned with time. They take the shape of an obsession, as he hears the inescapable clicking of the little wheels of his watch and he sees the unstoppable movement of the shadow on his curtain. As Kathryn Gibbons has put it: 'Quentin's obsession about time makes him a sort of human sun-clock' (1962:20).[46] His only action is initiated by his desire to escape from this obsession: he leaves his bed and turns the watch upside down. But because he can still

---

46 Daniel Singal has linked Quentin's 'overwhelming concern for things that tell time, accompanied by an inability to act in a temporal situation' (1982:174) to Erikson's 'identity diffusion': a failure to achieve a workable unity of ego identifications. As Erikson explains it: adolescence is a time when identifications with '*part aspects*' of important others must be organized into a 'functioning whole' (1959:55).

see the shadow on the curtain he must also turn his face to the wall. This position reminds Quentin of 'the eyes animals used to have in the back of their heads,'[47] which somehow reminds him of 'idle habits,' which reminds him of 'sister' and of 'death' ('That Christ was not crucified,' and earlier 'the good Saint Francis that said Little Sister Death'), and so on in full circle, back to time.

This circle from time to perverted sex, to sister and to death, and then back to time is repeated. It seems characteristic of Quentin's mind-style. Together with the lexical choices and the syntax of Quentin's text—the repeated parataxis in the narration of his actions and the use of progressives in the narration of his sensations—and with a constant returning to his father's words, this conveys a sense of 'stasis in motion,' of being caught up in a senseless repetition of meaningless events that leaves no room for change, for growth, for progress, for escape. The image that his text presents here—of Quentin turning his back on something he does not want to acknowledge—is reminiscent of the little boy Quentin in Benjy's text, crying and turning his face to the wall; unable to deal with the sight of Caddy's dirty drawers and the 'scrubbing' she consequently receives, and perhaps with his own responsibility for them. But, while Benjy can only present Quentin's behavior, Quentin can both present it and reflect on its causes. His despair, however, is never consciously expressed—except in a very roundabout way to his father. It shows itself only indirectly, through his mind-style.

The last sentences before the italics might have sounded cheerful enough, but in this ambience of gloom they easily acquire a cynical tone: 'Thinking it would be nice for them down at New London if the weather held up like this. Why shouldn't it?' The rhetorical question that Quentin poses himself seems to furnish its own answer in the form of an unexpected and unwelcome emotion: 'The month of brides, the voice that breathed.' This last sentence, still in regular type, runs on without quotation marks into the italics, showing how Quentin's emotion transfers his thoughts to earlier times, and calls up 'raw' memories: *She ran right out of the mirror, out of the banked scent. Roses. Roses. Mr and Mrs Jason Richmond Compson announce the marriage of.* Notice how this image of the mirror, and the need to 'frame' the situation, resembles Benjy's need for stability. The 'she' who runs away here is the same 'she' who left Benjy in despair. However, Quentin hastily cuts short these unwelcome memories, as can be seen from the return to regular type, by trying—unsuccessfully—to rationalize about them, and finally by putting them into some sort of frame—incest—that will at least succeed in forever tying her to himself: 'Roses. Not virgins like dogwood, milkweed. I said I have committed incest, Father I said. Roses. Cunning and serene.'

Quentin, it seems, cannot face the affective aspects of the world he evokes. Throughout the text one can find instances in which he abruptly tries to turn the 'raw' material floating inside his mind into more manageable rationalizations:

> *feeling Father behind me beyond the rasping darkness of summer and*
> *August the street lamps* Father I and protect women from one another from
> themselves our women
> (110)

---

47 One may find an allusion here to the Freudian 'primal scene': 'a love scene where the ignorant, fascinated child,' to use Robert's words, 'detects no love but only obscenity, a ridiculous paroxysm and an inconceivable outburst of savagery' (1980:198).

Seen the doctor yet have you seen Caddy
I dont have to I cant ask now afterwards it will be all right it wont matter
Because women so delicate so mysterious Father said. Delicate equilibrium
of periodical filth between two moons balanced.
(147)

Quentin, then, experiences two kinds of memories: his 'raw,' unreflected memories,
rendered in italics, and his conscious, rationalized memories, rendered in regular type.
The passages in italics, conveying Quentin's 'raw' memories, sound like Benjy and
have the same desperate concentration on Caddy, while his mediated, rationalized
memories honor his father's views. Quentin does not want to relive his memories as
they are. He tries to re-create them and present them to himself in such a way as to
render them powerless to hurt him any longer, but he must keep working on them
because their despair constantly threatens to surface again. One of the signs of
Quentin's psychic degeneration, as we shall see, is the growing inability of the
'scanner-device' of his ego to accomplish this task.

Just as Quentin deflates his memories of feeling by turning them into memories of
words, so he also protects himself against his pain by concentrating on less dangerous
sensations:

Why wont you bring him to the house, Caddy? Why must you do like nigger
women do in the pasture the ditches the dark woods hot hidden furious in
the dark woods.
And after a while I had been hearing my watch for some time and I could
feel the letters crackle through my coat
(105)

or by concentrating on the outside world:

Then why must you listen we can go away you and Benjy and me where
nobody knows us where The buggy was drawn by a white horse, his feet
clopping in the thin dust
(142)

Here, however, the loss of punctuation marks indicates a decreasing control.

Sometimes, when he is in the company of another person, Quentin even manages
to prevent his 'raw' memory before it starts, by concentrating on this companion, so
that the italics are skipped: 'Liquid putrefaction like drowned things floating like pale
rubber flabbily filled getting the odor of honeysuckle all mixed up. "You'd better take
your bread on home, hadn't you?"'(147). But as soon as there is silence again, the
dreaded memory surfaces anyway:

It was quiet, hardly anyone about *getting the odor of honeysuckle all mixed*
She would have told me not to let me sit there on the steps hearing her door
twilight slamming hearing Benjy still crying Supper she would have to
come down then getting honeysuckle all mixed up in it We reached the
corner.
'Well, I've got to go down this way,' I said. 'Goodbye.'
(148)

Quentin just barely manages to drive away his despair here, but when he is, ironically,
arrested for kidnapping and molesting a little girl, his resistance starts to break.

Finally, Quentin's behavior begins to show the confusion that exists inside him. His crazy laughter shows to the outside world how his thoughts and emotions are out of touch with each other: '"I'll h-have to qu-quit," I said. "It'll stop in a mu-minute. The other time it said ah ah ah," I said, laughing' (161). Quentin still tries to divert himself by concentrating on the outside world: 'I began to laugh again. I could feel it in my throat and I looked off into the trees where the afternoon slanted, thinking of afternoon and of the bird and the boys in swimming' (168f.). But concentrating on the outside world cannot save Quentin from this laughing:

> But still I couldn't stop it and then I knew that if I tried too hard to stop it
> I'd be crying and I thought about how I'd thought about I could not be a
> virgin, with so many of them walking along in the shadows and whispering
> with their soft girlvoices lingering in the shadowy places and the words
> coming out and perfume and eyes you could feel not see
> (169)

Although Quentin desperately tries to *think*, and to *think about thinking*, his emotional chaos shows itself. Almost anything will cause a dangerous emotion now, calling up a dreaded memory that can only be pushed off with tremendous effort:

> 'I think young gentlemen should drink wine, although my father, Gerald's
> grandfather' *ever do that Have you ever done that In the gray darkness a
> little light her hands locked about*
> 'They do, when they can get it,' Spoade said.
> 'Hey, Shreve?' *her knees her face looking at the sky the smell of
> honeysuckle upon her face and throat*
> 'Beer, too,' Shreve said. His hand touched my knee again. I moved my
> knee again. *like a thin wash of lilac colored paint talking about him
> bringing*
> 'You're not a gentleman,' Spoade said. *him between us until the shape of
> her blurred not with dark*
> (169)

Quentin's mind seems split; he still registers something of what is going on around him, but he is unable to join in the conversation, a discussion between his friends and the mother of one of them about the merits for 'young gentlemen' of drinking.

Finally his inner world overpowers the outer world, and Quentin drifts off into an actual hallucination:

> the honeysuckle drizzled and drizzled
> ...
> this is Quentin Im wet Im wet all over you dont have to if you dont want to
> (177)
> she took my hand and held it flat against her throat
> now say his name
> Dalton Ames
> I felt the first surge of blood there it surged in strong accelerating beats
> say it again
> her face looked off into the trees where the sun slanted and where the bird
> say it again
> Dalton Ames
> her blood surged steadily beating and beating against my hand

It kept on running for a long time, but my face felt cold and sort of dead, and my eye, and the cut place on my finger was smarting again. (187)

In this hallucinatory scene some kind of 'incest,' some kind of 'merge' occurs. In an illusionary delusion Caddy's blood, pulsing against Quentin's hand, flows together with his own blood as it runs down his face. The relaxation that this surrender brings—a 'delusion peace'—is conveyed through the relative simplicity of the language. We can appreciate how the extended metaphors that Quentin used before provided a screen that is not needed now. In this episode, Quentin's text is most like Benjy's, in its trance-like concentration on Caddy:

I had to stop and fasten the gate she went on in the gray light the smell of rain and still it wouldnt rain and honeysuckle beginning to come from the garden fence beginning she went into the shadow I could hear her feet then
Caddy
I stopped at the steps I couldnt hear her feet
Caddy
I heard her feet then my hand touched her not warm not cool just still her clothes a little damp still
do you love him now
not breathing except slow like far away breathing
Caddy do you love him now
(180)

The Psychostylistics of Mental Illness

The reader is almost forced, by now, to rely to some extent on a frame that organizes Quentin's mind-style in such a way that he is characterized not merely as a rather dependent and depressed young man, but as a person who is mentally ill. Critics have recognized this. Joseph Blotner, for instance, calls Quentin Benjy's 'psychotic older brother' (1984:213), 'His stream of consciousness,' as Bruce Kawin puts it, 'is not just chaotic and allusive, but frankly psychotic—a labyrinth in an earthquake' (1977:17). John Irwin argues that Quentin's narration shows the 'bipolarity typical of both compulsion neurosis and schizophrenia,' and he adds: 'The split is the result of the self's inability to handle ambivalence' (1980:29). Critics, however, have rarely analyzed such aspects on the basis of actual passages in the text. Quentin's text may be analyzed as a means of understanding his failure, ultimately, to create a world in which it is possible for him to live.

To extend the mental illness frame, one will have to distinguish between *symptoms*, *syndrome*, and *etiology*. Quentin's narration might be called 'schizophrenic' because his text shows as its major symptom a serious split between feeling and thinking. We can clearly see the phenomenon of splitting in Quentin's crazy laughing, which is recognized as abnormal by his surroundings: 'Watch him, Anse, he's crazy, I believe' (161); 'Quentin? Is he sick?' (169). Through his affective and cognitive behavior, Quentin creates not one more or less integrated world, but two separate, incomplete ones. Individuals in this situation will characteristically refuse to discuss this split between thinking processes and emotional processes, or acknowledge the mistakes this forces them to make. They will, 'when faced by circumstances which would force them to recognize the pattern of their operations... even use the threat, "You are driving me crazy," as a defense of their position' (Bateson 1972:262).

The syndrome that is called *schizophrenia*, which brings together a characteristic set of symptoms of which Quentin's narration presents some, refers to the state of living in two separate worlds. It amounts to an attempt to stay at least partially sane, to stay to some degree within a world that is shared with others.[48] The gap between thinking and feeling, therefore, must never be bridged, because this will inevitably cause a state of acute psychosis, a split both *of* and *from* reality: 'a temporary state in which various aspects of the environment are falsely perceived or interpreted' (Bernheim and Lewine 1979:9).[49] 'The outburst of the latent into the manifest psychosis,' Rolf Breuer argues, 'occurs when a person can no longer bear the split within himself and between himself and the world around; he seeks to reestablish the lost feeling of unity by repressing the awareness of division and by immunizing himself against it through breaking off contact with reality. The result is a state of absolute "nonfreedom"' (1980:115)—a very 'Faulknerian' word.

The symptoms may develop rather suddenly and quickly, within days, or gradually over a period of months, often during late adolescence, as in Quentin's case (cf. Ciompi 1989:16). Kaplan and Sadock mention as a precipitating event for a susceptible individual 'moving away to college' (1986:262). The anonymity of big cities seems to be one of the predisposing factors. Especially between the ages of fifteen and twenty-five, many new cases of the affliction are recorded among those who, like Quentin, come from rural areas to the big city. They are, it has been suggested, perhaps unable to read the signs and signals of such an environment and find themselves caught in a situation of multiple ambiguities and ambivalence.

There are many hypotheses concerning the etiology of schizophrenic and schizoid states of mind. As Bernheim and Lewine argue: '*Schizophrenia refers to the characteristically disturbed ways of thinking, feeling, and relating that develop in biologically predisposed individuals under certain personal and environmental circumstances*' (1979:21).[50] I shall not go into a discussion of any 'biological predispositions' here, whether genetic or intra-uterine, or even socially produced, such as an 'increased turn-

---

48 Eugen Bleuler (1857-1939) has coined the term *schizophrenia*, which means: 'split mindedness, in reference to the theoretical schism between thought, emotion, and behavior.' The diagnosis was based on the symptoms of thought disturbances (especially associative looseness); affective disorders (autism, ambivalence); hallucinations (or faulty perceptions); and delusions (or faulty cognitions). Later psychiatrists have added symptoms such as depersonalization (the perception of the self as strange); derealization and unreality (the perception of the outside world as strange), and the feeling that one's thoughts are echoed, blocked, or spread to other people (cf. Kaplan and Sadock 1988:253).

49 The term *psychotic* (according to the glossary of the American Psychiatric Association) refers to 'gross impairment in reality testing... When there is gross impairment in reality testing, the person incorrectly evaluates the accuracy of his or her perceptions and thoughts and makes incorrect inferences about external reality, even in the face of contradictory evidence... Direct evidence of psychotic behavior is the presence of either delusions or hallucination without insight into their pathological nature' (Kaplan and Sadock 1988:178f.).

50 For a recent overview of biological and environmental causes of the different forms of schizophrenia and the relations between these causes, see for instance *Research and the Complex Causality of the Schizophrenias* (1984), a report by the Research Committee of the Group for the Advancement of Psychiatry, and *Schizophrenia as a Systems Disorder* (1989), a special issue of *The British Journal of Psychiatry* edited by Hans D. Brenner and Wolfgang Böker.

over of brain monoamides' (Cools 1975:75f.; cf. Knapp 1990), which may lead to the 'sparking' of too many neurons in the brain, connecting an unusually large number of mental representations to form fuzzy concepts, and causing problems with the establishing of reality. Important as such aspects may be, they are not part of the fictional world created by Faulkner. The 'personal and environmental circumstances' that influenced Quentin's state of mind, on the other hand, are present in profusion and justify closer examination.[51] One approach that tries to explain the adverse influence of certain personal and environmental factors on biologically susceptible individuals is found in Gregory Bateson's concept of the *double bind*. In Chapter 1, I have discussed the double bind as a situation in which the individual, no matter what he or she decides to do, cannot be right because of the paradoxical messages contained, on different verbal and nonverbal levels, within the discourse with which he or she is habitually confronted.

One of the most serious problems with which Quentin is faced is his inability to understand and handle the ambivalence inherent in personal relationships and in his own character, his tendency to conceive of the world in terms of double bind patterns. To avoid failure, such a person learns to avoid the dilemma presented in the double bind. When confronted with ambiguity, he will behave in such a way that he 'shall be responsible for no metacommunicative aspect of his messages' (Bateson 1972:261). As Jay Haley points out, he will avoid 'indicating what is to take place in a relationship, and thereby avoid defining it' (1972:88). Because a failure to respond is also a 'meaningful' act, it will not do simply not to answer a question, for the silence itself uncovers 'that very sore point which is to remain concealed' (Breuer 1980:109).[52] It is the double bind that stipulates that any act will be the wrong one. The individual's suffering, then, is not caused by what Lyndall Gordon, discussing T.S. Eliot, refers to as 'a flawed other-self, left behind on the wrong side of the gap between frailty and perfection' (1988:30), but by a more fundamental and more agonizing hurt: not to be able to know which side *is* the wrong side, or the right.

Thus, by using vague and ambiguous terms, by speaking of irrelevancies, by 'flooding' his environment with obscure messages, by pretending not to hear or to understand, and especially by laughing, such a person tries to find ways out of an unbearable situation (Bateson 1972:621).[53] As Haley reminds us, the formal charac-

---

51 As Freud (1905) has put it: 'Neurosis will always produce its greatest effects when constitution and experience work together in the same direction. Where the constitution is a marked one it will perhaps not require the support of actual experiences; while a great shock in real life will perhaps bring about a neurosis even in an average constitution,' and he added: this 'view of the relative aetiological importance of what is innate and what is accidentally experienced applies equally in other fields' (Anna Freud ed. 1986:312f.)

52 Rosenbaum and Sonne present a letter by a schizophrenic patient to her doctor, which conveys clearly her craving for silence, yet her need to produce words, and her problems with the 'give-and-take' of dialogue:

Dear *Doctor* Smith

Oh, one *consented* to *be silent* have. Wish one went *be silent*. *Leave it* be. Let me *have* that I am *lucky*. Wish one is *silent-lucky*. *Let* me *have* that *it* is *luck* that *it* is *silence* that is *asked* for; oh, *be silent* is *luck, wish* that is *luck*. But have *luck* with silence *without that* on *paper*. Wish one is *lucky* with *it* (1986:112).

53 Norma MacDonald describes, in a moving way, the pain of the schizophrenic: 'My brain, after a short time, became sore with a real physical soreness, as if it had been rubbed with sandpaper until it was raw. It felt like a bleeding sponge' (quoted in Kaplan 1964:176).

teristics of any message can be broken down into the following elements:

I

am saying something

to you

in this situation

Thus, a person 'can avoid defining his relationship by negating any or all of these four elements': by denying that it is *he* who is speaking, by denying that anything is communicated, by denying that he is addressing another person, or by denying that the encounter takes place in the here and now (1972:89). In Bateson's words, he will, by responding in irrelevant ways, 'eliminate from his messages everything that refers explicitly or implicitly to the relationship between himself and the person he is addressing.' He will 'avoid the first and second person pronouns,' and 'avoid telling you what sort of a message [he is] transmitting—whether it be literal or metaphoric, ironic or direct' (1972:235).[54] Schizophrenia, in this view, is primarily a disorder of communication. 'If the patient cannot say "Yes" and cannot say "No" and cannot say "I cannot",' Haley explains, 'he must respond by labeling whatever he does as not related to the other person' (1972:103).

In the text this is visible as a breakdown of the deictic system, which, as I explained in Chapter 1, anchors a speaker to the situation he creates. The *I* may be masked, absent or fragmented, and the *you* silenced and replaced by a nonlocatable, nondeictic instance; definite deictics of time may become infinite, and local deictics of place may become global or even universal. In other words: the person 'speaks on "into the air"' (Rosenbaum and Sonne 1986:61). When the *I*, then, loses its 'body-bound identity,' body parts may become its acting, and speaking, counterparts. Quentin's text presents these forms of language distortion as fragmentation ('*My red hand coming up out of her face*' [153]), and synaesthesia ('My nose could see gasoline, the vest on the table, the door' [199]). The feeling that one is watching oneself behave, 'unsure whether to "own" the behaver or the observer' (Bernheim and Lewine 1979:56), cause the specific distortion of depersonalization that Quentin's language also suggests:

then I heard myself saying Ill give you until sundown to leave town
(183)

my mouth said it I didnt say it at all
(183)

As Bernheim and Lewine put it: 'Normal people have little difficulty in seeing themselves as *both* the actor and the observer. The schizophrenic, however, apparently must *choose* between the actor and observer' (1979:57).

Because of the fragmentation of the 'imaginary body,' the 'otherwise relatively firm boundary between internal and external, between self and surroundings,' gradually

---

54 Marguerite Sechehaye, in her 'Autobiography of a Schizophrenic Girl,' writes about her analyst: 'What did me the most amazing good was her use of the third person in speaking of herself, "Mama and Renee," not "I and you." When by chance she used the first person, abruptly I no longer knew her, and I was angry that she had, by this error, broken my contact with her. So that when she said, "You will see how together we shall fight against the System," (what were "I" and "you"?) for me there was no reality. Only "Mama," "Renee," or, better still, "the little personage," contained reality, life, affectivity' (quoted in Kaplan 1964:167).

becomes 'penetrable' (Rosenbaum and Sonne 1986:105). In Quentin's text, this is very clear from the unmarked deictic projection, with which he finally merges speech of several different persons:

> *Three times. Days. Aren't you even going to open it* marriage of their daughter Candace *that liquor teaches you to confuse the means with the end* I am. Drink. I was not. Let us sell Benjy's pasture so that Quentin may go to Harvard and I may knock my bones together and together.
> (200)

Linguistically speaking, the deviations of the afflicted individual may look like a regression towards an earlier, more primitive state of development: that of the young child, who also entertains fuzzy concepts. In a child, however, these are the result of immaturity of the brain, whereas in schizophrenia they seem to be caused by the disorganization of a well-developed symbol system (cf. Laffal 1979:33f.; cf. van Ree 1975:120ff.).

Julius Laffal has argued that concept formation, semantic organization and memory, may in principle be intact (1979:33). A person's conception of the world normally changes through social interaction. However, if social information is very unpredictable, unclassifiable and confusing, so that a person's own conceptualizations are constantly invalidated, he may give up trying to update the quality of his assumptions and close himself off from new information altogether. Shutting oneself out of speech situations, in its turn, will eventually cause idiosyncratic category extension, and thus a deviant conception of reality. As concepts cease to be the subject of reality testing, they tend to become larger and vaguer. They will lose their boundaries, and thinking as well as perceiving will become over-inclusive, employing 'generalizations and hypotheses of too broad, too involved, and too personal a nature' (Laffal 1979:22). At the same time, precisely because they cannot be invalidated any longer, they are used more and more as a psychological defense mechanism (cf. Laffal 1979:20ff.; van Ree 1975:120ff.).

As the deictic system collapses, operations upon and with language become more and more central in the individual's struggle to create a tenable situation. In Quentin's narration one can clearly see the increased importance of words, as 'part of an effort... to recapture the world of reality which had been lost' (Laffal 1979:19; Freud 1915:203). Thinking becomes '*metonymically substitutive*': concepts follow after each other not because they form part of an integrated conceptualization, but 'as a result of phonetic and semantic similarities and contiguities' (Rosenbaum and Sonne 1986:64). Such 'sliding' can easily be found in Quentin's text, where it finally seems to land on the crucial point:

> *the first car in town a girl Girl that's what Jason couldn't bear smell of gasoline making him sick then got madder than ever because a girl Girl had no sister but Benjamin Benjamin the child of my sorrowful if I'd just had a mother so I could say Mother Mother*
> (197)

Quentin's monologue, as 'language for oneself, caught between a threatening world within and a threatening world without,' becomes, to use Dorrit Cohn's words, 'an all too precarious refuge from both worlds' (1983:84). For him, concepts prevail over the world; his words are filled with sense, but they have no meaning in the outside world.

'The all too articulate Quentin,' Margaret Blanchard writes, 'escapes into words which signify no reality' (1969:565).

All symptoms in Quentin's mind-style point to the progressive fading of the boundaries of the self, which, as we saw, is evident even from the first pages of his text. But Quentin's narration also shows that schizophrenic language can be very poetic. Caught up in 'a set of paradoxical relationships with all of his responses labeled as wrong ones' (Haley 1972:109), the individual is forced to transcend into irony, laughter, imagination, poetry. As Silvano Arieti puts it, to the schizophrenic 'the word... itself becomes a masterpiece' (1981:75).

Quentin and the Family

Quentin's text provides a moving image of the lack of parental support from which he and his siblings have been suffering:

> When I was little there was a picture in one of our books, a dark place into which a single weak ray of light came slanting upon two faces lifted out of the shadow... It was torn out, jagged out. I was glad. I'd have to turn back to it until the dungeon was Mother herself she and Father upward into weak light holding hands and us lost somewhere below even them without even a ray of light.[55]
> (198)

The image presents a number of specific psychological experiences: the closeness, in the eyes of the child, of the parental figures 'holding hands'; the child's sense of despair ('us lost somewhere below'), and the unusual relationship that may come to exist between siblings caught in this situation.

At the beginning of his section, as we have seen, Quentin describes his sensations while lying in his bed at Harvard, unable to face the day: 'feeling the eyes animals used to have in the back of their heads when it was on top, itching' (87).[56] The resulting image forms a more overtly sexual version of the figure of exclusion that the parents 'holding hands' presents. Together they suggest that Quentin has difficulty moving beyond—and tends to regress to—the developmental stage that occurs shortly before the Oedipal phase, when the child has first learned to see its mother as a separate being and must then, as Melanie Klein has pointed out, come to terms with her relationship to the father and the measure of exclusion that this entails. A failure to accomplish this developmental task may be caused by a very early and traumatic separation from the mother (cf. Tustin 1988). As Minter puts it, the Compson children are 'held without gentleness'; though dismissed and ignored, they are 'still held fast.' They suffer from 'a malady that resembles claustrophobia no less than from fear of

---

55 Ironically, it is his father's story in the novel *Absalom, Absalom!* that forces Quentin to visualize a similar situation, this time concerning former inhabitants of his home-town: the moving image of a brother and a sister, whose closeness was 'not like the conventional delusion of that between twins but rather such as might exist between two people who, regardless of sex or age or heritage or race or tongue, had been marooned at birth on a desert island' (122).

56 Darl Bundren in *As I Lay Dying*, watching the officials who are taking him to the asylum, similarly reflects on the country's currency: 'A nickel has a woman on one side and a buffalo on the other; two faces and no back. I dont know what that is. Darl had a little spy-glass he got in France at the war. In it it had a woman and a pig with two backs and no face. I know what that is. "Is that why you are laughing, Darl?"' (235).

desertion' (1979:384). But Quentin remembers especially how his mother made her children into objects that she can distribute as she sees fit:

Jason I must go away you keep the others I'll take Jason and go where nobody knows us

(116)

I cannot stand it let me have Jason and you keep the others they're not my flesh and blood like he is strangers nothing of mine and I am afraid of them... I'll... try to forget that the others ever were

(119)

She talks about his brother Jason as her only love, tragically isolating him from the other children: 'he has never given me one moment's sorrow since I first held him in my arms I knew then that he was to be my joy and my salvation' (117). She rejects Benjy and Caddy for not living up to her expectations and for making her suffer so, but she does not mention Quentin at all. One of Quentin's obsessions on the last day of his life is his mother's failure to acknowledge him: *'if I'd just had a mother so I could say Mother Mother'* (197).[57]

Quentin's text does not present his very early experience directly, but his mother's paradoxical communication becomes very clear from Benjy's text:

Mother took my face in her hands and then she held me against her. 'My poor baby.' she said. She let me go.

(9)

Mother's verbal message here seems a loving one, which demands from Benjy a certain reciprocity that will affirm to her that her behavior is indeed loving, but her non-verbal behavior gives a conflicting message of rejection and retreat. Jay Haley has shown how such conflicting signals can easily produce a vicious circle. If the child retreats, the mother feels that she fails in being loving to her child, which will cause her to draw the child near. However, if the child reacts by approaching, she will feel her initial anxiety or dissatisfaction once more and force it to retreat again, and so on in circles (1972:109).

Benjy feels this dilemma; he senses that he must not rely on his mother and turns to his sister Caddy for security. But, while Benjy turns to the concrete earthliness of Caddy's voice, her smell, her loving arms, Quentin, to avoid the sin of incest, has to turn to an idea of her, a concept of Caddy as a virgin Goddess. It is clear that he, not being 'an idiot,' is not innocent enough to lie in her arms. As a 'half-baked Galahad' (126), Quentin has wanted to court his Lady, his idea of purity. It is thus that the incestuous closeness of the brother and the sister in *The Sound and the Fury* originates.[58] Contrary to the virgin Goddess or the Lady, Caddy is too accessible, too normal, too *real* to function as an icon. When she becomes sexually active, and thus proves to be made of flesh and blood, Quentin fails to keep her to himself: he fails to merge with her in death, as he drops the knife he holds to her throat; he fails to merge

---

57 Compare Darl Bundren in *As I Lay Dying*, who, Faulkner said, 'was mad from the first' (Gwynn and Blotner 1959:110): 'I cannot love my mother because I have no mother' (84).

58 The same development is found in Henry and Judith Sutpen in *Absalom, Absalom!* and, to a certain extent, in Darl and Dewey Dell Bundren in *As I Lay Dying*.

with her in love, the incest that would have to fly them off to hell together; and he fails even to defend her honor, by passing out when he faces his rival: her lover Dalton Ames (172ff.). All these failures, which he had desperately tried to keep out of his consciousness except in a rationalized or ironic form, crowd in on Quentin at the height of his psychosis.

As Bateson argues, when a person has learned to 'perceive his universe in double bind patterns' almost any element in the sequence of the double bind will cause panic and rage (1972:207). Such a person will constantly re-create his own double bind. It is essential, if one wants to understand Quentin's desperate act, to see the hopeless tangle in which he is caught up; his feeling self seeks to punish him for not doing what his rational self would never allow him to do. It is this feeling self, whose mind-style is embodied in the italics, that Quentin seeks to destroy by drowning himself. It is personified as his shadow, which keeps tying him to time and to the world, 'the instinctual claims of the body in its insistence upon life' (Jenkins 1981:160). This is perhaps why Quentin chooses the name day of St. Elmo, a saint protecting sailors against drowning, to drown himself. Notice the aggression in Quentin's perception and treatment of this shadow:

Trampling my shadow's bones into the concrete with hard heels

treading my shadow into pavement.

tramping my shadow into the dust.

(109,115,128)

This aggression is the displaced anger he unconsciously feels towards Caddy, which in itself is the displaced anger he unconsciously feels towards his mother.

He who never had a mother has had to let his Caddy go: *'She ran right out of the mirror'* (87). He has had to leave her to the love-making of another man, imagining again and again their passion:

the voice that breathed

roses roses the voice that breathed o'er Eden.

always his voice above the gabble voice that breathed

the voice that breathed o'er eden clothes upon the bed

the wild breath the yes Yes Yes yes

(87,92,120,121,171)

Quentin, it is clear, cannot count on Caddy to fulfill his needs. He has only his father to turn to. As the eldest son in the family, and with his intelligent and sensitive nature, he is the child who of all the children would most depend on his father. His father's nihilistic views, then, form the ultimate obsession on Quentin's last day.

The Impossible World of Quentin Compson

From the first page onwards, Quentin's mind-style shows how he is fascinated by his father's words, how he hangs on to them, and how sadly dependent, obedient and loyal he is to his father's views. This is most painful in the sections in which Quentin talks to his father about virginity:

And Father said it's because you are a virgin: dont you see? Women are

never virgins. Purity is a negative state and therefore contrary to nature.

It's nature is hurting you not Caddy and I said That's just words and he

said So is virginity and I said you dont know. You cant know and he said

Yes. On the instant when we come to realise that tragedy is second-hand. (132f.)

What Quentin is 'up against,' to use Bateson's words, is 'the false interpretation of his messages' (1972:199). His father takes Quentin's message and reclassifies it to suit his own neurotic impulses. These lines contrast splendidly with a passage in which Charles Mallison, in *The Mansion*, 'confesses' his love for his uncle Gavin Stevens:

> *Oh yes, I liked Father too all right but Father just talked to me while Uncle Gavin listened to me, no matter how foolish what I was saying finally began to sound even to me, listening to me until I had finished, then saying, 'Well, I dont know whether it will hold together or not but I know a good way to find out. Let's try it.' Not YOU try it but US try it.*
> (321)

One might have wished such an uncle for Quentin Compson. Quentin, desperately looking for a sense of togetherness such as that between Charles and his uncle Gavin, wants to be loyal to his father's point of view; therefore he should brush aside his obsessions. But the message that his father gives occurs within a specific nonverbal metacontext, which Quentin is forced to remember in his sister Caddy's words: *'Father will be dead in a year they say if he doesn't stop drinking and he wont stop he cant stop since I since last summer'* (142). As Jenkins has argued: 'Mr. Compson pretends to an intellectual understanding and acceptance of Caddy's predicament. But his emotional attitude towards Caddy's behavior is revealed in his progressive deterioration' (1981:142).

An understanding of the theory of the double bind can explain why the ambivalence in his father's behavior is fatal to Quentin: if Quentin wants to be loyal to his father's message he must be indifferent; if he wants to be loyal to his metamessage he must die of grief. Quentin cannot talk to his father about this dilemma, nor can he admit it to himself except in his psychosis, when he makes clear his inability to go on living:

> but if it was that simple to do it wouldn't be anything and if it wasn't
> anything, what was I
> (169)

Even greater confusion occurs when Quentin, perhaps partly 'to force him to take some action' (Irwin 1980:113; cf. Bleikasten 1976:114), 'confesses' to his father the incest he has not committed,[59] and the suicide he is already contemplating. His father does not believe him, and he, moreover, ignores or fails to understand Quentin's metamessage. Again, he uses his son's utterance for his own neurotic purposes:

> and i you dont believe i am serious and he i think you are too serious to
> give me any cause for alarm... and i i wasnt lying i wasnt lying and he you
> wanted to sublimate a piece of natural human folly into a horror and then
> exorcise it with truth and i it was to isolate her out of the loud world so that
> it would have to flee us of necessity
> (203)

---

59 Faulkner himself has said that Quentin imagined this discussion, that he 'just said, Suppose I say this to my father, would it help me, would it clarify, would I see clearer what it is that I anguish over?' (Gwynn and Blotner 1959:262f.). This, in fact, stresses the point that the double bind situation is created over and over again by the individual himself.

Finally, Mr. Compson father draws a conclusion that may be right enough but rudely
ends their discussion and dismisses his son:

> you cannot bear to think that someday it will no longer hurt you like this
> now were getting at it... you come to believe that even she was not quite
> worth despair perhaps and i i will never do that nobody knows what i know
> and he i think youd better go on up to cambridge
> (203f.)

These last words show the very depth of Quentin's despair. His father has finally
destroyed his only hope, his only reason for living. The only chivalrous thing left for
him to do, to suffer for his Lady, has been made worthless.

Quentin, still loyal and obedient, cannot detach himself from his father's views,
even if it kills him. Notice how his sense of self is diminished, as indicated graphologically in the pronoun *i*.[60] Quentin cannot but agree: time will kill his suffering;
it will not allow him to fill his life with this great suffering. He must escape time, or
else he will ultimately fail here too; and it is this 'prospect of ultimate failure' (Minter
1979:387) that causes Quentin's obsession with time and that sets him on the track that
leads relentlessly to his suicide. This, he thinks, will provide a solution for himself as
well as for his family:

> it will be better for me for all of us
> (204)

Quentin's personality is ruled by his obsession with the past and his fear of the
future,[61] but his motives are paradoxical. As A. Alvarez argues in his study of suicide, the suicidal person 'casts away his life in order properly to live.' What he hopes
to leave behind is his honor, 'a purified, idealized image of himself which lives on like
the memory of all those noble Romans who fell on their own swords with equanimity
for the sake of their principles, their reputations and their proper name in history'
(1973:103). Quentin's mind-style reveals his tragic and inescapable inability to create
order in his chaotic experience, which finally makes his world an impossible one.

Jason Compson

*then I got to thinking about when we were little and one thing and another
and I got to feeling funny again*

Just as one does not come to the Quentin section of the novel completely unprepared
but knows about Quentin from Benjy's memories, so one is also somewhat prepared
when Jason's section is reached. It has been argued that 'Benjy, though an idiot,
reveals the family situation more faithfully than Quentin, for the events Benjy
remembers tell us more than the efforts of Quentin to comprehend them' (Howe
1962:169). Although one must not equate quantity with fidelity, and although one may
wonder if what Quentin seeks is not deliverance rather than comprehension, it is

---

60 Faulkner explained the omission of capitals as follows: 'Because Quentin is a dying man, he is already
out of life, and those things that were important in life don't mean anything to him any more' (Gwynn and
Blotner 1959:18).
61 Cognitive psychologists speak of the 'negative triad' of the depressive narrative: 'I am worthless,' 'I can
rely on no support,' 'the future can bring no change in this situation.'

perhaps right to say that Benjy's plotless registration is more faithful to reality than Quentin's anguished interpretations.

Benjy's narration, after all, basically reflects the primitive version of reality we all shared once in our early childhood. The conceptual deviations apparent from his text, for instance of spilled water running *into* the table, may give a distorted representation of the world as grown-ups see it but do not make it unintelligible. Once one understands that Benjy's mind is limited and underdeveloped, it is possible to understand the concrete world he shares with his family. The reader feels it is certain, for instance, that the girl Quentin 'really' broke her water glass on the table, spilling its contents (81). Although biological reality is only part of a situation, for Benjy it is all there is. Social reality is non-existent to him. He has no idea of social rules and conventions and of the dialogues going on between people; he, one could say, treats them as parts of physical reality: as activity that he can perceive and that is in no way different from the flapping of a flag, which also shows movement and gives off sound.

Quentin's narration, on the other hand, also presents social reality: the culture in which he lives and his relationships with the members of his family. It consists for a large part of dialogues between others, between himself and others, and between different parts of himself. These voices all create different versions of reality. That this is upsetting to Quentin is evident from the way he describes some little boys he meets: 'They all talked at once, their voices insistent and contradictory and impatient, making of unreality a possibility, then a probability, then an incontrovertible fact, as people will when their desires become words' (134). For the same reason, Quentin is upset by the clocks at the jeweller's shop, all ticking away at contradictory times. Because Quentin cannot unify his own inner world, he longs desperately for a unity of the outer world.

We shall briefly consider the ways in which Jason is presented in Benjy's and in Quentin's texts. Benjy's narration conveys how Jason plays by himself, tattles on his brothers and sister, cuts up Benjy's paper dolls, walks with his hands in his pockets, sulks and whines, gets punished by his father, denounces his own family, and orders others around. At no time does he address himself to Benjy directly, help him or play with him. While Benjy's section presents the physical world of the Compson children, Quentin's story directs our attention away from this outside world. His narrative guides us inward, to the effects of the situation Benjy sets before us. From Quentin's section, as we have seen, it is clear that Mrs. Compson isolates and idolizes Jason, the only child she feels truly belongs to her and her family.

Such isolation always causes a deeply buried guilt in the child, as well as anger and contempt in the other siblings. Jason, it seems, unconsciously feels that he has something that his brothers and sister are missing and would want to take away from him if they could. His 'childish avarice, hands in his pockets even when it cost him a fall' (Blotner 1984:217) can be viewed as a symbolic act; his sense of self is based on not sharing, while his paranoia covers up the guilt he unconsciously feels at possessing something that should have been shared. He is a very lonely child, and there certainly is some truth in Mrs. Compson's complaint that when she dies she will leave Jason 'with no one to love him shield him from this' (118). She does not realize, however, that she herself causes this loneliness in Jason. Mr. Compson's behavior, on the other hand, is also very inadequate. For instance, all he does, according to Quentin, is to answer 'nonsense' (116) when his wife tells him her curious fantasies about taking Jason away with her. It should be clear that Jason, as a child, is just as helpless and unprotected against the devastating affection of his mother as Quentin is against her neglect. Jason can only protect himself by choosing to be unlikeable, by giving his brothers and sister a reason to hate him, so that at least he will have some sense of mastery over the situation in which he finds himself.

John L. Longley observes that Jason has sometimes been defended by critics who 'will pull the leg of the credulous public and pretend to see Jason with Jason's own paranoid vision: a long-suffering, put-upon man.' 'Some have gone so far as to endorse Jason's own justification of his embezzlement and perjury' (1963:145). Linda Wagner, on the other hand, points out that Jason, 'a man in his mid-thirties,' is 'dreadfully embittered because for seventeen years he has been supporting the entire rotting family'; 'he supports them with no preparation, no training, no breaks.'[62] Wagner argues that 'Quentin's concerns are also Jason's' and points out that 'the problems of honor, time, and human delicacy fall with more weight on Jason's shoulders than they ever did on Quentin's' (1971:4). It is not my aim to present Jason as a person who cannot help himself, or who has a right to behave as he does because of the problems that he faces. Jason may be called 'a villain' because he '*chooses* to do evil rather than good' (Longley 1963:141), implying that he performs his acts consciously. He does so, however, for a reason of which he is not aware. This reason may be examined from his mind-style.

From Quentin's section, even if Quentin is to some extent unreliable, it is obvious that Jason's behavior has its roots in the unhealthy environment in which all the children have had to grow up. Jason, who is out to hurt everybody but himself, is in his own way just as tragic as Quentin, who believes that he is out to hurt nobody but himself and thereby hurts everybody including himself through the aggressive act of his suicide; often 'not more than a hairline of difference will separate a villain from a tragic hero' (Longley 1963:139). My aim, in any case, is not to offer moral judgments, but to show Jason's mental self through his structuring of the world, of which his family background is an intricate part.

Jason's Mind-Style

Jason's text (pp. 206-305) does not have the divisions that his brothers' sections have in the form of passages in italics. I shall nevertheless follow the same procedure that I followed in my discussion of Benjy's and Quentin's mind-styles, and concentrate in the first instance on the two opening pages of Jason's narrative (206,207), in order to study the frames that can organize Faulkner's characterization of Jason.

If one considers Jason's linguistic choices, it is difficult at first glance to find specific patterns; no observable obsession with specific concepts and no convincing under- or overlexicalization appear. In addition, no remarkable syntactic pattern springs to the eye. Jason, in this respect, seems rather 'normal' as compared to his brothers. Faulkner himself called Jason 'the first sane Compson since before Culloden,' and Longley believes that 'Jason is "normal"... a recognizable human being that we have

---

62 As Faulkner himself expressed it: 'he assumed the entire burden of the rotting family in the rotting house' (Meriwether 1965:251).

seen many times' (1963:144). Apart from the use of colloquialisms such as 'bitch,' 'I says,' 'fix' and 'playing out of school,' which clearly set Jason apart from his brothers, the most obvious aspect of his narration, at this stage, is perhaps a certain feverish immediacy:

> Once a bitch always a bitch, what I say. I says you're lucky if her playing out of school is all that worries you. I says she ought to be down there in that kitchen right now, instead of up there in her room, gobbing paint on her face and waiting for six niggers that cant even stand up out of a chair unless they've got a pan full of bread and meat to balance them, to fix breakfast for her.

In this first paragraph of the encounter between Jason and his mother, there are no quotation marks, suggesting that this part of the text is still internal to Jason. In this respect, the paragraph resembles the passages in italics in the other sections. Jason's inner speech is in the form of an internal dialogue with his mother, as much of Quentin's is with his father. Quotation marks appear only in the second paragraph, where an external dialogue is presented.

As against Benjy's and Quentin's stories, all the attributive clauses *I says* used to introduce the dialogue in Jason's narration are in the present tense, which causes much of the immediacy mentioned above. The large number of these clauses, twelve in the first two pages if one counts 'what I say,' gives the text its characteristic ostensively assertive tone:

1 Once a bitch always a bitch, what I say.
2 I says you're lucky if her playing out of school is all that worries you.
3 I says she ought to be down there in that kitchen right now
4 'Well,' I says. 'You cant can you?'
5 'You never have tried to do anything with her,' I says.
6 'Yes,' I says. 'If she stayed on the streets.'
7 'I dont reckon she'd be playing out of school just to do something she could do in public,' I says.
8 'I dont mean anything,' I says.
9 'You asked me,' I says.
10 'Sure,' I says. 'I never had time to be.'
11 'I ought to know it,' I says.
12 'Not if you come down there interfering just when I get started,' I says.

Although a speaker must always be understood to 'do things' with his words (to try, at least, to create through language a situation in which he can feel himself 'at home'), Jason seems especially intent on having his listener understand and accept his own conception of reality. By keeping his deictic projection firmly anchored this way, he almost desperately guards his sense of self as separate from others.

Jason, with his profusion of attributive verbs, constantly draws attention to the fact that it is *he* who does the talking, that it is *he* who has the right to speak, and that it is *he* who is in charge of presenting the situation. Notice, however, that his text does not really present situations as actually existing. Of the twelve clauses listed above, six create hypothetical situations (*2,3,6,7,11,12*), while four negate possible situations (*4,5,8,10*). In one instance, Jason offers an assertion of such wide scope that it creates no specific situation (*1*). Only one sentence (*9*) contains a real assertion. Despite its assertive tone, then, Jason's discourse is not really assertive in content and shows that he, like Quentin, finds it hard to create the situation that he needs. Jason seems to feel as though he needs to force his addressee to acknowledge him constantly, as if he said: listen to me; it is *me* who is speaking. The reader feels this constant, obsessive call for attention. On the level of the embedded dialogue between Jason and his mother, his speech has the same ostensive tone. Although he seems to speak with ease and authority when he addresses his mother directly, Jason still needs to enhance the power of his words by using the ironic, opiniated sentence adverbs *well, yes,* and *sure,* and the tag question *can you?,* which must serve to prove to her, and to himself, how much he feels in charge of the situation.

If one looks closely at all the clauses of the dialogue with his mother that feature the pronoun *I,* one notices that Jason almost always assumes the role of the agent in actions:

1 I just answered your question.
2 I had to work.
3 I can quit the store and get a job
4 I can work at night.
5 I can watch her during the day
6 Not if you come down there interfering just when I get started
7 Everytime I try to, you come butting in

Critics have argued that Jason lives completely in the present but, curiously enough, none of these clauses really refer to a present action. Two actions are in the past (*1,2*), four actions are only stipulated (*3,4,5,6*), and one is repetitive but unaccomplished and not in the present (*7*). Again we see that Jason's language may sound assertive, but that it does not effectively create a situation in which he can act in the present. Two other clauses containing the pronoun *I* refer not to actions but to states. These states, however, are negated, and have a ring of self-pity:

I never had time to be.

I never had time to go to Harvard

This repetition seems to indicate that Jason, like Quentin in his own way, finds time working against him. As Cleanth Brooks points out: 'Jason, too, is harried by time, but in a very different way: far from wishing to obliterate it, he would like to catch up with it' (1964:328).[63]

No feelings are conveyed in Jason's narrative. The only clauses that refer to internal processes at all have the form of a negation, a stipulation, or both:

I dont reckon she'd be playing out of school

I dont mean anything

I ought to know it

These forms, like the sentence adverbs *well, sure* and *yes,* and the tag question *can you?* discussed above, serve to upgrade the abnormality of his mother's conceptualizations against which the normalcy of his own are supposed to stand out. By negating

---

63 This need to 'catch up' is also present in Quentin's text: 'and after a while I'd be afraid I had gotten behind and I'd count fast' (100); '*Mother Father Caddy Jason Maury getting so far ahead sleeping I will sleep fast when I door Door door*' (199). Both brothers, Quentin and Jason, express an elementary fear of being left behind that is also expressed in Benjy's howling: a primitive separation anxiety.

his thoughts, then, Jason, *does* convey something: not his thinking processes them-selves but his conclusions, which reverse those of his mother and ridicule her thoughts and feelings. Jason, in fact, deconstructs his mother's conceptualizations in order to be able to form his own.

As we have seen, all Jason's attributive clauses are rendered in the present tense. This pattern is broken only in two sentences:

She thought about that for a while.

Then she begun to cry again, talking about how her own flesh and blood rose up to curse her.

It seems that Jason's text, like Benjy's and Quentin's, is rendered in the narrative past or epic preterite, so that these two sentences in the past tense are the pattern from which the attributive clauses with their ostensive present tenses form characteristic deviations. These pervasive deviations from the narrative past stand out and so give the story its feverish immediacy. Although Jason does not refer to his own inner life, these two sentences in the past tense indicate some reflection on his part. At least he briefly stops his furious self-assertion to observe and interpret his mother's behavior here. As Jason presents it, Mrs. Compson thinks 'for a while,' but she does not reach any un-derstanding. Thus Jason unwittingly creates a situation that shows him clearly as his mother's child. Although he is not aware of it, the dialogue that he chooses to present makes clear that he is much like her; both reflect occasionally on their own behavior or that of others, but they do not go more than skin-deep. His mother's attention, at least, soon drifts to her own social position: 'But to have them think that... I didn't even know she had a report card... And now for Professor Junkin to call me on the telephone' (206).

This is not the only similarity between Jason and his mother. A second similarity, related to their lack of reflection, is their mutual inability to find a solution for the problems with which they are faced.

'But to have the school authorities think that I have no control over her, that I cant—' 'Well,' I says. 'You cant can you? You never have tried to do anything with her,' I says.

If you want me to control her, just say so and keep your hands off.

Everytime I try to, you come butting in and then she gives both of us the laugh.

Jason's usage of the pronoun *us* in this last passage conveys, without his awareness, and certainly against his will, his sense of their mutual dependency. But while Jason blames his mother for his ineffectiveness, she blames everybody *but* him: 'I dont mean you... You are the only one of them that isn't a reproach to me' (207). At fault is 'her own flesh and blood,' which 'rose up to curse her,' perhaps her husband and Quentin, who are dead now, and certainly Caddy, who is as good as dead to her; but more directly she speaks of Caddy's daughter Quentin.

With the verb-phrase *rose up* in the passage above, Mrs. Compson creates a position high above the plane of other human beings, as if she were a goddess or a queen against whom people can rise up ungratefully. As in Quentin's section, one sees how she isolates Jason by elevating him to this high sphere. Jason's reply is nothing but a confirmation of his mother's views; his ironic self-effacement presents his self-pity, but also his distorted sense of superiority: '"Sure," I says, "I never had time to be. I never had time to go to Harvard or drink myself into the ground. I had to work"' (207). With this perverted sense of superiority over the Compson side of the family, even if it is a real Bascomb characteristic that unites him with his mother, he attacks her as well. Jason does not hesitate to bring out his mother's confusion and ineffectiveness, and quotes her saying:

I didn't even know
How does she do it?
Where does she go?
What do you mean?
Do you think it will do any good?

He, moreover, intensifies the impression of her helplessness by the tone of his remarks to her:

You cant can you?
You never have tried
How do you expect to begin this late, when she's seventeen years old?

And, as if she were trying to assist Jason in despising her, Mrs. Compson keeps apologizing in the same helpless, self-pitying way that the other brothers record: '"I know I'm just a trouble and a burden to you," she says, crying on the pillow' (207).

The Psychostylistics of Paranoia

At the end of the second page of Jason's story, then, a frame must have presented itself to the reader. The lonely little boy who never had much to say has indeed learned to speak. However, the degree of ostension in his language—his need to use a profusion of attributive clauses and opiniated sentence adverbs, conveying without interruption that it is *he* who is in charge of the situation—seems to betray him and show the basic paranoic insecurity hidden underneath. A closer scrutiny of the actions in which he is engaged has rendered the same impression.

A paranoid personality disorder, such as Jason exhibits, makes a person suspicious of others. Such people constantly expect to be mistreated; they become secretive, and are continually on the lookout for signs of trickery and abuse. They are extremely jealous, overly sensitive and quick to take offence, as well as argumentative and tense. Their emotional responses are shallow, and they appear cold and humorless to others (cf. Davidson and Neale 1986:230). Persons with this type of delusional disorder, Kaplan and Sadock argue, 'use the defense mechanisms of reaction formation, denial and projection. Reaction formation is used as a defense against aggression, dependency needs, and feelings of affection. The need for dependency is transformed into staunch independence. Denial is used to avoid awareness of painful reality. Consumed with anger and hostility and unable to face responsibility for this rage, the individual projects his resentment and anger onto others. Projection is used to protect the person from recognizing unacceptable impulses in himself' (1988:271). Many of these characteristics are part of Faulkner's characterization of Jason and can be found in his mind-style.

Jason's tangled relationship with his mother is obvious. She pulls him up to her elevated level, isolating him as she has done since he was born ('he has never given me one moment's sorrow since I first held him in my arms I knew then that he was to be my joy and my salvation' [117]), and making herself indispensable to him. He puts her down and stimulates her helplessness, so that he can be sure she will always need him. It seems, then, as if the discussion between Jason and his mother serves only to stabilize and continue their distorted relationship, and has no function whatsoever in transmitting information or finding solutions to problems. Her helplessness serves to disguise the power she has over her son; his power must cover up the helplessness underneath.

Jason's dependence on his mother constantly betrays itself through his inner speech; all his thinking seems to direct itself to her:

> We ate a while. I could hear Ben in the kitchen, where Luster was feeding him. Like I say, if we've got to feed another mouth and she wont take that money, why not send him down to Jackson. He'll be happier there, with people like him... I says if they'd sent him to Jackson at first we'd all be better off today. I says, you've done your duty by him; you've done all anybody can expect of you and more than most folks would do, so why not send him there and get that much benefit out of the taxes we pay.
> (255)

His quasi-independent common-sense logic, perhaps an unconscious rebellion against his father's nihilistic philosophizing, is more pathetic than effective. As Irena Kaluza has pointed out, the connective *because*, for instance, 'becomes a mere signal of Jason's efforts to be logical and to present events in their cause-and-effect relations, while the connective's grammatical function gradually fades away' (1967:95):

> So he kept on patting her hand... with one of the black gloves that we got the bill for four days later *because* it was the twenty-sixth *because* it was the same day one month that Father went up there and got it and brought it home... and I says,
> 'Well, they brought my job home tonight' *because* all the time we kept hoping they'd get things straightened out and he'd keep her *because* Mother kept saying she would at least have enough regard for the family not to jeopardise my chance after she and Quentin had had theirs.
> (227; my emphasis)

No number of logical connectives in this passage will make Jason's speech logical.

From the first pages of his text it would seem that Jason's dependence on his mother is the most obvious aspect of his personality. This dependence is continually conveyed throughout the story. Jason returns, time and again, to his mother's possessive and perverted love for him. While he is in the house with her, he accepts her idolization with insincere, feigned exasperation, and after he has left her company, everywhere he goes, his memories return to her continuous, elaborate declarations of 'love,' addicted as he is to hearing them, if not from her then from himself. Jason's nonverbal behavior, as he presents it, constantly belies his verbal behavior, with which he tries to distance himself from his mother. He complies with her every demand: 'So I went out, then Mother called me back and cried on me a while. "You are my only hope," she says. "Every night I thank God for you"' (230). Jason's devaluation of his mother's feelings through his use of the predicate *cried on me a while* is also very clear here.

The remembrance of the day that Caddy's baby daughter Quentin was brought into the house calls up a memory of his father's funeral, not long afterwards. At that time

Jason hears his mother cry out in the same spirit: 'Thank God if he had to be taken too, it is you left me and not Quentin. Thank God you are not a Compson' (230). Not much later, precisely the same train of thought enters Jason's mind again. But this time he shows, even though he devaluates his mother's emotions, how this disturbed thinking is part of his own mind-style. The verb-phrase *like she says* gives added weight to his mother's thoughts, which, as the lack of quotation marks indicates, have been internalized by Jason in much the same way as Quentin internalizes his father's thoughts:

> Like she says, if one of you had to be taken, thank God it was you left me I
> can depend on you and I says well I dont reckon I'll ever get far enough
> from the store to get out of your reach.
> (Jason's section, 237)
> Like Father said down the long and lonely light-rays you might see Jesus
> walking, like.
> (Quentin's section, 86f.)

But Jason's narration, unlike Quentin's, immediately restores the distance between himself and the other. The irony and sarcasm of Jason's sentence is characteristic of his discourse. All his flattery and his compliance has the sting of resentment and self-pity, which is perfectly matched by his mother's self-delusion and hysterical insincerity: '"I know," she says. "I know you haven't had the chance the others had, that you've had to bury yourself in a little country store"' (254).

Jason's life, as well as that of his mother, is based on pretense. Each pretends to cherish the remembrance of the dead more than the other: '"I thanked God it was you left me if they had to be taken." "They were all right," I says. "They did the best they could, I reckon." "When you talk that way I know you are thinking bitterly of your father's memory," she says. "You have a right to, I suppose. But it breaks my heart to hear you"' (260). Moreover, although Jason delights in making his mother worry about his health, he pretends complete indifference to his own well-being:

> Little they cared how wet I got, because then Mother could have a whale of
> a time being afraid I was taking pneumonia.
> (231)
> 'I thought maybe you were sick,' she says. 'Having to hurry through your
> dinner like you did.'
> 'Better luck next time,' I says. 'What do you want?'
> (272)
> 'But I dont know what I'd do if anything happened to you, Jason.'
> 'I'm all right,' I says. 'Just a headache.'
> 'I wish you'd take some aspirin... I wish you'd take some aspirin.'
> 'Keep on wishing it,' I says. 'It wont hurt you.'
> (274)

Jason and his mother need no help from the outside, or, as Mrs. Compson herself puts it, 'We Bascombs need nobody's charity' (252). All they need is each other and a common enemy.

Caddy's daughter Quentin, tainted by 'blood like that,' which will make her 'do anything' (275), has to play the role of the black sheep. Pretending to save Quentin, Jason and his mother make life impossible for her. There clearly is more than a little truth in her anguished complaint:

> 'It's his fault,' she says. 'He wont let me alone'... 'It's his fault,' she says... 'He makes me do it. If he would just—' she looked at *us*... 'Whatever I do, it's your fault,' she says. 'If I'm bad, it's because I had to be. You made me.'
>
> (300; my emphasis)

In each of the few instances when Jason uses the pronoun *us* more or less sincerely, it is in connection with this mutual enemy Quentin, the embodiment of their sick relationship. Nobody will come between Jason and his mother, not while she is alive and probably not when she is dead:

> Like I say if I was to get married you'd go up like a balloon and you know it and she says I want you to be happy to have a family of your own not to slave your life away for us. But I'll be gone soon and then you can take a wife but you'll never find a woman who is worthy of you and I says yes I could. You'd get right up out of your grave you know you would.
>
> (284f.)

The essential passivity of Jason's nature shines through the thin coating of his frantic, unsuccessful endeavors and the ostensively assertive tone of his discourse. This passivity is a defensive response to his mother's attempts to control him through her weakness, her self-sacrifice, her flatteries, and the (in)direct accusations at the address of his father and the other Compsons.

Jason's dependency cannot be viewed in isolation from his father's inadequacies in dealing with his wife's anxieties: '"Dont be a fool," Father says... "Hush," Father says. "You're just upset"' (229). In the passage that presents his father's inadequacies in dealing with the rest of the world ('Father wouldn't even come down town anymore but just sat there all day with the decanter I could see the bottom of his nightshirt and his bare legs' [268]) one finds underneath Jason's usual sarcasm a genuine sadness at the decline of a father seen through the eyes of an adolescent boy who, after all, has a right to a better example of manhood. Jason may unconsciously want to do better than his father, but his behavior, in fact, only shows what he and his parents have in common. As Jenkins put it: 'Jason... delights in viewing himself as the victim, just as does his mother—and father. He torments and punishes himself in the bearing of his burden, his duty to his family and tradition which he deceptively believes he has disavowed and from whose' influence he believes he has freed himself' (1981:150).

If Jason's passive dependency on his mother is the most obvious aspect of his personality, his cruelty towards her and others is nearly as pervasive. We have already seen how his speech acts are intended to deconstruct his mother's conception of reality. One of his ways to do this is the 'art' of the rhetorical question, of which Jason proves to be master. Neither his mother nor his 'friends' and business partners can defend themselves against such 'questions.' Jason knows it; his insincere joviality, his nasty remarks, and the lack of reaction he receives are all related with perverted pride:

> 'Any of you boys made your million yet?' I says.
> 'You're smart, aren't you?' I says.
> He didn't say anything. He made like he was busy.
> 'You're getting a little too big for your pants,' I says.
> (249,250,250,250)

Dilsey's complaint, 'you's a cold man, Jason, if man you is' (238), puts into words what many in Jefferson must feel but are afraid to express.

With the condescending repetition of his question, Jason tries to assert his power over his niece Quentin and show his contempt of her: '"You will, will you?" I says. "You will will you?" She slapped at me. I caught that hand too and held her like a wildcat. "You will, will you?" I says. "You think you will?"' (210). As his generalizations show, not only she, her mother, Caddy, and her grandmother, Mrs. Compson, have his contempt, but all women:

> Just like a woman. Six days late. Yet they try to make men believe that
> they're capable of conducting a business.
> (218)
> I never promise a woman anything nor let her know what I'm going to give
> her. That's the only way to manage them.
> (222)

The same condemnation is applied to Jewish people and to blacks:

> 'I have nothing against jews as an individual,' I says. 'It's just the race.
> You'll admit that they produce nothing.'
> (219)
> I never found a nigger yet that didn't have an airtight alibi for whatever he
> did.
> (251)

Even his innocent brother, from whom Jason cannot reasonably expect any harm, has no right to compassion:

> you can send Ben to the Navy I says or to the cavalry anyway, they use
> geldings in the cavalry.
> (225)
> Rent him out to a sideshow; there must be folks somewhere that would pay
> a dime to see him
> (225)

In his sarcastic remarks about his brother Quentin, who wrecked the opportunities he received through his suicide, the underlying jealousy is finally very close to the surface:

> I says you might send me to the state University: maybe I'll learn how to
> stop my clock with a nose spray
> (225)
> At least I never heard of him offering to sell anything to send me to
> Harvard.
> (227)

It is clear that Jason is envious of anybody who has earned even the slightest degree of freedom. Thinking of his sister Caddy he remarks: 'I thought how she'd get around Dilsey and that Uncle Maury would do anything for ten dollars. And there I was, couldn't even get away from the store to protect my own Mother' (237). As a bachelor, at the age of thirty-five, Jason is still living with his mother, unable to leave her. One can understand how he feels trapped. When he sees his niece Quentin getting around Dilsey and misleading her grandmother, like her mother used to, all his anger at having been unable to escape must surface. His solution is the defense mechanism of putting passive into active. As William Freedman puts it, he inverts 'his confinement by imprisoning his family' (1961-1962:173). The degradation that Jason feels has its roots in his childhood insecurity. It was caused by his isolated position within the family, his fear of losing what should have been rightfully his—the love of his mother—and his 'guilt' over having this 'love' all to himself. Basic anxiety has caused Jason to move against people; his personality, as Faulkner presents it, is determined by the aggressive defense of 'arrogant-vindictiveness.' As Bernard Paris describes such a personality: 'Considerateness, compassion, loyalty, self-sacrifice are all scorned as signs of weakness; those who value such qualities are fools whom it is no crime to take advantage of, since they are just asking for it. The only moral law inherent in the order of things is that might makes right' (1974:61).

Jason's feelings of degradation have not been caused by his missed chance of acquiring a position in the bank of his sister's husband, as critics have argued (cf. Vickery 1954). His problems are much deeper and more insoluble. The luckless event of losing a chance he feels he should have had only revived and made actual the childhood obsession symbolized by his characteristic posture: 'hands in pockets.' His life-long fear of losing something that should have been rightfully his has been confirmed by his adolescent experience, and has caused his adult paranoia. This paranoia presently makes him imagine 'a conspiracy' (250) wherever he goes. Jason's paranoia is one more characteristic he shares with his mother. This paranoia is a family trait; it can easily be found in his mother's mind-style, where she speaks of the attitudes of her other son, Quentin, and her daughter, Caddy, towards herself and Jason: '"They deliberately shut me out of their lives," she says. "It was always her and Quentin. They were always conspiring against me. Against you too"' (302).

On his day of narration, April sixth, 1928, when Jason feels obliged to bring home his niece Quentin, who has run away with a lover from the carnival, everything seems to conspire against him. Even nature itself has its evil purposes: 'the sun getting down just to where it could shine straight into my eyes' (277). His self-pity reaches hideous forms as he struggles against the elements of nature: 'I had gotten beggar lice and twigs and stuff all over me, inside my clothes and shoes and all, and then I happened to look around and I had my hand right on a bunch of poison oak. The only thing I couldn't understand was why it was just poison oak and not a snake or something' (278). Jason's feeling that 'everyone is at fault and nothing can work right,' Jenkins argues, 'is clearly only a displacement and projection upon others of Jason's own inner chaos' (1981:151). It is clear that he must deconstruct the conceptualizations of others in order to construct some kind of order for himself. His 'inner chaos' is what he desperately tries to keep hidden, not because, as in Quentin's case, he is afraid it will destroy his sanity, but because he fears it will destroy his social position:

> And there I was, without any hat, looking like I was crazy too. Like a man
> would naturally think, one of them is crazy and another one drowned
> himself and the other one was turned out into the street by her husband,
> what's the reason the rest of them are not crazy too. All the time I could
> see them watching me like a hawk, waiting for a chance to say Well I'm
> not surprised I expected it all the time the whole family's crazy.
> (268)

Jason's sanity, then, seems to depend on counteracting the social disgrace brought upon his family by his siblings.

While Jason's dependency and insecurity are more obviously present in his story, his lack of reflection is the most interesting aspect of his mind-style, because it has the most profound influence on his static outlook on the world. His reflections, as we have seen, are only skin-deep, and resolve themselves at once into opinions full of contempt, self-righteousness, and boastful memories of his mother's dedication, that is, into examples of insecurity and dependency by which Jason 'pitilessly exposes himself' (Brooks 1964:339). There are a few instances, however, where this pattern is broken. Longley has argued that 'the entire pattern of Jason's life, both inward and outward, is perfectly adjusted to his needs and desires' (1963:147). That this *seems* to be the case may look like proof of his sanity, and Jason himself would certainly like us to believe it. As I shall show below, however, Jason's narration makes clear that his adjustment is by no means perfect; through the cracks in his varnish, one can see that he, like his brother Quentin, has feelings he must hide in order to keep sane.

As Cleanth Brooks writes, 'Jason is typically sardonic in his description of his father's funeral' (1964:338). I believe that a lot more can be said about this one long and relatively consistent return to the past. A close look at this memory will show that Jason remembers his mother's indirect reproach ('Other women have their children to support them in times like this' [226]), his uncle's drunkenness and the clove stems that he uses to hide the smell (226), their carelessness in leaving him behind in the rain, causing the fearful hope, or hopeful fear, that he will be able to 'please' his mother by catching pneumonia (231), and so on. He does not, however, mention thinking of his dead father. Throughout this passage, Jason avoids mentioning the word *funeral* and the word *undertaker*: 'and then they came and said they were ready to start' (225). In a similar way, he avoids using the word *grave*, by using instead the 'alien *it*' (Hurst 1987:80):

> trying to kick the mud off their feet and sticking to the shovels so they'd
> have to knock it off, making a hollow sound when it fell on it
> (230f.)
> When they begun to get it filled up towards the top Mother started crying
> sure enough
> (231)

These gaps in the story are of great importance. With his sentence adverb *sure enough*, Jason again devalues his mother's feelings in order to create the situation he needs: he does not want to realize what he is there for or what is really happening.

But after his mother and his uncle have left the cemetery and he is alone, 'watching them throwing dirt into it, slapping it on anyway like they were making mortar or something or building a fence' (231f.), his basic humanity, the universality of grief, begins to shine through: 'I began to feel sort of funny' (232). Jason's lack of knowledge of his inner self, his inability to listen to the voice of his unconscious—that is why Faulkner uses no italics in his section—together with his inexperience with expressing his feelings, gives this sentence its pathetic tone. Because his story is so utterly devoid of sincerity, this short lapse, or crack in his mask, stands out forcefully and causes some real compassion in the sensitive reader. But as soon as Jason meets his sister Caddy, who has kept herself hidden in the cemetery, this relative openness seems to vanish. In the first instance, he confronts his sister with his usual coldness: 'You dont give a dam about anybody... You'll talk mighty meek now. But you needn't have come back. There's not anything left' (232). It is clear that he projects his own greed upon Caddy. But Caddy's obvious despair at having been denied the right to share her grief over her father's death makes even him speechless: '"Why didn't they let me know?" she says. "I just happened to see it in the paper. On the back page. Just happened to." I didn't say anything' (233).

Caddy's words call up in Jason the great and fearful wound of his childhood, his own lifelong inability to share and to belong. Jason's uncharacteristic silence, easily overlooked, shows his compassion for his sister, and it is this compassion that enables him to share an experience: '*We* stood there, looking at the grave' (233; my emphasis). In the midst of 'the sound and fury' of Jason's discourse, this silent *looking* forms an oasis of peace. Caught off guard, Jason lets his memories run on into dangerous territory:

> then I got to thinking about when we were little and one thing and another
> and I got to feeling funny again, kind of mad or something, thinking
> (233)

A Glimpse of the 'Real' Jason

Again Jason starts 'feeling funny,' but clearly, he has no way to find out what it is that he feels or how he can put it into words. But at least he stops long enough to feel. Jason does not normally use progressives to refer to his actions. These actions, after all, are meant to seem instantaneous, firm and purposeful. Here, however, he uses four progressives in a row (looking... thinking... feeling... thinking), slowing down the pace of the passage and conveying its heightened intensity. However, as is only natural, Jason cannot preserve this feeling of sincere togetherness for very long; he soon hardens into his old self again. Still, his rationalizing clearly retains the connection between present and past neglect and loneliness; he still is 'the forgotten middle child' (Wagner 1971:4): 'now we'd have Uncle Maury around the house all the time, running things like the way he left me to come home in the rain by myself' (233).

Jason's reasoning, geared towards the deconstruction of this shared situation, immediately reasserts itself. This time it is stronger than ever because it must conquer the pain inside. It instantly destroys all there was momentarily between brother and sister:

> I says,
> 'A fine lot you care, sneaking in here soon as he's dead. But it wont do you
> any good. Dont think that you can take advantage of this to come sneaking
> back. If you cant stay on the horse you've got, you'll have to walk,' I says.
> 'We dont even know your name at that house,' I says. 'Do you know that?
> We dont even know your name. You'd be better off if you were down there
> with him and Quentin,' I says.
> (233)

But Jason does not easily regain his equilibrium on this day. To return to his adult obsession he must not only treat his sister with utter heartlessness again, by barely letting her get a glimpse of her baby daughter for the price of fifty dollars, he must also count her money again and put it away, as a replay of his childhood obsession.

Only then does he finally not 'feel so bad' any more: 'I says I reckon that'll show you. I reckon you'll know now that you cant beat me out of a job and get away with it' (236). Volpe has pointed out that 'Jason is actually keeping alive his bitterness to justify his own failure' (1964:120). His lost job opportunity—a result of Caddy's illegitimate pregnancy—after all dates from *eighteen years* before the day on which he tells his story. Yet, the present tenses of his attributive verbs keep reminding the reader of the actuality of these verbal exchanges for Jason.

When Caddy returns, almost insane with grief and longing for her child, Jason is once more brought into close contact with his inner self:

'Listen,' she says. 'If you'll get Mother to let me have her back, I'll give you a thousand dollars.'
(240)
'Wait,' she says, catching my arm... 'You promise, Jason?' she says, and me feeling her eyes almost like they were touching my face.
(241)

Once more Jason is able, if only for a very short time, to let the furious pace of his life slow down. With the isolated progressives—*feeling... touching*—Jason comes as close to his inner self as possible. It shows him at his most sensitive, his most honest, his most humane. He, who does not have 'a drop of warm blood' (240) inside him, as Caddy says, shows just like his brothers Benjy and Quentin how much his sister means to him. She, not his mother, is the only one who can come anywhere near his soul. But this is at the same time the reason why he must hurt her and her daughter Quentin more than anyone else.

Remembering how he 'solved' his problems with Caddy helps Jason deal with her daughter Quentin. Volpe has argued that 'Jason can survive as an adult while his brothers cannot because the vision of life that he brings out of his childhood approximates the reality of the world' (1964:120). I do not think that this is really clear from the text. Considering the exasperation of the people who have to deal with Jason, as well as his psychosomatic headaches, he does not seem to fit 'readily into modern society.' But by remembering his dissatisfactions and his 'triumphs,' he is finally able to get his life back into perspective.

The Inflexible World of Jason Compson

As we have seen, Jason's arrogance, pseudo common-sense and pseudo efficiency conceal the lonely, bewildered and embittered human being underneath. Of this human being, and his hunger for a common experience, a genuine shared reality, we have only seen a few short and furtive glimpses. Through the gaps in his story, Jason shows the feelings that his father's death causes in him; his progressives and his unusual silence create room for a certain measure of reflection, so that the use of the pronoun *we* can create for a moment a genuine shared situation between Caddy and himself, revealing the feelings that he has learned so carefully to hide from himself as well as from others.

Jason is a very vulnerable person. Like his brother Benjy, he needs a life that constantly shows exactly the right configuration. He, also, needs to 'pass his monument' on the right every time. To accomplish this, Jason will devaluate and deconstruct the conceptualizations of those around him. Only then is he able to create the situation that will sustain him. Nobody can say what would happen to Jason's soul if it were made to open up to love. Would he, like Benjy and Quentin, perish from the chaos inside? As it is, Jason manages to live on, his life one great struggle against his fellow man, but mostly against his own anguish and fear.

The Personalities of the Compson Children

Because in the novel *The Sound and the Fury* the three brothers Benjy, Quentin, and Jason Compson present themselves in the act of telling their stories, I have concentrated mainly on habitual *verbal* behavior: the 'consistent linguistic choices' (Fowler 1986:9) that each of them makes when describing his experience of the world in his own personal way. Experience, however, only has meaning if it can be related to something that went before: one's prior experience, stored in the memory, or the past experience of others, from which one has learned. This is why the past always remains 'alive,' or, as Faulkner expressed it beautifully through the voice of Gavin Stevens in *Requiem for a Nun*: 'The past is never dead. It's not even past' (80). It must be clear, then, that Benjy's, Quentin's, and Jason's concern with the past is in itself nothing remarkable. It is strange, however, that not one of them is able to create any future for himself. Normally a person will not only link his experience to the past, but will also extend it into the future in the form of hopes, dreams, plans, etc. Faulkner, in his essay 'To the Youth of Japan,' mentioned this universal importance to man of the 'freedom in which to hope and believe' (Meriwether 1965:84). The Compson brothers, however, do not possess this freedom; they are *confined* to a present that relates only to the past.

Jason Compson is confined psychologically by the 'love' of his mother, which he knows he will never be able to escape, by his general lack of initiative, and by his paranoia, which demands that he spend all his time guarding his possessions. His money, kept in a strong box in a drawer inside a dresser behind the locked door of his room, is a symbol of his state of mind. He lives in a world of precarious reality. He has corrupted and abandoned those aspects of biological reality that Bernstein mentions as 'the deepest universals we all share ... emotions, or affects' and that Faulkner himself called in his Nobel Prize Acceptance Speech 'the old verities and truths of the heart, the old universal truths... love and honor and pity and pride and compassion and sacrifice.' Jason has no need for or pride in cultural reality: the 'great traditions' of his native South, or the heritage of his ancestors. His sense of reality must depend on a constant re-establishing of interpersonal reality, of which his narrative style with its repeated ostentatious 'what I say'; 'I says'; and 'like I says' bears evidence. But Jason is utterly unable to establish the genuine human relationship based on mutual trust and respect that can create and sustain interpersonal reality. By forcing others to obey him, agree with him and grant him power, he creates the kind of 'pseudo-interpersonal' reality that is extremely unreliable and that can only intensify his paranoia. Such a 'pseudo-interpersonal' reality, or forced consensus, imprisons both Jason himself and those around him.

Quentin Compson has not abandoned the truths of biological reality: 'the kind of absolute intuitive knowledge, as intimate as the knowledge of one's own heartbeat or headache' that unites all mankind (Allen 1954:28), but he has come to distrust it. Life has taught him that things may not be what they appear to be. Uncertain of the meaning of his experience, in particular the loss of his sister Caddy, Quentin needs the advise and encouragement of those who came before, his elders. Cultural reality, embodied in the traditions of his native land, has taught him the values of honor, of purity, and of pride, but Quentin finds only an imperfect world in which such concepts cannot function. He must turn to his father as the only one who can help him establish order in the world of his experience. Mr. Compson's nihilistic views, however, present great problems for his son. What is more, the paradox between Mr. Compson's verbal and nonverbal behavior only intensifies Quentin's confusion. His loyalty prevents him from detaching himself from his father's point of view. This, unfortunately, deprives him of the chance to learn that his grief and his disappointment over the loss of his sister would not have vanished into thin air, but would have changed gradually into compassion, understanding and acceptance. Quentin is confined to his father's point of view, which he can neither escape nor accept. His only solution is to confine himself even more drastically, and more tragically, to the bottom of the Charles River.

Benjy's confinement, unlike that of his brothers, is largely physical. His life is lived behind gates and fences, and with the constant interference of his caretakers, because he 'cannot be trusted in normal public communion' (Freedman 1961-1962:22). His mental deficiency limits his understanding of experience to the most elementary aspects of biological reality, but, as Allen puts it, 'Benjy... in his idiocy, retains at least glimmering fragments of that truth that once was' (1954:45f.). What is more, Benjy's purity functions as a mirror that reflects such 'glimmerings' in others: in Caddy, who loves him truly; in Quentin, who gives him real support, and even in his father. Benjy, who can only understand his father's loving nonverbal behavior and fails to grasp his verbal nihilism, sees his father 'in light.' But Benjy also relentlessly reveals the lack of such 'glimmerings' in his mother and in Jason. He, who is 'not conscious of what he is doing,' thus 'emphasizes the old human virtues which the Compsons so rapidly are losing' (Allen 1954:49).

3

Multiple Voices in *As I Lay Dying*

The actions, the separate actions, I may have seen,
remembered. It was the imagination probably that
tied the whole thing together into a story. It's
difficult to say just what part of any story comes
specifically from imagination, what part from
experience, what part from observation. It's like
having... three tanks with a collector valve. And
you don't know just how much comes from which tank.
All you know is a stream of water runs from the
valve when you open it, drawn from the three tanks
—observation, experience, imagination

The motto of this chapter presents Faulkner's answer to the question of where he 'got the idea' for *As I Lay Dying* (Fant and Ashley 1964:96f.). The novel presents fifteen character-narrators: the seven members of the Bundren family and eight outsiders, neighbors, the doctor, the reverend and others, all of whom report on their own behavior and that of their fellow characters. Each of them, one could say, uses the same 'three tanks' that Faulkner himself used: *observation*, *experience* and *imagination*. In addition, the reports often include as well the underlying cause-effect relations of behavior, sometimes made explicit in the text through causal connectors such as *because*, *so*, and *therefore*.

A speaker may use his observation to report on the actions of others. Darl Bundren, for instance, reports how his younger brother Jewel 'steps in a single stride through the window. Still staring straight ahead, his pale eyes like wood set into his wooden face' (3). Speakers use their experience when remembering a fellow character's past, or habitual, behavior, as Anse Bundren does with regard to his son Darl: 'he tends to his own business, just because he's got his eyes full of the land all the time' (32). Speakers use their imagination, finally, to reflect on the other characters' feelings or thoughts, as Cora Tull does with regard to Darl's emotions: 'He just stood and looked at his dying mother, his heart too full for words' (22). Speakers may also observe their own behavior as if from the outside, for instance Vardaman: 'Then I begin to cry. I can feel where the fish was in the dust' (49); they may entertain memories of themselves at an earlier time, as in the case of Dewey Dell: 'Once I waked with a black void rushing under me. I could not see' (107); or they may report reflections about themselves, as Darl does: 'I cannot love my mother because I have no mother' (84). As this last example shows, these observations may also include the assignment of cause-effect relations to behavior.

Fifteen different narrators can create a lot of ambiguity. Thus it is possible for Cora and Vernon Tull to report that it is Darl who is upset about leaving his mother's deathbed to earn 'a quick three dollars': 'Darl almost begged them on his knees not to force him to leave her in her condition. But nothing would do but Anse and Jewel must make that three dollars' (19). They believe that Jewel would not 'miss a chance to make that extra three dollars at the price of his mother's goodbye kiss.' (19). Yet, Darl's own verbal behavior is limited to his remarks:

It means three dollars

We'll need that three dollars then, sure

It means three dollars... Do you want us to go, or not?
(15,16,18)

Jewel's behavior, on the other hand, suggests that he is unable to face the seriousness of his mother's illness: '"Ma aint that sick," Jewel says' (16). According to Cora 'it was between her [Addie] and Darl that the understanding and the true love was' (22). Yet she reports Addie herself as saying: 'He [Jewel] is my cross and he will be my salvation. He will save me from the water and from the fire. Even though I have laid down my life, he will save me' (154), while the father, Anse, tells his children: 'You never pure loved her, none of you.' This ambiguity concerns not only the reporting of behavior in contradictory ways, but also the idiosyncratic assignment of cause-effect relations to this behavior.

In *As I Lay Dying*, then, the different speakers are characterized in two ways: through mind-style, or *characterization from the inside*, and through the reports of others, or *characterization from the outside*. Because of its idiosyncrasy, attribution forms the most obvious hinge between the two processes of characterization. As I argued in Chapter 1, it tells us something about both the attributor and the attributee. Darl's observation that Vardaman's pale face is 'fading into the dusk like a piece of paper pasted on a failing wall' (45) makes clear, for instance, something about Vardaman's shock at his mother's death but also about Darl's obsession with void. This idiosyncrasy also applies to the explicit labels that characters receive from their fellow characters. When Vardaman repeats many times 'My mother is a fish' (74,89,180,182), this perhaps makes clear something about Addie but especially about Vardaman himself. When Darl says: 'Jewel's mother is a horse' (89), this may explain something about Addie, but it also reveals something about Jewel, about Darl himself, and about the different relations between the family members.

In Faulkner's works such labels often take the form of similes. Anse in particular receives many such labels, which liken him to 'a dipped rooster' (40), 'a scarecrow' (65), 'a felled steer' (66), 'a failing steer' (147), 'an old tall bird' (147), or 'a tall bird hunched in the cold weather' (156). In the simile appearance and behavior come together, ultimately suggesting that appearance is the final expression of habitual behavior. Jewel's eyes are especially described in a detailed way, most often by his brother Darl. But while Darl sees Jewel's eyes in terms of bleached chips of wood, to their younger brother Vardaman they are 'like marbles' (89). Here again, the ways Jewel's eyes are described tell us something of the describer as well as of the described.

In this chapter I shall discuss the characterization of the Bundren children, Cash, Darl, Jewel, Dewey Dell and Vardaman Bundren, in the order in which they appear in the text. I shall focus thereby on the influence of 'the voice of the other' on the mind-style of the individual, and concentrate especially on the voice of the mother, Addie.

Addie Bundren

My children were of me alone, of the wild blood boiling along the earth

In her own section there are few direct indications of Addie's verbal (or nonverbal) behavior towards her children. This does not mean that her voice has no influence. On the contrary, its influence is extensive and starts already with their names. It is important to realize that a child uses its own name to refer to itself before it can use the pronoun *I*. It is the name, rather than the concept *I*, that initially organizes the self (cf. De Levita 1965:173). If a child's name is a traditional one—if it is named, for instance, after a predecessor, as is the case with the children of *The Sound and the Fury*—it grows up with a clear sense of its place in the family. If a child receives a name that has a distinct meaning in the world, such as the name 'Jewel,' this becomes a factor in establishing its sense of self. As an introduction to the study of the children's personalities, we shall first turn to Addie's mind-style, as it is presented in the only section that is narrated by her.

By the time the reader reaches Addie's monologue, past the middle of the book, she has been the object of the other characters' actions, observations, memories and imaginings for a long time. She has been nursed by her daughter Dewey Dell, and propped up in bed so that she can see her oldest son Cash working on her coffin. She has been visited by her doctor, Peabody, and by her neighbors, Vernon and Cora Tull and their daughters. Her dead body has been consecrated by the Reverend Whitfield. Her youngest son Vardaman has caught a big fish, which he aims to show to mother, and he has bored holes in her coffin so that she can breathe. In contrast to all this commotion, Addie's third son, Jewel, has tried to defend his mother's peace and quiet: 'I said if you'd just let her alone. Sawing and knocking, and keeping the air always moving so fast on her face that when you're tired you cant breathe it' (13). Her privacy is important to him, as a discussion between him and his father, reported by Darl, makes clear:

> 'She wanted that like she wants to go in our own wagon,' pa says. 'She'll rest easier for knowing it's a good one, and private. She was ever a private woman. You know it well.' 'Then let it be private,' Jewel says. 'But how the hell can you expect it to be—'
> (17)

When Addie's section in the text has been reached, the whole family has set out for Jefferson to bury Addie with her relatives, as she wanted; and the three oldest boys have had to rescue her body from a flooded river.

Addie's behavior has been observed by the members of her family. Firstly, her verbal behavior has been virtually nonexistent. Once, according to Peabody, she said 'Cash... you, Cash!' in a voice that was 'harsh and strong' (42), while Darl has reported that she shouted 'You, Cash... You, Cash!' in a voice that was 'harsh, strong, and unimpaired' (43). Addie's nonverbal behavior was limited almost entirely to the movements and expressions of her eyes. Only once did she raise herself, lay back, and turn her head. Apart from this, she only looked at Cash, at Anse, at Peabody, who felt her eyes 'shoving' at him, driving him from the room (41), and especially at Vardaman, at whom she not only looked but whom she also watched. Apparently she did not once look at her daughter: 'Dewey Dell leans down, trying to press her back. "Ma," she says; "ma." She is looking out the window, at Cash' (43).

Addie's eyes have been described to resemble 'two candles when you watch them gutter down into the sockets of iron candle-sticks' (7); 'lamps blaring up just before the oil is gone' (41). These eyes touched, 'not with sight or sense, but like the stream from a hose touches you, the stream at the instant of impact as dissociated from the nozzle as though it had never been there' (39f.). The actual moment of her death has been reported in reference to these eyes: 'the life in them, rushing suddenly upon them; the two flames glare up for a steady instant. Then they go out as though someone had leaned down and blown upon them' (44). The separate observations of Addie's behavior and appearance all tie in neatly within the traditional 'deathbed frame': her face 'wasted away so that the bones draw just under the skin in white lines' (7); her hands 'laying on the quilt like two of them roots dug up and tried to wash and you couldn't get them clean' (13); her body 'no more than a bundle of rotten sticks' (40), making 'no more of a hump than a rail would' (7). Only the fact that her voice is described as 'unimpaired,' which implies that it was always 'harsh and strong,' may tell us something about Addie's personality at this point.

The memories that different speakers have of Addie's habitual behavior contribute to this sparse information. The text of Darl, the second brother, provides the clearest indications of his mother's habitual behavior in the past: she always 'whipped' and 'petted' his younger brother Jewel more. This observation is immediately motivated: 'He is a head taller than any of the rest of us, always was' (16). When Jewel was still a baby, she 'would sit in the lamplight, holding him on a pillow on her lap' (130). When years later she believed Jewel ill, she would worry about him and get Dewey Dell 'to do his milking' and 'fix him special things to eat and hide them for him' (115). Darl's text not only commemorates his mother's behavior, it also posits her feelings, and motivates them in a self-assured way: 'I knew that she was hating herself for that deceit and hating Jewel because she had to love him' (115); 'She cried hard, maybe because she had to cry so quiet; maybe because she felt the same way about tears she did about deceit, hating herself for doing it, hating him because she had to' (122).

Cora Tull's text is another source of information concerning Addie's habitual behavior and feelings. However, contrary to the impression created by Darl's text that Addie was especially close to Jewel, Cora 'saw' that 'with Jewel she had just been pretending, but that it was between her and Darl that the understanding and the true love was' (22). Nevertheless, she believes that Addie, 'lost in her vanity and her pride,' had 'closed her heart to God and set that selfish mortal boy [Jewel] in His place' (154). Cora Tull also imagines her neighbor's habitual feelings: 'She lived, a lonely woman, lonely with her pride, trying to make folks believe different, hiding the fact that they just suffered her' (20), and she reports that this woman is 'dying alone, hiding her pride and her broken heart. Glad to go' (21). The text of Addie's husband Anse also expresses his wife's wish to die. As many speakers report it, he repeats again and again how her mind was 'set on it' (29,41,99,101). In addition, he explicitly characterizes her as 'a private woman' (17); a self-sufficient woman ('She was ever one to clean up after herself' [18]), and a dedicated mother to her sons: 'couldn't no woman strove harder than Addie to make them right, man and boy: I'll say that for her' (34).

If one superimposes the various reports of Addie's behavior, whether observed, remembered or imagined, certain personality themes present themselves. Addie seems to have been a hard-working, private and proud woman, honest, hard on herself, lonely, and perhaps somewhat harsh and selective in her affection for her children.

Addie's Mind-Style

In Addie's section (pp. 155-163), the reader is immediately confronted with Addie's own reports of her habitual behavior at some unidentified time in the past:

I would go down the hill to the spring where I could be quiet and hate them.

I would have to look at them day after day... and think that this seemed to be the only way I could get ready to stay dead

I would hate my father for having ever planted me.

I would look forward to the times when they faulted, so I could whip them.

I would think with each blow of the switch: Now you are aware of me!

These memories are difficult to understand because of the indeterminacy of the personal pronouns. It is unclear to whom the pronouns *them, they,* and *you* refer. The (re)-reader may remember, at this point, that Darl reported about Cora that 'she taught school too, once' (10), and read the 'too' to mean: like my own mother, suggesting that Addie refers to her school-children here. The same indeterminacy exists with regard to the pronoun *it* and the demonstrative *this*: 'especially in the early spring, for it was worst then'; 'this seemed to be the only way.' It seems that these pronouns have no circumscript references, but evoke more diffusely Addie's state of mind at the time.

The text of Addie's memories returns here to her father's nihilistic views: 'I could just remember how my father used to say that the reason for living was to get ready to stay dead a long time.' This nihilism is reminiscent of Mr. Compson in *The Sound and the Fury*. Both fathers express a stifled hatred of the world in which they live. This strong negative emotion must include their children, who are necessarily a part of this world, and who, during their early nurturing, are dependent on it. Thus the children inherit their fathers' hatred and include it in their own conceptualization of reality and their own sense of self. The text shows clearly how Addie, like Quentin Compson, is loyal to her father's views, as she herself replaces the verb *live* with the verb phrase *get ready to stay dead*. In Quentin's text the hatred that co-exists with a tremendous loyalty and admiration for his father has led, perhaps through reaction-formation, to a state of paralysis or stasis, an inability to act in the outside world.[64] When this hatred must find expression, it is directed against the self, disguised as suffering or the self-effacement of suicide. Addie has found a different solution; her text shows how the hatred for the one on whom she was dependent is acted out in the world, displaced unto the school-children that are dependent on her.[65]

Three lexical fields are of importance on the first page of Addie's text. The first one contains elements of nature: 'spring,' 'quiet,' 'sun,' 'trees,' 'smelling,' 'damp,' 'rotting leaves,' 'new earth,' and 'planted,' all linked to the theme of fertility. The second set relates to the negative, punishing side of morality: 'secret,' 'selfish,' 'faulted,' 'whip,' 'switch,' 'hate.' Opposite terms are conspicuously absent; there is no openness, no selflessness, no virtue, no tenderness, no compassion, no love. The third

---

64 Reaction formation is 'the management of unacceptable impulses by permitting expression of the impulse in antithetical form. This is equivalently an expression of the impulse in the negative' (Kaplan and Sadock 1988:144). Here unacceptable feelings of hatred towards the father are expressed as their opposites: admiration and loyalty.

65 This defense mechanism is sometimes called 'turning passive into active': the subject, here, makes others suffer what she herself has had to endure, thereby changing her own role from a passive into an active one.

set contains elements related to death: 'rotting,' 'blood,' 'dead.' The three sets are interrelated in a way that seems characteristic of Addie's mind-style. Addie looks for solitude in nature, not to get closer to herself or to have her sense of self revitalized, but to indulge uninterruptedly in her hatred. Her need to inflict punishment on others is fertilized by nature. Her sense of morality—the ability to distinguish between right and wrong—is no cause in itself but functions only to create an opportunity for the displacement and acting out of her anger on the children in her care. As her text shows, this anger, even if it is displaced away from the self, clearly remains self-hatred: 'When the switch fell I could feel it upon my flesh; when it welted and ridged it was my blood that ran.'

The suffering that Addie inflicts on herself by way of others has a clear purpose: to prove to herself the reality of her existence, which her father denied. Where Quentin Compson was unable to counteract his father's conceptualizations—the worthlessness of life in general, and the worthlessness of his (Quentin's) own life in particular—Addie's sadism allows her to find a 'solution' outside herself. Her narration is ultimately directed at the father: 'Now you are aware of me! Now I am something' (155). That it is this complex and only superficially acknowledged void in Addie's life that makes her marry Anse Bundren is suggested by the causal connector *so* immediately after this passage: 'And so I took Anse' (156).

Addie and Anse

The second and third pages of Addie's text (156,157) contain memories of her first encounters with her husband-to-be. The clauses that show the first-person pronoun all contain an action verb in the past perfect, whereby Addie conceptualizes herself as purposeful, determined, active: a performer of completed actions that create a definite, circumscript situation:

I saw him pass the school house
I learned that he was driving four miles out of his way to do it.
I noticed then how he was beginning to hump
I went to the door and stood there when he passed.
I looked up that day and saw Anse

By contrast, almost all the clauses that have Anse as a subject contain verbal ing-forms:

he was driving four miles out of his way
he was beginning to hump
his head turning slow to watch the door
Anse standing there... turning his hat round and round in his hands
he... driving his eyes at me
he... turning the hat in his hands.
he... holding his eyes to mine
he... watching my face.

Such clauses already suggest around Anse an atmosphere of indecision and of incompleteness, a lack of energy and a fear of initiative, reinforced by the repetition of the adjective *slow* used as an adverb: 'the wagon creaking slow, his head turning slow.' In this way, the slowness is not only a characteristic of the movement but an attribute of the object as well: Anse's head does not just move slowly; it is a slow head.[66]

Many similes that will come to characterize Anse through the years are significant in this respect as well: 'he looked already like a tall bird hunched in the cold weather'; 'his eyes... like two hounds in a strange yard.' The contrast between Addie's energy and decisiveness and her future husband's inertness is emphasized, moreover, by the way the text presents their discussions. She asks all the questions and he gropes for words, barely saying anything except a twice repeated 'that's what I come to see you about' when the lack of 'womenfolks' in his life is mentioned. The identical form of the two answers presents Anse as an unimaginative soul, not someone Addie can respect. That Addie, indeed, does not respect him is clear from the cynical way she traps Anse in a word game. Tricking him with words, she deliberately misleads Anse into thinking that unlike him she does have relatives, just so she can enjoy his bewilderment and his concern over having to meet 'town folks' and be judged by them:

'I aint got no people. So that wont be no worry to you. I dont reckon you can say the same.'

'No. I have people. In Jefferson.'

His face fell a little. 'Well, I got a little property. I'm forehanded; I got a good honest name. I know how town folks are, but maybe when they talk to me.......'

'They might listen,' I said. 'But they'll be hard to talk to.' He was watching my face. 'They're in the cemetery.'

'But your living kin,' he said. 'They'll be different.'

'Will they?' I said. 'I dont know. I never had any other kind.'

Thus the little self-assertion that Anse has ventured into: 'I got a little property. I'm forehanded; I got a good honest name' is taken care of. Addie's aggression clearly comes to the surface in the form of the word-game, while the source of her hatred shows itself in its content. The lack of nurturing at the source of her life has left its trace: 'I never had any other kind.' Addie's behavior shows itself as a distressing tangle of desires, fears and defenses.

Immediately after this scene, Addie's cynical logic is repeated: 'So I took Anse.' The text once again links the marriage to Addie's ability to inflict violence and suffering on another person, and to feel contempt. Through her verbal as well as her physical violence, Addie is able to act out her hatred. Her marriage will provide an opportunity to continue displacing her rage against her father. Two aspects of Addie's language are important in this respect: the power of the causal connector *so*, creating Addie's personal logic, and the energy of the verb *took*, which launches her relationship with Anse and which clearly brings out its inequality. This relationship is soon to become even more unequal, when the verb *took* is replaced by the verb *suckle*: 'I would think that if he were to wake and cry, I would suckle him, too' (158). This 'possible world'

---

66 Anse, in fact, forms a striking example of the poor white described by W.J. Cash: 'a striking lankness of frame and slackness of muscle in association with a shambling gait, a boniness and misshapeliness of head and feature, a peculiar sallow swartness, or alternatively a not less peculiar and a not less sallow faded-out colorlessness of skin and hair' (1969:25). For this type of Southerner, 'lacking lands and markets which would repay any extensive effort as a farmer, lacking any incentive which would even serve to make him aid the women at tasks which habit had fixed as effeminate, it was the most natural thing in the world... to sink deeper and deeper into idleness and shiftlessness' (1969: 26).

in which Addie takes away Anse's maturity soon evolves into one in which she even takes away his life: 'I believed that I would kill Anse' (158), a 'possible world' soon presented as if real: 'And then he died. He did not know he was dead' (160).

Symbiotic Longings and the Distrust of Words
While Addie's anger thus quickly diminishes and destroys its own outlet, leaving itself once more to stand naked, certain changes in her life seem at least for a short while to work a positive change in her. The birth of her first child Cash teaches Addie the victory of genuine feeling over words: 'When he was born I knew that motherhood was invented by someone who had to have a word for it because the ones that had the children didn't care whether there was a word for it or not' (157). Notice how Addie's text acknowledges here for the first time a kinship with other women ('the ones that had the children'), which must be seen in the light of the fact that she has not mentioned her mother or any other female relative or friend.[67] Consequently, Addie achieves some insight into her violence towards the school-children: 'I knew that it had been, not that they had dirty noses, but that we had had to use one another by words like spiders dangling by their mouths from a beam, swinging and twisting and never touching' (158).

In a moving way the text allows its subject to explore the sources of her only partly acknowledged anger and to look into the primitive needs that lie beyond. It presents the pre-verbal closeness to another human being that Addie experiences through her child: 'Cash did not need to say it to me nor I to him' (158). This preverbal, motherly discourse—Kristeva's 'semiotic' (1986)—is based on a complex of visual, auditory, gustatory, kinesthetic, tactile, and olfactory stimuli. It is not, however, without tension or conflict. Notice, in this respect, the aggressive quality of the verb that describes the weaning of her babies: 'I refused my breast to Cash and Darl after their time was up' (161). In addition, Addie's text keeps emphasizing the ostentatious certainty and decisiveness of her conclusions through the repeated attributive clause *I knew that*, which occurs even six times in just one paragraph (157f.). The text also makes clear her aggression, for instance through the use of negations to convey essentially positive experience: 'the ones that had the children didn't care'; 'Cash did not need to say it.' A similar effect is created by the use of terms that cause a collocational clash within the sentence in which they occur, for instance the verb *violated* in the sentence 'my aloneness... had never been violated until Cash came' (158). Such collocational clashes convey the ambivalence of Addie's feelings.

Addie's feelings of relative peace and fulfillment cannot survive when her second son, Darl, is born. The repeatable character of the experience of childbirth devaluates it for her. This is clear already from the way the text shapes the start of her relationship with Darl: 'Then I found that I had Darl. At first I would not believe it' (158). If we compare these verbs with those that conceptualize Addie's relationship with her husband and with her first-born son: 'I *took* Anse'; 'I *knew* that I had Cash' (emphasis added), the diminishing power and decisiveness is obvious. Through the verbal forms *find* and *would not believe it*, the text makes clear that she does not acknowledge Darl's

---

67 Addie is another of Faulkner's victims of an absent mother and an embittered father.

existence in the active way in which she took possession of her husband Anse and accepted her first-born Cash.

Once having felt her hunger for symbiosis Addie, in a Lacanian way, blames *the word*, repeatable like child-birth, which stands between the subject and experience, signifying even the very absence of the experience. Displacing her disappointment and anger on her husband Anse, she blames his word, *love*: 'He had a word, too. Love, he called it. But I had been used to words for a long time. I knew that that word was like the others: just a shape to fill a lack' (158). Although Addie started her relationship with Anse by tricking him with words, she now accuses him of having tricked her with his word. To defend herself against Anse's word, she repeats his name to herself so often that it becomes a receptacle in which the human being is captured and presumably made harmless: 'I would think: Anse. Why Anse. Why are you Anse. I would think about his name until after a while I could see the word as a shape, a vessel, and I would watch him liquify and flow into it like cold molasses flowing out of the darkness' (159).

While Addie's text thus dehumanizes and immobilizes Anse inside the senseless shape of his name, Addie tries by the same process of repeating her sons' names to liberate them from the world of words, so that they remain to her pure experience: 'And when I would think *Cash* and *Darl* that way until their names would die and solidify into a shape and then fade away, I would say, All right. It doesn't matter. It doesn't matter what they call them' (159). With these operations on words, Addie gains a form of mastery over the presence and absence of objects. They constitute her version of Freud's 'da-fort' game (1920). The operations generate two distinct solutions for Addie. In the passage about Anse, she employs the power of the word to reshape the object into its own form and thus destroy it. In the passage about her children, she calls up the power of words to loosen themselves from the objects for which they stand, in order to dispel these same words and create a pre-verbal directness of experience.

We see here how Addie, paradoxically, needs a profusion of words—many of which are negations of other words that are evoked as well—to create a world in which these words would not be necessary, thus showing how a real return to a pre-verbal situation is impossible. Addie seems aware of this. In a third passage, she complains about the power of words to leave experience behind, the power she herself has just made use of to free her children: 'I would think how words go straight up in a thin line, quick and harmless, and how terribly doing goes along the earth, clinging to it, so that after a while the two lines are too far apart for the same person to straddle from one to the other' (160).[68]

---

68   A similar outrage over the power of words is found in Quentin Compson's text in *The Sound and the Fury*: 'They all talked at once, their voices insistent and contradictory and impatient, making of unreality a possibility, then a probability, then an incontrovertible fact, as people will when their desires become words' (134). The distrust of words that Faulkner thematizes through the personalities of Quentin Compson, Addie Bundren and others extends beyond the narrow scope of the psychiatric implications of symbiotic longings. It is a typical characteristic of thought at the beginning of this century, when concepts such as heroism, patriotism and honor seemed to have lost their value. Faulkner spoke of 'mouthsounds; the loud and empty words which we have emasculated of all meaning whatever—freedom, democracy, patriotism' (Meriwether 1965:65f.). In *The Sound and the Fury*, he placed these feelings at a time when second- and third-generation Southerners asked themselves whether the large and important phrases of the Civil War had

So far, Addie's text has presented three major periods in her life that are crucial to an understanding of her personality. The first concerns Addie's life as a schoolteacher and includes her marriage to Anse Bundren. As we have seen, the text here presents three interrelated lexical fields: one of nature, one of (negative) morality, and one of death, foregrounding the aggression in Addie's personality. The second episode, of the birth of her older children, confronts her with primitive needs and fears that lie beyond her aggression. The text here focuses on Addie's operations on words, which provide her with a certain mastery over the presence and absence of objects. A third period is obsessively concerned with the concept of sin. Addie's obsession with sin, together with her need to act out this obsession in the outside world, stems from primitive feelings of guilt over an all-consuming anger towards an inadequate and damaging father.

Addie is in a sense right, then, to attribute the existence of the sin to God: the father 'who created the sin' (161). It is indeed the voice of the father—*her* father—that brings about, through its nihilism, the emptiness and worthlessness at the source of his daughter's sinful anger. The text emphasizes this emptiness through its lexical choices: 'gaps,' 'lacks,' 'cries,' 'darkness,' 'terrible nights,' 'orphans.' Their impact is heightened by collocational clashes such as 'hearing the... voicelessness,' and by the powerful similes in which they function, which aim to verbalize truths that are beyond words:

> like the cries of the geese out of the wild darkness in the old terrible nights,
> fumbling at the deeds like orphans to whom are pointed out in a crowd two
> faces and told, That is your father, your mother.
> (160)

Notice incidentally how, albeit in a negative and impersonal context, the concept of *mother* is presented.

The Expiation of Sin

The text presents Addie's attempts to master her feelings of guilt through the acting-out of her sinfulness. The mental activity verbs that have Addie as subject are different from the ones used before: *I believed*, versus *I knew*. If we compare these attributive verbs, it is clear that the certainty of her assertions has diminished. However, the form of the attribution itself—the that-clause—still shows the control of an assertion founded on a conscious conclusion. The frequent repetition of the predicate *would think of...* *sin*, suggests the compulsive, enduring nature of Addie's mental activity:

> I would think of sin
> I would think of him as dressed in sin.
> I would think of him as thinking of me as dressed also in sin
> I would think of the sin as garments which we would remove
> (161)

The clauses above materialize the sin in the form of a garment that can be put on and taken off at will.

This 'play' with sin serves the mastery of guilt feelings, just as operations on

actually had any meaning. In *As I Lay Dying*, the time is the period after World War I. The characters hope to find underneath the emptiness of the word the 'real truth' of experience.

words serve the mastery of absence, while at the same time offering a solution to lone-liness by enabling the guilt to be shared. That this 'he,' who came 'swift and secret' through the woods, is not Addie's husband—the 'slow' one already 'beginning to hump'—is clear. By sharing her sin with a religious man, an 'instrument ordained by God who created the sin, to sanctify that sin He had created' (161), Addie magnifies it in order to better exorcize it, so that after the birth of her third child 'the wild blood boiled away and the sound of it ceased' (162). Addie's text acknowledges the existence of her illegitimate son Jewel—child of the reverend Whitfield—in the following way: 'Then I found that I had Jewel. When I waked to remember to discover it, he was two months gone' (161). If one compares these verb phrases (*found* and *waked to remember to discover*) to the ones that Addie's text uses to present her relationship to Anse, Cash and Darl (*took*, *knew*, and *found... would not believe it*), one clearly observes a diminishing control, a progressive splitting from reality, as if the distance between the dreamlike state of her mind and the earth-bound functioning of her body has gradually increased.

Depression and Death

The next two children, Dewey Dell and Vardaman, are of her body but not of her soul. As the verb phrases present them, they are motherless from birth, used only to settle her account with Anse:

> I gave Anse Dewey Dell to negate Jewel. Then I gave him Vardaman to replace the child I had robbed him of.
> (162)

After this, Addie believes she can 'get ready to die' (162). She has, in fact, been dying ever since the birth of Jewel, when she believed her 'duty to the alive' to be fulfilled.

Now that she has indeed died, and her family is performing its duty in bringing her to her last resting place, very few references to her behavior or feelings are made. Vardaman repeats a few times that his mother 'is a fish,' and that 'Jewel's mother is a horse' (182). Anse emphasizes once more her hard work: 'a slaving and a slaving,' and her pride: 'she wouldn't have us beholden.' He points to her wish to have them all present: 'She would want us all there,' and he emphasizes her self-sacrifice in bringing them all up: 'You all dont know... The somebody you was young with and you growed old in her and she growed old in you, seeing the old coming on and it was the one somebody you could hear say it dont matter and know it was the truth outen the hard world and all a man's grief and trials. You all dont know' (217).

Addie's text, then, reviews three major periods in her life, in which she successively works through her aggression, her symbiotic needs—and in connection with this her distrust of words—and her feelings of guilt. After the birth of her youngest children, for at least five or six years, Addie had been getting 'ready to die' (162). In the different periods that Addie describes, her family members were a part of the situation that she needed to create to sustain herself: Anse is thus linked with aggression, Cash with symbiosis, Darl with denial, Jewel with guilt, and Dewey Dell and Vardaman with death. Addie's section provides material that can be used to show the influence of her mind-style on the developing personalities of her children.

Darl Bundren

I cannot love my mother because I have no mother
As the voice of the first monologue, Darl is the only narrator of *As I Lay Dying* who
is known from his own section before others present his behavior. Because it forms the
beginning of the book, Darl's first section (pp. 3,4) also has the important function of
presenting a setting for the whole novel.

Darl's Mind-Style
The dominant lexical field of Darl's text constitutes a rural scene, with concrete entities
such as 'field,' 'path,' 'cottonhouse,' 'straw hat,' 'cotton,' 'bluff,' 'spring,' 'reins,'
'wagon,' 'gourd' and 'willow branch.' A sub-set presents the details of the cottonhouse, with its 'logs,' 'roof,' 'window,' 'walls' and 'floor.' A separate set pertains to
carpentry, with 'chips,' 'boards,' 'adze blade,' 'planks,' 'trestle,' 'edges' and 'box.'
The first set is related to the proper name *Jewel* and the pronoun *I*, while the second
set is related to the proper name *Cash* exclusively.

If one looks at the modification of these nouns, one notices both a contrast and a
similarity between the two sets. The contrast exists between the 'rough logs' of the
cottonhouse in the first set and 'the smooth undulations' of the boards in the second set,
as well as between the 'frayed and broken straw hat' and the 'empty and shimmering
dilapidation' of the cottonhouse in the first set and the 'finished box' in the second set.
Thus the text invests these two areas of interest with a contrast between imperfection
and perfection, and ties Darl himself to the area of imperfection. The similarity
between the two sets consists of the eroticizing modifications attached to the noun
'path' in the first set and to the nouns *boards* and *planks* in the second. The path that
the text thus presents is described in terms of tactile imagery as hard and smooth and
with soft corners; the planks are constituted through both visual and tactile imagery to
be 'yellow as gold, like soft gold,' possessing 'flanks' with 'smooth undulations.' Both
perfection and imperfection are thus eroticized.

Within the first set, *path* is the noun with the largest frequency. In addition, it is
predicated in a most active way: it 'runs,' it 'turns,' it 'circles' and it 'goes on,' to be
followed by the speaker and his companion. A large number of the clauses that have
Darl as subject, or Darl and this companion, present this situation:
Jewel and I... following the path
I... follow the path
we go on up the path
I... mount the path
Such clauses cast Darl in the role of performer of a simple, rather indolent physical
action. Other clauses that have Darl as subject likewise cast him in the role of
performer of a simple physical action:
Jewel and I come up from the field
I turn
I come around the corner.
I pass him
I reach the top
I go on to the house

The verbs used here are either transitive or complemented by a prepositional phrase; one verb is implicitly reflexive: 'I turn [myself].' Darl's text, then, is concerned with the relations, spatial and influential, between himself and important entities. The only clause that contains a stative verb—'I am fifteen feet ahead of him'—has this same focus.

When one considers the pronoun systems that the text utilizes it becomes clear that the first-person pronoun is almost always paired with the proper name Jewel or the corresponding third-person pronoun:

Jewel and I come up from the field

I am fifteen feet ahead of him

Jewel's frayed and broken straw hat a full head above my own.

I turn... Jewel fifteen feet behind me

he crosses the floor... as I come around the corner.

Three times the plural forms are used: 'anyone watching us'; 'when we reach it'; 'we go on up the path.' In contrast, the first person pronoun is only once used in relation to Cash: 'When I reach the top he has quit sawing... he is fitting two of the boards together.' In this instance, however, the activity is simultaneous but not shared. The scene created by this second lexical set completely lacks the intimacy of the first-person plural pronoun.

Textual characteristics clearly show how Darl almost constantly observes himself in relation to his brother Jewel. In order to do so, however, he takes the point of view of a distanced 'anyone' who is able to perceive 'Jewel's frayed and broken straw hat' a 'full head' above Darl's own. Less explicitly, Darl continues this throughout the presentation of the walk, splitting himself into an acting participant and an observing, detached, anonymous 'anyone,' who knows that Jewel, who is fifteen feet behind and invisible to him, is 'looking straight ahead'; 'steps in a single stride through the window'; and 'crosses the floor in four strides.' One must conclude, then, that Darl's text makes no distinction between perceived worlds and imaginary worlds here.

The text uses the simple present as its basic tense, conflating event time with narrating time. Progressives are used in adverbial clauses, creating a sense of simultaneity, as for instance in: 'Still staring straight ahead... he crosses the floor.' A few post-modifiers present the adverse effects of the past on the present, as for instance in: 'rough logs, from between which the chinking has long fallen.' Finally, the modals *could* and *will* create a stipulative world: 'Addie Bundren could not want a better one, a better box to lie in. It will give her confidence and comfort.'

The text of Darl's first section, then, creates a world in which the contrast between perfection and imperfection is important, in which the past has its adverse effects on the present, and in which inanimate objects are eroticized. Generally speaking, the spatial and influential relations between the speaker and the animate and inanimate objects around him are the constant focus of attention, at times causing a splitting of consciousness. We shall see in the following sections how this worldview, created by Darl's own verbal behavior, evolves throughout his text, and how it is influenced by, and influences in turn, the reports of Darl's behavior made by others.

Darl and Cash

Darl is the second child in the family; apparently he was born shortly after Cash. As

Cash puts it: 'me and him was born close together' (217). To Cash this is important, and it explains his closeness to his brother. The text of Darl's first section presents his admiration for Cash's work. This is clear elsewhere as well from the amount of loving detail in his description of Cash: 'Cash works on, half turned into the feeble light, one thigh and one pole-thin arm braced, his face sloped into the light with a rapt, dynamic immobility above his tireless elbow' (68). Their complicity shows itself in the quality of Darl's memories: 'So we didn't tell'; 'But Cash and I knew' (117).

Darl's feelings of responsibility for his brother are clear from the viewpoint shifts that he uses to imagine and verbalize Cash's image of their dying mother's face as it 'seems to float detached' upon the darkness, 'lightly as the reflection of a dead leaf' (46), and from the help he gives Cash in verbalizing his reflections on Jewel:

He looked at me, his eyes fumbling, the words fumbling at what he was
trying to say. 'It aint always the safe things in this world that a
fellow.......'
'You mean, the safe things are not always the best things?'
'Ay; best,' he said, fumbling again. 'It aint the best things, the things that
are good for him....... A young boy. A fellow kind of hates to see.......
wallowing in somebody else's mire.......' That's what he was trying to say.
When something is new and hard and bright, there ought to be something a
little better for it than just being safe, since the safe things are just the
things that folks have been doing so long they have worn the edges off and
there's nothing to the doing of them that leaves a man to say, That was not
done before and it cannot be done again.
(117)

The closeness between the brothers is also clear from the concern Darl shows for his brother's comfort after he has been injured, but it is most apparent from Darl's direct appeals to Cash, reported by Cash himself, when he is helpless in front of the rest of the family and the officials that have come to take him away:

I thought you would have told me... I never thought you wouldn't have.
I thought you'd a told me. It's not that I... Do you want me to go?
(220,221)

Darl and Cash were the only children for nearly ten years. During this time, Darl might have developed the typical carefree behavior of a younger child protected by an older brother and cherished by his mother. Darl's personality, however, seems to have moved towards remoteness and isolation. The text of his first section has already conveyed a need to split into an acting self and a distanced observing self.

Public Views of Darl

It is the distance from others that is the most frequently reported aspect of Darl's habitual behavior:

Darl was different from those others.
(19)
It was Darl, the one that folks say is queer, lazy, pottering about the place
(22)
Darl... that sits at the supper table with his eyes gone further than the food
and the lamp, full of the land dug out of his skull and the holes filled with

distance beyond the land.

(23)

Many narrators go further than simply to observe Darl's peculiar behavior. Cash, for instance, defends his brother: 'I see all the while how folks could say he was queer, but that was the very reason couldn't nobody hold it personal' (220); and he extends this apology even to an external audience: 'It was like he was outside of it too, same as you' (220). Anse shows his irritation: 'How many times I told him it's doing such things as that that makes folks talk about him' (93). He also attributes causes to Darl's behavior: 'he was alright at first, with his eyes full of the land, because the land laid up-and-down ways then; it wasn't till that ere road come and switched the land around longways and his eyes still full of the land, that they begun to threaten me out of him, trying to shorthand me with the law' (32). Anse, here, gives a very good example of how attribution may reflect the attributor's mind-style, telling us more about the attributor himself than about the attributee. It is obvious that Anse translates Darl's behavior into his own terms, complaining again, this time via Darl, about the road that was built right by his house. There is no indication, however, that such considerations are a part of Darl's problem.

Something similar is the case with the attributions of Vernon Tull: 'I reckon I am blessed in having a wife that ever strives for sanctity and well-doing like she says I am. Now and then a fellow gets to thinking about it. Not often, though. Which is a good thing... I have said and I say again, that's ever living thing the matter with Darl: he just thinks by himself too much' (63f.). The attribution does tell us something about Darl this time but it also reflects Tull's personality and his relationship with his wife Cora, who herself even knows the solution to Darl's problem: 'all he needs is a wife to straighten him out' (64). Cora's solution, again, characterizes especially herself and her interest in Darl as a prospective husband for one of her daughters. She commemorates her daughter Eula's interest in Darl, and quotes her words: 'I reckon Cash and Darl can get married now' (30). She observes Eula's behavior with obvious pleasure: 'Someone comes through the hall. It is Darl. He does not look in as he passes the door. Eula watches him as he goes on and passes from sight again towards the back. Her hand rises and touches her beads lightly, and then her hair' (8). Armstid comments on the strangeness of Darl's paraverbal behavior:

> He said it just like he was reading it outen the paper. Like he never give a durn himself one way or the other... in that voice like he was just listening and never give a durn himself.
>
> (176)

Tull, finally, considers Darl's eyes and the way he looks at people:

> He is looking at me. He dont say nothing; just looks at me with them queer eyes of hisn that makes folks talk. I always say it aint never been what he done so much or said or anything so much as how he looks at you. It's like he had got into the inside of you, someway. Like somehow you was looking at yourself and your doings outen his eyes.
>
> (111)

From Tull's text, it seems as if Darl's inner emptiness reflects the personalities of others as in a mirror.

Darl and Addie

The strange distance that is such a disturbing aspect of Darl's behavior can be linked to his mother's disbelief of his existence: 'I would not believe it.' Even his name, Darl, with its loving reverberations of 'darling' is unreal. It seems as if his mother's disbelief has become Darl's own disbelief and has disturbed the normal development of his ego strengths.[69] As his text shows, Darl is constantly concerned with the concept of identity, perhaps because of the tendency to 'split' already recognized in the first section. The mere incidence of the verb *be* in his monologues indicates how pervasive is his struggle to stabilize his sense of self:

In a strange room you must empty yourself for sleep. And before you are emptied for sleep, what are you. And when you are emptied for sleep, you are not. And when you are filled with sleep, you never were. I dont know what I am. I dont know if I am or not. Jewel knows he is, because he does not know that he does not know whether he is or not. He cannot empty himself for sleep because he is not what he is and he is what he is not. Beyond the unlamped wall I can hear the rain shaping the wagon that is ours, the load that is no longer theirs that felled and sawed it nor yet theirs that bought it and which is not ours either, lie on our wagon though it does, since only the wind and the rain shape it only to Jewel and me, that are not asleep. And since sleep is is-not and rain and wind are *was*, it is not. Yet the wagon *is*, because when the wagon is *was*, Addie Bundren will not be. And Jewel *is*, so Addie Bundren must be. And then I must be, or I could not empty myself for sleep in a strange room. And so if I am not emptied yet, I am *is*.

(72)

In this crucial scene, Darl's concern is in part with his younger brother Jewel. However, the reflection tells us more about Darl himself than about Jewel. The text shows, in fact, how Darl's jealousy of his brother's sense of self forces him to 'deconstruct' it: 'Jewel knows he is, because he does not know that he does not know whether he is or not.' In this way Darl elevates Jewel's supposed lack of awareness as a more serious problem than his own lack of identity, even if he secretly envies Jewel's natural sense of self.

This endeavor forms part of an intellectual exercise with which Darl desperately tries to create himself as a reality. His very self-consciousness, however, stands in the way of a sure sense of self. Notice the extreme number of negatives and negations: 'are not,' 'dont know,' 'does not,' 'cannot,' 'never,' 'is not,' 'unlamped,' 'no longer,' 'not yet theirs,' 'not ours,' 'not asleep,' 'is-not,' 'will not,' 'could not,' 'am not,' and the repeated 'empty' and 'emptied,' taking the form of an obsessive rumination. Only in the last sentence of this section does Darl relinquish his obsession with identity. In this wonderfully poetic sentence, he comes closer to giving voice to his feelings of loneliness than anywhere else in his texts:

How often have I lain beneath rain on a strange roof, thinking of home.

---

69 Jeffrey Berman, discussing Sylvia Plath's *The Bell Jar* speaks of 'ego strengths: the ability to tolerate frustration and imperfection, the renunciation of pathological modes of gratification, the capacity for reality testing and problem solving' (1987:135).

The linguistic forms of Darl's text create a highly ambiguous mind-style, calling up concepts while at the same time denying them. Faulkner makes use of very unusual forms to create this effect:

> How do our lives ravel out into the no-wind, no-sound, the weary gestures
> wearily recapitulant: echoes of old compulsions with no-hand on no-strings:
> in sunset we fall into furious attitudes, dead gestures of dolls. Cash broke
> his leg and now the sawdust is running out. He is bleeding to death is Cash.
> (191)

Again we see how a speaker's observations of others can tell us more about the observer himself than about the observed. With Darl's observation of Cash's bleeding leg—'the sawdust... running out'—the text conveys not just Cash's interest in carpentry but especially Darl's own feelings of increasing emptiness and worthlessness.

He continues here a tendency already pervasive in the first section of his text through its focus on the disintegration of the 'dilapidated' cotton-house and the 'frayed and broken' straw hat. In addition, the text emphasizes Darl's loathing of insincerity: the 'phoniness' of 'weary gestures'; 'dead gestures.'[70] The train of thought that the bleeding leg arouses in Darl combines his concern with disintegration ('ravel out'; 'running out') with his fear of his own impulses ('echoes of old compulsions'), his lack of control ('no-hand on no-strings'), and his anger ('furious attitudes'). Not much later Darl muses: 'If you could just ravel out into time. That would be nice. It would be nice if you could just ravel out into time' (193). His simultaneous fear of and fascination with annihilation are now combined into a dangerous mixture often found in the suicidal, and reminiscent of Quentin Compson in *The Sound and the Fury*.

In some ways, Darl Bundren also resembles the autist Benjy Compson in *The Sound and the Fury*. Frances Tustin argues that the cognitive and affective defects found in autists may also exist in some neurotic individuals, here overlaid by relatively competent behavioral patterns. Such individuals show, on a subconscious level, a tremendous fear of disintegration: a dread of 'falling apart,' of 'spilling away,' of 'exploding away,' of 'losing the thread of continuity which guarantees their existence' (1986:23). The fear of disintegration, Tustin believes, is caused by a traumatic separation from the mother before any real sense of self has had a chance to develop.[71] The result, she argues, is a terror of the 'damaging mother,' warded off by 'disinterested and disowning conceptualizations.' This disowning is clear in the text of Darl Bundren, who explains to his brother:

> I cannot love my mother because I have no mother
> (84).

---

70 Darl's disgust of 'phoniness' links him with the characters in many twentieth-century American novels, such as those by J.D. Salinger. Think, for instance, of Franny Glass, in *Franny and Zooey*, Seymour Glass in 'A Perfect Day for Bananafish,' not to mention Holden Caulfield in *Catcher in the Rye*. The complaint here shows reverberations of Hamlet's complaints on 'customary suits of solemn black,' 'windy suspiration of forc'd breath,' 'the fruitful river in the eye,' 'the dejected haviour of the visage,' and 'all forms, moods, shapes of grief' that are mere 'actions that a man might play' (Act I Scene II, ll. 77-86).

71 As Tustin puts it: 'The Fall from the sublime state of blissful unity with the "mother" who, in early infancy, is the sensation-dominated centre of the infant's universe, is part of everyone's experience. However, for some individuals, for a variety of reasons, different in each case, the disillusionment of "coming down to earth" from this ecstatic experience has been such a hard and injurious experience that it has provoked impeding encapsulating reactions. It has been the pebble which provoked the landslide' (1986:25).

He constantly refers to his mother by her full name, as if she were a mere acquaintance: 'Addie Bundren could not want a better one, a better box to lie in' (4). In addition, when he helps to carry the coffin, he does so 'balancing it *as though* it were something infinitely precious' (88, my emphasis).

The traumatic separation from the mother that lurks behind such 'disinterested and disowning conceptualizations' can be suspected. One only has to think of Addie's disbelief of Darl's existence—'Then I found that I had Darl. At first I would not believe it' (158)—and the aggression with which she terminated the breast-feeding of her children: 'I refused my breast to Cash and Darl after their time was up' (161). The process of weaning, as Melanie Klein has argued, causes the infant to feel 'that he has lost the first loved object—the mother's breast—both as an external and as an introjected object, and that this loss is due to his hatred, aggression and greed.' Weaning, she explains, thus 'accentuates his depressive feelings and amounts to a state of mourning,' so that, 'whenever in later life mourning is experienced, these early processes are revived' (1975:44). Darl's final disintegration indeed coincides with the death of his mother. Darl's need to love a mother can only show itself in the text through its projection in his brother Cash, whose behavior towards their mother is conceptualized by Darl with much tenderness: 'He [Cash] lays his hands flat on Addie, rocking her a little' (133). This utterance, again, tells us as much or more about the attributor, Darl, than about the attributee, Cash.

Darl and Jewel
While Darl thus projects his need to love a mother in his older brother, he displaces his anger unto his younger brother: the brother who is his mother's 'Jewel.' Again and again, Darl forces on his brother the painful awareness of his mother's dying and death. He does so in a detached, impersonal language that constantly denies his own involvement, leaving Jewel alone in his grief:
'Jewel,' I say... 'Do you know she is going to die, Jewel?'
'Jewel,' I say, 'do you know that Addie Bundren is going to die?'
Jewel, I say, she is dead, Jewel. Addie Bundren is dead
'It's not your horse that's dead, Jewel,' I say.
(35,36,48,84)
These words force on Jewel a bitter awareness of a tragedy for which he is not yet ready. Other clauses call into question Jewel's parentage:
Jewel... whose son are you?... Your mother was a horse, but who was your father, Jewel?
(195)
Jewel, I say. Who was your father, Jewel?
(196)
To this Jewel reacts immediately: 'You goddamn lying son of a bitch... You goddamn lying son of a bitch' (195), indicating that the issue was already alive for Jewel and thus suggesting that the kind of remark belongs to Darl's habitual behavior. There is, however, a great loneliness in Darl, mixed in with his need to hurt, which shows itself in the desperate call for attention: *Jewel, I say... Jewel, I say* (45).

The text combines the concepts *mother* and *horse*, creating them as equals in their relationship to Jewel. Thus it is as if Darl sees Addie's dedication to Jewel—'she always petted him more'—reduplicated and eternalized in that of the horse. We have the opportunity here to touch on a crucial aspect of Darl's text. Many critics have emphasized Darl's clairvoyance, which allows him to narrate Jewel's adventures with his horse, as well as such crucial scenes as his mother's dying minutes, while he himself is not present. A more 'realistic,' and perhaps more satisfying, view is also possible.[72] At times Darl simply predicts accurately what is going to happen, for instance that Jewel will catch up with them by cutting across and meeting them 'at Tull's lane' (92). As Charles Palliser puts it, 'Darl's apparent ability to foretell the future by supernatural means is really based on his knowledge of how his family will react to predictable circumstances' (1987:624). When a situation is not predictable, for instance the violent participation of his siblings in his arrest, Darl cannot foresee it.

Indeed, Darl is an astute observer of habitual behavior, which has made him an expert on personality. This makes it possible for him to extend his knowledge of his family's actions beyond what he can observe. Peabody's text, after all, confirms almost to the letter the accuracy of Darl's report of his mother's last words to Cash, a scene at which he is not present. The world that Darl's text creates in this instance is not so much a prediction of the future as a fantasy of the present, which is in a way a continuation of the past. Notice, in this respect, how the scene with the horse begins:

'Where's Jewel?' pa says...
'Down to the barn,' I say. 'Harnessing the team.'
Down there fooling with that horse. He will go on through the barn, into
the pasture. The horse will not be in sight.
(9f.)

Here the modal forms *will go* and *will not be* do not suggest a real world but instead a 'possible one,' a world that might have been. That the rest of the account is presented as if it were an actually perceived world should not be surprising. We have already seen in the first section of his text that Darl tends not to distinguish between perceived worlds and imagined worlds.

The linguistic choices in Darl's fascinated reports of Jewel's relationship with his horse show more than anything the strong desires that Darl cannot voice for himself. The forms of behavior that he attributes to Jewel and his horse all symbolize basic needs that cannot be fulfilled in Darl's own life: his need for control, for beauty, for mutuality and for love. Darl attributes to Jewel a respectful control over the horse: '"Come here, sir," Jewel says. He moves. Moving that quick his coat, bunching, tongues swirling like so many flames' (10). He attributes to the movements of his brother and the horse an almost mythical beauty: 'Then Jewel is enclosed by a glittering maze of hooves as by an illusion of wings; among them, beneath the upreared chest, he moves with the flashing limberness of a snake' (11). By means of description Darl creates their unity: 'They stand in rigid terrific hiatus, the horse trembling and groaning. Then Jewel is on the horse's back. He flows upward in a stooping swirl like

---

72 Darl's text is not the only text that shows this kind of 'clairvoyance.' Addie, for instance, 'knows' that Jewel will be her 'salvation,' that he will save her 'from the water and from the fire' (154); Anse 'can see same as second sight the rain shutting down... a-coming up that road like a durn man' (33); Cash reacts to Darl's unexpressed thought of their mother holding Jewel on a pillow on her lap (130), and Dewey Dell 'knows' that Darl 'knows' of her pregnancy 'without the words' (24).

the lash of a whip, his body in midair shaped to the horse' (11). Throughout, the similes have to convey an impression that is beyond words. Finally, Darl imagines the closeness of man and horse through strife and through love:

Without looking back the horse kicks at him, slamming a single hoof into the wall with a pistol-like report. Jewel kicks him in the stomach; the horse arches his neck back, crop-toothed; Jewel strikes him across the face with his fist and slides on to the trough and mounts upon it... 'Eat,' he says... 'You sweet son of a bitch,' he says.

(12)

The same mixture of control, violence and love is imagined again later, when Darl's text is presented in italics, suggesting the less conscious nature of the mental activity: *'He applies the curry-comb, holding himself within the horse's striking radius with the agility of an acrobat, cursing the horse in a whisper of obscene caress'* (169). It seems as if Darl's emptiness and fear must be counteracted by a form of magical thinking that can provide the badly needed power and control. The text fills the gaps created by Darl's absence at moments that are important for him.[73] He receives satisfaction from 'seeing' the horse's dedication to Jewel and from 'hearing' his mother's preference for Cash because he is now, like the artist, the creator and master of the painful scenes.[74]

Beneath Darl's magical thinking, then, one finds his jealousy of his siblings. We have already seen his irritation over Cash's ostentatious behavior. Darl's closeness to his older brother, however, seems to keep his feelings in check. Jewel's position is naturally more threatening to Darl. As the youngest child for nearly ten years, and already insecure about his worth and his place in the world, he had to adjust to the presence of a younger brother whose place with his mother was special from the beginning. As we have seen, feelings of rivalry are evident from the very first lines of the novel. Darl constantly observes the position of his brother in relation to himself: 'I... ahead of him'; 'Jewel's... hat... above my own'; 'Jewel... behind me'; 'five feet apart'; 'Jewel... in front' (3f.). He feels threatened by his brother's height, and he attributes idiosyncratic consequences to this physical characteristic. It explains, he thinks, at least part of his mother's preference for his brother ('that's why ma always whipped him and petted him more'), and the name she gave him: 'That's why she named him Jewel' (16).

Darl fears his brother's hard eyes, yet he is obviously fascinated by them. He has to present these eyes to himself again and again in the form of similes:

pale eyes like wood set into his wooden face

eyes... like pale wood in his high-blooded face.

eyes like pale wooden eyes.

---

73 We will see in the chapter on *Light in August* how a whole community can fill gaps in a way that amounts to a shared psychosis.

74 In *Beyond the Pleasure Principle* (1920), Freud advanced what has become known as his 'repetition-compulsion theory.' As Jeffrey Berman writes: 'Freud used this idea to explain the tendency to repeat traumatic situations for the purpose of mastery, thus making possible the adaptive and integrative functions of the ego.' Thus Darl's verbal behavior, here, may be seen to serve, to use Berman's words, 'a counterphobic purpose' by allowing him to 'recreate distressing experiences to gain control over them' (1987:285). In Darl's case, however, this creative and basically constructive solution has turned into a destructive fixation.

eyes... pale as two bleached chips in his face.
eyes.. two colors of wood, the wrong one pale and the wrong one dark.
(3,16,17,131,168)

The bleached wood Darl associates with Jewel clearly contrasts with 'the golden wood' he associates with Cash, showing the difference in his feelings for his brothers.

Virtually every one of the many sections narrated by Darl starts with a physical description of Jewel, showing the importance for Darl of his brother's self-contained behavior and appearance:

Jewel and I come up from the field

We watch him come around the corner and mount the steps.

He has been to town this week: the back of his neck is trimmed close

He sits erect on the seat, leaning a little forward, wooden-backed.

He goes on towards the barn, entering the lot, wooden-backed.

He comes up the lane fast... light and erect in the saddle

He sits the horse, glaring at Vernon

On the horse he rode up to Armstid's and *came back on the horse*

Against the dark doorway he seems to materialise out of darkness, lean as a race horse

(3,15,35,84,87,95,113,167,201)

How much Jewel's image has become an obsession for Darl is clear from the passages in italics:

'You're welcome to the house,' Armstid said. *He had that wooden look on his face again; that bold, surly, high-colored rigid look...* 'She would appreciate it,' pa said.

(168)

But after Armstid gave pa a drink, he felt better, and when we went in to see about Cash *he hadn't come in with us. When I looked back he was leading the horse into the barn* he was already talking about getting another team

(169)

Darl's obsession causes a loosening of deictic anchoring in his text, with the pronoun *he* shifting to Jewel in the middle of his report of his father's behavior, without formal indicators. These observations present Darl's fascination with the image Jewel creates through his appearance, his postures and his behaviors, and with the impact this image has on others. Although Darl's own place, as he creates it for himself, is mostly outside the realm of physical action—in the first section his action is limited to 'following the path'—he seems to long, like Addie, for a deed that can fill the void he cannot fill with words. In this respect Cora Tull is right when she believes Darl to be 'the only one of them' that has 'his mother's nature' (19). Perhaps she is even right that, in a way, 'between her and Darl... the understanding and the true love was' (22).

Darl and the Younger Siblings

Darl's relation to his sister Dewey Dell is determined by her sexuality:

She sets the basket into the wagon and climbs in, her leg coming long from beneath her tightening dress: that lever which moves the world

(91)

Squatting, Dewey Dell's wet dress shapes for the dead eyes of three blind
men those mammalian ludicrosities which are the horizons and the valleys
of the earth.
(150)
The text here conceptualizes parts of Dewey Dell's body, making them into objects.
Dehumanized and eroticized, they become like the boards out of which Cash is making
their mother's coffin, with their flanks that show 'smooth undulations,' and even like
'the path' with its smoothness, its hardness and its 'soft right angles.' In the second
quote Darl conceptualizes himself as the only seer among the blind, thus, like Quentin
Compson, keeping his sister's sexuality to himself. Observe also how this raises the
issue of having to defend her honor when Darl presents his sister's unspoken question:
'Are you going to kill him?' (35).

Darl is capable of warm feeling. We have seen his concern over Cash's comfort.
Even towards Jewel he can show patience and tenderness: '"Goddamn you," Jewel
says. "Let Jewel take the end of the rope and cross upsteam of us and brace it," I say.
"Will you do that, Jewel?"' (132). Darl's relation to Vardaman is clearly that of an
older brother. As Vardaman reports it, Darl explains with much patience to his brother
the sounds that come from the coffin with the decomposing body of their mother:
'"Hear?" Darl says. "Put your ear close... She's talking to God... She is calling on
Him to help her... She wants Him to hide her away from the sight of man... So she
can lay down her life"' (197). Perhaps this scene provides an explanation for Darl's
'mad' act of arson.

The Mind-Style of Madness
Faulkner himself observed that Darl 'was mad from the first' (Gwynn and Blotner
1959:110).[75] The observations of many narrators suggest the same, by emphasizing
the habitual quality of his withdrawn and inappropriate behavior. As we have seen,
Darl's concentration on the verb *be* shows his obsession with identity, occasionally
expressed directly: 'I dont know what I am. I dont know if I am or not' (72). We have
seen, in addition, how his text conveys his extreme ambivalence through different
forms of negation. Both are clear signs of weak ego-functions. Darl's text also shows
a tendency to develop the deictic loosening that is characteristic of psychotic language
(cf. Rosenbaum and Sonne 1986), and it is curiously devoid of expressions of his own
affect. Through the habitual use of the defense mechanism of rationalization, Darl
systematically suppresses his emotions. As we have seen, when Darl's language
occasionally shows signs of affect breaking through, this is made harmless through displacement and through the effects of stipulation, generalization, understatement and
irony.

While Darl's affect, then, is largely eliminated from his verbal behavior through
rationalizing and philosophizing, his paraverbal behavior becomes more and more
deviant through his 'crazy laughter.' This behavior is not only socially inappropriate

[75] The classic symptoms of schizophrenia applicable to Darl Bundren according to Bleikasten include
'withdrawal from reality, loss of vital contact with others, disembodiment and splitting of self, obsession
with identity, sense of isolation and deadness, and armageddonism,' the sense that the world is coming to
an end (1973:90).

('we hadn't no more than passed Tull's lane when Darl begun to laugh. Setting back there on the plank seat with Cash, with his dead ma laying in her coffin at his feet, laughing' [93]), it is also psychologically aberrant. We see here the same split between feeling and thinking that is obvious in Quentin Compson's text in *The Sound and the Fury*. As in Quentin's text, this laughter is incomprehensible and frightening to others: 'He begun to laugh again... He sat on the ground and us watching him, laughing and laughing. It was bad. It was bad so. I be durn if I could see anything to laugh at' (221). As the journey with the smelling corpse and the vultures circling overhead becomes more and more 'ridiculous,' Darl's behavior may seem the only 'reasonable' comment on it. Such a view, however, ignores the painful split within Darl's personality, as well as his isolated social situation. It is obvious, in any case, that his laughter stands in a complex way for his inconsolable sadness.

Finally Darl's text, like Quentin Compson's, shows the dissolution of ego-boundaries. Borders between inner and outer have disappeared when Darl starts referring to himself through second- and third-person pronouns:

Darl has gone to Jackson. They put him on the train, laughing, down the long car laughing, the heads turning like the heads of owls when he passed. 'What are you laughing at?' I said. 'Yes yes yes yes yes.'

...

'Is it the pistols you're laughing at?' I said. 'Why do you laugh?' I said. 'Is it because you hate the sound of laughing?'
They pulled two seats together so Darl could sit by the window to laugh. (235)

A Hidden Side of Darl

The unusual situation of the hideous journey with the decomposing corpse of his mother, however, has brought out a hidden aspect of Darl's personality. If it is true that Darl sets fire to the barn in which his mother's coffin is kept—Darl's text does not mention the deed but other narrators speculate on it or hint at it—Darl is after all able to perform a deed for his mother. He thereby also comes closer in spirit to his brother Cash, who believed that one of them 'would have to do something' (216) to save her from the rest of the degrading trip after Jewel rescued the coffin from the flood 'against God in a way' (216). Darl's deed also brings him close to sharing his mother's fate. Setting the barn on fire can be seen as a deed that symbolizes his final loyalty to his mother. It makes him share her fate by bringing him a kind of death in the form of his 'capture and deportation' to the Jackson insane asylum. Darl's insanity thus turns out to be an act of 'homage' to the mother he never had.

Jewel Bundren

It would be just me and her on a high hill

By the time Jewel's first section (pp. 13,14) has been reached, his name has been mentioned by Darl more than twenty times, not counting the third-person pronouns referring to him. Darl's obsessive interest in Jewel, as well as Jewel's supposed lack of awareness of it or lack of reaction to it, has become clear. By 'looking straight ahead,' 'still staring straight ahead,' Jewel seems to guard his own space, much to the regret of Darl. This observation, however, may tell us more about Darl, the observer, who is desperate for a reaction from his younger brother, than about Jewel, the observee. To understand Jewel's personality, we must first examine Jewel's own mind-style.

Jewel's Mind-Style

While in Darl's highly organized text it was easy to distinguish two major lexical sets that begin to create the physical setting of the novel, Jewel's text does not present categories that are easy to isolate. This is mainly because his text does not conceptualize a specific sense of place, time, or participants, but only a confused and disorganized set of attitudes. When Darl's text, for instance, presents the noun *window*, the entity is conceptualized specifically as one of the two facing windows of the cottonhouse. Jewel's 'window,' in the first sentence of his text, remains unclassified, unattached to any larger structure. In addition, the one clause that shows present tense and may thus anchor the time of narration to the event time—'I can see the fan and Dewey Dell's arm'—creates a specific context only because of the deathbed scene described by Cora Tull (7). In the same way, the pronouns in Jewel's text are left unattached. It is Darl's detailed introduction to the scene that makes it possible to understand that the 'he' occurring in nearly every sentence is Cash, and the 'she' is their mother.

If one studies the clauses that have Jewel himself as subject, one notices that Jewel places himself in the role of speaker in virtually every case:

I told him to go somewhere else.
I said Good God do you want to see her in it.
Because I said If you wouldn't keep on sawing and nailing at it
I said if you'd just let her alone.

These speech acts, however, have taken place at some unidentified time in the past. Their impact, at the time of narration, is focused on the expression of an attitude or set of attitudes. One instance is formally a command, another is a rhetorical question (notice the absence of the question mark) and two contain the modal construction *if you would*, which evokes an alternative world that depends for its realization on the actions of others, thus showing Jewel's helplessness in front of these others.

All the constructions conceptualize Jewel's desires or needs at the time of narration. Two sub-clauses explicitly attribute cause-effect relationships to certain events:

It's because he stays out there, right under the window, hammering and sawing
Because I said If you wouldn't keep on sawing and nailing at it

These sub-clauses, however, are left dangling, without main clauses specifying the nature of these events. As they stand, the constructions draw attention to their paired verbal -ing forms. Such forms, occurring throughout the text, are the most pervasive grammatical set of Jewel's first section:

hammering and sawing
knocking and sawing
waiting, fanning themselves

sawing and nailing
sawing and knocking, and keeping the air always moving
Together with the clauses 'One lick less. One lick less. One lick less,' these echoes convey most painfully Jewel's despair over his mother's disturbance and its relentless continuation. But they convey perhaps most forcefully Jewel's own helplessness to do anything about it.

Jewel and Addie

In his confused way, Jewel is trying to conceptualize the causes of his mother's condition, to understand his brother's Cash's behavior through analogy ('It's like when he was a little boy') and to create alternative worlds that circle around yet avoid an awareness of his mother's actual situation:
If you wouldn't keep on sawing and nailing at it
if you'd just let her alone.
If it had just been me... if it had just been me... it would not be happening
The last clause clearly conceptualizes an alternative world in which Jewel himself is the actor:
It would just be me and her on a high hill and me rolling the rocks down the hill at their faces, picking them up and throwing them down the hill faces and teeth and all by God until she was quiet and not that goddamn adze going One lick less. One lick less and we could be quiet.
(14)
We notice here that Jewel's dreamworld includes his mother, for whom he wants peace, without Cash's 'goddamn adze going,' without Dewey Dell's fan 'keeping the air always moving,' and without 'them others sitting there, like buzzards' (13).

Jewel's dream of the closeness between himself and his mother can be linked with her conceptualization of him. As we have seen, Addie's own text emphasizes the dreamlike quality of their relationship ('When I waked to remember to discover it, he was two months gone' [162]), as well as its peacefulness ('Then there was only the milk, warm and calm, and I lying calm in the slow silence' [162]). The name that she gave him, Jewel, reflects the great value he has for her and symbolizes his physical beauty. According to Cora she calls him her salvation and makes him her God: 'He is my cross and he will be my salvation. He will save me from the water and from the fire. Even though I have laid down my life, he will save me' (154). Thus, Jewel is explicitly linked to his mother's feelings of guilt (the cross) and their exorcism through sin. Addie's feelings are clear also from her nonverbal behavior as presented by Cash and Darl: 'When he was born, he had a bad time of it. Ma would sit in the lamplight, holding him on a pillow on her lap. We would wake and find her so. There would be no sound from them' (130).

Jewel lives out his mother's conceptualization of him through his every posture, gesture and action, and by his exclusive devotion to her. His endeavors to undo her hopeless situation are not only found in his own section. Darl reports that Jewel refuses to consider the seriousness of his mother's condition: '"Ma aint that sick," Jewel says. "Shut up Darl"' (16). Darl's reports of Jewel's behavior again emphasize how Jewel creates a personal conceptualization of the causes of his mother's illness, a conceptualization that he can handle because he can place it in the context of his jealousy of

his older brother. This is a feeling with which he has long been familiar:
'It's laying there, watching Cash whittle on that damn.......' Jewel says.
(17)
With Cash all day long right under the window, hammering and sawing at
that—
(18)
Like Jason Compson in *The Sound and the Fury*, Jewel is unable to utter the word
coffin. As Darl puts it, he speaks 'harshly, savagely, but he does not say the word.
Like a little boy in the dark to flail his courage and suddenly aghast into silence by his
own noise' (17). Darl's reports again show that he understands his brother's affects,
but that he cannot afford to acknowledge his empathy.

Jewel and the Need for Space
Throughout the text one recognizes the space that Jewel creates around himself. He
occupies a special place in the Bundren family, between the two oldest children, Cash
and Darl, and the two youngest, Dewey Dell and Vardaman. Space is essential to an
understanding of Jewel's personality. As Darl puts it, it literally allows him to grow
up taller 'than any of the rest of us' (16). Jewel, it seems, has always needed this space
for himself. Cora Tull mentions him 'flinging into tantrums or sulking spells' and
'inventing devilment to devil her' (19), and Darl mentions him 'peakling around the
house' (16). The whole episode in which Jewel secretly works for Lon Quick, sneaking
out of the house at night to earn himself enough money to buy the horse he wants,
testifies to this same characteristic.

Jewel's space exists around him as he 'sits the horse,' and it is constantly
emphasized through his behavior. He does not allow others to enter his space. His
nonverbal behavior, as observed mainly by Darl but also by others, constantly fore-
grounds how, in his self-sufficiency and his pride, he is able to ignore others:
He does not look at us.
He has not once looked back.
He has not looked back.
He passes us swiftly, without looking at us
Jewel sits the horse, gazing straight ahead.
Jewel does not look back.
(15,35,91,96,106,214)
Nor does he let his pace be determined by others:
but Jewel will not wait.
He will not stop.
But he will not wait.
Jewel does not stop.
(88,88,88,89)
His habitual posture ('motionless,' 'poised,' 'upright,' 'wooden-backed'); his habitual
expression ('wooden-faced,' eyes 'pale like wood'), and his habitual tone of voice

('harsh' and 'savage'), all make him seem untouchable, impregnable.[76]

Jewel's verbal behavior, as presented by others, creates and preserves this space in the same way. As we saw already in his first section, his discourse consists largely of imperatives full of impatience, usually aimed at ending any conversation between himself and others, and at dismissing them:

Shut up, Darl.

Ah, shut your goddamn mouth

Pick up... Pick up, goddamn your thicknosed soul!

Then turn loose

Get to hell on back to your damn plowing

Well, goddamn it, let's get across, then

Then go on back to the goddamn bridge and walk across

You go to hell

Get out of the way... Get out of the water.

(16,16,87,88,111f.,131,131,131,147)

When Jewel pronounces a question, it almost always contains the strong rhetorical element that was noticed in his first section, which again discourages conversation and dismisses people:

Who the hell asked you to follow us here?

(112)

Goddamn it, do you want to wait until he sets fire to the goddamn team and wagon?

(215)

Only when Jewel speaks to his horse is his tone different. To his horse, the only creature that is allowed to approach him, Jewel allows himself to speak 'in a soothing murmur' (133): '"Go on," he says. "I aint going to let nothing hurt you. Go on now"' (130).

Having to handle the coffin with his mother's body, and having to smell her decomposing body, brings out violent physical reactions in Jewel:

In his face the blood goes in waves. In between them his flesh is greenish looking, about that smooth, thick, pale green of cow's cud; his face suffocated, furious, his lip lifted upon his teeth.

(87)

Jewel's face goes completely green and I can hear teeth in his breath.

(87)

'Come on,' he says in that suffocating voice... his face suffused with fury and despair.

(88)

It is no wonder that Jewel immediately needs to distance himself again, riding his own horse instead of the wagon with the others and upsetting his father: 'I told him not to bring that horse out of respect for his dead ma, because it wouldn't look right' (93). When he is on his beloved horse, within his own space, Jewel's image is quickly

---

76 Jewel clearly forms an example of Karen Horney's 'detached personality,' who cannot let himself be influenced or pressurized in any way. As we shall see, his hidden compliant tendency only comes out under unusual circumstances.

restored: 'He sits erect, poised, looking quietly and steadily and quickly this way and that, his face calm, a little pale, alert' (127f.).

It seems necessary for Jewel always to keep his space. If this is impossible, he loses his poise. Upon reaching the city without the horse, when he uses his characteristic verbal behavior on a stranger and is consequently threatened with a knife, Jewel becomes uncharacteristically docile. Suddenly, and for once, he acts in accordance with his position as Darl's younger brother, obeying him without comment. Darl reports it in the following way: '"Hush," I say. "Tell him you didn't mean it." "I didn't mean it," Jewel says' (214). After this episode, Jewel refuses to join his family: 'He does not get on, even though the wagon has started again. "Get in, Jewel," I say. "Come on. Let's get away from here." But he does not get in' (214). The degradation of this role-switching confrontation, which Jewel cannot undo by mounting his horse, perhaps provokes the extreme violence against Darl that the next section presents:

'Catch him and tie him up,' Jewel said.
(215)
Kill him. Kill the son of a bitch.
(221)

A Hidden Side of Jewel

Knowing how threatening the absence of space is to Jewel's sense of self, it is now possible to feel the full impact of the unusual behavior that his mother's death brings out in him. Not only does he allow his father to ride his horse ('Him and Jewel stood in the lot talking a while, then Anse got on the horse and rode off. I reckon that was the first time Jewel ever let anybody ride that horse' [172]), but it is also Jewel himself who trades his horse for a pack of mules to transport his mother's body to Jefferson. Like his brother Darl, Jewel suffers for his mother; like him, he joins her in a kind of death, losing that which he loves and needs most.

Dewey Dell Bundren

I wish I had time to let her die

Dewey Dell feels herself invisible to the world: to her father, who is 'too busy letting neighbors do for him'; to her older brothers, one of whom 'dont care about anything,' one of whom keeps on 'sawing the long hot sad yellow days up into planks and nailing them to something,' and one of whom 'sits at the supper table with his eyes gone further than the food and the lamp' (23). Dewey Dell's conceptualization of herself as totally alone is confirmed by the conceptualizations of her by others. Again and again she is stereotyped, made anonymous and fragmented by the voices around her. Even the people who know her name refuse to pronounce it, referring to her as 'a tom-boy girl' (7); 'that near-naked girl' (22); 'sister' (55); 'that gal' (111,126); 'the gal' (109,110,112,123,139,171,172,174); 'the girl' (39,40,41,99,101,102,103); 'that girl' (100). Others generalize her appearance away from her and call her 'country woman' (224); 'one of them black eyed ones' (224); others again present her behavior or her life in a stereotypical way, or prescribe a stereotype way to approach her:

She kind of bumbled at the screen door a minute, like they do
you have to let them take their time.

You have to humor them. You save time by it.
in the eyes all of them look like they had no age and knew everything in the
world
Her face was lowered a little, still, like they do in all their dealings with a
man
But it's a hard life they have
(183,183,185,185,186)

Some voices focus on parts of her body—those parts that are disturbing—fragmenting
her into less than herself: an arm 'keeping the air always moving so fast' (13); a leg
'coming long from beneath her tightening dress' (91); eyes like pistols (100,101), and
'mammalian ludicrosities' (150).

At best Dewey Dell is conceptualized in terms of the persistence of her caring
behavior:

Dewey Dell still a-fanning her with the fan.
The girl is standing by the bed, fanning her.
The girl does not stop the fan.
her arms outflung and the fan in one hand still beating with expiring breath
into the quilt.
(28,39,40,44)

Her behavior seems to be appreciated by her father ('Dewey Dell a-takin good keer of
her' [40]), but the remark serves mainly to give Anse an excuse for not having called
the doctor sooner. In a similar way, Anse uses Dewey Dell's behavior as an example
('He touches the quilt as he saw Dewey Dell do' [48]), but he does so largely because
he needs a model to make his own behavior seem appropriate. But while Dewey Dell's
behavior is taken for granted or used for the observer's own purposes, it is also
criticized. She is seen as

keeping the air always moving so fast on her face that when you're tired
you cant breathe it
(13)
always standing over Addie with a fan so that every time a body tried to
talk to her and cheer her up, would answer for her right quick
(22)
not stopping the fan, speaking up quick, keeping even him [Darl] from her.
(22)

The first quote, however, must be understood in the light of the sibling rivalry in the
Bundren family; the last two present Cora Tull's interest in the subject, and her endeavors to advance Darl as his mother's favorite.

Dewey Dell's Mind-Style
Dewey Dell's own section (pp. 23,24) extends the rural setting of the novel that was
created by Darl's text. Her lexical set is very limited, however, and contains much
repetition: 'row' (twice); 'land' (twice); 'woods' (twice); 'shade' (three times) and
'sack' (seven times), conveying especially Dewey Dell's obsession with the sacks in
which she and the farmer Lafe put the cotton they are picking. This first section of
Dewey Dell's text contains an amazing number of clauses with first-person pronouns:

1 me and Lafe picked on down the row.

2 I did not think
3 we picked on
4 I said will I or wont I
5 I said if the sack is full when we get to the woods it wont be me.
6 I said if it dont mean for me to do it the sack will not be full
7 I will turn up the next row
8 I cannot help it.
9 I had to do it
10 I cannot help it.
11 we picked on towards the secret shade
12 our eyes would drown together touching
13 I didn't say anything.
14 I said 'What are you doing?'
15 I could not help it.
16 I could not help it.
17 I saw Darl
18 I knew he knew
19 I would not have believed that he had been there
20 I said 'Are you going to tell pa'
21 I said it
22 I can talk to him without knowing with hating
23 'What do you want, Darl?' I say.
24 'When is she going to die?' I say.
25 'Then why are you taking Jewel?' I say.

Three of these clauses put Dewey Dell in the role of agent of the simple shared action of picking cotton (*1,3,11*), which is directly linked to the most frequently used noun in the text: *sack*. Many clauses cast Dewey Dell in the role of communicator (one in negated form), whereby her lover Lafe and her brother Darl are linked as past and present speech partners (*4,5,6,13,14,20,21,22,23,24,25*).

The other clauses all cast Dewey Dell as the experiencer of an internal process. A majority of these are negations, functioning directly or indirectly as denials of responsibility: 'I could not help it.' The text's logical connectors *if...then* and *because* are used to obtain permission to give in to desire:

Because I said if the sack is full when we get to the woods [then] it wont be me. I said if it dont mean for me to do it [then] the sack will not be full and [then] I will turn up the next row but if the sack is full, [then] I cannot help it.

The presented worldview is motivated by three separate desires. First of all there is the desire for a sexual relationship, which is linked to and shared with Lafe: 'our eyes would drown together.' In connection with this desire, one can understand the repeated modification of the noun *shade* through the adjective *secret*. Secondly, there is the urge to disclaim responsibility for the consequences. The text conveys this also by presenting the woods and the shade as the active subjects of their sentences ('the woods getting closer and closer and the secret shade') instead of the real actors Dewey Dell and Lafe. Thirdly, there is Dewey Dell's need for her family's attention and protection. This need, as we have seen, is an essential element of the relation between Dewey Dell and the other characters of *As I Lay Dying*.

Dewey Dell and Addie

Addie's text contains almost no reference to her daughter. Unlike the births of her brothers, Dewey Dell's birth seems to have made no impression on her mother at all. In this sense Dewey Dell is more 'motherless' than Darl is. By announcing her existence the way she did—'I gave Anse Dewey Dell to negative Jewel' (162)—Addie effectively cancels her as soon as she is born. If Dewey Dell was not acknowledged by her mother when she first saw her, the same seems to happen when her mother last sees her. As Darl presents it, Addie ignores Dewey Dell's last request for attention, favoring her oldest brother Cash:

'Ma,' she says; 'ma.' She is looking out the window, at Cash... 'You, Cash,' she shouts... 'You, Cash!'
(43)

Yet, Dewey Dell's text shows that she does not deny the importance of her mother, as Darl does. Her complaint is simply that she cannot conceptualize her mother's death. The text, with its double modifications of earth, links Addie's corpse, which must be yielded to the earth before Dewey Dell is ready for it, to Dewey Dell's feeling that she herself, being pregnant, is 'like a wet seed wild in the hot blind earth' (58) before she is ready for it:

I heard that my mother is dead. I wish I had time to let her die. I wish I had time to wish I had. It is because in the wild and outraged earth too soon too soon too soon. It is not that I wouldn't and will not it's that it is too soon too soon to soon.
(106)

To fill her void Dewey Dell, like Darl, seeks comfort in erotic experiences. Her closeness to the family cow, the only other female in her vicinity, answers her need for intimacy and recognition. Thus her text conceptualizes its breath as blowing 'in a sweet, hot blast,' through her clothes, against her 'hot nakedness, moaning' (56). The ambiguous 'quasi-clause' *moaning* may designate either Dewey Dell's or the cow's behavior, thus linking them in their desire.

Another coping strategy is formed by Dewey Dell's mothering behavior, through which she can give others what she herself lacks. This mothering behavior seems to form a contrast with Dewey Dell's desperate quest for an abortion. As such it resembles the paradoxes in her mother's relationships to her oldest children, although, as Dewey Dell's text makes clear, for her it is not that she 'wouldn't,' but that it is 'too soon.' Perhaps we find another reflection of the paradox in the name that Addie gave her daughter. Dewey, in Mississippi, is normally a man's name.[77] Cora Tull's characterization of Dewey Dell as a 'tom-boy girl' seems to attend to this, while the collocation 'dewy dell' (valley of dew) seems to prefigure Dewey Dell's most telling self-conceptualization as 'a wet seed wild in the blind earth.'

---

77 In her biography of Faulkner's friend and mentor Phil Stone, however, Susan Snell mentions that according to Stone 'there was a girl up the railroad tracks named Dewey Dell.' This girl introduced him and his friends to sex when he was ten years old (1991:37f.).

Dewey Dell and Darl

Darl's text, especially, shows a fascination with Dewey Dell's caring behavior, even if it is never directed to him:

Dewey Dell stoops and slides the quilt from beneath them [Addie's hands] and draws it up over them to the chin, smoothing it down, drawing it smooth.
(47)
Suddenly Dewey Dell is behind us in the water. 'You make him come back,' she says. 'Jewel!' she says... 'You, Jewel!' Dewey Dell says.
(146)
'Jewel,' Dewey Dell whispers.
(148)
Dewey Dell squats and lifts Cash's head. 'Cash,' she says, 'Cash.'
(148)
Dewey Dell wipes his mouth on the wet hem of her dress
(149)
Dewey Dell has laid Cash's head back on the folded coat, twisting his head a little to avoid the vomit.
(149)
Dewey Dell wiped his mouth again... 'What is it, Cash?' Dewey Dell said. She leaned down. 'His tools,' she said... Dewey Dell lifted Cash's head so he could see.
(167)
Dewey Dell undressing him.
(168)
Dewey Dell wipes his face with the hem of her dress.
(196)
'Jewel!' Dewey Dell cries; 'Jewel!'... 'Jewel! Jewel!'
(204f.)

These reports are confirmed by those of others, for instance by Armstid ('the gal leaned down and wiped his mouth' [172]), and by Vardaman ('Dewey Dell leans back and wipes Cash's face' [181]). But it is Darl's habitual state of mind that determines the number of observations and the quality of their detail. Notice, for instance, how Darl's report of Dewey Dell's verbal behavior ('"Cash," she says; "Cash"' [148]) parallels his report of his mother's dying words ('"Cash," she says; "you, Cash!"' [42]). Notice also the parallel between Darl's report of Dewey Dell's interpretation of her mother's dying gaze ('"It's Jewel she wants," Dewey Dell says' [43]) and his report of his sister's own concerns ('"You, Jewel! Jewel," she whispers'). Darl's conceptualizations, then, repeat the patterns of preference for his brothers; his fascinated observations serve, like his conceptualizations of Jewel and his horse, to give him a sort of mastery over a painful situation.

This fascinated watching of Dewey Dell, which probes into the essential void in which she, like her brother, finds herself, allows Darl to capture the misery of his sister's unwanted pregnancy. Dewey Dell relies on traditional family codes of behavior when she says: '"Are you going to tell pa are you going to kill him?" without the words' (24). Darl echoes the unvoiced question: 'She just keeps on saying Are you going to tell pa? Are you going to kill him?' (35).[78] Naturally, both siblings understand the social code. Thus, by answering 'Why?' Darl refuses to be a brother to her; he disowns her just as he disowns his mother. Yet, Dewey Dell's conceptualization of a solution to her problem—'He [doctor Peabody] could do so much for me if he just would' (53)—is captured by Darl in the very essence of the loneliness it entails: *'She will go out where Peabody is,.. and she looking at him, saying You could do so much for me if you just would. If you just knew. I am I and you are you and I know it and you dont know it'* (47f.).

Dewey Dell's mind-style, like her brother Darl's, is characterized by negative space, void. Unlike Darl, who creates his own void, Dewey Dell seems passively confronted by it, as her dream reveals: 'Once I waked with a black void rushing under me. I could not see' (107). In contrast to Darl, who denies or distorts his affect, Dewey Dell is able to feel as well as to express her emotions, and to attribute cause-effect relations to them: 'It's because I am alone' (53). Because Darl's own loneliness, unlike the loneliness of Dewey Dell, remains unacknowledged, Darl cannot afford his feelings of empathy to reach consciousness. His imagined discourse shows the essential coldness of his communicative behavior: 'I said to Dewey Dell: "You want her to die so you can get to town: is that it?"' (35).

Darl's very astute observations of his siblings allow him to stir up their most painful obsessions and then deliberately to misinterpret them. This causes Dewey Dell's mind to form the idea of murder: 'I rose and took the knife... and I killed Darl' (107), and it explains why, in the end, she jumps on him 'like a wild cat.' Through this kind of behavior Dewey Dell shows the essential strength of her character: a strength that allows her to perform actions in her own interest, a strength that keeps her sane.

Vardaman Bundren

She went away when the other one laid down in her bed

Like his sister Dewey Dell, Vardaman often remains unnamed by characters who are quite aware of his name yet call him 'that boy' (26,65,76,124,139,172,173,174,178); 'the boy' (40,109,123); 'that poor boy' (30); 'Bud' (55); 'this boy' (64); 'the chap' (99); 'that chap' (103); 'the poor little tyke' (30) and 'the durn little tyke' (40). But unlike his sister, Vardaman is habitually viewed with tenderness and compassion. Especially Vernon Tull carefully notes Vardaman's appearance and behavior:

That boy comes up the hill. He is carrying a fish nigh long as he is. He slings it to the ground and grunts 'Hah' and spits over his shoulder like a man. Durn nigh long as he is.
(26)
Vardaman picks it up again. He goes on around the house, toting it in both arms like a armful of wood, it overlapping him on both ends, head and tail. Durn nigh big as he is.
(27)

---

78 Dewey Dell's addition: 'if he had said he knew with the words I would not have believed that he had been there and saw us' (24), shows her awareness of the deceptive nature of words, and again shows her mother's influence on her personality.

The attention that the sonless Tull gives to Vardaman obviously reflects his own desire to be the father of a son. It points at the same time to the neglect that Vardaman experiences from his own father, in whose conceptualization he is as worthless as his brothers: 'Well, I reckon I aint no call to expect no more of him than of his mangrowed brothers' (34).

Many voices confirm the lack of care that his father, who 'is looking out over the land' (27) and who 'calls him without looking around' (27), provides. Doctor Peabody notices Vardaman's loneliness and defeat: 'He sits on the top step, small, motionless in faded overalls. When I came out he looked up at me, then at Anse. But now he has stopped looking at us. He just sits there' (41). Obviously, one of the reasons for the compassion Vardaman receives is his small size. He is not, however, as young as he might seem from these reports. Some years earlier, when Jewel was secretly working to earn money to buy his horse, Vardaman was already able to take over some of his chores (115). We shall have to study Vardaman's own sections to get an idea of his developmental level, and we shall do this occasionally by comparing his mind-style to that of Benjy Compson in *The Sound and the Fury*, whose mind is arrested at the level of a very young child.

Vardaman's Mind-Style

The lexical choices of Vardaman's first section (pp. 49-52) function to extend the rural set constituted by the texts of Darl and Dewey Dell with 'porch,' 'fish,' 'overalls,' 'trees,' 'chickens,' 'barn,' 'bushes,' 'rocks,' 'dirt,' 'stall,' 'wagon shed,' 'stick,' 'hitch-rein,' 'breast-yoke,' 'buggy,' 'cow,' 'milk,' 'path,' 'hill,' 'spring' and 'wood.' The nouns are almost all of a rather simple, general type. In addition, very few of these nouns are modified; one can find a few simple adjectives referring to sense perceptions and to size: 'cool,' 'hot,' 'warm' and 'long.' Unmodified, generalized nouns, and nouns modified in this crude fashion, classify entities in the world in a simple and child-like way. The two adjectives that classify entities in terms of activity—'sucking' and 'flopping'—are more complex and thus present Vardaman's more detailed interest in actions.

The modification of nouns through the use of a prefix is an unusual form: 'not-fish,' and 'not-blood.' These forms immediately remind one of Darl's text: 'no-wind,' 'no-hand on no-strings.' Their function, however, is very different. While Darl uses such forms destructively, to devaluate his own worldview or that of others—worlds that he cannot face—here they are used constructively, to conceptualize entities for which the language does not have a word. What, after all, does one call a fish after it has been cut into pieces, and what does one call blood that has been washed away? The text includes several instances of nominalization: 'the warm smelling' (twice); 'the crying' (three times); 'snuffings and stampings'; 'a gaudy splotching'; 'hearing.' Such nouns can function as subject or object, or in a prepositional phrase, but they all show again the importance that actions have for Vardaman.

A large number of the clauses that have Vardaman as subject, all in the present tense, show his concentration on his own actions and experiences as they occur. They can be divided into four main groups. The first consists of only a few verb phrases that present stipulative worlds, for instance: 'If I jump off the porch.' Such verb phrases, generally speaking, present the subject as a 'dreamer.' In this case, however, the stipulative world is almost immediately transformed into a real one: 'I jump from the porch.' Vardaman is not much interested in contemplating possible future worlds. The only alternative world that interests him is the world of the past, when his mother was still alive.

The temporal proximity between the death of the fish he had meant to show to his 'ma' and the death of his mother causes Vardaman to link the two events. The clauses in the past tense present his endeavors to deny his mother's death through a form of undoing of both events: 'Then it wasn't so. It hadn't happened then.' The adverb *then* evokes a point in time to which Vardaman would like to return. This, however, is impossible: 'now she is getting so far ahead I cannot catch her.' Notice that the text conceptualizes abstract temporal distance in terms of more concrete spatial distance: the distance that a fish could swim.

A second small group of verb phrases contains the construction *begin to* ('Then I begin to run'; 'Then I begin to cry') and present Vardaman's awareness of a change in his pattern of activity. The accompanying adverbial *then* places this change within the time scheme of his other actions.

A third group consists of those predicates that contain a simple action verb, most often intransitive, such as *run, come, jump*, but occasionally transitive, such as *find it, throw it away*. These predicates place the subject in the role of agent of a simple action. Several times, the text presents as an intransitive a verb that is usually transitive, for instance: 'I strike.' This is not because Vardaman does not understand transitivity, as was the case with Benjy Compson. He is able to use transitivity, but he hesitates to conceptualize his violence as directed against the animals. In these clauses, Vardaman presents his furious anger over his mother's death, displaced thrice, first on doctor Peabody, who 'came and did it,' then on Peabody's team, and finally on the farm cow: 'I aint a-going to milk you.' These displacements help him to face his mother's condition; Vardaman can begin the complex process of mourning.

Finally, a large group of verb phrases includes the auxiliary *can*, for instance: 'I can feel'; 'I can hear'; 'I can go'; 'Then I can breathe again'; 'then I can cry'; 'I can smell'; 'then I can leave'; 'I can see.' Each instance of the clause 'I can' creates a contrast with its unstated opposite 'I cannot,' and thus also conveys the meaning of a change in Vardaman's condition, this time from a state that is conceptualized as negative to a state that is conceptualized as positive. In connection with this, the adverb *then* moves beyond the realm of a simple temporal progression towards the realm of cause and effect. The parallelism of the repeated 'I can... I can... I can... I can' forcefully conveys Vardaman's relief at his renewed abilities. This applies especially to the most frequently repeated form 'I can cry,' which is extended even further through nominalization: 'the crying can.'

Many of these clauses center around a mental verb that casts the speaker in the role of experiencer of an internal process. Vardaman, unlike his brother Darl, is in touch with his own feelings. Sometimes one finds synaesthesia, when the mental verb has an object that does not seem to fit its meaning, for instance: 'I can hear the bed and her face and them'; 'I can hear wood, silence.' These mental verb phrases are often complemented by small-clauses, creating a trance-like atmosphere:

I can feel the floor shake

I can hear the stick striking
I can see it hitting their heads... missing altogether
I can hear her turn
I see him dissolve
I can see hearing coil towards him, caressing, shaping

In contrast to its scanty use of adjectival modification, the text shows a tremendous amount of adverbial modification. The small-clauses above form only one type of verb modification. Many verbs phrases are accompanied by postmodifying prepositional phrases, conveying the direction of an action in relation to the physical body, such as 'under the skin, under my hand'; 'up from under my hands, up my arms.' The prepositional phrases at first present a goal-directed activity, generally away from his mother's body and towards a comforting hiding place: 'towards the back'; 'to the edge'; 'from the porch'; 'into the warm smelling.' Later, when his anger expresses itself, they present haphazard, frenzied movement: 'into the ground'; 'into the dust'; 'into the air.' Occasionally prepositional phrases present the place of the action: 'in the dark'; 'in the wagon shed'; 'in the dust.'

Very often the modification consists of a progressive in a clause with adverbial characteristics, for instance:

I can breathe, vomiting it.
I cannot see, running in the sucking dust
I can cry, looking at the stick.
I can cry quietly, watching the top of the hill.
I can cry quiet now, feeling and hearing my tears.

These clauses present the complexity of Vardaman's activity. A few times the text shows adverbial modification through similes. Here words seem insufficient to express the necessary details: 'If I jump I can go through it [the barn] like the pink lady in the circus,' and 'the buggy wheeling onto two wheels and motionless like it is nailed to the ground and the horses motionless like they are nailed by the hind feet to the center of a whirling plate.' It is clear that Vardaman can imagine himself as an agent in a circus act, and that he has been struck by the 'Faulknerian' stasis in motion of a merry-go-round.

State verbs, all in the present tense, occur in only a small portion of the final part of the section. They present an awareness of the strange and wonderful emptiness that occurs when the organism repairs itself after forceful emotions have found expression: 'I am not crying now. I am not anything... I am not anything. I am quiet' (52). Although critics have often based their discussions of Darl's and Vardaman's basic similarity on passages like these, this restorative emptiness is quite different from Darl's destructive ruminations over not-being.

The text shows a certain indeterminacy in its pronoun system. The pronoun *it*, for instance, wavers between various unnamed, related but slightly different referents: 'it wasn't so'; 'It hadn't happened'; 'he... that came and did it' (repeated thrice). Vardaman seems to avoid mentioning states and events that have to do with his mother's death. However, when his anger finds expression, he is able to name the referent of the proverb-pronoun *did it* in the above repetition: 'You kilt my maw!... You kilt her!' Other pronouns can only be understood in reference to previous sections. The pronoun *he*, for instance, changes its referent from doctor Peabody, whose visit to the house coincides with Addie's death, to Jewel's horse, whose kicking starts a chain of violent reactions in Vardaman, enabling him eventually to reach a stage where he can grieve.

The Psychostylistics of Mourning

The process of mourning is clearly not a straightforward one starting with denial and working through anger towards acceptance. Vardaman approaches the enigma of his mother's death with renewed energy, but he does so on a new, more intimate level as the colloquial elements of the text suggest: 'Then hit want. Hit hadn't happened then. Hit was a-laying right there on the ground. And now she's gittin ready to cook hit' (52). Instead of focusing on guilt, the text finally concentrates on the phenomenon of death itself. Jewel's horse, now vanishing in the twilight 'as though the dark were resolving him out of his integrity, into an unrelated scattering of components,' is the most important emblem of Vardaman's mind-style at this point in the text.

While all visual elements of the horse fade in the darkness, Vardaman understands that the animal itself does not disappear; he can, after all, still 'see hearing coil towards him, caressing, shaping his hard shape—fetlock, hip, shoulder and head; smell and sound.' He is aware that he can keep the horse present through his concentration. With the help of his words, which give form to this concentration, Vardaman is able to conceptualize the abstract understanding not only that the horse *is* but also that he, Vardaman, *is* separate from it. He tries to understand the situation of the fish, and thus of his mother, through analogy. Although the fish has become 'not-fish,' which stands in a complex way for the fact that his mother has become 'not-mother,' it may still exist in a different form even when it is 'cooked and et.' And he, Vardaman, can exist separate from it. Thus the section can conclude: 'I am not afraid.'

Vardaman's text, focusing on the conceptualization and classification of abstract entities taking place in a young child under painful circumstances, may be compared to Benjy Compson's text in *The Sound and the Fury*. Benjy's arrested mental development allows only for the classification of concrete objects, or abstract objects in terms of concrete objects, and refuses to admit the notion of change. Vardaman's text shows the more advanced mind-style of an inexperienced individual in his endeavors to understand the sudden and drastic changes of his world. These changes cause a certain measure of regression, so that he seems younger than he is fact is.

Throughout the text Vardaman tries to conceptualize and classify the changing attributes of his siblings in relation to their identities and his own connection with them:

And Dewey Dell hasn't got a broken leg and I haven't. Cash is my brother. (181)

Jewel hasn't got a horse anymore. Jewel is my brother. Cash is my brother. Cash has a broken leg... Cash is my brother. Jewel is my brother too, but he hasn't got a broken leg. (194)

My brother is Darl. He went to Jackson on the train. He didn't go on the train to go crazy. He went crazy in our wagon. Darl (234)

But most important, of course, is Vardaman's changing relationship to his mother.

Vardaman and Addie

There is very little to say about the way in which Addie's relation to her youngest son started. All that Addie's text makes clear is that she gave Vardaman to his father Anse, to 'replace the child' she had 'robbed him of' (162). This means that Vardaman is not canceled like his sister, whose function was to 'negate' Jewel, but it does mean that he is as motherless as she is. Still, doctor Peabody reports that just before she dies she 'watches the boy' (40), and Darl imagines that she 'looks at Vardaman' (44) while she completely ignores Dewey Dell. There are no other indications of Addie's behavior towards Vardaman, except that she presumably made him do some of Jewel's chores and sent him to look for Jewel at one time (119). However, that his mother is important for Vardaman is clear; when he catches a large fish, his first thought is 'to show it to ma' (26).

Vardaman was perhaps named after the historic figure James K. Vardaman, the '"Great White Chief" of the Hillsmen,' who became governor in 1903, and who worked for better schools in the Hills (Peirce and Hagstrom 1984:459).[79] It is possible to see this as Addie's deliberate choice, since she was after all a schoolteacher. In that case, Addie may have had high hopes for Vardaman, which may have influenced his development positively. Vardaman, in any case, has not turned away from those around him. The text emphasizes constantly that he turns to others for examples of appropriate behavior. As Vernon Tull presents it, he 'spits over his shoulder like a man' (26); he 'cusses it [the fish] like a grown man' (27); and his own text shows him cursing the cow 'like Jewel does' (51). He is able to address Cash with his fears, even if Cash does not respond: 'Are you going to nail her up in it, Cash? Cash? Cash?' (59). He clearly admires Darl: 'Darl is strong and he was coming in slow and so I knew he had her,' (137), as well as Jewel: 'Jewel would a whipped him' (214). He relies on Vernon Tull for help and he constantly turns to Dewey Dell for support.

Working Through

Although the text of Vardaman's first section may seem violent and destructive, close analysis shows a constructive working through of the process of mourning as described by Freud (1917). This process is not a smoothly ongoing one. The healing conceptualizations are not stable, but waver between different possibilities. The text, here, shows the importance of social constructions. This marks the largest difference between Darl's text and that of Vardaman. Darl's conceptualizations are immune to the influence of others. Vardaman, however, even if he firmly and confidently conceptualizes his dead mother as a fish that continues to exist in some form although it is cut into pieces and eventually 'cooked and et,' is still influenced by his family's completely different

---

79 James K. Vardaman was also a racist. 'The Negro, he said, was a "veneered savage," who, "like the mule, has neither pride of ancestry nor hope of posterity." "Why sqander money on his education," Vardaman said, "when the only effect is to spoil a good field hand and make him an insolent cook? ... The way to control the nigger is to whip him when he does not obey without it"' (Peirce and Hagstrom 1984:459). In his essay 'Mississippi' (*Holiday* April 1954), Faulkner spoke of those who 'voted indefatigably for the Vardamans,' naming their sons after him, and argued that they originated 'in bitter hatred and fear and economic rivalry of the Negroes who farmed little farms no larger than and adjacent to their own, because the Negro, remembering when he had not been free at all, was therefore capable of valuing what he had of it enough to struggle to retain even that little and had taught himself how to do more with less' (Meriwether 1965:13).

conceptualizations. These conceptualizations, made concrete when Addie's body is placed in the coffin, force Vardaman to work through a traumatic past experience: 'I got shut up in the crib the new door it was too heavy for me it went shut I couldn't breathe because the rat was breathing up all the air. I said "Are you going to nail it shut, Cash? Nail it? *Nail* it?"' (59).

To tackle his fear, Vardaman needs to create a different conceptualization: 'It was not her. I was there, looking. I saw. I thought it was her, but it was not. It was not my mother. She went away when the other one laid down in her bed and drew the quilt up. She went away' (60). In order to be part of the family, Vardaman tries to bring together the two conceptualizations in one:

> It was not her because it was laying right yonder in the dirt. And now it's all chopped up. I chopped it up. It's laying in the kitchen in the bleeding pan, waiting to be cooked and et. Then it wasn't and she was, and now it is and she wasn't. And tomorrow it will be cooked and et and she will be him and pa and Cash and Dewey Dell and there wont be anything in the box and so she can breathe.
> (60)

Thus Vardaman succeeds, for the time being, in creating a worldview that will lessen his fear—his mother will not suffocate, as he himself almost did—while at the same time securing his place within the family. The doubleness of his conceptualization, however, remains a problem, making his actions, as Tull's text presents them, erratic. Even though he believes that the woman who 'laid down in her bed' is not his mother, he opens the window so that the rain can keep her (the fish) wet. Also, his family's behavior continues to disturb his conceptualization and causes him to drill holes in the coffin for her to breathe, even though he believes that there would not be anything in the box. The very short text of the third section reconceptualizes confidently: 'My mother is a fish' (74). But, as soon as his father mentions that Addie is in the wagon ('We'll all go in the wagon with ma, like she wanted'), Vardaman loses confidence in his conceptualization and has to repeat: 'But my mother is a fish. Vernon seen it. He was there' (89).

This time, to find a solution, Vardaman returns to a discussion he had earlier with his brother Darl, as the repeated 'I said' makes clear. In Darl's remark that 'Jewel's mother is a horse,' Vardaman recognizes the similarity with his own conceptualization. If Darl can explain this conceptualization to him, Vardaman seems to think, he can perhaps through analogy understand his own conceptualization of his mother. Unwittingly, Vardaman touches here upon Darl's personal obsession:

> 'Jewel's mother is a horse,' Darl said.
> 'Then mine can be a fish, cant it, Darl?' I said.
> Jewel is my brother.
> 'Then mine will have to be a horse, too,' I said.
> 'Why?' Darl said. 'If pa is your pa, why does your ma have to be a horse just because Jewel's is?'
> 'Why does it?' I said. Why does it, Darl?'
> Darl is my brother.
> 'Then what is your ma, Darl?' I said.
> 'I haven't got ere one,' Darl said. 'Because if I had one, it is *was*. And if it

is was, it cant be *is*. Can it?'
'No,' I said.
'Then I am not,' Darl said. 'Am I?'
'No,' I said.
I am. Darl is my brother.
(89f.)

Even remembering this conversation is frightening to Vardaman, so that, when he recalls it, he must return frequently to the family relations that are real to him ('Darl is my brother'). Darl plays a cruel game with his brother, but one wonders how far he can be blamed for it. His lack of restraint here signals an essential loss of control over his mind-style, which had not occurred before. Vardaman, in his innocence, even tries to help Darl when the latter denies his own existence: '"But you *are*, Darl," I said.'

When the coffin is in the water, Vardaman once more becomes certain that his mother is a fish: 'she could go faster than a man'; 'she could go faster than a man or a woman'; 'I hollering catch her darl catch her head her into the bank darl' (136). Vardaman, like all children, still believes grown-ups to be completely powerful, and he trusts their motivations to parallel his own. A general task of growing up consists of learning and accepting that this is not the case. Vardaman has to learn it, or re-learn it, at a difficult time:

Then he comes up out of the water. He comes a long way up slow before his hands do but he's got to have her got to so I can bear it. Then his hands come up and all of him above the water. I cant stop. I have not got time to try. I will try to when I can but his hands came empty out of the water emptying the water emptying away
'Where is ma, Darl?' I said. 'You never got her. You knew she is a fish but you let her get away. You never got her. Darl. Darl. Darl.'
(137)

Vardaman's mind-style keeps touching on the conceptualization he knows his family holds; his social nature forces him to align his own conceptualization with theirs. His psychological immaturity, however, does not yet allow him to do so. Looking with Darl at the buzzards that circle above the coffin, he says: 'I wouldn't let him light on her' (180), but he adds almost immediately: 'But my mother is a fish.'

Suddenly, on a more unmediated level, which the text as usual signals in italics, Vardaman makes an important discovery:

Jewel *has gone away. He and his horse went away one supper time*
'It's because she wouldn't have us beholden,' pa says...
Is it because Jewel's mother is a horse Darl? I said... That's why Jewel and I were both in the shed and she was in the wagon because the horse lives in the barn and I had to keep on running the buzzard away from
(181)

As Vardaman conceptualizes it, Jewel has gone away because he wants to be with his mother. Notice how the attribution formula *it's because*, which his father uses and which Vardaman immediately repeats, is an example for him and helps him understand. This conceptualization allows Vardaman at one stroke to understand both his brother's behavior and his own. But it leads again to the unacceptable conceptualization that his mother is in the coffin, and this prevents him from finishing his sentence. Vardaman must again regress to his idiosyncratic worldview:

> But Jewel's mother is a horse. My mother is a fish. Darl says that when we
> come to the water again I might see her and Dewey Dell said, She's in the
> box; how could she have got out? She got out through the holes I bored,
> into the water I said, and when we come to the water again I am going to
> see her. My mother is not in the box. My mother does not smell like that.
> My mother is a fish
> (182)

When Jewel comes back without his horse, Vardaman slowly learns to accept the death of his mother. Together with Darl, he is able to approach the coffin and imagine her inside: 'We hear her. We hear her turn over on her side. "Listen," Darl says. "She's turned over," I say. "She's looking at me through the wood"' (197).

Vardaman feels that he can understand Darl's behavior in analogy with his own self-assigned task of chasing the buzzards: '"Where is Darl?" they said. "He is out there under the apple tree with her, lying on her. He is there so the cat wont come back"' (207). He thinks he understands Darl's grief after the fire almost burnt their mother, and he tries to console him: '"You needn't to cry," I said. "Jewel got her out. You needn't to cry, Darl"' (208). Of course Vardaman misunderstands the reasons for Darl's grief, but the gesture tells us that he, in contrast to Darl, has learned to share the conceptualizations and purposes of his family. It was a hard lesson. As Darl puts it: 'He too has lost flesh; like ours, his face has an expression strained, dreamy, and gaunt' (209). Vardaman has had to face the emptiness that death causes. His last section conveys how he now sees the world in terms of this emptiness:

> I hear the cow a long time, clopping   on the street. Then she comes into
> the square. She goes across the square, her head down   clopping   She
> lows. There was nothing in the square before she lowed, but it wasn't
> empty. Now it is empty after she lowed. She goes on,   clopping   . She
> lows.
> (233f.).

Cash Bundren

> *If I could have just moved, even set up*

Cash is a man of deeds. Before one reaches the first of the sections that present him as a narrator (p. 73), his actions have been observed by many other narrators. All present him sawing, knocking, hammering, trimming, working on his mother's coffin. The first one to give a characterization of Cash is Darl:

> a good carpenter, Cash is. He holds the two planks on the trestle, fitted
> along the edges in a quarter of the finished box. He kneels and squints
> along the edge of them, then he lowers them and takes up the adze. A good
> carpenter. Addie Bundren could not want a better one, a better box to lie
> in. It will give her confidence and comfort. I go on to the house, followed
> by the Chuck.   Chuck.   Chuck.
> of the adze.
> (4)

Although the passage seems to indicate Darl's admiration of his brother it also conveys

a certain irritation. The irritation is even clearer in Jewel's text:
> It's because he stays out there, right under the window, hammering and
> sawing on that goddamn box. Where she's got to see him. Where every
> breath she draws is full of his knocking and sawing where she can see him
> saying See. See what a good one I am making for you.
> (13)
> that goddamn adze going One lick less. One lick less. One lick less until
> everybody that passes in the road will have to stop and see it and say what
> a fine carpenter he is.
> (13)

It is clear that Jewel is not just worried about his mother's comfort, but that he is also jealous of Cash. Jewel remembers how Cash was always keen on helping his mother: 'It's like when he was a little boy and she says if she had some fertilizer she would try to raise some flowers and he taken the bread pan and brought it back from the barn full of dung' (13). One wonders, incidently, how Jewel knows this, since he is more than ten years younger than Cash and therefore could not have observed him as a little boy. Perhaps the source of this information is Darl so that he and Jewel not only consider Cash's actions exaggerated but also share an irritation over their ostentatiousness.

Cash's physical appearance, as it is presented by various narrators, suggests a hard worker. The presentations emphasize especially his arms with their evidence of hard work:
> his sweating arms powdered lightly with sawdust
> In the lamp his sawdusted arms looked like sand.
> His shirt is blotched with sweat. He has not washed his hands and arms
> (46,54,55)

Cash's appearance thus forms a strong contrast with his 'dangle-armed' father.

Cash and Addie

Cash is the only one of the children capable of keeping a direct contact with their dying mother, who, as Dewey Dell observes, is 'just watching Cash yonder' (7). Both doctor Peabody and Darl quote Addie's only words before she dies, directed at Cash:
> Beyond the porch Cash's saw snores steadily into the board. A minute later
> she calls his name, her voice harsh and strong. 'Cash,' she says; 'you,
> Cash!'
> (Peabody, 42)
> She is looking out the window, at Cash stooping steadily at the board in the
> failing light... 'You, Cash,' she shouts, her voice harsh, strong, and
> unimpaired. 'You, Cash!'
> (Darl, 43)

Dewey Dell imagines the importance that Cash's work has for Addie: 'Maybe she wont go until Cash' (54). Anse, quoted by Darl, emphasizes the fact that Cash's work satisfies his mother: 'It was her wish... she will rest quieter for knowing it and that it was her own blood sawed out the boards and drove the nails' (18). It is Anse's worry that Cash should be able to keep working on the coffin: 'Cash'll need to eat quick and get back to work so he can finish it in time' (47).

Cash is a man of few words. When he is quoted, it is almost always done by Darl.

His very first quoted words in the text concern the moment of his mother's death: 'Cash comes to the door, carrying the saw... "She's gone," Cash says' (45f.). These first words immediately turn to the central moment of the text. But it is his nonverbal behavior, rather, that characterizes him:

Cash does not look at him [pa].
Cash does not answer.
Cash looks down at her face.
He is not listening to pa at all.
He does not approach the bed.
He stops in the middle of the floor... his face composed.
Cash is not listening.
He is looking down at her peaceful, rigid face
Cash is not listening.
After a while he turns without looking at pa and leaves the room. Then the saw begins to snore again.
(46)

The carefully presented absence of any behavior other than the extended looking at his mother's face gives the moment its intensity. As Darl presents it, Cash refuses to acknowledge his father's presence, almost as if following his mother's instructions.

Since Darl is not present at this occasion, the whole scene is one of imagined observation. Darl imagines his brother's mental representation of Addie's face, and verbalizes the impression for him in his own poetic language:

her peaceful, rigid face fading into the dusk as though darkness were a precursor of the ultimate earth, until at last the face seems to float detached upon it, lightly as the reflection of a dead leaf.
(46)

The specific lexical choices seem to echo those of Addie herself: 'darkness,' 'earth,' 'dead,' 'leaf.'

All other presentations of Cash's verbal behavior, until we reach the first of his own sections, concern his responsibility for the coffin:

'Give me that plank,' Cash says. 'No; the other one.'
'Get something to cover the lantern,' he says.
'Why dont you go on to the house, out of the rain?' Cash says.
'You go on in,' Cash says. 'Me and Vernon can finish it.'
'You get on to the house,' Cash says.
'I'm going to bevel it,' he says.
(67,68,69,69,70,70)

Again one notices how in Darl's conceptualization Cash consistently prevents his father from getting involved with what he, Cash, is doing, making sure that his mother needs only him.

The different narrators' presentations of Cash's behavior make his special relationship with his mother clear. Cash has always wanted to do things for his mother and by doing things for her he can deal with her death. In Darl's and Jewel's conceptualizations, Cash's behavior consists of *acts* that ostensively communicate his proficiency, which is a subject of discussion not only for his family but among others as well: 'Vernon Tull says he brings each board up to the window for her to see it and say it is all right' (39). As Darl presents it, Cash acts in silence in front of his mother's image:

> He looks up at the gaunt face framed by the window in the twilight. It is a composite picture of all time since he was a child. He drops the saw and lifts the board for her to see, watching the window in which the face has not moved. He drags a second plank into position and slants the two of them into their final juxtaposition, gesturing toward the ones yet on the ground, shaping with his empty hand in pantomime the finished box. (43f.)

The most essential thing, in this respect, is that Cash is Addie's eldest son. He was received by her in an exclusive atmosphere of closeness between mother and child that quickly excluded his father. In his mother's conceptualization of him, as indicated in her text, Cash is the solution to a problem: 'And when I knew that I had Cash, I knew that living was terrible and that this was the answer to it' (157). Cash, in fact, seems to embody his mother's need not just for the deed in preference of the word but for the deed as the solution to a problem. Cash's love for his mother is in the deeds he performs for her; because she has wanted it to be so, he does not need the word love.

Cash's physical appearance is captured best in the image of his powerful, faithful arm working for his mother: 'Cash is wet to the skin. Yet the motion of the saw has not faltered, as though it and the arm functioned in a tranquil conviction that rain was an illusion of the mind' (68). This skillful arm, however, stands in opposition to the impaired leg, caused by an earlier fall off a church roof. As Vardaman puts it:

> Cash comes to the hill, limping where he fell off of the church.
> Cash turns and limps up the path.
> (51,52)

The limp causes Cash to have to relinquish his role to Jewel when they carry Addie in her coffin to the wagon:

> 'We better wait,' Cash says. 'I tell you it aint balanced now. We'll need another hand on that hill.'
> 'Then turn loose,' Jewel says. He will not stop. Cash begins to fall behind, hobbling to keep up, breathing harshly; then he is distanced and Jewel carries the entire front end alone
> (88)

The passage shows Cash's concern with balance in the context of his unbalanced gait and its consequences for his role as oldest brother.

Cash's Mind-Style

Cash's first section (p. 73) immediately confirms the observations of others. The lexical choices—'bevel,' 'surface,' 'nails,' 'seam,' 'joints,' 'stress,' 'house,' 'bed,' 'crosstie,' 'coffin'—constitute a set pertaining to carpentry, as shown also in Darl's mind-style in his first section. Another set, relating to death, overlaps with the first through the word *coffin* that belongs to both of them, and contains also the nouns *body, grave, earth, hole*. The text shows very little modification of nouns, which gives it a naive, unsophisticated quality. Only three of the nouns in the second set are accompanied by adjectives, all of them simple ones: *dead body, old grave, natural hole*.

Verbal modification is more important and shows Cash's understanding of the various aspects of actions, for instance: 'Water moves easiest up and down or straight across'; 'the earth sinks down on the bevel.' The number of logical connectors is large, and, in contrast to Jewel's text, the subclause containing the connector comes complete with its main clause, for instance: 'The animal magnetism of a dead body makes the stress come slanting, so the seams and joints of a coffin are made on the bevel.' Cash's text conceptualizes the world in terms of clearly defined categories that relate to each other logically. Yet his use of the connector *except* makes clear his awareness that these neat categories can leave out an existing possibility, when the stress in a bed is not 'sideways.' Cash cannot continue his train of thought, which involves the concept of sex, as is shown by an ellipsis in his text.

There are only two sentences that show Cash as subject: 'I made it on the bevel'; 'So I made it on the bevel.' The two are identical except for the logical connector in the last one, which finds its justification in the section as a whole. Both present Cash as self-sufficient actor. The section shows Cash as a man who sees himself as an agent who understands the different aspects of actions, and who thinks logically about their various consequences. In the first of five sections narrated by Cash, he discusses the reasons why he makes his mother's coffin 'on the bevel.' His concern is with *stability*: 'There is more surface for the nails to grip. There is twice the gripping-surface to each seam.' Left to his own resources, Cash is in control and capable of a perfect job. Tull's text emphasizes the high degree of perfection of the coffin, 'with every joint and seam bevelled and scrubbed with the plane, tight as a drum and neat as a sewing basket' (77f.). Cash's perseverance is clear when, without one complaint, he repairs the coffin after Vardaman has bored holes in it. As Tull puts it:

> He could cut up a tin can and hide the holes and nobody wouldn't know the difference. Wouldn't mind, anyway. I have seen him spend a hour trimming out a wedge like it was glass he was working, when he could have reached around and picked up a dozen sticks and drove them into the joint and made it do.
> (77)

The Need for Balance

In his very short second section (p. 86), Cash is concerned with a subject that is closely related to that of the first section he narrates, namely *balance*. His problem here, however, is that he has to rely on the other members of his family, who do not share or even understand his concern. It is clear that Cash finds it difficult to communicate verbally with the members of his family. While his nonverbal behavior is controlled, complete and self-contained, his verbal behavior is incomplete and halted:

> It wont balance. If you want it to tote and ride on a balance we will have—
> I'm telling you it wont tote and it wont ride on a balance unless—
> It wont balance. If they want it to tote and ride on a balance, they will have

Three times he is unable to finish. Notice how only the first attempt shows the personal pronoun *we*, while the later ones do not seem to include Cash himself any longer. Moreover, the ellipses occurring at exactly the same place in his discourse seem to indicate that Cash tries to, but cannot, envision disturbing his mother's body after her coffin has been closed. The texts of the other members of his family reflect Cash's concerns over the coffin. Darl's text presents how Cash keeps repeating: 'It aint balanced right for no long ride' (96); 'It aint on a balance' (130,131). The coffin with Addie is not in balance, Cash believes, because 'them durn women' (80,81) put her in 'head to foot so it wouldn't crush her dress' (78). Nobody, however, takes the reasons for his concerns seriously.

Love of stability and balance is Cash's obvious psychological characteristic. It is important to realize that both his father's and his mother's texts testify to a lack of balance in their mind-styles. We have seen already his mother's tendency to divorce the horizontal from the vertical: 'how words go straight up in a thin line, quick and harmless, and how terrible doing goes along the earth' (160). In his father's text a similar division is noticeable: 'When He aims for something to be always a-moving, He makes it long ways, like a road or a horse or a wagon, but when He aims for something to stay put, He makes it up-and-down ways, like a tree or a man' (31). In contrast to his parents, Cash constantly tries to create for himself a world of stability and balance, symbolized by the diagonal—'slanting'—line of the bevel.

When the wagon with the coffin has to cross the flooded river, Cash initially shows himself in control. Again he deliberately excludes his father, by ordering him to 'walk across on the bridge' (112). As Darl conceptualizes it, Cash physically comforts his mother, laying his hands 'flat on Addie, rocking her a little' (133). Taking up his role as the oldest brother and leader, Cash 'takes the reins and lowers the team carefully and skillfully into the stream' (133). But, as Tull later presents it to his wife, Cash had to lean over more and more, 'trying to keep the coffin braced so it wouldn't slip down and finish tilting the wagon over' (139). When it nevertheless did tilt, Tull remembers: 'Cash went outen sight, still holding the coffin braced' (139). Again one recognizes Cash's fidelity to his mother. Lying on the bank of the river, unconscious and with his leg broken, Cash even comes to resemble his mother as she 'lay dying': his face as if 'sunken a little, sagging from the bony ridges of eye sockets,' his body 'pole-thin in his wet clothes' (142). When the family finally continues the journey, he is as close to her as he can be, lying tied to the coffin 'on top of Addie' (167).

Cash's third section (p. 151) is the shortest one of all and consists of the two sentences he speaks after he regains consciousness: 'It wasn't on a balance. I told them that if they wanted it to tote and ride on a balance, they would have to...' Again Cash cannot finish his sentence, or include himself in an action that would disturb his mother's body. His actions from now on are limited to making sure that his physical condition does not delay the journey. He must therefore pretend that he is not in pain:

> It's just the bumps... It kind of grinds together a little on a bump. It dont bother none... It dont bother none... Aint no time to hang back. It dont bother none.
> (181)

But Darl also observes his brother's nonverbal behavior. His facial expression, which had been 'composed' before, is now 'interrogatory, intent, and sad' (192). When his family nevertheless tries to do something for him and stabilizes his leg by pouring cement over it, he is more worried about getting cement on the coffin than about his own comfort, arguing still: 'I can last it'; 'I could last it' (192); 'I could have lasted. It dont bother me none' (193). He himself takes the blame for his increasing discomfort ('It was the sun shining on it, I reckon. I ought to thought and kept it covered' [195]; 'I ought to minded it' [196]), and he is grateful for a little water poured on it to cool

it off. Darl and Vardaman present his verbal behavior:
   I'd be obliged
   I'm obliged... It feels fine.
   I feel fine... I'm obliged to you.
   I feel fine... I'm obliged to you.
   (195,196,198,198)
To doctor Peabody Cash finally even defends his family when the former shows his
contempt for the stupidity of their 'treatment':
   They just aimed to ease hit some... Hit never bothered me none... It never
   bothered me much
   (222)

Cash and the Family

Cash's loyalty, then, is not limited to his mother, but includes his whole family. He
does not want to be left at Peabody's, and he uses the pronoun *we* even though he is
in pain and unable to move: 'We got the digging to do' (217); 'We'll get her under-
ground' (219). During the last part of the journey, Cash is forced by his broken leg to
abstain from deeds and make use of words. His two final sections are therefore much
longer. One can imagine how Cash thinks that Darl's fate would have been different
if he could have used deeds instead of words, and could have defended his brother physically from those who took him to the insane asylum after he set fire to a neighbor's
barn. Cash's text, in any case, creates a stipulative world in which his brother's situation would have been different: 'If I could have just moved, even set up' (221). In
the real world, as Cash conceptualizes it, he can only express his amazement at the behavior of others: 'it was Dewey Dell that was on him before even Jewel could get at
him' (220). Cash has to content himself with words; and his words are much less effective than the deeds of the others.
   Much of his third section (pp. 215-221) consists of rationalizations with which
Cash tries to make his brother's 'capture and deportation' acceptable to himself: 'It
wasn't nothing else to do. It was either send him to Jackson, or have Gillespie sue us'
(215). But at times he cannot help but wonder:
   Sometimes I aint so sho who's got ere a right to say when a man is crazy
   and when he aint.
   (215f.)
   But I aint so sho that ere a man has the right to say what is crazy and what
   aint.
   (221)
Again we can see that Cash's concerns are with balance; in this case with one man
balanced against those that judge him: 'Sometimes I think it aint none of us pure crazy
and aint none of us pure sane until the balance of us talks him that-a-way' (216). Notice here, and in his whole fourth section, the profusion of negations, stipulations, modals, adverbs of circumstance and so on, which make clear the complexity of Cash's
feelings. Even if he has shown few emotions, he is sensitive enough to ponder the
question of why Darl might have set Gillespie's barn on fire: 'when Jewel worked so
to get her outen the river, he was going against God in a way, and when Darl seen that
it looked like one of us would have to do something, I can almost believe he done right

in a way' (216). It is clear that Cash admires the deed, even if 'nothing excuses setting fire to a man's barn and endangering his stock and destroying his property' (216).

Cash acknowledges the closeness between himself and Darl, quoting many times Darl's concerned empathy with him:

We better take Cash to the doctor first.

Let's take Cash to the doctor first

Dont you want to go to Peabody's now, Cash?

Do you want to go to Peabody's

I'll drive you to Peabody's and come back for them.

You let me take you back to Peabody's

(217,217,217,218,218,219)

Cash's text also attributes causes to Darl's concern: 'It's because me and him was born close together, and it nigh ten years before Jewel and Dewey Dell and Vardaman begun to come along' (217).

A Hidden Side of Cash

The extraordinary experience that brings out unexpected behavior in Cash, then, is not the rescuing of his mother's coffin from the flood—this only confirms his habitual behavior—but the 'capture and deportation' of the brother to whom he feels closest. Immobilized as he is by his broken leg, Cash is forced to experience an unknown and complementary side of his personality; through his extraordinary verbal behavior he shows how he is capable of sensitive reflection and of self-expression. That this unusual behavior is nevertheless characteristic of Cash is clear from the same emphasis on balance.

We have come to Cash's last section, which is also the last section of the book. The oldest son of the family is given the final word. Curiously enough, Cash's text omits naming the object of the family's difficult journey once it has been reached: 'and so when we got done with the shovels' (239). Earlier Cash's text had in the same way avoided mentioning the grave itself: 'But when we got it filled and covered and drove out the gate' (220). The passage reminds one of Jason Compson in *The Sound and the Fury*, who dreaded mentioning his father's grave, using the same 'alien *it*' (Hurst 1987:80).[80] While Cash's fourth section showed almost exclusively the pronoun *I* with a mental activity verb, which conceptualized his lonely position within 'the sound and fury' of his family's deeds, this fifth section shows, through the pronoun *we* and action verbs that Cash includes himself once more in the activity of the family:

So when we stopped there

So when we got done

So we went back to the house.

So we set in the wagon

And so pa come back and we went

(239,239,239,239,240)

Notice the self-assured inevitability created here by the causal connector *so*, which has replaced the uncertainty of the fourth section now that Cash can involve himself again

---

80 Jason Compson saw his father's undertakers 'trying to kick the mud off their feet and sticking to the shovels so they'd have to knock it off, making a hollow sound when it fell on it' (230f.).

in deeds. Nevertheless, before he ceremoniously grants the last word to his father, his final thought is for the brother he feels most 'kin to':
But it is better so for him. This world is not his world; this life his life. (242)

The Personalities of the Bundren Children

In my discussion of the personalities of the Bundren children I have focused on their mother's early conceptualization of them, including the names she chose for them. An important influence on the children's personalities turned out to be their order of birth, that is, the specific place each of them occupies in the family. And although my emphasis was on habitual behavior, it became clear that the specific situation with which fate confronted them all was able, at least in some of them, to bring out unexpected aspects of their personalities. Thus Cash found out that he could speak; Jewel found out that he could share, and Darl found out that he could act.

Cash's place as the eldest brother in the family makes it natural for him to function as the leader of the undertaking. This role of 'being the oldest' (217) dictates his sense of responsibility, and shows why he can ignore their inadequate father more easily than the others and is even able to remove him from the scene. It also explains the fact that Darl uses him as an example for his sexual experiments, 'wondering if Cash was yonder in the darkness doing it too' (9f.). The role of oldest brother also justifies the fact that the last section in the novel is his. Darl's place in the family led to his closeness to Cash, because they were 'born close together' (217). Having an older brother who was already an expert on deeds, Darl has become an expert on words. This explains why Vardaman turns to him, not for an example of how to behave but for an explanation of life's mysteries. Darl's role as man of words explains why the first section in the novel is his, and why he narrates more sections than any other narrator. Jewel's place between the older siblings and the younger ones, not having to belong to either, forms the origin of his sense of freedom and his aloofness. Dewey Dell's place as only daughter in a family of sons causes her to expect her brothers' obedience inside the house and their protection outside of it, even if she achieves neither. Vardaman, as the youngest child, is open to the examples, the guidance and the care of his older siblings (cf. Wladis Hoffman 1991).

Addie's conceptualization of Cash as a solution to a problem adds to the natural inclinations of an oldest child. Her active acceptance of him—'I knew that I had Cash'—has provided him with a stable position in the world. Her tendency to divorce the word from the deed, in order to try to rediscover the purity of experience, can be linked to Cash's desire to show his love for his mother through deeds. In contrast, Addie's denial of Darl's existence—'I would not believe it'—links up with his precarious sense of self and his consequent fear of disintegration. Addie's denial parallels Darl's feeling that he has no mother. His need for rationalization distances him even further from his mother and her need for the purity of the deed, but it may also, paradoxically, tie him to her, reminding her of her own defenses. Jewel's special place with his mother is best captured by his name. In her conceptualization he is hardly a flesh-and-blood human being but rather the product of her dream, her rescuer from the water and the fire, both her cross and her salvation: the traditional 'brilliant bastard.' His dreamworld contains just the two of them, mother and favorite son, 'on a high hill,' and all his activity is directed towards establishing this world. The name that Addie gave to her daughter shows her paradoxical feelings towards her own role as a woman and a mother. Dewey Dell's conceptualization of her situation as 'a wet seed in the earth too soon' can be linked to this name. Her images of emptiness and void convey the loneliness of a child that was given away to balance an account. Vardaman, although he was given away by his mother to a man who was already dead but did not know it, can perhaps through his name be linked to her hope that education will provide escape. Small, motionless and in faded overalls, he at least receives his mother's sincere attention in her dying minutes.

My discussion has shown the paradoxes of Addie's personality. Addie felt that she had been tricked by words, yet she always needed them desperately herself and used them to trick others. She understood words to be 'a shape to fill a lack,' and she conveyed her belief that words were invented by people who never had the feeling. Words to her represented the gaps in the lacks where the deeds should have been. Addie's husband Anse seems never to have understood this paradox, but her children, who were created by it, have understood it to some extent. In their different and paradoxical ways, they try to live up to her expectations of them and perform acts for which they can stand: Cash stoically works on her coffin and Jewel saves it from the river and the burning barn, so that the promise made to her can be fulfilled. Darl, who needs words even more desperately than his mother, tries to save her dignity by setting the barn in which her coffin is kept on fire, to burn her and spare her the degradation of the trip with her decomposing body. For the younger children it is more difficult to act out her conception of them, because they never really belonged to her. Still, the pregnant Dewey Dell continues to carry out her duty to the world as 'a wet seed' in the soil, for the 'wild blood' of the earth; and Vardaman, in his magical child's world, recreates his mother as a fish that, like his mother, keeps sliding out of his hands.

4

Light in August and the Issue of Unreliability

*Unanimity does not change prejudice into truth;
it only makes it more dangerous*

Voice is *the* route to characterization in William Faulkner's *The Sound and the Fury*. Each of the Compson brothers Benjy, Quentin and Jason, in his own separate section, presents himself as an utterer of sounds, a speaker of words, a *voice*. From the recurring elements of voice the reader distills a knowledge of this speaker's mind-style and worldview, and thereby of his personality. The speaker himself is not necessarily, or usually, aware of the personality he shows. What he tells about himself and his view of the world, including his own personality, may not at all be in accordance with the knowledge the reader acquires from his verbal behavior. Jason Compson, for instance, may present himself consciously as one in charge of his surroundings, but his mind-style, as we have seen, shows him to be a rather helpless, bewildered, pathetic individual. In my discussion of *As I Lay Dying*, the emphasis was on the contribution of the voice of the other to the personality of the individual. Attribution theory can be used to explain that the voice of the speaker characterizes the speaker himself as well as the one spoken about: the attributor as well as the attributee. Thus it is clear that Darl Bundren's observation of his brother Cash's nonverbal behavior—'he [Cash] lays his hands flat on Addie, rocking her a little' (133)—can tell us as much about Darl himself as it does about Cash.

While in *The Sound and the Fury* and *As I Lay Dying* the link between voice and personality is clear, in *Light in August* this relationship is much less apparent. As Sister Kirstin Morrison points out, in *Light in August*

> voice function is more subtle and consequently understanding of it more
> necessary... the reader's unawareness of the fact of voice and lack of
> sensitivity to its function easily result in misunderstanding of the novel in
> general and of the character of Joe Christmas in particular. Only with an
> understanding of voice—its place in the narrative, its relation to character,
> its effect on the reader—only then can the reader appreciate *Light in August*
> and the complexity and dimensionality of Joe Christmas, his manifestation
> as person.
> (1982:143)

The greater complexities of voice in *Light in August*, as compared with *The Sound and the Fury* and *As I Lay Dying*, stem in part from the fact that *Light in August* is a third-person novel narrated by an external, or 'extradiegetic,' narrator (Genette 1986). Thus, while my first chapters discussed the character as a speaker, this chapter will concentrate on the character and his text as they are conveyed through the voice of this extradiegetic narrator.[81]

Often, the narrator does not reveal much about himself. Even so, as Shlomith Rimmon-Kenan observes, 'there is always a teller in the tale, at least in the sense that any utterance or record of an utterance presupposes someone who has uttered it'; there are, however, 'forms and degrees of perceptibility of the narrator' (1987:88f.). As Valerie Shaw puts it: 'Even if he is merely an onlooker, the narrator must participate somehow in the story's action, or in the unfolding of meaning; he cannot be a completely transparent lens, but must have a fictional identity of his own' (1986:115). Every narrator, even a very covert or hidden one, presents the setting and the characters, identifies with attributive clauses the speakers whom he quotes, and relates the time of the events to the time of narration through tense. Because a speaker's presentation might be more or less accurate with regard to certain aspects of the story, I shall begin with a discussion of the concept of the reliability of the narrator, or, to use Félix Martínez-Bonati's term, with the question of 'narrative objectivity' (1981:21).

My interest in the subject of *reliability* in connection with personality in the novel *Light in August* originates in my amazement at critical works that label its major character as 'this colored Romeo... the amoral mulatto' (Geismar 1971:89), or as 'a black man who looks white' (Jehlen 1976:84), and speak of 'the fact of his Negro blood' (Brown 1967:436). Relatively few accounts characterize Joe Christmas as a black or a mulatto without hesitation; a majority, however, do not question his status as murderer. One critic writes: 'Joe finds that he has to kill her, and does' (Brooks 1971:60), the that-clause suggesting a conscious conclusion reached by Christmas. Another even goes beyond the text to present Christmas as 'a man of whom we might say that it is surprising not that he commits one murder but that he has not committed more, a man apparently capable of any violent and repulsive deed' (Waggoner 1966:103). A third points out that 'we are told how Christmas murders Miss Burden' (Chase 1971:18). Only a few critics are more careful in their labeling (cf. Fadiman 1975), and add modals such as *probably* and *presumably* to their discussions of Christmas's murder of Joanna Burden.

I shall argue that such endeavors to gain mastery over the text duplicate the very events that the story is about. As Homer Pettey wrote in connection with *Sanctuary*, Faulkner's narrative 'compels his reader into a complicitous role with the novel's events' (1987:73). Although there is talk of Joe Christmas having raped and murdered Joanna Burden, we are not *told* that he murdered her, let alone being told *how*. My discussion of Joe Christmas's personality, in any case, will unsettle and problematize such readings. It does not in the first place explore the question of how, why, or even if Joe Christmas committed the murder, but instead how Faulkner entices the reader to participate in acts of labeling and prejudice that *make* him the murderer. This project has led me to the issue of *reliability*, and thus to the question of the validity of a remark made by one of the major internal narrators of *Light in August*:

If public talking makes truth, then I reckon this is truth.

---

81 In the following discussion, when I speak of 'the narrator,' I shall refer to the 'extradiegetic narrator.'

Reliability and Credibility

The concept of *reliability* is concerned with the establishment of 'mutual knowledge' (Werth 1984:55). Depending on a listener's estimation of the speaker's reliability, he may be willing to enlarge his own world—the collection of 'facts' that he, consciously or unconsciously, holds to be true of the world—by accepting those that he cannot perceive for himself. No one can experience all aspects of the world for himself. Depending on one's physical, psychological, historical and social position in the world, certain aspects of it will be directly included in one's perception of how things are, while others must be taken on trust. However, in the process of the 'negotiation of reality' between a speaker and his listener, the important factor is not so much the reliability of this speaker, but his *credibility*: his ability to inspire a certain measure of trust in his listener. One can distinguish, then, between *reliability* and *credibility*: reliability refers to the speaker's ability to know the truth and speak it, while credibility refers to the ability of a speaker to inspire trust in his listener, or the degree to which his observations are taken to be correct. This is the difference between trustworthiness and being trusted. Reliability lies solely in the speaker, while credibility, one could say, is a 'joint venture' of speaker and listener.

In social psychology, which can be defined as 'an attempt to understand... how the thought, feeling, and behavior of... individuals are influenced by the actual, imagined, or implied presence of others' (Allport 1968:3; quoted in Berkowitz 1980:11), research has been done on credibility. Leonard Berkowitz, for instance, poses the important question clearly and simply, under the heading of 'The Credible Communicator':

> Communicators' qualities, especially their credibility, affect their likelihood of convincing the audience. Communicators are more likely to be persuasive if people are favorably disposed towards them. But what is involved in this favorable disposition, and how do these characteristics operate?
> (1980:291)

The question of credibility goes back at least as far as Aristotle. His concept of the *ethos* referred to '"a favorable disposition" of the listener towards the speaker.' It 'appears to denote the degree of trust a listener is willing to place in the message of a speaker,' and 'reflects a willingness to rely upon or show confidence in the speaker and his message' (Giffin 1967:106). In his *Rhetoric*, Aristotle contended that the listener's estimation of the speaker is based on his perception of three characteristics: firstly, how correct the speaker seemed to be; secondly, how honest the listener thought he was; and thirdly, his intentions towards the listener. Numerous modern analyses of audience-reactions show variations and extensions of these same three factors, for instance: (i) the degree to which the speaker seems to know what he is talking about—his obvious expertise or authoritativeness; (ii) his personal attractiveness; (iii) his interest and enthusiasm; and (iv) his apparent motivation to manipulate or even deceive his audience (Berkowitz 1980:292).

The distinction between reliability and credibility is an important one. A speaker, after all, may seem utterly unreliable and yet receive tremendous credibility, for instance because he fulfills the needs of his listeners (as do the leaders of religious sects). On the other hand, a speaker may seem perfectly reliable and nevertheless receive no credence at all, for instance because his status is low (think of members of minority groups).[82] The distinction between reliability and credibility is not usually made in narratology; it is, however, of the utmost important for a full understanding of the story of Joe Christmas in *Light in August*. To introduce the distinction into narratological theory, I shall examine the four credibility factors mentioned above—authoritativeness, attractiveness, interest and motivation—in terms of their applicability to a theory of reliability and credibility in fiction.

Authoritativeness
The speaker's own estimation of his authoritativeness can give important information to his listener when it is encoded into the language he uses through modal constructions, that is, through 'signals to the listener/reader of the speaker's attitude to his situation' (Verdonk 1988:118). One of the functions of modals is to specify 'the degree of assurance or commitment with which a speaker vouches for a proposition' (Fowler 1986:57). When a speaker, for instance, uses the epistemic modals *ought to* or *should*, he signals that he is not certain of the validity of his statement. The doubt expressed by the speaker thus communicates itself to the listener, who must decide whether or not to incorporate these views of the world into his own conceptualization of it.

Here, as Paul Werth argues, the listener's estimation of the speaker's authoritativeness is a very important factor. In his example *Bert should have finished painting by now*, it makes a difference whether the sentence is spoken by Bert's wife, who presumably knows his work-habits, or by a casual acquaintance. To account for this difference, Werth proposes a 'multivalued theory of truth' (1981:23) that can provide a set of 'degrees of possibilities' according to which the proposition expressed is 'true ... likely to be true... possible... likely to be false... or false.' Consequently, it is 'certain... probable... possible... improbable... or impossible' that a certain listener will include the proposition in his conceptualization of reality. According to Werth, 'high authoritativeness... increases the probability tendency associated with the modal... low authoritativeness decreases it' (1981:23). In other words, if the modal construction *ought to* means *it is probable* in a neutral context, it will be 'upgraded' to mean *it is (almost) certain* when it is pronounced by an authoritative speaker. Think, for instance, of a surgeon putting in the last stitch of a cardiac valve replacement and saying: *This ought to do it.* Conversely, if *ought to* is used by a speaker with low authoritativeness, it will be 'down-graded' to mean merely *it is possible*, or even *it is improbable or dubious*.

In such cases, Werth argues, a listener may even be tempted to interpret the epistemic modal (dealing with uncertainty) as a root modal (dealing with obligation), as when a would-be mountaineer comes to a hike in tennis shoes and says: *These shoes ought to be good enough*, meaning: *They had better be good enough; I haven't brought any other ones.* Of course, the same scale of authoritativeness also applies for root

82 As Christopher Lasch has argued, 'the rise of mass media makes the categories of truth and falsehood irrelevant to an evaluation of their influence. Truth has given way to credibility, facts to statements that sound authoritative without conveying any authoritative information... President Nixon's press secretary, Ron Ziegler, once demonstrated the political use of these techniques when he admitted that his previous statements on Watergate had become "inoperative"... Not their falsity but their inability to command assent rendered them "inoperative"' (1978:74f.).

modals. It makes a difference if a mother says to her child: *You should take a shower and go to bed* or if it is the little girl next door who says the same thing. Modal adverbs and sentence adverbs, such as *certainly, surely*, and *perhaps*; adjectival versions, such as *it is certain that*; and verbs of knowledge and prediction, such as *seem, believe, guess* and *foresee*, are subject to considerations of authoritativeness in the same way. But even if speakers use no modal constructions to qualify the certainty of their statements, the influence of authoritativeness must be recognized. If my dentist says: *That tooth looks all right from the outside but it has a cavity on the inside*, I am more willing to believe him than if a taxi-driver tells me the same thing. In the same way, if the baby-sitter calls me at work and tells me the baby just took its first steps, I am more easily convinced than if the doorman tells me this. Naturally, a speaker can show his authoritativeness through his verbal behavior, but also through his para- and nonverbal behavior: his tone of voice, his facial expressions, his posture and his gestures.

Obviously, professionals and witnesses have high authority, and so have those who have proven to be right on previous occasions.[83] It seems important, however, that it be clear from the start that the speaker has authority, or that he make this manifest early on in the conversation, at least by the middle of the message (Sternthal, Phillips and Dholakia 1978:289). This will prevent the listener from arguing against the speaker in his mind; it will force him to hold back counter-arguments, and consequently, perhaps, to listen better. Even witnesses of events, however, may be less authoritative than they seem. As Berkowitz puts it, 'individuals selectively attend to the world around them and transform the information they receive from their surroundings in terms of their usual ways of understanding things' (1980:160f.). Moreover, a speaker often communicates material that has been in his memory for some time. Berkowitz explains, 'the trouble is that the information does not just lie in the memory store safe and untouched... We may want to be accurate, but the delayed message we transmit may not be a faithful report of what we have really seen or heard' (1980:161). In the meantime, potentially harmful or painful events may have been forgotten, or in neurotic persons have been sharpened.

Attractiveness

Although it may seem less important than authoritativeness, personal attractiveness can certainly be a factor with respect to credibility. Two questions seem of importance here: firstly, which factors determine personal attractiveness? and secondly, what makes an attractive person seem reliable? Psychological experiments have provided the following observations with respect to personal attractiveness. All else being equal, a person will usually be attracted to another person (i) whom he meets often, provided they are of similar status; (ii) who shares similar values and beliefs; (iii) who satisfies some psychological need, for instance by possessing complementary abilities; (iv) who is competent or intelligent; (v) who has a pleasant appearance, is beautiful or handsome; and (vi) who is pleasant and agreeable, yet not dull (Berkowitz 1980:160f.). The

---

83 Michel Foucault has argued that the discourse of authority is a practice 'that systematically forms the objects' of which it speaks (1972:49). The socially important question is who is entitled to speak, and from what institutional site (1972:51).

second question posed above is less easy to answer. In fact, individuals, when asked, tend to deny that they have greater trust in the reliability of attractive speakers. Many experiments, however, have shown that such mechanisms nevertheless work on an unconscious level (cf. Osgood & Tannenbaum 1955).

To explain this, suppose for a moment that an individual is attracted to another but does not trust his words. Such a situation implies a certain 'cognitive conflict.' As Lawrence Pervin puts it: 'There is movement in human organisms, as living systems, towards integrated functioning and reduction of conflict' (1984:489). This means that an individual will strive to establish congruence between his concept of self and his experience and between his different concepts, including different self-concepts, in order to lessen or avoid 'inconsistent sets of knowledge or cognitions' (Berkowitz 1980:88). Leon Festinger has studied inconsistencies between conceptualizations and the conflict these arouse under the heading of 'cognitive dissonance.' As he argues: two cognitions 'are in a dissonance relation if, considering these two alone, the obverse of one would follow from the other.... x and y are dissonant if not-x follows from y' (1957:13). The implications of dissonance are especially forceful with respect to behavior. As Berkowitz explains, 'dissonance occurs when the individual holds at any one time two or more cognitions that have contradictory implications for his behavior: One cognition implies, "Do this," and the other indicates, "Do the opposite"' (1980:88). Cognitive dissonance, as Worchel and Cooper argue, gives rise to an 'unpleasant psychological tension,' which has 'drive-like properties that are much like those of hunger and thirst,' in that the experiencer 'is "driven" to reduce that tension' (1979:117).

To accomplish reduction of tension, an individual may do one of four things: he may change one of his cognitions to make it more consistent with the other; he may add new cognitions to bridge the gap between the two; he may alter or deny the importance of the cognitions and their conflict; or he may disclaim his own responsibility for the ensuing behavior. Discussing this last tendency within the context of psychoanalytic practice, Roy Schafer has argued that 'the art of disclaiming is a basic lesson in our socialization' (1980:70). By using expressions such as 'I don't know what's gotten into me'; 'I couldn't get away from the thought that...'; or 'the impulse overwhelmed me,' the speaker presents himself as a victim of 'happenings,' the origins of which lie outside his own 'sphere of influence' (1980:70). This 'art of disclaiming,' a mild and socially accepted form of delusion, is usually effective in reducing ambivalence. However, an individual may be especially disturbed by conflicting cognitions if he has already publicly committed himself to one of the cognitions (cf. Brehm & Cohen 1962); if he himself is responsible for the inconsistency (cf. Wicklund & Brehm 1976); or if he has a pre-existing inability to handle ambivalence (Bateson 1972:206f.). The Batesonian double bind, discussed in Chapter 2, in connection with Quentin Compson's personality, is an especially vicious form of cognitive dissonance whereby one of the conflicting cognitions is, as it were, included in the other.

If we return to the question at hand, these mechanisms to reduce tension may serve to heighten mentally the credibility of an attractive speaker, or, if this is impossible, to lessen the attractiveness of a speaker thought to be unreliable; to add new information to 'smoothe out' the conflict, for instance the information that the speaker is too young to know what he is talking about, so that it is possible to find him unreliable yet still find him attractive; to decrease the importance of the issues, for instance, by 'realizing' that the speaker's words are not important, that his attractiveness was never noticed, or that reliability has nothing to do with attractiveness; or to disclaim responsibility for the obvious lack of ability to regulate and understand one's own conduct. Such mechanisms, as I have stressed before, are automatic and unconscious, and serve to protect the individual from psychological suffering and harm. They are blocked, for instance, in schizophrenic states, leading to more grotesque and socially unacceptable forms of delusion.[84]

The theory of cognitive dissonance, although in essence very simple, is extremely far-reaching in its implications. It may help us to understand not only the question under discussion here, and the double bind situation at the root of certain psychic disorders, but also the spreading of rumors, the resistance to new information—the 'inertia of mental attitudes' (Foucault 1972:10)—and the attitude changes caused by the public voicing of private opinions, all of which are of importance in *Light in August*.

Interest and enthusiasm

Interest and enthusiasm, which are conveyed through the speaker's tone of voice, facial expressions, gestures and posture provide, like authoritativeness, an indication of the speaker's self-confidence. Self-confidence is a very persuasive phenomenon, and it easily heightens the confidence of a listener; the speaker, after all, seems to know what he is talking about (cf. London 1973). Interest and enthusiasm, moreover, convey the speaker's love for his subject, which may easily imply elaborate exposure, and thus suggest knowledgeability or authority. Authoritativeness, as we saw, in its turn increases credibility.

For interest and enthusiasm, as well as for authoritativeness, the degree of exposition is crucial. Too much will have an adverse effect, making a listener doubt the speaker's conscious or unconscious motivation. Listeners will often sense that a speaker who is enthusiastic in an exaggerated way may well be trying to hide his depression; a speaker who is abnormally attentive may well be trying to hide his boredom; and a speaker who behaves in an extremely authoritative way may well be trying to compensate for his insecurity. Doubt is also created if qualities of tone of voice, facial expression and posture do not match up with each other or with the words that are spoken.

Motivation

The listener's evaluation of the speaker's motives is perhaps the most elusive aspect of credibility, since motives, contrary to authoritativeness, attractiveness, enthusiasm and interest, are often meant to stay hidden from the listener. No speaker, after all, will consciously communicate motives that might decrease his credibility. Nevertheless, the listener may sense that the speaker's hidden motive is to get something from him, for

---

84 Virginia Woolf, who in *Mrs Dalloway* gives a convincing presentation of schizophrenic thinking in the character of Septimus Smith, writes: 'He must somehow see through human nature—see its hypocrisy, and insincerity, its power to recover from every wound, incapable of taking any final impression' (Holograph Notes, 19 Nov. 1922; 22 July 1923; quoted in Henke [1981:13]). R. Laing considers this the result of the schizophrenic person's 'inner honesty' (1965:83). Jeffrey Berman likewise argues that the schizophrenic is 'more skeptical of all types of would-be and as-if attitudes than the rest of us' (1987:162).

instance permission or favors, or to pass something on to him, for instance an un-pleasant job or an unwanted responsibility, blame or guilt, rather than to present in-formation or to exchange ideas. And because, as Donald Spence puts it, 'in any bargaining session, truth takes the back seat' (1982:95), the listener will not lend much credence to the speaker's overt message in such cases.

Majority Opinion

One last factor, although it is not a characteristic of the speaker, is also important with respect to credibility, namely majority opinion. It has become clear that people tend to trust those who are also trusted by a majority of others (cf. Giffin 1967:118).

What should have become clear in this discussion, in any case, is that credibility is a 'real' and important phenomenon in our everyday life. It is largely a matter of reading between the lines; a message usually does not directly, or even in a conscious way, communicate its reliability. It is important to keep the conceptual difference between *reliability* and *credibility* in mind. The speaker may seem reliable, but to a certain listener his credibility may, for whatever reason, be low, or the speaker may seem unreliable but his credibility may be high. The theoretical concept of *mind-style* is especially well suited to the exploration of reliability and credibility in fiction.

Reliability and Credibility in Fiction

Our understanding of the concepts of reliability and credibility in real-life situations forms the basis of our understanding of them in fiction, and vice versa. This does not mean, however, that they necessarily function in the same way in all respects. I shall therefore explore the specific functions of reliability and credibility as narratological concepts on different levels of narration.

As I have argued, the notions of reliability and credibility in real life serve the creation of shared conceptualizations of the world. In this way, speech-partners expand the reality that they already share. This reality is always minimally made up of the biological foundation of their humanness (biological reality), but usually contains many social aspects as well (cultural and interpersonal reality). In fiction, this creation of shared conceptualizations occurs on different 'narrative levels' (Genette 1986:227ff.): that of the (extradiegetic) narrator and his narratee, and that of the different characters. Each level presents its own biological, cultural and interpersonal reality shared by the fictional speech-partners. Reliability and credibility, then, because they function to expand the physical and social reality that speech-partners already share, function on one narrative level rather than between two different ones. The purpose of communication is the expanding of a shared world, sometimes desired by both partners, sometimes forced by one upon the other. But to do this, the speech-partners must share the same level of reality. When a reader judges a fictional speaker, then, he must ask himself what this speaker's own speech-partner(s) would think of his judgments, that is, the reader must 'step into the shoes' of a listener who exists on the same narrative level as the speaker and take over his point of view (cf. Rabinowitz 1981:413).

To judge an extradiegetic narrator, then, the reader must 'become' the extradiegetic narratee; to judge an intradiegetic narrator, he must 'become' the intradiegetic narratee. The more realistic the story, the easier this will be. Thus, the character Septimus

Smith, in Virginia Woolf's novel *Mrs Dalloway*, is unreliable because his views do not fit in the world that he shares with his wife, his psychiatrist, and other characters, who all know that flowers cannot grow through one's flesh. The external world surrounding Septimus Smith is one in which such things do not happen. The story, of course, does not state this explicitly, but the reader can be sure of it because these characters share a world that is realistic in that it is biologically much like our own world, in which such things cannot happen. The norms that the reader falls back on, in this case, are the laws of biological reality, which all people share simply because their mental apparatus is of the human type. They can also be cultural ones, shared not by humanity as a whole but by specific groups of people.

Instead of this realistic world in which the unreliable speaker Septimus Smith lives, the narrator might have presented a world in which flowers *do* grow through one's flesh. In such a world it would be harder to judge the reliability of speakers, since the frame knowledge obtained from experience in our own world may or may not apply. Therefore, we do not know what other curious things might be 'true' in such a world, and consequently, we do not know how to identify judgments to which a speaker's fellow characters could reasonably object. To use John Woods' words, Sherlock Holmes 'could have travelled backwards in time and could have squared the circle' (1974:31), but such a story, in which 'alien norms' are established, is harder to read, and it is likely that the reader will fall back on his own frames of reference.[85] Because of the reader's tendency to fall back on frames that exist in his own world, the story-world remains apart from the actual world only for as long as and to the extent that its frames are explicitly supported in the text. As Rolf Breuer has put it, the work of art is a 'hybrid': a 'universe in itself, which follows its own laws and cannot therefore be judged by standards extrinsic to it,' but at the same time a 'reflection of the real world around it,' which 'can and indeed must be judged by extrinsic standards' (1980:112).[86]

The Narrator

Let us focus on the power of the extradiegetic narrator to present the story-world and thereby posit the 'existence' all its objects and phenomena. Some fictional works present this power overtly, and play with it in an interesting way. The narrator of 'City of Glass' by Paul Auster, for instance, introduces his protagonist as follows:

> As for Quinn, there is little that need detain us. Who he was, where he
> came from, and what he did are of no great importance.
> (1988:3)

Similarly, the narrator of *The Radiant Way* by Margaret Drabble corrects her own

---

85   Young children, whose frames of reference are yet flexible, are notoriously more receptive to works such as *Alice in Wonderland* than are fifteen-year-olds who have never encountered the story before (cf. Lippman 1971).

86   'Through this twofold and in fact contradictory relation to reality,' Breuer argues, 'the artist resembles the schizophrenic, whose illness, roughly speaking, consists in creating a counter-world in which he is the absolute lord and master, though at the risk of losing contact with the reality around him' (1980:112). As Peter Brooks points out, Freud's description of the 'Zwischenreich' (1914)—a place 'both artificial and a piece of real experience' (1987:10); an 'artificial space' that is nonetheless 'the place of real investments of desire from both sides of the dialogue' (1987:12f.)—is very much like the literary text.

digression, thereby setting the limits of her exposition:

> But that is another part of this story, and not to be pursued here, for Brian
> is not a woman... Forget I mentioned him. Let us return to Liz, Alix and
> Esther.
> (1988:88)

The narrator in the first excerpt asserts himself, from the very first page of his story, as a definite authority. This heightens his credibility throughout his narration of the unusual series of events that forms the story. The narrator in the second excerpt might, from this utterance alone, receive much less credence; not because she does not know her 'facts,' but because of her uncertainty about what should be told and what should not, or her (pretended?) lack of mastery over her own impulse 'to tell it all.'

It should be remembered that these words are not directed at the reader, of whom the narrator has no notion, but at a narratee on the same level of narration as the narrator. However, because the world presented in these excerpts is very much like the real world, and because the narratee is completely covert—he is only evident as 'the appellative element' that is immanent in the utterance of the speaker (Martínez-Bonati 1981:85)—it is easy for the reader to step into his shoes. As Genette explains: 'the more transparent the receiving instance and the more silent its evocation in the narrative, so undoubtedly the easier, or rather the more irresistible, each real reader's identification with or substitution for that implied instance will be' (1986:260). The narratee might, however, have been less covert, for instance if his judgments had been included in the narrator's utterance in the following way:

> Although I can see on your face that you think differently, who he was,
> where he came from or what he did are of no great importance.

> Although you just said you think you should know more about Brian, let us
> return to Liz, Alix and Esther.

In these cases the narratees' disagreement is acknowledged, which makes them more overtly present as fictional persons. Consequently, for many readers a greater distance is created between the reader and the story. Thus it is harder to step into the narratee's shoes.

As we can see from these examples, it is possible, here, for the narrator to continue his or her story in spite of the narratee's objections. This would be highly unlikely if the narratee's protests concerned certain other aspects of his message, for instance:

> As for Quinn, although you deny his existence, there is little that need
> detain us. Who he was, where he came from, and what he did are of no
> great importance.

Such a story cannot easily unfold itself. The disagreement is somehow serious enough to divert attention away from the protagonist Quinn, on the intradiegetic level, towards the conflict between the narrator and his narratee, on the extradiegetic level. If this happens, the story shifts from one narrative level—the world of the characters—to another narrative level—the world of the narrator and narratee. In other words, the extradiegetic level becomes diegetic, and consequently, the narrator is no longer an extradiegetic one. We must assume, then, that for a narrator to present a story in which he or she is extradiegetic, certain information must be taken as 'true' by his or her narratee. The narrator must be credible to the narratee, at least with respect to certain aspects of the story, or else there can be no ongoing narrative. Or, to turn this around, if the extradiegetic narrator can function as story-teller, the narratee must be presumed to grant credence to certain aspects of the story. If not, this speaker and his listener could not remain extradiegetic; their disagreement would become the focus of the story.

But if the narratee is assumed to agree, so must the reader, who, as we saw, takes over the point of view of this narratee. Thus, as Martínez-Bonati explains, 'comprehension of a narrative requires in general... a particular receptivity to the narrator's words; we must extend to them a subtle form of fundamental credence... in order for the narrative to move forward' (1981:31). This is the reason why, as many critics have pointed out, the reader is partial to the narrator's words. Lubomír Doležel speaks in this respect of the narrator's 'force of authentication' (1988:490). Because the narratee obviously gives the narrator credence, the reader, who takes over his or her point of view, does so as well. The credibility of the narrator, like all credibility, is a creation of this speaker *and* his listener, who desires structure: a *story*. To believe a narrator, then, is to follow the 'rules of the game' of story-telling, which is a convention, but which, like many conventions, also reflects psychological needs.[87]

To conclude: a speaker's discourse contains two types of information. Firstly, there are his assertions (propositions with their presuppositions and inferences), which must be taken as true for the story to proceed. These assertions can of course turn out to be untrue, but they are taken as 'facts' of the story-world as long as there is no evidence to the contrary. Secondly, there is another type of information, consisting of the speaker's personal opinions *about* these 'facts.' This information does not influence the continuation of the story in the same way, that is, it does not necessarily have to be 'true' for the story to unfold itself.

The Apophantic Content of Sentences

As Felix Martínez-Bonati explains, Aristotle discusses in his *De Interpretatione* the 'apophantic' sentence as one that is 'capable of being either true or false, or, more exactly, one in which either truth or falsehood inheres.' Such sentences posit 'states of affairs or circumstances as being facts, and are either true or false with respect to what is the case' (1981:25). No sentence, however, contains these 'facts' in a pure state, so that it is better not to speak of apophantic sentences, but to describe the apophantic content of a sentence or an utterance as that abstraction of it that contains the pure proposition as it might be expressed in a logical formula. All propositions that can be abstracted from a story together form what Martínez-Bonati has called the 'mimetic stratum' of the speaker's language, and he argues: 'we do not encounter the mimetic stratum as a linguistic stratum. We only encounter it as *world*; as *language* it disappears' (1981:37).

This must not be taken to mean, however, that this 'mimetic stratum' really imitates or shows a world. As Genette points out, 'the very idea of *showing*... is completely illusory... no narrative can "show" or "imitate" the story it tells. All it can do is tell it in a manner which is detailed, precise, "alive," and in that way give more or less the *illusion of mimesis*' (1986:163f.). It is this 'illusion,' of course, to which

---

87 That so-called postmodern novels can frustrate this need in various ways only goes to prove its existence.

Martínez-Bonati is referring. The 'mimetic stratum' is a stratum of language, and as such it naturally consists of words. It does not, however, use words to imitate an existing world, but rather to create one in the imagination: a world that comes into being through the narrator's description of it.[88] The 'mimetic stratum' of literature might more properly be called the 'creative stratum,' since it creates conceptualizations of a world that never existed.[89]

Naturally, the mental representations that this 'creative stratum' calls up in different listeners are not identical. If a speaker conveys the proposition *there stood a tree*, some listeners will 'see' a world containing something like an elm tree, and others something much more like an oak, depending on the semantic network in the individual's mind. This may not be important for the story. However, if a speaker does not want his listeners to follow the connections of their own semantic networks in this way, he must 'arouse in them more specific images and associations,' which will, to use Spence's words, 'add a certain texture and tone to what is being described—the chordal accompaniment, so to speak, to the melodic line' (1982:42). The propositions of the 'creative stratum,' then, do not imitate an existing world, but rather create a 'possible world' in the individual's mind, by specifying what this particular world must be like in order for these propositions to be true. In other words, they can create a world precisely because of the existence of these 'facts' and their inferences. If, for instance, the proposition at the beginning of Faulkner's *Light in August* < Lena think > is taken to be true, a world is put before our eyes in which this is the case. The existential presupposition of the speaker < Lena exist >, as well as the inferences that can be made as a result of biological frame knowledge, for instance < Lena breathe >; cultural frame knowledge, for instance < Lena female >, and those based on personal experience, are automatically included. Notice that the tense of the verb is not reflected in the formulas above, as it is not part of the world that is created but forms, as a deictic, a link between this newly-created world and the world of the narrator, which he shares with his narratee. Tense, we could also say, functions to link two worlds, or two narrative levels, rather than to give substance to either one of these levels. Simply speaking, present tense will present Lena's world as being simultaneous with the world of the narrator's speech act, and past tense or future tense will place her world at a distance from the narrator's speech act, either backwards or forwards in time.

Let us turn to the first sentence of *Light in August* now, and consider it in more detail:
Sitting beside the road, watching the wagon mount the hill toward her, Lena thinks, 'I have come from Alabama: a fur piece.'

---

88 From the narrator's point of view, of course, it may well be mimetic; in other words, the narrator may 'imitate,' in words, a situation that, to him, really exists, about which he may not be completely correct or knowledgeable, as is the case in *Light in August*, and from which he must select certain aspects and leave out others. (cf. Doležel's 'pseudomimesis' 1988:480).

89 This world does, of course, imitate the real world to a greater or lesser degree. W.F. Harvey, for instance, speaks of 'the *angle* of mimesis' (1965:16), presenting a scale that indicates how closely a certain literary work resembles life. The angle of mimesis of *Light in August* would be relatively 'narrow,' then, as compared to *As I Lay Dying*, because it follows more closely the laws of biological 'reality.' The angle of mimesis, however, can never be 0 degrees.

The apophantic content of this sentence is made up of the following propositions, facts or primitive states of affairs: <Lena sit beside road>, <Lena watch wagon>, <wagon mount hill toward Lena>, <Lena think *I have come from Alabama: a fur piece*>. It includes as well the existential presuppositions <Lena exist>, <road exist>, <wagon exist>, and the inferences <Lena female>, <Lena human>.

Together these propositions, with their basic presuppositions and inferences (logic and pragmatic), form the creative stratum of the narrator's language; they are the 'facts' of the story-world.[90] Notice that the narrator's representation of Lena's thought is also part of the apophantic content of his utterance. The narrator, here, creates a world in which it must be taken as a fact that the person Lena really entertains this thought. In other words, the thought is authentic.[91] The thought itself is presented as if it were a sentence that Lena (silently) speaks to herself. The narrator's representation of this sentence, however, is not a sentence proper, but a pseudo-sentence, an object that represents the thought that Lena entertains.

The virtue of such a pseudo-sentence is, as Martínez-Bonati puts it, 'to make present an authentic sentence from *another* communicative situation (whether real or merely imaginary)' (1981:79). In other words, the sentence has transmigrated from one world (that of Lena, in which it is an instance of her verbal behavior), to another world (that of the narrator's verbal behavior, in which it is an object representing Lena's verbal behavior, and in which it also has other implications). The sentence that Lena (silently) speaks to herself, then, is one object among many in the world that the narrator creates. Even if this sentence is fiction to the reader, or to the narratee, it must be considered authentic or 'true' for the story to move ahead. It does not, however, have to contain 'the truth.'[92]

We have seen, then, that an external narrator normally receives a form of elementary credence. Yet he might, for instance, present contradictory propositions or false logical deductions (in realistic stories these include violations of biological reality, among which are obvious shifts in chronology and geography; cf. Moore 1989). This would be the case, for instance, if Faulkner's narrator in *Light in August* had started his story in the following way:

Sitting beside the road, watching the wagon mount the hill toward her, Lena

---

90 John Woods calls these fictional propositions 'bet-sensitive.' 'We may classify a sentence containing empty singular terms as bet-sensitive,' he argues, 'if a bet, that so-and-so did such and such, can be won or lost according as the sentence "so-and-so did such and such" or a contrary of it is rightly assented to, yet not lost even given that "so-and-so does not exist" is rightly assented to' (1974:13). If I say, for instance, that Lena walks from Alabama to Jefferson and you say she takes the train, you are wrong and I am right; in other words, it is possible to bet on how Lena came to Jefferson.

91 As Dorrit Cohn puts it, 'just as dialogues create the illusion that they render what characters "really say" to each other, monologues create the illusion that they render what a character "really thinks" to himself.' This rule, she argues, 'is most convincingly proved by its exceptions. Certain mental quotations are introduced by warnings that they are to be understood not as literal reproductions' (1983:76). Such 'unreal' or 'anti'-monologues are common in *Light in August*, for instance: 'If the child had been older he would perhaps have thought...'; 'With more vocabulary but no more age he might have thought...' (152). Gene Moore speaks of '"imaginary" direct discourse (or perhaps *unheimliche Rede*?), which is formally indistinguishable from direct quotation in all respects except that the quoted statement is explicitly marked with *as-if*, as hypothetical, speculative, or imaginary' (1989:18).

92 Likewise in *Absalom, Absalom!*, as we shall see, it is true that Thomas Sutpen says 'Her mother had black blood,' but it is not certain that she did; the sentence is 'authentic,' as it is presented by the external narrator, but it does not necessarily convey 'the truth.'

thinks, no longer alive, 'I have come from Alabama; a fur piece.' If such contradictions were present, it would be difficult for the narratee, and with him for the reader, to picture the world that is created. As Martínez-Bonati puts it, 'the imaginary effort of the reader to constitute the pertinent feature of the narrated world would collapse' (1981:106). The reader cannot accept both propositions—< Lena think > and < Lena not alive >—at the same time, because the presupposition of the first one, < Lena alive >, is cancelled by the second one.

Even in such a case, however, the narrator would not necessarily lose his credibility if it were possible to consider his stance to be figurative or ironic (Lena's narration would resemble that of Addie Bundren in *As I Lay Dying*, who also thinks after she has presumably died already). A simple but instructive example can be found in Chapter XV of *Light in August*. All through the list of the collective activities of the people of Jefferson, we find inconsistencies: a town cannot wonder, speculate, forget, condone, or blind its eye. No town can say 'they are crazy.' In other words, the narrator, here, presents a quote that cannot possibly be authentic or 'true.' This, however, will not make him unreliable, because to the reader it is clear that he is speaking figuratively. Only when a metaphorical reading is impossible as well (but when can that be?), will the narrator lose his credibility. Only then would the questioned sentences fail to create a world at all, so that, as Martínez-Bonati puts it, 'attention would fall back on the speaker and his state of mind' exclusively (1981:106). The reader must now assume the questioning stance of the narratee, and the story is no longer about the embedded world of Lena, but about the narrator's imaginings or hallucinations. In that case, however, the narrator is no longer an extradiegetic one.

Summarizing, the narrator is conventionally considered reliable with respect to the 'facts' of the story-world that he presents, or the apophantic content of his discourse. The reader who judges the narrator's ability to speak 'the truth' shares the point of view of an 'ideal' addressee who exists on the same narrative level as this narrator, which makes possible the unfolding of the story. Without a basic trust in those elements of a story that can be captured in logical formulas—its 'bare' propositions—there *is* no ongoing narrative. Thus, only in those cases in which contradictions cannot be resolved as figures of speech (because the text's predominant mode is literal?) does the narrator's authoritativeness with regard to the 'facts' of the story-world become questionable. However, authoritativeness is not, as we have seen, the only factor used to determine credibility. Apart from the apophantic content of his message—the 'facts' of the story-world—a narrator also conveys non-apophantic elements: whether personal opinions, judgments or generalizations.

The Non-Apophantic Content of Sentences
The non-apophantic features of a narrator's text include special lexical choices, generalizations and abstractions, modals, deictics and phatic expressions, as well as his use of thematization, which are not transparent like the 'creative stratum' of his discourse but remain visible as language. These elements, which are present to a smaller or larger degree in all texts, evoke the mind through which the world is seen. They suggest the personal presence of a speaker, whose value schemes will be judged in terms of those of his listener. Thus they may decrease or increase his credibility. To give a simple example, the sentence *potatoes are tasty* or *tomatoes are disgusting* will be considered

(more or less) 'true' by someone who values these foods (more or less) in the same way as the speaker.

Through the non-apophantic content of his discourse, one could say, the narrator posits his own subjectivity, or 'creates' himself as an individual with specific personal views concerning the world he presents. Even if the narrator's propositions are consistent, and have to be taken as 'facts,' his way of putting them may raise doubts in his listener's mind. Related information will then be viewed with suspicion, accepted with reservations, or held in abeyance—in a 'pending file' (Werth 1984:54,72)—awaiting further evidence. To return, for a moment, to the example of Paul Auster's 'City of Glass': that the character Quinn exists belongs to the necessary 'facts' of the world created by the narrator; that the listener need not know anything about this Quinn, however, belongs to the personal opinions of the narrator.

Opinions, strictly speaking, lie outside the realm of 'fact'; they are not capable of being true or false. Faulkner's work makes clear again and again that even opinions shared by many others are not 'the truth,' as my discussion of the personality of Joe Christmas will show.[93]

The Speaking Character

In the previous section I have discussed the power of the narrator to present the story-world, and the authoritativeness that this implies. The same power, however, is not possessed by the speaking character 'inside' the story. As Martínez-Bonati puts it: 'For the fundamental understanding of all narration, the requirement is that the mimetic sentences of the narrator, but not those of the character, be accepted as true' (1981:31). The world in which the character lives has been created for him by a narrator. It is clear that this forms a big difference with the narrator's freedom to create a world. Any other world the character might create for himself cannot be *the* world of the story. Character-speakers have, in Doležel's terms, a 'lower degree of authentication authority' (1988:490) than narrators. A character, even if his story is consistent, can only create the story-world as long as the narrator does not interfere. As soon as this happens, the character shows the limitations or idiosyncrasies of his own inner world. Thus, the world created by a character, no matter how consistent, may at any time be overruled by the narrator, and this applies to the character's quotes of other speakers' words as well. The delegation of basic narration to a character can therefore only occur in the absence of the narrator's text. A first-person novel, such as *The Sound and the Fury* and *As I Lay Dying*, must thus be understood as starting with implicit quotation marks: a trace of the presence of a narrator who introduces the character's story.[94]

The context in which the character exists, then, determines his reliability. If the context with all its ramifications contradicts him, he reveals himself as unreliable; if the context supports the character, he will appear reliable for the time being. The world of the unreliable speaking character, then, does not contrast with the norms and values

---

93 Faulkner's work challenges 'the notion of consensus.' As Linda Hutcheon explains this challenge in postmodern terms: 'Whatever narratives or systems that once allowed us to think we could unproblematically and universally define public agreement have now been questioned by the acknowledgement of differences.' The result is, she argues, that consensus 'becomes the illusion of consensus' (1990:7).
94 Compare for instance Faulkner's last novel *The Reivers*, which starts with the attributive clause 'Grandfather said:...,' after which first-person narration continues throughout the text.

of the narrator, with those of the implied author, or with those of the work itself, as critics have argued, but with his own context: the apophantic content of the narrator's message, that is, the 'bare' propositions that create the facts of the story-world. Irony will occur if the narrator has created a world containing certain 'truths' that the unreliable character does not speak, obviously because he does not know them. What he thinks is the case, then, contrasts with what the narrator has conveyed about the story-world: the world the other characters recognize as *the* world. Speaking characters are often not unreliable so much as limited, as was the case with Benjy Compson in *The Sound and the Fury*. In other instances, the character is unreliable because he is a liar; he knows 'the truth' about the story-world that the narrator has created, but refuses to speak it. Sometimes the character is both limited and deceitful.

Thus, if the assertions of a character contradict those of the (extradiegetic) narrator, the character is always the one who is in error. Whether this private 'other world' of the speaking character is in itself consistent or not, the attention is always drawn away from it towards the state of mind of this character.

Narrative Complexity in *Light in August*

The basic narration in *Light in August* rests with a narrator who stays outside the story. Sometimes this narrator seems to disappear almost completely from the narrative, virtually leaving only the apophantic content of his message, and thereby making the reader feel as though he has, as François Pitavy puts it, 'apprehended *immediately* the objects or actions described or reported' (1982:180). In such episodes, one finds short sentences, verbs that describe the presented actions in a direct and exact way, neutral attributing clauses, or none at all, to introduce quotes, and very few adverbs and adjectives, for instance:

> McEachern was waiting, holding the strap. 'Put it down,' he said. The boy laid the book on the floor. 'Not there,' McEachern said, without heat. 'You would believe that a stable floor, the stamping place of beasts, is the proper place for the word of God. But I'll learn you that, too.' He took up the book himself and laid it on a ledge. 'Take down your pants,' he said. 'We'll not soil them.'
> (164)

Except for the adverbial phrase 'without heat,' the episode is narrated in an objective way. Exactly because of its directness and concentration, it is also very compelling. A. Alvarez, in the context of his own work on 'Auschwitz stories,' speaks of a 'curt' and 'icy' style, 'stripped of feeling as of ornament, in which the monstrous lunacies of life' are 'allowed to speak for themselves, without comment and therefore without disguise' (1973:242). Such episodes can be panoramic or focus on one character exclusively:

> He got back into bed and lay again on his back, his eyes wide and still upon the ceiling. He could see her motionless shadow, shapeless, a little hunched. Then it went away. He did not look, but he could hear her kneel in the corner, gathering the broken dishes back into the tray. Then she left the room. It was quite still then.
> (170)

When the narrator is more clearly present in the text, he may still follow closely one of the characters. Often the lexical choices that the narrator conveys can to a large extent be understood as typical of the character, for instance Hightower's 'faintly overbearing note of levity and warmth' in the sentence: 'Sometimes it would seem to Hightower that he would actually hale Byron into the house by a judicious application of pure breath, as though Byron wore a sail' (342f.).

Of course such lexical choices are a matter of *voice*. They are not necessarily in the character's own idiom, but may show an 'amplification,' or 'augmentation,' of the character's own voice (Pitavy 1982:173). The following episode, for instance, shows this in a movement 'upwards' towards consciousness, as Joe Christmas recovers from the beatings he has received:

> He was in the hall without having remembered passing through the door, and he found himself in another bedroom while he still hoped perhaps not believed that he was moving toward the front door. It was small too. Yet it still seemed to be filled with the presence of the blonde woman, its very cramped harsh walls bulged outward with that militant and diamondsurfaced respectability... Then the whiskey began to burn in him and he began to shake his head slowly from side to side, while thinking became one with the slow, hot coiling and recoiling of his entrails: 'I got to get out of here.' (244f.)

The excerpt begins with a sentence in which the narrator presents Christmas's physical and emotional behavior, after which it turns, without transition, not to the narrator's judgment of the room's atmosphere, nor to an external description by the narrator of Christmas's thoughts, but to the actual awareness of Christmas's mind, which precedes his conscious thought 'I got to get out of here.'

There obviously is help from the narrator here, but what is conveyed is ultimately the mental activity of Joe Christmas. As Faulkner himself justified this: 'it is a writer's privilege to put into the mouths of his characters better speech than they would have been capable of, but only for the purpose of permitting and helping the character to justify himself or what he believed himself to be.' Throughout large portions of the text, then, the distinctions between the narrator's voice and that of the character are blurred. Together they form one authentic, or 'true,' 'heightened voice': defined by Sister Kirsten Morrison as 'a voice that is rooted in the mind of the character, a voice that issues from that mind yet is not bound by the limits of intelligence and sensibility which that mind has by nature, a voice heightened to perception and articulation of which the mind itself is incapable' (1982:150).[95] This heightened voice makes it possible to convey the character's mental activity in an authentic way and at the same time reveal his inability in the field of communication.

Heightened Voice
Benjy's voice in *The Sound and the Fury*, the voice of a dumb 'idiot,' is perhaps the best and most elaborate example of heightened voice, but equally interesting examples are Vardaman's and Darl's verbal behavior in *As I Lay Dying*. Sister Kirstin Morrison, discussing Addie Bundren, speaks of 'that innermost center of her which exists free of

---

95 Toolan speaks of 'substitutionary speech,' and distinguishes also 'substitutionary perception' and 'substitutionary cognition' (1990:110ff.; cf. Fehr 1938).

body, that speaks expressing the beliefs and motives which constituted her person yet which she could never have clearly articulated or consciously perceived' (1982:150). In these examples, the heightened voice is of the autonomous monologue type, but heightened voice is also found in episodes of narrated monologue (free indirect discourse). In this way, 'a mind's vague ruminations,' as Dorrit Cohn calls them, may reach 'conceptual expression' (1983:104). Such episodes may be understood to convey the emerging into consciousness of preconscious material that was suspended 'on the threshold of verbalization' (Cohn 1983:103). Thus it often has the exclamation-like quality of discovery, and may be followed by conscious verbal behavior expressing the same discovery, as in the following passage:

> It was the woman: that soft kindness which he believed himself doomed to be forever victim of and which he hated worse than he did the hard and ruthless justice of men. 'She is trying to make me cry,' he thought, lying cold and rigid in his bed
> (185)

Narration, in such a passage, is what Cohn calls 'a kind of mask, from behind which sounds the voice of a figural mind,' bearing 'the stamp of characteristical limitations and distortions' (1983:102). It is, after all, not the narrator who believes 'it was the woman,' but Joe Christmas, whose emerging consciousness reveals his characteristically distorted views and his fear of women. Heightened voice, however, is not the same as narrated monologue. It can be found in psychonarration as well.

While narrated monologue is always difficult to distinguish from figural narration (cf. Cohn 1983:106), psychonarration normally shows itself clearly through the mental verbs in the attributing clauses, with which the narrator not only indicates the specific mental activity of the character but may also give information as to the 'truth' of the reported mental representations. As we have seen in Chapter 1, the attributive verb changes its meaning from perception verb to cognition verb when moving from the small-clause via the to-infinitive and how-clause to the that-clause, or to put it differently: the perception aspect of the activity gradually decreases in favor of the cognition aspect, showing that the classifications *cognition* and *perception*, also, are prototype categories with fuzzy boundaries and overlap. It would therefore be a 'futile exercise,' to use Cohn's words, to 'delimit psycho-narration sharply from the narration of sensations that impinge on a character's mind, from within or from without' (1983:49). Mental activity arises from both external and internal stimuli, and normally involve both perception and cognition. As Rudolf Arnheim has pointed out:

> the cognitive operations called thinking are not the privilege of mental processes above and beyond perception, but the essential ingredients of perception itself. I am referring to such operations as exploration, selection, grasping of essentials, simplification, abstraction, analysis and synthesis, completion, correction, comparison, problemsolving, as well as combining, separating, putting in context. These operations are not the prerogative of any one mental function; they are the manner in which the minds of both man and animal treat cognitive material at any level.
> (1954:13; quoted in Kinney 1978:17)

The mental verbs, however, do not always appear in psychonarration. Especially those that focus on external stimuli such as seeing and hearing are often left out, as in:

> In his underclothes and barefoot he left the cabin. [He saw that] it was a
> little lighter outdoors... Ahead, rising from out a close mass of trees, he
> could see one chimney and one gable of the house. [He noticed that] the
> house itself was invisible and dark.
> (116)

What Cohn calls 'figural narration,' conveying what the character sees or hears without stating this explicitly by means of an attributive clause such as *Christmas saw that*, is in fact a form of psychonarration. Thus, the distinction between pure narration and psychonarration is effectively blurred, just like the distinction between pure narration and narrated monologue. Heightened voice is found, then, in psychonarration, narrated monologue and internal monologue, but it is also encountered, in Faulkner's work, as episodes in italics that 'quote' the subject's most hidden 'raw' mental representations in a direct, if 'amplified,' way. An example that shows beautifully the movements of the human mind that can be expressed this way is found in the following excerpt:

> Joe thanked him. Then he could look at the calf and say, aloud: 'That
> belongs to me.' Then he looked at it, and it was again too fast and too
> complete to be thinking: *That is not a gift. It is not even a promise: it is a*
> *threat* thinking, 'I didn't ask for it. He gave it to me. I didn't ask for it'
> believing *God knows, I have earned it*
> (200)

Heightened voice is authentic, or 'true,' in that it presents the character's mind as it 'really' works. But it does not necessarily convey 'the truth,' in the sense that such episodes do not necessarily 'have the narrator's approval,' as André Bleikasten has suggested (1987:95). They do, however, have his sympathy or understanding. The narrator is involved, but he does not necessarily condone.[96]

Sometimes, however, the narrator goes further, and shows his compassion or sympathy more explicitly, for instance when he emphasizes Christmas's tender age: 'He was *just* eight then' (171; my emphasis). Sometimes he also indicates his agreement, as when he uses the attributing verb *know*: 'It was only as he put his hand on the door that he became aware of complete silence beyond it, a silence which he at eighteen *knew* that it would take more than one person to make' (235; my emphasis). There are other cases in which the narrator goes beyond the heightened voices that he presents, for instance when he conveys information that cannot be in the conscious or unconscious mind of any of the characters present at that specific point in the story:

> All the men in the village worked in the mill or for it. It was cutting pine.
> It had been there seven years and in seven years more it would destroy all
> the timber within its reach.
> (4)
> he [Christmas] was too young yet to escape from the world of women for
> that brief respite before he escaped back into it to remain until the hour of
> his death.
> (133)

---

96 This is, in fact, the same kind of mistake that is made by readers who believe that the characters' words have the author's approval, and accuse Faulkner of the racism and misogyny that his characters often show. (cf. Joyce Carol Oates 1983).

Although in such cases the narrator seems omniscient in that he can look into the past as well as the future, as his modal adverbs show he does not claim unlimited authority on all the subjects that he himself considers worthy of mentioning: 'He would not look up then. He would not move, *apparently* arrested and held immobile by a single word' (123; my emphasis); '*Perhaps* he thought of that other window which he had used to use and of the rope upon which he had had to rely; *perhaps not*' (253). In the first example the narrator limits himself to an exclusively external point of view, such as an onlooking character might have: an 'invisible eyewitness' (Lanser 1981:266); in the second example he bases his expectation on his own prior knowledge of the character.

The Narrator's Reliability
If a narrator's knowledge is limited, he does not necessarily lose his reliability. To the contrary, the careful way in which this narrator consciously limits his own authority on the relevant issues rather seems to increase it. As we already saw, much of his text is objective in that through the apophantic content of its propositions it presents the characters, including their mental activity, as 'objects' in the story-world.

Yet, in a few places the narrator reverts to generalizations that may hold implications with regard to specific instances in the text, such as: 'now and then a negro nurse-maid with her white charges would loiter there and spell them [the words on Hightower's sign board] aloud *with that vacuous idiocy of her idle and illiterate kind*' (62f.; my emphasis). In the holograph manuscript this sentence even reads 'with that ~~dull~~ stupid and vacuous idiocy of her idle and illiterate *race*' (Ms. 24; my emphasis; 'dull' crossed out by Faulkner). In the context of the plot of *Light in August*, this passage may be very important. Close reading of the paragraph in which the quoted sentence occurs makes it likely that it presents the heightened voice of one of the characters, most likely that of Gail Hightower. Yet, if this part of the text were to present the narrator's generalized opinion of blacks, the reader might well doubt his ability to present Joe Christmas's actions objectively.[97] The narrator, in such a case, is so much a part of the community he presents that he may not only fail to explore and analyze its ideology, but may even fail to present its objects correctly. The sensitive reader, in any case, may well be influenced by this possibility, depending on his own world-view.[98]

---

97 The narrator's ideology, or in Susan Sniader Lanser's terms, the 'external ideology' that 'serves to comment on, symbolize or illustrate an internal element of the story,' and the 'internal ideology' that 'emerges more organically from the textual actions themselves' (1981:218), would to a large extent fall together. Lanser introduces the 'axis of coincidence,' which 'measures the relation between... the various systems of norms... belonging to the communicators implied in and by the work.' On this axis, she argues, 'various degrees of ambivalence and questioning as well as opposition can be marked' (1981:218f.).

98 Ultimately, all the speakers in *Light in August* who discuss the position of blacks in relation to whites or the relation of whites in relation to blacks, including the narrator and also Christmas himself, do so from their own positions as whites and from the context in which their own sense of identity was formed. This, of course, presents a '*strange loop*' similar to the one that occurs if one tries to judge one's own reliability or one's own sanity (cf. Hofstadter 1980:696). It also applies to the author himself. Faulkner has often been accused of misrepresenting blacks and their existence. However, as Thadious Davis puts it, he 'never knew or wrote about "black" people as we today know and understand the term. He wrote about "The Negro," the white man's own creation,' and she adds: 'the reiteration of this fact is one of the simplest ways of defining the social and cultural concerns reflected in Faulkner's world' (1983:2). To use Jerome Bruner's words: Faulkner's work presents 'a "right version" of a possible world for his time and place,' depending

To conclude: I have shown how Morrison's concept of *heightened voice* is a useful one with which to describe and understand Faulkner's concentration on voice in *Light in August*. This heightened voice can be found in all sorts of narration, whether it should formally be called figural narration, psychonarration, narrated monologue, or quoted monologue using italics. In all these instances the narrator does not *talk about* Joe Christmas's conceptualizations, but conveys them in a direct, if 'heightened,' way. Since so much of the text consists of this heightened voice of the character, voice is a most fruitful route to characterization, as it was in *The Sound and the Fury* and *As I Lay Dying*. In this third-person novel, voice creates an even more intricate and expansive inside view of the way in which fictive persons structure their worlds, thus forming a window into the individual as well as the collective mind.

Internal voices

But so often the practiced and chronic liar deceives only himself; it is the man who all his life has been selfconvicted of veracity whose lies find quickest credence.

In this section, I shall examine the voices of the most important intradiegetic speakers (speaking characters) in *Light in August* chapter by chapter and examine their reliability as well as the credence they receive from others.

In the first chapter, the extradiegetic narrator concentrates on young Lena Grove's progress on foot towards Jefferson, where she hopes to find Lucas Burch, the father of her unborn child. The narrator conveys the world as she experiences it, but he relies especially on quoted monologue and dialogue. He records what she says, for instance: 'I dont reckon I need any promise from Lucas. It just happened unfortunate so, that he had to go away' (19); he records what she thinks, for instance: 'And then he will see me and he will be excited' (9); and he indicates in italics a kind of non-analytic associative movement of mind, for instance: *Then it will be as if I were riding for a half mile before I even got into the wagon* (8). These last 'raw,' or unreflected, mental representations, going 'idle and swift and smooth,' are 'filled with nameless kind faces and voices' (9), because Lena's naive, trusting nature tends to disarm the stern farmers that she meets on her way. Only on a few occasions does the narrator distance himself from Lena, to tell something that is not in Lena's mind, for instance when he mentions that she is telling 'more than she knows she is telling.'

Although there is no reason to doubt the authenticity of these quotations, one cannot take for granted that they contain 'the truth.' Lena's faith in Lucas Burch is clear from the beginning, for instance from the words she speaks to her brother after the sudden disappearance of her lover: 'He's going to send for me. He said he would send for me' (6), but her views clash with the narrator, who in a paragraph that voices the brother's views, refers to Lucas Burch as one of those 'sawdust Casanovas' (6). As we have seen, when the views of a character clash with those of the narrator, the

---

for its development on 'the destruction of earlier forms of reticence' (1986:146). As Walker Percy puts it, in the introduction to his uncle W.A. Percy's *Lanterns on the Levee*, 'it is hardly proper to judge a man's views of the issues of his day by the ideological fashions of another age' (1990:xii).

character is conventionally the one in error.[99] When the views of one character clash with those of another, it may be difficult to know which is the more 'truthful.' Lena, in any case, is not a speaker with high credibility in the novel. She is immediately identified as a stranger: '"She aint come from nowhere close," Armstid said. "She's hitting that lick like she's been at it for a right smart while and had a right smart piece to go yet"' (10), which in itself decreases her credibility to the local farmers.

Lena's obvious naiveté is another reason for the farmers to doubt her. Her world-view is questioned by many of them, for instance by Mrs. Armstid:

And you believe that he will be there when you get there. Granted that he ever was there at all. That he will hear you are in the same town with him, and still be there when the sun sets.

(22)

It is clear that Lena's views are not trusted by the other characters, who consider her vanished lover 'a scoundrel who deserted her in trouble,' and who believe 'that she will never see [him] again, save his coattails perhaps already boardflat with running' (28). But her simple trusting nature—'I reckon a family ought to all be together when a chap comes. Specially the first one. I reckon the Lord will see to that' (23)—nevertheless elicits admiration. She even receives some sort of 'deeper,' more elementary credence from the farmer Armstid that, to him, overcomes her unreliability: 'I reckon she knows more than even Martha does, like when she told Martha last night about how the Lord will see that what is right will get done' (27). The end of her story will prove Lena right.

In Chapter II, the narrator shifts his focus from Lena Grove to Byron Bunch, one of the workers at the planing mill where Lena hopes to find the father of her unborn child. The similarity of their last names—Bunch and Burch—has led to the mix-up between the two men that has directed Lena to Jefferson, and that involves Bunch in her search. The chapter basically summarizes Bunch's views of the arrival of two fellow workers at the mill: a certain Joe Christmas, three years earlier, and a certain Joe Brown six months earlier. This Joe Brown, as Bunch soon understands, is really the missing father-to-be Lucas Burch. In this chapter the narrator relies heavily on psychonarration. With his choice of the attributing clause at the beginning of the chapter 'Byron Bunch *knows* this' (33; my emphasis), the narrator seems to indicate agreement. In other words, he seems to vouch for the 'truth' of the reported views. One cannot be sure, of course, how far the influence of the verb of knowledge stretches; Bunch also merely 'believes' or 'thinks' things at times. But his privileged position is reinstated throughout the chapter, for instance: 'And then Byron *knew*. He *knew* then why the other worked in the Sunday clothes... He *knew* as well as if the man had told him' (37).

While the narrator thus chooses explicitly to endorse the views of Byron Bunch, whom he also consistently calls by his first name, he does not do the same for the other speakers in this chapter, to whom he refers as 'the men,' 'the others,' 'one,' or 'the

99 Stephen Meats, in his 'The Chronology of *Light in August*,' refers to this when he writes: 'Byron Bunch reports that Brown arrived at 8:00 P.M. Because the 9:00 time is in an omniscient passage [better called narrator-text because the narrator is not omniscient, as he himself states many times], I will assume it to be correct' (1982:230).

first ones.' The effect is that the narrator brings to life a world in which Bunch, the only one who 'knows,' is isolated from the anonymous group of workers whose discourse does not necessarily contain reliable information. Bunch's isolated position is clear from the reactions of the other workers as well. He has been at the mill for seven years, but remained 'a man of mystery among his fellow workers' (52), and although the narrator, as we just saw, vouches for the reliability of much of what he thinks, Bunch's credibility is not high: 'One or two of the others looked at Byron. They smiled a little... "I reckon Byron stays out of meanness too much himself to keep up with other folks," the other said. They looked at Byron' (46). Because Bunch is created as a privileged speaker, at least in this part of the text, his lack of credence reflects back on the reliability of 'the others'; as Bunch himself puts it: 'most of what folks tells on other folks aint true to begin with' (59).

In Chapter III the narrator again shifts focus, this time to the former minister of Jefferson, the Rev. Gail Hightower. Together with Hightower, the reader is made to look out of the window of the house in which this minister has become totally estranged from society after the death of his wife. Hightower, who as a minister should have had high authority, is now a stranger with an unappealing appearance, a 'fifty-year-old outcast who has been denied by his church' (52). This episode, consisting of a few pages at the beginning and the end of the chapter, frames in typically Faulknerian images of stasis and suspension a different section, in which the narrator follows Bunch's memories, presumably as he walks towards Hightower's house to tell him about his feelings for Lena. These memories do not, for the most part, concern Bunch's personal experience, but concentrate on the stories the townspeople have told him earlier about the tragedy that caused Hightower's retreat from society.

In his discussion of the narrative complexity of *Light in August*, Hugh Holman expresses the view that Bunch 'is himself the retrospective narrator for a good deal of Hightower's early story' (1958:156). Yet, Bunch's thoughts and memories are not narrated directly by himself, but instead through the mediation of the extradiegetic narrator. These memories concern almost nothing but gossip and rumors, and gossip about rumors:

> they told Byron how the young minister was still excited even after six
> months, still talking about the Civil War and his grandfather, a cavalryman
> (65)
> They told Byron how he seemed to talk that way in the pulpit too, wild too
> in the pulpit, using religion as though it were a dream
> (66)
> They told him how the wife was a small, quietlooking girl who at first the
> town thought just had nothing to say for herself.
> (66)
> But the town said that if Hightower had just been a more dependable kind
> of man, the kind of man a minister should be... she would have been all
> right too.
> (66)
> And they told Byron how after about a year in Jefferson, the wife began to
> wear that frozen look on her face
> (67)

they told Byron how she stood there, in the aisle now, shrieking and
shaking her hands at the pulpit
(69)
they told Byron... how the wife was hardly cold in the shameful grave
before the whispering began. About how he had made his wife go bad and
commit suicide because he was not a natural husband
(76)

This second- and third-hand information dates from more than twenty-five years
earlier, and it has been in Bunch's memory for close to seven years. Perhaps because
he not only understands man's vulnerability to rumors but also recognizes his own
vulnerability—'I reckon I aint no better than nobody else' (59)—Bunch tries to refrain
from narrating these stories as if they were 'the truth.' In any case, neither Bunch
himself nor the extradiegetic narrator endorses these views of Hightower's tragedy.

Gossip and Rumors

To explain the power of gossip and rumors, let us turn for a moment to the findings
of social psychologists on these subjects. As I have argued before, an event can never
be perceived exactly as it is; the mental representation that the mind makes of it is
always a personal one, because the individual fits the event into a personal worldview.
This personal representation, moreover, does not stay constant throughout the years,
among other things because the unconscious workings of the mind tend to delete or
sharpen those aspects that are potentially harmful to the individual. Generally speaking,
the conceptualization of the event evolves with the individual worldview as a process.
Voicing a conceptualization, in addition, always alters it, mainly because the
description of an event to others depends very much on the demands of the situation,
including in particular the demands, or the imagined demands, of an audience. What
one remembers of a much discussed event, then, is not so much the event itself as the
style and the form in which it was discussed with others.

When rumors go 'from mind to mind,' certain alterations tend to occur that turn
out to be fairly systematic. First of all, the information is leveled, that is, details that
are ambiguous or difficult to place are left out, whereby the story becomes easier to
understand; secondly, the information is sharpened, or focused more directly on a few
important details; and thirdly, the presuppositions already existing in the listener's mind
(frame knowledge) are assimilated, so that they form part of the story when it is retold.
To gain more insight into this last aspect, the social psychologists Allport and Postman
conducted a startling experiment in which groups of people were made to spread a
story among themselves about a white man threatening fellow travellers on the subway
with a razor. In over half of the groups that formed 'gossip chains,' the razor moved,
in the course of the retelling, from the hand of the white man to the hand of a black
fellow traveller. As the investigators argued, this can be seen as a 'clear instance of
assimilation to stereotyped expectancy. Black men are "supposed" to carry razors,
white men not' (1958:54ff.; quoted in Berkowitz 1980:162f.).[100] Such stereotyped

---

100 Rumors, as Allport found out, can even be based on hallucinations that incorporate such frame
'knowledge.' 'Police,' he writes, 'received a telephone report from a woman who claimed to have witnessed
with her own eyes the killing of a white man by a mob of Negroes. When the squad car reached the scene

expectancy clearly shows the dangers of conceptual frames; we shall see that it plays a large role in *Light in August*, and, curiously enough, in its critical reception as well.

Many investigators have tried to explain the spreading of rumors, and several theories have been proposed. Most stress the importance of ambiguity. If an event is both highly important and ambiguous, people will find it hard to decide what their reaction should be. Dissonance theory, with its emphasis on conflicting concept-ualizations, can explain why people tend to streamline their versions of the event, spread their stories to find confirmation for their own views, selectively attend to any new information, and ignore that which opposes these views. As Berkowitz puts it, 'a person's motivation to communicate about some important matter is directly related to the intensity of the cognitive conflict within him' (1980:166). These rumors will be soothing, not only to the speaker but to others as well, because they offer explanations, even if they are not correct. Often, however, rumors are disruptive rather than soothing. Such rumors, it was found, are usually not spread by those who are closely involved in the event but by those who follow it from some distance. This may in part be understood as a form of 'ego-enhancing,' as someone with interesting information will always be valued by others because people enjoy, as Faulkner calls it in *Light in August*, an 'emotional barbecue' (317). In addition, Leon Festinger (1957) has suggested that people at some distance from an upsetting event will often experience strong fears as they unconsciously imagine themselves in a similar situation. Yet they sense at the same time that there is not enough reason for this emotion. Instead of recognizing their own empathy, they may well react by exaggerating the impact or falsifying the nature of the event that caused the fear, in order to justify their reactions.

In Chapter IV, the extradiegetic narrator summarizes and explains what Byron Bunch tells Hightower about the responsibilities he feels towards Lena. He, 'having been chosen by circumstance to represent Jefferson to her... did not hope nor intend to avoid that responsibility' (91). The chapter concentrates on Bunch, 'talking quietly, thinking, remembering' (90), his story filled with 'voices, the hushed tense voices about the town' (92). The emphasis, throughout, is on the question of reliability and credibility, and the relationship between the two, as where Bunch has to lie to his landlady:

> He looked straight into cold, already disbelieving eyes, watching her in turn trying to read his own, believing that she read what was there instead of what she believed was there. They say that it is the practiced liar who can deceive. But so often the practiced and chronic liar deceives only himself; it is the man who all his life has been selfconvicted of veracity whose lies find quickest credence.
> (93)

Bunch's involvement with Lena clearly changes his status as speaker. Since he has fallen in love with her, his reliability has become questionable.

Most of the information that is conveyed through Byron's consciousness is con-cerned with the story of Joanna Burden's murder and with the disappearance of Joe Christmas. The information on which he bases his story may well be at least third-

the police found a group of girls playing hopscotch and could find no trace of violence nor any support for the woman's story. Other citizens, as excited as she, no doubt believed the tale and spread it' (1979:64).

hand, because Bunch was with Lena at the boarding house 'at the very time when it was all coming out down town at the sheriff's office, at the very time when Brown was telling it all; about him and Christmas' (95). Even the people from whom Bunch must have received his information were not really present; they had to remain outside the sheriff's office because the officials 'had locked the door,' leaving the windows 'lined with folks' faces against the glass' (106). Thus, Bunch's quotations of Joe Brown's crucial words—'I'm talking about Christmas... The man that killed that white woman... He's got nigger blood in him' (107f.)—may not be authentic, or 'true,' let alone that one can automatically assume that they contain 'the truth' about Christmas. It is important to remember, at this point, that although quotations made by the extradiegetic narrator are normally authentic, quotations made by a speaking character need not be. In *Light in August*, then, where so much of the information is based only on rumors, all quotations made by speaking characters should be viewed critically.

In contrast to the previous chapters of the novel, in which nothing is certain, Chapter V presents Christmas's own point of view under the direct authority of the external narrator. This chapter consists of a meticulous report of Christmas's last day in Jefferson, his motions, speech, and different levels of thought. The same directness that characterizes this last chapter is also found in Chapters VI through XII, which present Joe Christmas's life from his first memories in the orphanage at the age of five up through his last visit with Joanna Burden and his flight from Jefferson. Many of these chapters start with an allusion to the deepest levels of memory. These chapters, to be discussed in detail in the next section, are of ultimate importance for the exploration of Christmas's personality. Here it becomes clear, for instance, that the janitor and the dietician at the orphanage, the two people at the root of the rumors that Christmas is a black man, are both insane, with 'mad eyes looking into mad eyes, mad voice talking to mad voice as calm and quiet and terse as two conspirators' (140).

In Chapter XIII, the story has shifted again to the present, and with that, to the rumors that are spreading through town. This time, they are not those of long ago, remembered by Bunch, but those that started 'within five minutes' after the fire was discovered. Before Joe Brown has told his story to the sheriff, 'the casual Yankees and the poor whites and even the southerners who had lived for a while in the north' already 'believed aloud that it was an anonymous negro crime committed not by a negro but by Negro' (315). This means, in a sense, that any black man will satisfy them. The story that Joe Christmas is the murderer of a white woman will be believed as soon as it is 'clear' that he is a black man. In the second part of this chapter, Byron Bunch is the main speaker, telling Hightower that he also believes the rumors. This is, at least, what his report 'I told her it was a nigger killed a white woman. I didn't lie then. I reckon I was so glad I never had to lie then' (334) indicates. But Bunch's motives, as Hightower understands them, are not unselfish. Anxious to spare Lena's feelings, he is relieved to be able to tell her that her runaway lover is not involved in any way: 'I have kept it from her that it was the man she is hunting for that told on the murderer... I have kept that from her' (334). Bunch, set on believing for Lena's sake and because of his love for her, that Joe Brown, the father of Lena's child, is not a criminal, is now too much involved to be credible to Hightower, a man sensitized by his own tragedy: '"And that," Hightower thinks, "is the first lie he ever told me. Ever told anyone, man or woman, perhaps including himself... Or maybe it is not lie yet because he does not know himself that it is so"' (336). Although Hightower's reliability may be questioned as well, he enforces the reader's impression that Bunch is normally reliable, but has now changed status.

Chapter XIV consists of the narrator's direct report of Christmas's last day in Jefferson, before he is taken prisoner. This chapter, which we shall study extensively in the following section, is as crucial as Chapters V through XII, because it offers reliable information concerning Joe Christmas's personality. In Chapter XV the attention is focused on the psychonarration of a collective consciousness: the shared mental representations of social reality. Within the first two pages (375,376) one finds:

> the town in general did not know
> as far as the town knew
> the town found
> Soon it became known
> The town looked upon them both
> The town wondered
> then it forgot to speculate
> the town learned
> it wondered about this
> then forgot it
> the town either forgot or condoned
> that which in a young man it would have crucified
> It just said, 'They are crazy'
> Or perhaps what it condoned was
> the town blinding its collective eye

In this town, Christmas—'that white nigger that did that killing up at Jefferson last week' (379)—lets himself be caught.

The largest part of Chapter XVI is concerned with the story of Christmas's family background as told by his grandparents. They are helped and supplemented by Byron Bunch, who at an earlier time heard parts of the story from the woman. The discussion concerns especially the identity of Christmas's father. 'It was a fellow with the circus' (412), Bunch says, and although Christmas's mother presumably told her father that he was 'a Mexican,' the grandfather 'knew somehow that the fellow had nigger blood' (413). The verb *know* seems to indicate that Bunch agrees. Hines, who considers the child of his daughter and this circus man a punishment 'wrought upon him' for his own sins, believes that it was the devil himself who told him Christmas 'was a nigger' (416). The old man Hines is clearly not a reliable speaker, and his quotations of Christmas's early concern with racial differences are not necessarily authentic. In any case, the external narrator's scrupulous report of the decisive moments in Christmas's early life never mentions such a concern.[101] But even if the quotes were authentic, the old

---

101 Regina Fadiman comments on omissions and inconsistencies such as these between the narrator's story and Hines's story, which have often been ascribed to careless revisions. This sounds as if Faulkner intended the narrator to mention Christmas's early concerns with race—before the incident with the dietician—but forgot to do so. Fadiman argues that 'all contradictions and inconsistencies of fact ultimately affect critical interpretations of the work.' It is like saying that 'Cezanne meant to shadow his apples with green paint but had only blue at hand. Still, the fact of the blue paint remains in the painting and it is the blue with which a critic must contend' (1975:164, note 1). Whether Faulkner failed to correct inconsistencies out of

man certainly gives far too much weight to the little boy's normal curiosity about why someone is 'a nigger,' and his question about whether God is 'a nigger.' In the meantime, Bunch's motives, and thereby his reliability, are again questioned by Hightower. As the following conversation between Hightower and Bunch shows, Bunch himself is now aware that his 'bargaining' decreases his credibility: '"Ah Byron, Byron. What a dramatist you would have made." "Or maybe you mean a drummer, a agent, a salesman," Byron says. "It's a poor thing. I know that. You dont need to tell me."' (429)

Chapters XVII and XVIII show Byron Bunch's growing awareness of the lies his love for Lena have forced him to tell: 'I must have knowed, to have done what I have done: the running and the lying and the worrying at folks' (440). Accordingly, the narrator now returns to his ostentatious support of Bunch's views: 'He *knew* now what it was that seemed to lurk clawed and waiting' (440); 'He *knew* now why he neglected to engage a doctor' (440); 'Then he *knew*' (443; my emphasis). This awareness of his own motives prompts Bunch to set things straight; he finally arranges for Lucas Burch, alias Joe Brown, to meet with Lena and the baby and then prepares to leave town. The rest of the chapter focuses on this meeting between Lena and her former lover, who shows just how unreliable he is when he says to her: 'You just leave it to me. Dont you worry none. I aint never give you no reason yet to worry, have I? Tell me that' (476). But, although the reader knows of his unreliability, Lena still gives him credence.

Chapter XIX starts again with psychonarration of social reality: with what 'the town wondered' on 'that Monday night' (489), and especially with the question of why Christmas fled to Hightower's house. Was it 'like to like' (implying that both men are homosexuals), 'sheer chance,' or 'wisdom' (489)? All these views may well be wrong. In opposition to these rumors, the narrator presents the version of Gavin Stevens, the District Attorney. Throughout his text, Stevens makes it clear that he is not telling 'the truth,' but only expressing his personal beliefs. For instance:

I think I know why it was
I believe that all she wanted was that he die 'decent'
I imagine that after thirty years
Very likely that was the first time
But of course I dont know what she told him.
(491,491,491,493,494)

Much like the narrator's text, Stevens's story shows a caution that contrasts with the rumors 'blown from mind to mind': the 'myriad voices' of the town. The modals, modal adverbs and verbs of knowledge and prediction that Stevens uses communicate his doubt to his addressee, a college friend from Harvard. But although his conceptualizations may sound hesitant, they will certainly be 'upgraded' (Werth 1981) by this addressee because Stevens is an authority on matters of crime. Stevens, in any case, knows how to combine stray observations into a 'story' and thus answers his listener's need for consistency with a forceful, coherent 'possible version' of 'the truth.' Gavin Stevens certainly is a credible speaker, even if he remains unendorsed by the narrator. The narrator's account of Christmas's death, in this chapter, includes Hightower's lie,

---

carelessness, or whether he left them or created them deliberately, as they stand they cannot fail to suggest the unreliability of Hines.

whereby his desire for 'justice' gains a victory over his general depression, his fears, and perhaps even his religion and his love of 'the truth.' His compassion, which, as Richard Chase puts it, is 'a purely naturalistic intuition of his own solidarity' with other people (1971:23), forces the ex-minister to tell a lie in the name of god, and to use the rumor that he is a homosexual in the name of 'a higher truth'; 'Men... Listen to me. He was here that night. He was with me the night of the murder. I swear to God' (512). Chapter XX continues this development in Hightower, whereby he, albeit briefly, approaches 'the truth' of his own tragic life.

Chapter XXI, finally, is recounted by a stranger, a furniture dealer from the East, who has his own motives for remembering the story of Lena and Byron's unfolding relationship and for telling it to his addressee. He found it interesting 'at the time' and 'amusing enough to repeat,' but the anecdote is meant especially to please, and perhaps excite, his wife, as they are both 'not old either' and he has 'been away from home... for more than a week' (545). That this speaker is not necessarily reliable is clear; his purpose, in any case, is not to tell 'the truth,' but to make the story 'interesting in the retelling' (545).

The Reliability of the Internal Voices
While the narrator, as we saw, often limits his information, the townspeople in their easy gossiping are by no means so careful. The carelessness with which 'the town' draws its conclusions is evident. 'The voices with no time for "perhaps,"' as Richard Godden has called them, 'will gather at the scene of the crime and in the barbershop, to tell the story of a "nigger"' (1980:245). Apart from the narrator and 'the town,' we hear many other speakers in the novel. Sometimes these speakers are engaged in discussions with other speaking characters, such as Lena and Mrs. Armstid in Chapter I, or Hightower and Byron Bunch in Chapter XVII; sometimes, they present to others or to themselves actual 'stories' with some sort of beginning, middle and end, and with stretches of deictic projection. The reliability of these speakers, however, can never be taken for granted. As we have seen, there are many reasons to suspect the 'truths' they present.

Although I agree with Harold Hungerford that 'the reliability of the narration is almost never in question,' I cannot concede that 'except for Lucas Burch, the characters of *Light in August* are truthful people' (1983:184). Not all the characters are truthful in that they intend to speak 'the truth.' As his involvement with Lena grows, Byron Bunch, for instance, shows many times that he half senses, and finally knows fully that he is not telling 'the truth.' The talk that 'went here and there about the town, dying and borning again like a wind or a fire,' also presents various versions of what happened, all perhaps equally untrue. Byron Bunch himself points to the town's habitual behavior: 'the town had had the habit of saying things... which they did not believe themselves' (80), inventing evil 'in other people's names.' Individually, people may hesitate about whether Joe Christmas is really a black man. They may call him a 'white nigger,' object that 'he dont look any more like a nigger than I do' or be 'sensitive' enough to notice that 'it was like he never knew he was a murderer, let alone a nigger too,' but nobody speaks out on his behalf, even after Percy Grimm has killed him.[102] This includes Bunch himself, who knows perfectly well that Joe Christmas 'never admitted that he killed her,' and who admits that 'all the evidence they got against him is Brown's word, which is next to none' (430).

We see, then, that the people of Jefferson are not always truthful. But even if they were truthful in the sense that they think they are telling 'the truth,' and honestly desire to tell 'the truth,' their accounts could not be presumed to contain only reliable information. If Mr. Hines, for instance, is truthful in that he believes what he presents is 'the truth,' he is nevertheless totally unreliable because he is mentally ill. Even Gavin Stevens's authoritative and careful account of Christmas's escape and death is little more than a 'silly last speech' (Jehlen 1976:91), since he seeks to determine 'which of Joe Christmas's last impulses were Caucasian and which Negroid,' and thus not only takes it for granted that Christmas's father was indeed a black man, but also implies that 'black and white are fixed physiological entities ratifying a caste system' (Godden 1980:236). This, after all, would mean that 'race itself is the problem, that one must be either black or white because these are inherently incommensurate identities' (Jehlen 1976:91), and would consequently change Christmas's tragedy from a social one into a physical one, comparable to Benjy Compson's.[103] Even if Gavin Stevens is a figure of authority in Jefferson and, as an attorney, authoritative on the subject of crime; even if he is therefore credible perhaps, and even if he is basically truthful in that he intends to speak the truth, in this respect he is not reliable.

In this section I have studied, as a preparation for an examination of the personality of Joe Christmas, the texts of some of the most important speaking characters of *Light in August* with regard to their reliability, or the degree to which they can be trusted to convey 'the truth,' and with regard to their credibility, the degree to which they are trusted by others to tell 'the truth.'

Joe Christmas

Why did God make me an outcast and a stranger in mine own house (Du Bois)
Joe Christmas's characterization begins in metaphor, as he is named by the foreman in the planing mill:

'His name is Christmas,' he said.
'His name is what?' one said.
'Christmas.'
'Is he a foreigner?'
'Did you ever hear of a white man named Christmas?' the foreman said.
'I never heard of nobody a-tall named it,' the other said.
The text immediately establishes Christmas's status of difference: a 'foreigner,' a

---

102 The lynching of Christmas is of a special kind, recognized and described by social psychologists, whereby the killing is committed not by a mob, but by an official member of 'communal law' (cf. Collins 1982:77). As Allport puts it, 'The fact that lynchings are not prevented, that lynchers, even when known, are seldom apprehended and almost never punished, reflects the silent acquiescence of police officials and courts. The entire process, therefore, partakes of a "social norm"—and cannot be explained entirely in terms of the mental life of the lynchers' (1979:61f.).
103 Of course one might argue that this is indeed Faulkner's intention; all the emphasis on social constructions such as rumors and gossip, however, seems to indicate that it is not.

'nobody a-tall.' Byron Bunch understands the importance of this act of naming, and he understands 'how a man's name, which is supposed to be just the sound for who he is, can be somehow an augur of what he will do' (35). Christmas will be named again and again by others, and we shall see how these acts of naming are indeed related to 'what he will do.'

The first thing to notice about Joe Christmas's own discourse, when he enters the story in Chapter II, is that it is extremely sparse; as the narrator presents it:

The newcomer turned without a word.

He did not talk to any of them at all.

He still had nothing to say to anyone, even after six months.

(35,36,38)

Christmas's first words in the text are spoken to Byron Bunch: 'How much do they pay for overtime?' (37). This question immediately lets Bunch 'know' that the man has not eaten for days, and makes him offer the newcomer a share of his lunch. Christmas's next verbal act, presented by the narrator through Bunch's consciousness, is a refusal of the offered food. Even though Christmas has, as Bunch 'knows,' 'in all likelihood... lived on cigarettes for two or three days now' (37), he responds with a rude 'I aint hungry. Keep your muck' (37).

Christmas's voice next appears when Bunch repeats what some unidentified townsmen told him they witnessed in a barbershop one night, when Christmas was angry with Brown for speaking about their joint activities:

And Christmas saying in that quiet voice of his, that aint pleasant and aint mad either: 'You ought to be careful about drinking so much of this Jefferson hair tonic. It's gone to your head. First thing you know you'll have a hairlip.'

(87)

With this punning on hair- and harelip, and the consequently reported act of violence against Brown, Christmas seems to reveal his brutal nature early on in the novel. One must remember, however, that this information is at least third-hand and unendorsed by the narrator. The description of the event is at best partly 'true,' and the quotation is unlikely to be completely authentic; besides, what is reported here is certainly not all that happened and perhaps not even the most crucial part of the event. Christmas's first words were quoted directly by Bunch, who seems relatively reliable at least until his involvement with Lena starts. In contrast, this last information is based solely on rumors (only the observation about Christmas's voice: 'that quiet voice of his, that aint pleasant and aint mad either' [87], is first-hand). It must therefore reflect the atmosphere of misgivings that already surrounds Christmas by the time of the incident in the barbershop.

Public opinion has been against Joe Christmas from the beginning. It is clear that this stranger, who 'looked like a tramp, yet not like a tramp either' to the workers at the planing mill, and who 'did not look like a professional hobo in his professional rags,' yet had 'something definitely rootless about him' (33), was baffling and annoying from the start because he could not be *classified*. As Gordon Allport observes, people tend to be 'guarded and tentative' in their response to a stranger:

The story is told of a group of farmers who were gathered in a country store when a young stranger walked in. 'Looks like a little rain,' the

stranger ventured affably. No one spoke. After a time one farmer queried, 'What may your name be?' 'Jim Goodwin, my grandfather used to live just a mile up the road.' 'Oh, Ezra Goodwin.—Ye-es, it does look like a little rain.' In a sense strangeness is itself a mark of visibility. It signifies, 'Go slow until the stranger can be fitted to a category.'
(1979:129)

But Christmas cannot be fitted into any category. What is more, his face, described through Byron's consciousness as 'darkly and contemptuously still' (34), immediately inspires violent words: '"We ought to run him through the planer," the foreman said. "Maybe that will take that look off his face"' (34).

Joe Christmas's voice, unclassifiable like the rest of him, is heard next when Byron Bunch tells Hightower what Joe Brown supposedly told the sheriff and what Byron himself overheard from 'them talking about it on the porch' (96). These rumors are again focused on Christmas's alleged violence. As Bunch puts it:

The he [Joe Brown] told how he found out that night that sooner or later Christmas was going to kill her or somebody... And Brown said... that he kind of said something back to Christmas, not meaning to make him mad, and Christmas said, in that still way of his: 'You dont get enough sleep. You stay awake too much. Maybe you ought to sleep more... Maybe from now on.'
(103)

These quotations of Christmas's words are at least third-hand; Byron Bunch, after all, does not quote Christmas, but he is either quoting the townsmen who quote Joe Brown's quotes of Christmas's words, or he makes them up himself. In any case, he is not likely to be reliable.

Even though the people who spread the rumors could not hear Brown's quotations of Christmas's words very well (as we saw, they remained outside the sheriff's office with their faces pressed up against the glass), and even though Brown is an unreliable narrator to begin with (his motive is clearly to blame Joe Christmas and to collect the reward) critics have taken this piece of discourse as early evidence of Christmas's murderous intentions. But if one considers the complicated gossip chains involved and the context of the reward offered, it is by no means certain that Joe Christmas meant to kill anyone, or even that he came into his cabin on the Saturday morning of the fire at about seven o'clock to say to Brown 'I've done it... Go up to the house and see' (104). Although Joe Brown stresses his own reliability to the sheriff ('I'm just telling you the truth... That's what you asked for' [105]), his story should be viewed with suspicion.

When Byron Bunch tells Hightower that the sheriff asked Brown why he never made his suspicions about Christmas's intentions public, he again draws attention to the alleged violence of Christmas. He repeats what he overheard while sitting with Lena, including what he believes are Brown's quotations of Christmas's words. These words were meant to explain why he, Brown, did nothing to prevent the crime for which he is now blaming Christmas. As Brown supposedly put it:

One time he even admitted it, told me he was part nigger. Maybe he was drunk when he done it: I dont know. Anyway, the next morning after he told me he come to me and he says (Brown was talking fast now, kind of glaring his eyes and his teeth both around at them, from one to another) he

said to me 'I made a mistake last night. Dont you make the same one'... I
knowed my life wouldn't be worth nothing if I ever crossed him
(108)

These crucial words, however, are Bunch's quotations of the town's quotations of
Brown's quotation of Christmas's words.

If this account of the instances of Christmas's own voice in the first four chapters
of *Light in August* seems complicated and hard to follow, it is because the intricate patterns of telling and retelling through which Faulkner chose to convey these instances
are complicated and hard to follow. A failure to appreciate this complexity has led
readers to attribute the reported actions and the quoted discourse to Joe Christmas without realizing the unreliability of the accounts.[104] Such readers fall into a trap that is
similar to the one into which Byron Bunch falls. Bunch, who did not have any suspicions about Christmas's race, and who knew so well when it concerned Hightower's alleged homosexuality that all it takes for rumors to spread is 'that idea, that single idle
word blown from mind to mind' (77), immediately takes Brown's word (or what he assumes were Brown's words) for it that Christmas is black. Surprisingly, it is immediately 'true' for Bunch not only that Christmas is black, but also—it follows almost
automatically—that it is *he* who committed the act of violence upon the white woman.
The people of Jefferson are quick to make the case even more 'delicious' by adding
rape; hoping 'that she had been ravished too: at least once before her throat was cut
and at least once afterwards.'[105] Bunch believes the unreliable Joe Brown because,
as he tells Hightower, 'even a liar [meaning Joe Brown] can be scared into telling the
truth' (110), but most likely because Christmas's status in town is even lower than
Brown's own after Christmas's racial background has been 'found out.' Only Hightower, a man broken by his own tragic mistake, and a man, moreover, who has himself
suffered on account of rumors, avoids this trap when he asks the pertinent question:

Is it certain, proved, that he has negro blood? Think, Byron; what it will
mean when the people—if they catch....... Poor man. Poor mankind.
(109)

Hightower, of course, knows what it will mean: if Christmas is black, he will be found
guilty and be punished by the community before he is even tried.[106]

At the end of the fourth chapter, then, the reader has very little direct evidence of

---

104 Faulkner himself referred to the unreliability of his speakers when he pointed out that sometimes, in
his work, opinions come from 'the sort of people whose opinions one would not put too much faith in'
(Meriwether & Millgate 1980:126f.).
105 Prejudice has it that blacks are inclined to sexual violence and promiscuity. Because American slavery
was '*racial* slavery,' J. R. Pole argues, 'the slave personality became conflated with the Negro personality.'
As early as 1765, he writes, the French *Encyclopédie* used 'slave' and 'Negro' almost interchangeably
(1976:209). Both were considered 'lazy, irresponsible, cunning, rebellious, untrustworthy, and sexually
promiscuous' (Davis 1975:41).
106 As John Barker points out: 'The 1920's... were a period of increased lynchings, of a powerful Ku Klux
Klan, and of the resurgence of racist practices and myths' (1982:262). He mentions, for instance, the
lynching of an untried 'Negro' in Atlanta, who was 'burned at the stake,' and of whose body small pieces
'were being hawked as souvenirs' (1982:251). John B. Cullen describes an earlier case in Oxford Mississippi
(1908), whereby he himself—at the age of 14!—captured a black man whom he thought was 'a good
nigger,' but who was accused of murdering a white woman. This untried black man was eventually lynched
and castrated, and his body was hung from a walnut-tree outside the courthouse of Oxford (1954:90ff.).

Joe Christmas's own voice. Accounts of his discourse are very scarce; only five separate instances can be found, and of these only one can be considered authentic. From the narrator's text, and from Byron Bunch's personal observations, which are unendorsed by the narrator, it may be inferred that Christmas is reticent and withdrawn, yet also provocative, and he rudely refuses food offered as a token of friendship. All other accounts of Christmas's voice, even if they are credible to the community, are definitely unreliable. Firstly, this information is never endorsed by the extradiegetic narrator. Secondly, it is based on rumors, and rumors, as we have seen, present streamlined, disambiguated versions of events. These disambiguated versions, paradoxically perhaps, seem to lead away from 'the truth,' suggesting that sometimes truth is not served by resolving ambiguities, but is rather preserved in them. Thirdly, each time they are retold, rumors incorporate the expectations and prejudices of the teller, the frames on which his understanding is based. They contain, as well, the demands of the audience of the teller, its expectations and its prejudices.

In this case, these expectations and prejudices include the misgivings that already surround Christmas, especially his seemingly conscious and deliberate refusal to be classified. In this he is the opposite of Joe Brown, who is transparent and talkative, and who is immediately understood and classified by anyone who meets him, even though his real identity remains unknown. In other words, the townspeople collectively distrust and dislike Christmas because they are not allowed to 'know' him. His appearance, his manner, his voice, and even his name give no unambiguous clues as to his personality, his background, or his purpose in life. As one of the men representing 'the town' puts it later: 'He never acted like either a nigger or a white man. That was it. That was what made the folks so mad' (386). People are 'dying' to name him, or to have him named by others. One can sense the marshal's satisfaction, for instance, when this finally happens: 'A nigger... I always thought there was something funny about that fellow' (108).

This distrust of Christmas not only colors the conceptualizations of those present in the barbershop, who witnessed Joe Christmas's abusal of Brown, or those outside the sheriff's office looking in, who witnessed Brown's betrayal of Christmas. It also progressively distorts the stories about him as they are 'blown from mind to mind.' Such an 'inflammable story,' as Allport puts it, 'flies down the street, becoming sharpened and distorted at each telling' (1979:64). Later on, precisely as happened in Allport and Postman's experiment, 'the town' turns the story around 180 degrees; instead of Brown's betrayal of Christmas, which seemed clear until Christmas was labeled 'a nigger,' the story is now that 'the nigger... pretending to be a white man' tried 'to lay the whiskey and the killing both on Brown and Brown told the truth' (385). When the story is finally recounted to Hightower in the text, Bunch is likely to have distorted it still further.

All in all, then, the repeated sequence of perceiving, telling and retelling makes it possible that Christmas's part in the hostilities at the barbershop as compared with that of Brown is blown all out of proportion. And after Joe Brown has labeled Christmas as a black man, the observers and speakers, who are all white, can be expected to exaggerate Christmas's part in the violence even more.

The Framing of Joe Christmas

It is perhaps enlightening at this moment to return to social psychology. In an experiment conducted by Birt Duncan, for instance, white Californian university students perceived a '"somewhat ambiguous," certainly less than blatant shove' as an act of violence if the harm-doer was black and the victim was white. If the harm-doer was white and the victim black, however, the exact same behavior was labeled as 'aggressive behavior, dramatizing, playing around, and so on (any category but violent behavior)' (1976:596). In addition, if the harm-doer was black, his behavior was considered the outcome of stable personal dispositions, that is, his violence was considered 'typical,' or part of his personality, and of blacks in general. If, on the other hand, the harm-doer was white, this same behavior was considered the result of external circumstances and not inherent in his personality, let alone typical of whites in general.

It seems, then, that 'the threshold for labeling an act as violent is lower when viewing a black actor than when viewing a white actor' (Duncan 1976:591). Besides, this behavior is considered characterological or racial in blacks, whereas it is considered situational or accidental in whites. As Phoebe Ellsworth argues more generally: 'attributional asymmetry is true of a large variety of unequal power relations: the low status person's negative behaviors are dispositional, the high status person's reactive' (1980:196). 'If this finding is so readily available for college subjects,' Duncan concludes, 'its generalizability to other subject populations can be expected to be even more dramatic' (1976:597). This expectation certainly seems to apply to the world created in *Light in August*. Duncan's warning, though it pertains to the 'real world,' is a relevant addition to critical readings of the novel:

> One may be tempted to ask... have blacks been the victims of mislabelings
> or errors, in cases where there was a 'reasonable doubt...'? In court
> testimonies, this could have grave consequences.
> (1976:597)

That Faulkner was interested in such 'mislabelings' is clear. One only has to think of Lucas Beauchamp, in *Intruder in the Dust*, whom everybody, including Gavin Stevens, considered guilty of murder. Just imagine where he would have been without the help of young Charles Mallison.

All this does not mean that Christmas is not a violent person; it only shows that any conclusion concerning his personality is premature. The reader certainly is tempted to evoke a frame whereby Christmas can be labeled as violent, but a careful reading must yield an awareness that such a frame is largely built on prejudice. Violence is certainly associated with Christmas, but it remains to be seen just how far this violence is projected unto him by others, or provoked in others by him. How much does it really originate within Christmas himself as a result of a specific situation or of his character? It is important to realize, in any case, that no account of Christmas's violence has as yet been endorsed by the narrator. Through the account of the different contexts in which Joe Christmas's actions are placed, one is made conscious of the difficulties involved in knowing 'the truth.' One becomes aware of the dangers of social frames, and sensitized to the nature of prejudice. 'Public talking' does not 'make truth,' or in other words: 'unanimity does *not* change prejudice into truth; it only makes it more dangerous.'

The Mind-Style of Joe Christmas

From Chapter V onwards the narrative situation changes drastically, because Joe Christmas's behavior is now presented on the direct authority of the narrator. The first three pages (pp. 112-114), present a few instances of his verbal behavior, directed at Joe Brown:

Shut it

Shut it!

Will you be quiet now?

Will you?

Will you now?

These words are reminiscent of the ones that Jason Compson in *The Sound and the Fury* speaks to his niece Quentin: curt imperatives and rhetorical questions, orders that convey an inability to discuss grievances. But while Jason acted largely out of his own neurotic preoccupations (the 'war' of the Bascombs against the Compson side of the family), Christmas seems much more directly provoked.

Firstly, Brown is drunk, so that any serious discussion is out of the question. Secondly, in contrast to Brown's own account (as the rumors have it) that he meant no harm and would only 'tease' Christmas until he realized 'that Christmas was mad and that it wasn't no time to joke him' (103), Brown (who is after all Christmas's guest) does not stop his laughing when Christmas repeatedly orders him to be quiet so that he can sleep. Only after Christmas has hit him in the face viciously and repeatedly with his right hand, while holding him down with his left, does Joe Brown stop his nerve-racking laughter. He does not, however, become quiet but only more annoying and even nasty:

Take your black hand off of me, you damn niggerblooded—... You're a nigger, see? You said so yourself. You told me. But I'm white. I'm a wh—

(113)

With these words Brown obviously touches something buried deep inside Christmas, who as a result becomes increasingly violent, almost choking Brown. It is clear now that Christmas is capable of violence under certain circumstances; whether it can be said that he has a violent personality, whether his violence is habitual, remains to be seen.

For the first time now, while describing this violent behavior, the narrator moves inside Christmas's mind and conveys its unreflected contents, as usual in Faulkner's texts rendered in italics:

Something is going to happen to me. I am going to do something

(114)

These 'raw' mental representations floating through Joe Christmas's mind have been used by critics as evidence that he was already planning to murder Joanna Burden. The fact, however, that they are unreflected makes any 'planning' in the usual sense impossible. Besides, even if they were, the constructions seem to indicate that Christmas feels on the brink of being overwhelmed by a power beyond his control, so that he seems a victim rather than an agent (cf. Duvall 1987:105).

The first-person pronouns of Christmas's text ascribe roles to him that are unique to his personality (cf. Hurst 1987). In the clauses discussed above, which were addressed to Brown, first-person pronouns are not found, while in the clauses that do contain them, the only addressee is Christmas himself. This reinforces the impression of Christmas as one who has withdrawn from his fellow human beings. It must be noticed that Christmas's text never uses the pronoun *we*, which even Jason Compson's text shows occasionally. Many of the clauses that possess first-person pronouns present Christmas as the experiencer of an external process or action:

1 God loves me too
2 God loves me too
3 she started praying over me
4 she started praying over me.
5 I have been tricked, fooled.
6 she lied to me
7 She ought not to started praying over me.
8 if she hadn't started praying over me.
9 she ought to have had better sense than to pray over me.
10 She ought not to started praying over me.
    (115,115,115,116,116,117,117,117,117,123)

The large amount of repetition gives the passage, continuing over many pages, an obsessive quality. Many of these clauses are concerned with an act of praying, which is interpreted as negative and victimizing (*3,4,7,8,9,10*); two clauses present Christmas as the victim of deceit (*5,6*). Only two clauses (*1,2*) present Christmas as the experiencer of a more positive external process—loving—but this experience fades as soon as it forms itself in Christmas's mind: 'He could see it like a printed sentence, fullborn and already dead *God loves me too* like the faded and weathered letters on a last year's billboard *God loves me too*' (115).

A larger number of clauses present Christmas as the experiencer of an internal process:

1 me not knowing that too
2 I have not gone to sleep.
3 I do not know what time it is
4 I have not yet been asleep
5 Perhaps I believe
6 Why in hell do I want to smell horses?
7 Damned if I haven't
8 Damned if I haven't slept again.
9 All I wanted was peace
10 That's all I wanted
11 That dont seem [to me] like a whole lot to ask.
12 What in hell is the matter with me?
13 I heard ten strike last night too. And eleven. And twelve.
   But I didn't hear one.
    (115,115,115,115,116,119,121,121,123,127,127,129,130)

All these internal processes are somehow invested with doubt and ineffectiveness. The only instances that convey them in a more positive way paradoxically sound like conclusions to his life. The 'raw' sensation *All I wanted was peace* (*9*), and the conclusion 'That's all I wanted' (*10*), both seem to convey resignation to an inevitable fate. One sentence perhaps captures best the ambiguity of Christmas's mind-style: *Something is going to happen. Something is going to happen to me* (130). It is unclear whether this sentence refers to an internal process or an external one, and the suggestion is that Christmas himself does not know. There are very few clauses in which Christmas presents himself in the role of agent:

1 *I am going to do something*
2 I must have hurt his nose more than I knew
3 Maybe I have already done it
   (114,119,122)

Not one of these sentences, however, designates a definite activity in the present; and all convey confusion and bewilderment, an inability to understand the internal or external influences that force Christmas into action.

As the lexical fields of his text show, all of Christmas's conceptualizations revolve around his need for rest, sleep, peace, and love. But it appears somehow to be too late. This sense of time being up is reinforced by farewell rituals, some of which are reminiscent of Quentin Compson in *The Sound and the Fury* on the last day before his suicide: the meticulous grooming; the pouring away of the whiskey; the glimpse of Brown in the barbershop ('It was as if he had just paused there for Brown to look at him' [125]); his very self-conscious last walk through the town with 'his blood... talking and talking' (128); his heightened awareness of time ticking away; and the conclusion reached concerning his purpose in life: 'That's all I wanted' (127).

The early chapters of *Light in August*, then, tempt the reader to evoke a frame whereby Christmas's character could be labeled as withdrawn and rude, and possibly given to violence. These chapters (II, III, and IV) give a subjective, outside view of Christmas, determined by the feelings of uncertainty that he arouses in others. As Sister Kirstin Morrison puts it, all statements here seem to 'corroborate on the level of incident the general impression left of Christmas in Chapter 2: a thug, cold, silent, cruel' (1982:160). Chapter V, on the other hand, shows him, from his own mind-style, to be lonely, confused and depressed: a victim rather than a harm-doer. The new information of this chapter clearly creates a tension within the reader's frame for understanding Christmas's personality and should be reason enough for reconsidering this frame, especially since here the reader is given 'his first objective look at Christmas' through the narrator's text. The narrator, as Sister Morrison points out, still 'exteriorizes, speaks *about* certain thoughts of Christmas's mind rather than opens to view the workings of that mind. But it is a hint of the interiorization that is to come' (1982:161). It is clear that Christmas is capable of violence when provoked, and that he is unable to understand fully his own state of mind and thereby his actions in the world, but most pervasive of all is the intimation of an approaching disaster that he is unable to avert: a 'something' that he cannot name.

Christmas's Tragedy

From Chapter VI onwards, the narrator moves deeper into the mind of Joe Christmas, to those 'raw' memories that are 'in and out of remembering but in knowing constant' (131): those experiences that have determined his personality. These mental representations concern Christmas's own image of the little boy he once was: the five-year-old, among the other orphans 'in identical and uniform blue denim' (131), whose 'primal image' is an empty corridor 'in a big long garbled cold echoing building,' where he, 'like a shadow, small even for five years, sober and quiet as a shadow' (131), could vanish without being seen. These early images already stress Christmas's lack of identity, his loneliness, and his rootlessness, characteristics that tie in closely with Bunch's characterization of him, as well as with his own mind-style. Joe Christmas does not know his own background; his history has been lost, and 'to lose one's history is,' as Martin Luther King said in a speech honoring W.E.B. Du Bois, 'to lose one's self-understanding and with it the roots for pride' (quoted in Barker 1982:242).

The first words that are heard out of young Christmas's mouth: 'Well, here I am' (134), mark his symbolic birth in the text. Spoken 'with complete and passive surrender' (134), they still convey something of a naive faith in his own worth as a human being and the possibilities of receiving care from others, which also pervades the words of Lena Grove as she arrives in Jefferson. They show that he has not lost faith in humanity even though he obviously has already suffered deprivation. They will, however, also mark a turning point in his life, because with these words the little boy vomits the toothpaste he has been eating while he is forced to hear his caretaker's secretive and guilt-ridden attempts at love-making when he hides in her room. The boy does not understand these acts, nor does he pay much attention to them: 'He was not listening; he was just waiting, thinking without particular interest or attention that it was a strange hour to be going to bed' (133).

Still, it is then, when he is accused of spying on her, that he hears, out of the mouth of the woman whose task it is to feed him, the cursed label: 'little nigger bastard' (135),[107] forever linking his person—his very identity—with food and filth, with womanhood and sin, with guilt and a need for punishment to 'get it over with' (136). Little Joe Christmas takes upon himself here, for the first time, the role of scapegoat: 'he believed that he was the one who had been taken in sin' (135).[108] The themes of identity, women, food, filth, sin, guilt and punishment return throughout his life. While some critics have argued that Christmas's problem is more with women than with his allegedly mixed blood, this early experience shows the genesis of a complex of themes, any one of which will be capable of calling up the dreaded whole. But because these themes and their interrelations are, for the most part, hidden from consciousness, Christmas himself cannot name, investigate or understand them.

There is no indication of any violence in Christmas's personality while he is young; quite to the contrary, he seems like a sweet little boy, 'a large toy: small, still, round headed and round eyed, in overalls' (138). It is clear, however, that he has an acute awareness of cruelty in others. One glance at the man who will become his foster father reveals to him signs of unnecessary harshness: 'a blunt clean hand shut, even on

---

107 The dietician's story, as she tells it to the matron of the orphanage, is so full of lies that one cannot have much confidence in her observation that the other children have been calling him 'nigger' before this time. The narrator does not convey that Christmas was called 'nigger' in his narration of Christmas's early youth. Christmas had been aware, though, that he was 'different from the others' (152), but he attributes this to the fact that the old man who turns out to be his grandfather watches him continuously.

108 As Dinnah Pladott has argued, such 'sacrificial victims... are blinded and deluded by an artificial *hamartia*. This tragic *hamartia* leads them to accept unquestioningly, as their natural state, their isolation and exclusion from human love and companionship.' They are 'barred from experiencing any form of illumination: their circumscribed capacities constitute the very crux of their tragedy' (1985:100).

the soft felt of the hat, into a fist' (156). It is a premonition of the severe corrections that the orphan is expected to need and that he will soon receive, tantamount to real persecution.

The Psychostylistics of Persecution

No one, Gordon Allport argues, 'can be indifferent to the *abuse* and *expectations* of others' (1979:143); inevitably the persecuted person will have to create ego-defenses. 'Persecution-produced' behavior, which is meant as a defense behind which the vulnerable personality hides, becomes incorporated into the personality, part of it. To use Pole's words: 'the mask melts into and transforms the face' (1979:205). As a result of persecution, Christmas's personality becomes more and more detached and resigned (cf. Horney 1950). Such a person 'pursues neither love [as Quentin Compson did], nor mastery [as Jason Compson did]; he wants, rather, to be left alone, to have nothing expected of him and to be subject to no restrictions' (Paris 1974:62).

The little boy who was already vulnerable because of his rootlessness, his lack of identity and his loneliness, who said little, not out of spite but because he had little experience in the world ('he was not old enough to talk and say nothing at the same time' [159]), becomes progressively withdrawn.[109] Characteristically, he tries through 'reticence and dignity [to] create the impression of quiet poise' (Allport 1979:147):

'Do you know it [the catechism] now?' he [the foster father] said. The boy did not move. 'No,' he said.
(163)
he too walked erect and in silence, his head up.
(163)
He stood, slight and erect. When the strap fell he did not flinch, no quiver passed over his face.
(164)
The boy didn't answer, rigid, erect
(165)
'Come,' McEachern said, trying to lead him to the feed box. 'Sit down here.' 'No,' the boy said... 'Are you all right? Are you sick?' 'No,' the boy said. His voice was faint, his face was quite white.
(166)

Christmas's withdrawal from those around him is clear from his own text as well. Almost all of his verbal behavior consists of the single words *no* and *nothing*, and the short sentence 'I dont know.' Only once does he use the word *yes*, but in this case it is a depersonalized untruth: 'His mouth said it, told the lie. He had not intended to answer at all. He heard his mouth say the word with a kind of shocked astonishment' (180). One finds here for the first time the dissociation between feeling and (verbal) action that becomes a characteristic of Christmas's most confused moments, as well as the roots of his withdrawn yet poised behavior at the planing mill, which is interpreted as provocative and which immediately generates violent thoughts in his fellow workers.

---

109 There is, at first instance, no indication that Christmas 'refuses to learn the catechism his foster-father commands him to memorize,' as Doreen Fowler argues (1986:152). As the text shows, he finds it impossible to speak about things that he cannot understand. In this he is the opposite of others, who love nothing better.

The need to live behind such a mask of 'reticence and dignity' always creates a certain measure of unconscious fear that someone, eventually, will be capable of shattering it. Especially a woman, Christmas feels, might do this, for instance his foster mother: '"She is trying to make me cry," he thought... "She was trying to make me cry. Then she thinks that they would have had me"' (185f.). Still, his character is not too fixed to give his first love, the waitress Bobby, a chance to go behind the mask and make him cry:

> Then he found that he was crying. He had not cried since he could
> remember. He cried, cursing her, striking her. Then she was holding him.
> Even the reason for striking her was gone then. 'Now, now,' she said.
> 'Now, now.'
> (218f.)

In addition to withdrawal, persecution also leads to hypersensitivity, and to a constant preoccupation with the problem that is felt to cause the persecution. Christmas's problem during his early childhood is that he is somehow guilty of not speaking words that he cannot understand. He fails to understand the dietician's need for secrecy and therefore fails to promise her he will be quiet. This failure is explicitly connected to the question of his race when she calls out desperately: 'Tell!... Tell, then! You little nigger bastard! You nigger bastard!' (138). Later he fails to speak the words of the catechism, again exposing himself to punishment and, worst of all, making him guilty and in need of being 'prayed over.'

To him it is always the woman-caretaker who is the cause of his guilt, through her continuous acts of implicating him in her secretive and sinful passions. As Christmas concludes much later: 'It was the woman who, with a woman's affinity and instinct for secrecy, for casting a faint taint of evil about the most trivial and innocent actions' (185). This is clearly Christmas's own generalization, conveyed through heightened voice and does not reveal the narrator's beliefs on the subject. The narrator, however, shows his compassion by voicing Christmas's thoughts in this involved way. Christmas's tendency to associate womanhood with secrecy and guilt, stemming from his early experience with the dietician and projected unto his relationship with his foster mother, is certainly reinforced when he finds out that his girl, Bobby, is a prostitute. The link between women, secrecy and guilt will play a role again in his relationship with Joanna Burden. Because he is so sensitive to any sign of secrecy in a woman's behavior, Christmas is always ready to interpret his foster mother's behavior in this negative way, making it hard or impossible to trust her, to look at her even, and to accept her love or her food as a token of her love:[110]

> He walked stiffly past her, rigidfaced, his face rigid with pride perhaps and
> despair.
> (164)

---

110 He may, to a large extent, be right. Although it is not my purpose, here, to study the characterization of Mrs. and Mr. McEachern, certain aspects of their relationship and their religious background point in the direction of her almost having to be secretive. The narrator points to this when he says: 'he *knew* that... she would want him to sin in order that she could help him hide it' (210; my emphasis) and, by using the attributive verb *knew*, gives the impression that he agrees with this view. This does not mean, however, that he subscribes to the generalization that Joe makes about 'woman's affinity and instinct for evil,' which does not feature the attributive verb *knew*.

He heard her approach across the floor. He did not look... He had not once looked at her. He had not moved. 'Joe,' she said. He didn't move. 'Joe,' she said... She did not touch him. 'I aint hungry,' he said... While she watched him he rose from the bed and took the tray and carried it to the corner and turned it upside down, dumping the dishes and food all onto the floor.

(169f.)

One senses very clearly the helplessness, rather than wilfulness, behind Christmas's behavior. Notice, again, the extreme caution that the narrator observes when he describes Christmas's state of mind ('pride *perhaps* and despair'; my emphasis).

These observations can explain Christmas's rude refusal of food in Chapter II. His words, spoken at the age of eight in Chapter VII—'I aint hungry'—are identical to those he speaks twenty-five years later at thirty-three, when Byron in his 'motherly' way offers him a share of his lunch. And while he manages to allow the not very motherly Bobby to feed him in the impersonal setting of a restaurant,[111] he cannot eat with Joanna in the intimate setting of her kitchen, and continues to eat the food she sets out for him alone. After becoming Joanna's lover, it is almost inevitable that he should repeat the act of violence once directed to his foster-mother's food:

He went directly to the table where she set out his food. He did not need to see. His hands saw; the dishes were still a little warm, thinking *Set out for the nigger. For the nigger.*

He seemed to watch his hand as if from a distance. He watched it pick up a dish and swing it up and back and hold it there while he breathed deep and slow, intensely cogitant. He heard his voice say aloud, as if he were playing a game: 'Ham,' and watched his hand swing and hurl the dish crashing into the wall

(261)

The old link between identity—his 'niggerhood'—and food is evident here. A certain measure of depersonalization takes place as the neurotic complex is called up. As in Benjy and Quentin Compson's texts in *The Sound and the Fury*, and as in Vardaman Bundren's text in *As I Lay Dying*, there is synaesthesia: 'His hands *saw... thinking*.' In addition, the small-clauses ('He watched it [his hand] pick up'; '[he watched it] swing it up and back'; '[he watched it] hold it there"; 'He heard his voice say'; '[he] watched his hand swing') present his experience without expressing intellectual mediation. Paired with the adverbial phrase 'intensely cogitant,' these small-clauses present the eerie, paradoxical quality of Christmas's depersonalized state of mind. The same construction was already found at the root of Christmas's neurotic complex, in the incident with the dietician. At this time there is at first an intellectual awareness, as indicated by the narrator's use of the that-clause: 'he found that he had been sweating,' after which awareness starts to fade, as the small-clauses indicate, and Joe Christmas becomes 'turned in upon himself, watching himself sweating, watching himself smear another worm of paste into his mouth' (134).

---

111 This allows Christmas to conceptualize her in an impersonal way. The holograph manuscript reads here, he could think of her 'as just a face without a body: his face without his body thinking of her face without body, as he might think of a flower' (Ms. 71).

Though the question of Christmas's background is not raised during the time of his growing up with the McEacherns—no suspicion that he might have mixed blood is ever voiced—the issue seems never to leave Christmas's mind completely. As Olga Vickery puts it, 'Joe himself is imbued with its possibility' (1971:29). More than once, he considers using the 'bad news' of his identity as a revenge:

> Sometimes he thought that he would tell her alone. Have her who in her
> helplessness could neither alter it nor ignore it, know it and need to hide it
> from the man... To say to her in secret, in secret payment for the secret
> dishes which he had not wanted: 'Listen. He says he has nursed a
> blasphemer and an ingrate. I dare you tell him what he has nursed. That he
> has nursed a nigger beneath his own roof, with his own food at his own
> table.'
> (184)

Persecution often leads to such imagined acts of revenge. It is unlikely, however, that Christmas means his 'confession' to Bobby that he might have mixed blood only as an act of revenge or self-destruction, as some have argued. His text shows a genuine need for love and intimacy:

> He told her quietly and peacefully, lying beside her, touching her. Perhaps
> he could not even have said if she listened or not. Then he said, 'You
> noticed my skin, my hair,' waiting for her to answer, his hand slow on her
> body.
> She whispered also. 'Yes. I thought maybe you were a foreigner. That you
> never come from around here.'
> 'It's different from that, even. More than just a foreigner. You cant guess.'
> ...
> 'I got some nigger blood in me.'...
> 'I think I got some nigger blood in me.' His eyes were closed, his hand
> slow and unceasing. 'I dont know. I believe I have.'
> (216)

This need to be known by a loved person is a universal human need; it is certainly not 'something strange' or 'going "one up" on a woman' (Adamowski 1971:244). When Bobby refuses to believe Christmas, or even to discuss the possibility and thereby acknowledge an uncertainty that is so much a part of his sense of self, he does not seem to be very upset. Yet his caressing becomes mechanical, somewhat depersonalized; he had been 'touching her with his hand' (215), but now he lies there, 'not moving, his hand not ceasing' (216). It seems as if Christmas pulls out part of his emotional investment, even if their involvement continues.

The relationship of Christmas and Bobby ends in a bout of violence inflicted upon him by one of her friends. In order to save her own skin, Bobby, like the dietician and like Joe Brown later, provides Christmas with a label: 'He told me himself he was a nigger! The son of a bitch!' (240). The words of Bobby's friend, as they go through Christmas's mind, foreshadow in a real way his final destiny: '*We'll find out. We'll see if his blood is black,*' and then, when they have already wounded him: '*We'll need a little more blood to tell for sure*' (241). After this, for more than fifteen years, Christmas uses the myth of his mixed blood as a way to get out of his involvements with women or as a form of revenge. But he will still try to find recognition. Twice again, out of a genuine need to be known by a friend, he tries to communicate his doubts about his identity, and twice again he is betrayed.

Even though persecution usually leads to the secret warfare of cunning and revenge, it may well lead, in the end, to an actual confrontation. In the part of the text that describes Joe Christmas's adolescence, there is a slow progress toward such a confrontation between him and his foster father:

They faced one another.

For a while longer they faced one another.

Perhaps they were looking at one another.

Now he looked at the other.

Again they stood face to face.

They could not distinguish one another's face now.

(179,179,179,179,179,180)

Facing him, the two of them almost toe to toe, he struck at Joe with his fist.

Joe took the first two blows; perhaps from habit, perhaps from surprise. But he took them, feeling twice the man's hard fist crash into his face.

Then he sprang back, crouched, licking blood, panting. They faced one another. 'Dont you hit me again,' he said.

(181)

Persecuted as he has been, humiliated and provoked, Christmas still controls himself and does not revert to violence. But he now nurtures a conscious wish for further confrontations that can establish his independence: 'I wish he would try to follow us. I wish he would try to stop me' (189). Clearly, he cannot and will not accept any more persecution.

When his foster father, then, calls his girlfriend Bobby a 'Jezebel' and a 'harlot' (224), Christmas hits him with a chair:

Stand back! I said I would kill him some day! I told him so!

He cried aloud, 'I have done it! I have done it! I told them I would!'

(227,228)

One should not conclude from these utterances that Joe Christmas commits here his first premeditated murder. Many sons with oppressive fathers have openly or silently expressed such a wish in a fit of anger; it represents an ultimate act of rebellion, but it cannot usually be taken literally. Besides, there is no indication that the man is really dead. His death, for Christmas, is a symbolic one. 'Exulting perhaps... of having put behind now at once and for all the Shalt Not' (228), he, in any case, has placed himself beyond his father's persecution, whether he is dead or not. Later, when interrogated by Bobby's friends—'If you croaked the guy, say so' (237)—he tells them simply and openly: 'I dont know, I tell you!... I hit him. He fell down' (238). The issue is not important to Christmas. His freedom from persecution is everything to him. At this moment, when he has gained his freedom and nothing seems to stand in the way of his life with Bobby, she betrays him in virtually the same words Joe Brown would use almost two decades later.

When Joe Christmas turns up many years later at Joanna Burden's back door, his rootlessness is unchanged. His persecution-produced behavior seems a fixed part of his personality. He is obviously sensitive to questions of race. When a little boy tells him that 'colored folks' look after Joanna, it is 'at once... as if the boy had closed a door between himself and the man who questioned him' (250). When he nevertheless climbs into the house, he seems 'to flow into the dark kitchen: a shadow,' his behavior and appearance reminiscent of the little boy in the orphanage, 'returning without a sound and without locomotion to the allmother of obscurity and darkness' (252f.). Christmas is still capable of starting a relationship with a woman. But like Bobby, Joanna Burden is older and she seems to him not very feminine—'mantrained muscles... mantrained habit of thinking'—certainly nothing like the dietician. His disgust of women, originating with this early caretaker, forces Christmas to experience Joanna as not really a woman at all: *'Under her clothes she cant even be made so that it could have happened...* "My God," he thought, "it was like I was the woman and she was the man"' (258). But, even though he experiences Joanna as not very feminine, she is still sufficiently female to remind him constantly of the other women in his life. When Joanna and he have become lovers, and she seems to him more passive, less masculine, he feels compelled to throw her dishes with food against the wall, just as he threw his foster mother's food on the floor, and he stays away from her for six months. But even though he has a habit of leaving women, and he thinks of leaving now, this time he cannot bring himself to go. What he really hopes is that 'she'll make the first sign' (263), a sign that he is worthy of her love.

Characteristically, after they have become intimate enough to talk about their backgrounds—'sitting side by side on the cot in the now dark cabin' (264)—and he has told her that he might be 'part nigger,' Christmas feels as though he has 'fallen into a sewer' (281). Although we can believe the narrator when he conveys Joanna's 'imperious and fierce urgency that concealed an actual despair at frustrate and irrevocable years' (283), the text focuses primarily on Christmas's problematic understanding of womanhood and his fear of female passion. Through heightened voice the narrator conveys that it is *he* who finds her naked 'in the wild throes of nymphomania,' that it is *he* who sees her 'wild hair, each strand of which would seem to come alive like octopus tentacles,' and that it is *he* who hears her 'breathing: "Negro! Negro! Negro!"' (285). Whether Joanna's behavior is pathological or not, it is Christmas who feels again labeled, trapped and implicated in the sinful life of a woman. As he experiences it, she begins 'to corrupt him,' and he begins 'to be afraid. He could not have said of what' (285).

What he cannot name, of course, is the old neurotic complex that is called up and that causes him once more to depersonalize. He begins 'to see himself as from a distance,' and to experience himself as 'a man being sucked into a bottomless morass' (285). When Joanna talks about wanting his child, it is *his* preoccupation with cunning and revenge that makes him sense at once: *'She wants to be married That's it. She wants a child no more than I do,'* and that makes him think: 'It's just a trick... I should have known it, expected it. I should have cleared out of here a year ago' (290f.). Yet the complexity of his feelings is clear when he finds her note on his cot and he prepares himself 'like a bridegroom, unaware of it' (293). Critics have commented again and again on Christmas's lack of feeling, and have called him a psychopath. A careful reader cannot, however, miss the struggle between his longing for love and his fear of involvement.

Christmas finds himself unable to leave Joanna, just as he was unable to leave

Bobby after he found out that she was a prostitute. Complicating matters further, another man has now entered the scene. Christmas has by this time invited Joe Brown to live with him in his cabin, and he is afraid that his 'shameful' relationship with Joanna may become known to Brown. Consequently, he feels trapped between two threats: that Brown 'might learn about the woman in the house and do something irrevocable' (296), and that 'because of the fact that for over a month now she had done nothing at all, made no move at all... she might do anything' (297). His memories of betrayal by women haunt him, and he imagines her 'alone and idle in the house all day, with nothing to do save to decide whether to betray him at once or torture him a little longer' (297). It seems inevitable, then, that he should lie sleepless at night, desperately thinking 'I have got to do something. There is something that I am going to do' (297).

One note on his bed in the cabin, however, awakens Christmas's hunger for love and intimacy. Taking no time even to read Joanna's message, he pictures himself naively 'on the verge of promise and delight' (299):

> 'All that foolishness,' he thought, holding the yet unopened paper in his hands; 'all that damn foolishness. She is still she and I am still I. And now, after all this damn foolishness'; thinking how they would both laugh over it tonight, later, afterwards, when the time for quiet talking and quiet laughing came: at the whole thing, at one another, at themselves.
> (299)

If these thoughts convey Christmas's naïveté, they also make clear his genuine longing for affection. But he is gravely disappointed when the betrayal that he has heard uttered twice by women is now made into an ultimate act of self-conviction that Joanna forces him to perform. He, who for fifteen years had been 'obsessed with the idea that he must choose' (Vickery 1971:27) and was unable to do so, must now 'ignore his own uncertainty, admit his black blood, his sinfulness, and his dependence for salvation on her and her God' (Vickery 1971:35).

Christmas's 'niggerhood' has shrunk him to one in need of special protection and education.[112] Even if Joanna's intentions were good, 'the call to "grow up," addressed to adults is,' as Rodger Cunningham puts it, 'implicitly infantilizing and hence double-binding.' It imposes a 'contradictory situation in which the subject cannot succeed and from which he cannot escape as long as he accepts the given terms' (1987:48).[113] Such '"humane" and "enlightened" emphasis' on the person's own

---

112 Joanna Burden here resembles one of the so-called '"romantic racists," [who] sincerely believed that native Negro intelligence lacked the hard, analytical characteristics that had made European and American civilization, and the inference was that in an exposure to untrammelled competition in that society, the Negro would suffer and fail. Unless he were specially protected, or educated into its hard, competitive ways, he would go under' (Pole 1976:214). This refers to 'a pervasive white belief that Negroes could not look after themselves, and that without white protection they would degenerate and even die out. This belief persisted after the Civil War' (Pole 1976:199). The 'Yankee schoolma'am,' Cash writes, 'who, in such numbers, moved down upon the unfortunate South in the train of the army of occupation, to "educate" the black man for his new place in the sun... was, of course, no proper intellectual, but at best a comic character, at worst a dangerous fool, playing with explosive forces which she did not understand. She had no little part in developing Southern bitterness' (1969:140).
113 There is in Christmas, perhaps, also the reflection of a more widespread fear of the North existing in the South 'as a culture dominated by "female" notions and, sometimes more literally, by the sort of women who... "write books; patronize abolitionist societies; or keep a boarding school"... a misogynist's nightmare' (Gray 1989:61).

good, he argues, constitutes a denial of his own 'goodness and personal validity' (1987:66). By imposing this double bind Joanna fulfills her father's prophecy that she would never succeed in lifting this 'black shadow' to her own level.[114] It is clear, in any case, that the situation puts Christmas beside himself:

'To school,' his mouth said.
'To school,' his mouth said. 'A nigger school. Me.'
'learn law in the office of a nigger lawyer,' his mouth said.
'But a nigger college, a nigger lawyer,' his voice said, quiet
Tell niggers that I am a nigger too?
(303,303,303,304,304)

Again the text shows how Christmas's body moves as if on its own account. Although Joanna recognizes his speech acts as questions, and answers 'yes' to all of them, only the last one is a real question indicated with a question mark.

It seems as if in pronouncing this question, Christmas finally realizes that he can refuse. With this realization, he finds himself again: 'Then it was as if he said suddenly to his mouth: "Shut up. Shut up that drivel. Let me talk"' (304). Finally the tables are turned, and Christmas, having been labeled falsely again and again, now takes his turn to label the woman, repeating many times the cruel classifications 'old,' 'worn out,' 'not any good anymore':

You're old. I never noticed that before. An old woman. You've got gray in your hair.
(304)
There is not anything the matter with you except being old.
(304)
That's all. You're just worn out. You're not any good anymore. That's all.
(305)

The last months of their life together, from May until August, seem to repeat Christmas's childhood years. Joanna's discourse imitates his foster father's, while his own words are identical to those he uttered as a little boy:

her voice repeated its tale: '....... not to school, then, if you dont want to go.... Do without that....... Your soul. Expiation of.......' And he waiting, cold, still, until she had finished: '....... hell....... forever and ever and ever.......'
'No,' he said.
(306)

The Gap in the Text

The text picks up here where Chapter V leaves off, in fact overlaps it, suggesting that all of the intervening chapters convey what goes through Christmas's mind in a flash while he is sitting against a tree, watching Joanna's house. As if he knows that he is

---

114 Faulkner himself once said about Joanna Burden: 'Maybe she had begun to assume the attitude of so many Southern people that it [the inferior position of blacks] couldn't be changed and altered because the Negro would be incapable of change...' He, however, admitted that he did not remember the book very well: 'And that's another book that I will have to read again' (Gwynn and Blotner 1959:112). Joanna, in any case, is doing her best to bring about a change in Christmas.

going to die, his whole life, and all the things that have made him what he is, pass before his eyes. When he hears twelve strike, Christmas moves towards the house, his head empty, his mind blank. He enters Joanna's bedroom with his razor in his hand, 'not open yet,' suggesting that he plans to open it later. But the determined mood that he had been in before ('then it was time'), and that continues while he stands over the bed in which Joanna is lying, vanishes. As the narrator explains it, 'his body seemed to walk away from him. It went to the table and his hands laid the razor on the table and found the lamp and struck the match' (309).

Just as his mouth has in the past said things that he did not plan, his body now performs actions that he has not planned and that cancel out his prior intentions. Whatever his plans were—and it may well be that he intended to kill Joanna at once, or possibly himself—he is unable to execute them. While they thus face each other, she sitting in the bed, he standing by the table, Joanna tries once more to get him to pray:

'Will you kneel with me?' she said. 'I dont ask it.'

'No,' he said.

'I dont ask it. It's not I who ask it. Kneel with me.'

'No.'

They looked at one another. 'Joe,' she said.

'For the last time. I dont ask it. Remember that. Kneel with me.'

'No,' he said.

(310)

There is no violence in Christmas's voice, just stubbornness and poise, and the pride that characterized him as a little boy. He sees her take from under her shawl a gun, yet he does not jump but merely turns away his gaze, as if ready to die: 'He was watching the shadowed pistol on the wall; he was watching when the cocked shadow of the hammer flicked away' (310).

It is important to notice the repeated progressives: *he was watching; he was watching* that are used in this description of Christmas's behavior. They give the action an indefinite duration and suggest a certain resignation on the actor's part to what is happening, in accordance with characteristics of Christmas's own mind-style as shown on the same night, in Chapter V. They certainly do not suggest quick or violent action on the part of Christmas. It is again as if Christmas is ready to meet the fate that he has, unconsciously, been awaiting: the punishment, perhaps, that he has looked for all his life. But these progressives suggest at the same time that the narrator does not have sufficient evidence to convey the completion of the action. He seems to disappear together with the characters whose actions he communicates.

Many critics have tried to fill the following ellipsis in the text. Daniel Singal, for instance, explains how 'he... decapitates her with a razor in symbolic castration' (1982:185). But, as I have argued before, although the townspeople tell one another that Christmas murdered Joanna Burden, and possibly raped her before and after he did so, we are not told that he killed her or how. Olga Vickery's discussion treats of 'Joanna's act of raising the pistol and Joe Christmas's use of the razor,' which are both 'projected as shadows against the wall' (1971:31). There is, however, no such shadow of the razor. In fact, there is no mention of the razor at all after Christmas has laid it down on the table.[115] John Duvall argues that Christmas kills Joanna in an act of self-defense—'justifiable homicide'—but certainly not legally of murder.[116] 'What the text suggests,' Duvall writes, 'is that... Joe, in addition to being non-black, is non-murderer' (1987:108). It is hard to imagine, however, that Christmas would have cut Joanna's throat in such a way that her head almost came off completely when she was moved, just to stop her from shooting at him a second time. At that time he does not even know yet that the gun contains another bullet and he is surprised when he discovers this later. Slashing someone's throat, in any case, is an unlikely way to defend oneself against a pointed gun. All Christmas had to do was to take the gun away from her, which he did in any case since he is still clutching it without being aware of it much later.

Because the narrator has been following Christmas closely, the ellipsis in the text suggests his own lack of knowledge as well as the blank state of Christmas's mind. This state lasts from Christmas's final visit with Joanna, shortly after midnight on Friday, through his ride in the car of a young couple 'late Friday night' (326). During this time, Christmas's body seems to have moved on its own, not as far as one can tell from the text, towards violence but rather away from it. Moving away from the bed, putting the razor on the table and lightening the lamp, it behaved not merely as 'non-murderer,' as Duvall suggests, but even as 'non-killer.' The narrator has previously shown various ways of filling in a blank in the conscious or even unconscious mind of Christmas, for instance as he did just prior to the last visit with Joanna:

He was not thinking *Maybe she is not asleep either* tonight. He was not thinking at all now... He just sat there, not moving... He didn't think even then *Something is going to happen. Something is going to happen to me*
(130)

Here the narrator conveys Christmas's behavior and makes clear, albeit in negative terms, something about his state of mind. At other times, he has used modals to suggest a certain state of affairs with respect to Christmas's mental activity, and has thereby introduced, in a most circumscribed and careful way, a number of possibilities for the reader to contemplate. That the narrator does not do even this much after Joanna has pointed her gun at Christmas is extraordinary. It leaves the reader in essentially the same dilemma as the townspeople. In a sense, one could say, the reader is 'forced into the shoes' of the townspeople, and is tempted, like them, to solve the enigma in a prejudiced way.

I have already discussed the tendency of critics to follow the lead of the people of Jefferson without giving this gap in the text much thought. Following the community's belief that Christmas is a murderer is just one way, and the most obvious one, to fill the ellipsis, stemming from a failure to read large portions of the text critically. Another way to resolve the enigma is, as Stephen Meats has suggested, to assume that Brown murdered the woman after Christmas knocked her unconscious. As Meats sums

115 The razor Christmas appears to have in his possession much later may well belong to the black man, Roz, 'with that nekkid razor in his hand' (357).
116 John Duvall points out: 'A general principle for justifiable homicide in Mississippi law that could have provided a precedent in 1932 was established in 1879 in *Cannon v. Mississippi*: "That one has malice against another does not deny him the right to kill that other in self-defense"' (1987:107).

up the case that might have been made against Brown had he not betrayed Christmas: he was seen in the house; he tried to conceal the body of the murder victim; he most likely set fire to the house... he ran after he was discovered at the scene, and later he told an obvious lie in an attempt to claim the one-thousand-dollar reward. (1971:272)

But the story that Meats makes up to support this case against Brown is also just a story to fill a gap, a 'shape to fill a lack.' James Snead has argued that Brown, with his dark complexion and the scar by his mouth that is mentioned again and again, definitely 'looks more like a "foreigner" and "nigger" and "murderer" than Christmas does' (1986:92),[117] but this is just as prejudiced as taking Christmas to be the murderer because Brown says he is a 'nigger.'[118] Still, it illustrates well the unreliability of people who assume, with much less information about his personality than the reader has, that Christmas is the murderer.

The rest of the story of Christmas's life is a public affront. An arbitrary man is fetched: '"Get me a nigger," the sheriff said. The deputy and two or three others got him a nigger' (319). The man is whipped until he provides two names: those of Joe Brown and Joe Christmas. As we have already seen, it was Brown, supposedly, who was found at the site of the crime, behaving in a compromising way. Brown, the stories tell, 'kept on saying how there wasn't nobody upstairs and that the upstairs was all afire anyway and there wasn't any use trying to save anything from up there,' so that the countryman who speaks to him suspects that 'there was something wrong from the way the drunk man was trying to keep him from going upstairs' (99). In addition, it must be clear to the people of Jefferson as well that Brown's story is meant to save his own skin and at the same time earn him the reward. His story, as Bunch reports it, labels Christmas as a 'nigger,' and thereby transfers the suspicion from his own head to Christmas's. Three times, like Judas, Brown repeats the words that turn public opinion around:

'That's right,' he says. 'Go on. Accuse me. Accuse the white man that's trying to help you with what he knows. Accuse the white man and let the nigger go free. Accuse the white and let the nigger run.'
(107)

What the townspeople do not know, but what the reader should have noticed, is that Brown's version of the events is not just incredible because of his obviously selfish motives. It cannot represent a true account of the happenings since it clashes with the narrator's account of the same events. Christmas, in the narrator's words, 'had not been to the cabin since early morning' on the Friday of the murder (309), and therefore Brown could not have seen him 'get up about dawn and go out' on Saturday morning

---

117 In the manuscript Christmas is described as having rust-colored hair, hazel eyes, and a thick, smooth pallor (Ms 63); as Fadiman writes, 'perhaps Faulkner felt that these visual details would conflict with the ambiguity he preferred not to resolve' (1975:111). Still, in the final text it is clear that no one had ever imagined Christmas to be a black man.

118 Regina Fadiman's suggestion that 'once Christmas has committed a murder, it is immediately assumed by the formerly unsuspecting members of the white community that he is a Negro' (1975:206) seems to me to be mistaken; as I have argued, the causal sequence is rather the reverse: Christmas is presumed to be the murderer as soon as he has been identified by Joe Brown as a Negro.

(104). Although the narrator's account of Christmas's actions on this Saturday morning is not completely clear, it seems highly unlikely, since Christmas was running away from Jefferson, that he would have come back to the cabin to tell Brown what he had done. Besides, if Christmas had returned, and if he had murdered Joanna, one imagines that he would have been covered with blood, so that Brown could not seriously have thought that 'Christmas just beat her some' (104).[119]

The Danger of the Frame

It is not my purpose to prove that Christmas is innocent, although it is tempting to think that a little friend like Chick Mallison from *Intruder in the Dust* could have made a difference here also. My intention is, rather, to place some question marks behind statements by critics such as 'he commits, after all, a terrible murder' and 'of course he murders Joanna.' From the text one cannot decide if this is true. Perhaps Christmas was capable of such an act of violence against someone whom, as we saw, he loved as much as he was capable of loving anyone; perhaps not. Such an act is hard to execute, even if one has the intention and the motive, and even if violence is part of one's personality. But for the reader to conclude, in line with public opinion, that he is guilty, it is necessary to close the gap in the story. This gap, however, stubbornly resists closure. The reader knows much more than the people of Jefferson about Christmas's prior actions and his prior experiences, on the basis of which his personality can be deduced and possible motives or intentions construed. These might make an act of murder understandable, even 'in character,' *if* it had been committed. However, basing a conviction on prior actions or possible motives alone, especially if these are ambiguous and if their report is unreliable to begin with, is as much an act of prejudice as basing it on race.

The question of who committed the murder is perhaps what the Japanese call a MU question (cf. Hofstadter 1980:246ff.). It demands of the listener to be 'unasked,' because no answer to it can possibly be correct. The question was asked wrongly and should be recast. As the narrator of Robert Pirsig's *Zen and the Art of Motorcycle Maintenance* puts it, MU means that one must 'enlarge the context of the question ... restudy the question' (1982:321f.). The story of Joe Christmas, in any case, is not a story of how a murderer gets caught; it is the story of a man who is suddenly believed to be black, and who is therefore considered capable of rape and murder; a man who is convicted (even by critics) without sufficient evidence, and without a trial, and who is murdered by the brutal act of lynching.[120] The community has constructed for itself a black man and a murderer: a scape-goat.

The chapters after Christmas's last visit with Joanna describe how he painfully surrenders to the role that has been created for him by the people. This, however, is no proof of his final identity or of his guilt, as has been argued. It is only evidence of the power, and the danger, of the frame. As 'the sound and fury of the hunt' (364) dies

---

119 It is also curious, if Christmas were the murderer, that the young man with whom he hitched a ride 'a mile or two beyond the scene of the murder, with a pistol' (326) did not mention any blood. Christmas could not very well have washed and changed before he approached the car, still clutching the gun. This is a pragmatic inference based on frame knowledge: where there is a slashing of throats, there is blood.

120 Faulkner himself expressed his disturbance over 'the lynching of Negroes not for the crimes they committed but because their skins were black' (Meriwether 1965:37).

away, Christmas walks around, seemingly aimless, in a state of depersonalization and dissociation. Gradually he loses whatever unity of self he once possessed. His discourse starts to show perseveration ('he began to say over and over to himself *I have not eaten since I have not eaten since*' [365]), and he experiences visual, olfactory and auditory hallucinations: 'he smelled negro. Motionless (he was sitting against a tree beside a spring, his head back, his hands upon his lap, his face worn and peaceful) he smelled and saw negro dishes, negro food... It seemed to him that he could hear without hearing them wails of terror and distress quieter than sighs all about him, with the sound of the chewing and the swallowing' (368). This section of the text basically re-captures the spirit of Chapter V, but Christmas's mental activity is increasingly conveyed through psychonarration rather than through quoted or narrated monologue. At first he can still think about his goals in life, as he had done in Chapter V ('That was all I wanted... That was all, for thirty years. That didn't seem to be a whole lot to ask in thirty years' [364]), but more and more small-clauses suggest a loss of conscious awareness. Finally, his body seems to leave him also, giving a false impression of unearthly strength:

> his mind did not need to bother to remember why he was running, since the running was not difficult. It was quite easy, in fact. He felt quite light, weightless. Even in full stride his feet seemed to stray slowly and lightly and at deliberate random across an earth without solidity, until he fell. Nothing tripped him. He just fell full length
> (366)

Christmas's identity fades until he finally gives in to the labels that obviously must be stamped upon him. After he 'surrenders' at Mottstown, there is no more internal view of him; it is as if by assuming the label *Negro*, Christmas has no more 'inside.' His personality evaporates, obliterated by the frame stamped upon him. This does not mean that he is a 'Negro murderer'; it does not prove anything. It shows only what social frames, expectations and prejudice are capable of.

The Unknowability of Personality

In my introduction to this chapter, I have argued that Faulkner entices the reader into performing the same acts of prejudice that the people of Jefferson engage in, even though the modal constructions in the narrator's text constantly foreground this narrator's own lack of insight and understanding. These constructions provide alternatives, and convey time and again the indeterminacy of events and the ultimate unknowability of causes of behavior, feelings and emotions, and of personality.[121] They open up, problematize and undermine the disambiguated, streamlined versions of 'the town,' and create a world that allows no such destructive closure. Thus they form an important contradiction to the 'truth' assumed by the majority.

---

121 With his hesitant narrator, Faulkner is an example of those narrative artists who, to use Richard Hull's words, have 'operated an aesthetic and ethic of not knowing their characters' (1992: 33). This narrator is one who 'in the end does not know and does not want to know,' avoiding 'complicity in power schemes' (1992:44).

What, then, makes the reader vulnerable to implication in what Duvall calls the 'same ideology that the text problematizes'? Two thoughts on this subject can be mentioned here. Firstly, as we have seen, much of the information reaches the reader through the voice of Byron Bunch. Bunch is introduced in the first chapters as a reliable speaker, which obviously lends him credibility long after his reliability has in fact become questionable. Secondly, the story of Joe Christmas's labeling by the community and his consequent lynching is constantly complicated by his own search for identity. As an orphan, he longs to be *named* by others. When he tells his girlfriend Bobby:

I think I got some nigger blood in me... I dont know. I believe I have.
(216)

she refuses to believe him. She even refuses to discuss the possibility of his mixed blood and thereby acknowledge the uncertainty that is so much a part of his personality. Joe Christmas is not relieved by having the possibility of his mixed blood denied or made unimportant. He cannot, because his very identity depends on this possibility.

If, as Richard Gray writes, 'it is a traditionally Southern strategy to place the black on the margins of language,' Christmas's place is completely outside of it. What he needs is to find a voice, a language: what Donald Kartiganer calls an 'available myth, or version of reality, that will allow him to live the entirety of his contradictory being' (1982:97). Even more than if he had really been black, he is denied 'the dignity of an adequate definition' (Gray 1989:146): the dignity of having 'a name.' Therefore, as Kartiganer writes, he will drive 'incessantly towards identity, fiercely defying all attempts to define him by reduction to less than his awareness of himself' (1982:97). But the situation is more complicated than this. Christmas will defy *all* attempts to define him, whether reductive or not. Detachment was his solution to the unbearable situation of his youth, and it has become part of his character (cf. Horney 1950). With his hypersensitivity to influence, pressure, or ties of any kind, he is doomed to refuse the very act of complete definition by a fellow human being for which he longs. His problem is not only 'one man's agonizing struggle to phantom his identity against an entire community's to name him' (Ruppersburg 1978:33). It is also a struggle against himself: a struggle between his need to be named and his need to stay free of the influence of others, which he has learned to fear. His character is strung out between acts that force others to name him and acts that seek to escape the same process. This paradox keeps him struggling for the very thing he is trying to escape: the act of being named, of becoming a person. The center of Joe Christmas's text, and of his personality, remains an absence: a lack that no shape can fill.

5

Absalom, Absalom!
A Novel of Attribution

*It wasn't only the old houses and the old families,
the old names, the antiquarian side of provincial
or state history. It was also the past as a wound:
the past of which the dead or alienated plantations
spoke, many of them still with physical mementoes
of the old days, the houses, the dependencies, the
oak avenues.*
(V.S. Naipaul)

Faulkner's novel *Absalom, Absalom!*, like his other works, is a novel of attribution, thematizing the assignment of cause-effect relations to human behavior. This assignment of motives to human actions, in which the individual automatically engages, serves to determine this individual's own future behavior, and it characterizes him through his mind-style. Nowhere in Faulkner's oeuvre, however, are his characters so much involved with behavior in a past that cannot be recaptured as in *Absalom, Absalom!* Throughout the text, the different speakers contemplate questions of behavior and worldview during the turbulent times of the American Civil War, but they especially ponder the question of why Henry Sutpen shot his friend and schoolmate Charles Bon: a piece of local history or myth. Implicitly or explicitly, these speakers ask of themselves and each other that their ruminations show 'at least some regard for cause and effect even if none for logical sequence and continuity' (308), thus drawing attention to the fact that these ruminations are constructions: stories expressing suggestions, beliefs, hopes, fears, expectations and conjectures, which present their personalities as products of this past.

Miss Rosa Coldfield

and only I, a child, a child, mind you
The very first word of Miss Rosa Coldfield's story, told to Quentin Compson on a 'long still hot weary dead September afternoon' of 1909, is indeed a causal connector, with which Miss Rosa attributes causes to her own behavior: 'Because you are going away to attend the college at Harvard they tell me' (6). This, presumably, is the reason why she has asked Quentin to come and see her. Up to this point, the text of *Absalom, Absalom!*, with which an external narrator presents the encounter between the elderly Miss Rosa and the young Quentin, has focused on Quentin's mental activities—his thoughts, visions, imaginings—as conveyed explicitly through attributive clauses such as: 'Quentin thought of...' (3); 'Quentin seemed to watch...' (5). These mental activities seem to be stimulated by the strange surroundings of Miss Rosa's house and by the story she tells: a 'history' that causes him to have to listen to 'two separate Quentins': 'the Quentin Compson preparing for Harvard in the South, the deep South dead since 1865 and peopled with garrulous outraged baffled ghosts,' and 'the Quentin Compson who was still too young to deserve yet to be a ghost but nevertheless having to be one' (5). The passage, presented through heightened voice, presents Quentin's

perception of the postbellum South as a dead land, and the Southerners as a loquacious, incensed and perplexed people who are neither dead nor alive. He resents having to be one of these people, in a situation he feels he cannot escape.[122]

Although we shall concentrate in this chapter on Miss Rosa's discourse as it is introduced by an external narrator, it is Quentin's own ordering and attention span—his mental activity—that divides Miss Rosa's text into several longer and shorter sections. The selections that Quentin's mind makes are thus indicative of his own mental state. They exhibit the situations that Quentin internalizes even if he ostensibly tries to deny this to his father by saying 'why tell me about it? What is it to me?' (10).

Matters of Mind-Style

Logical connectors are an important characteristic of the first section of Miss Rosa's story:

So I dont imagine
since Northern people have already seen to it
So maybe you will enter the literary profession
(6,6,6)

They abound throughout her text, especially in those places where Miss Rosa tries to find reasons for the behavior of Thomas Sutpen, the man who married her sister Ellen, and to account for his impact on herself and the community of which she is a part. One of her sentences even contains as many as five logical connectors:

So he quit coming to church himself; now it would be just Ellen and the children in the carriage on Sunday morning, so we knew now that at least there would be no betting now, since no one could say if it was an actual race or not, since now, with his face absent, it was only the wild negro's perfectly inscrutable one with the teeth glinting a little, so that now we could never know if it were a race or a runaway
(25)

Miss Rosa's text returns here to a time before the Civil War, so her story is in essence the conjecture of a very young child. Retrospectively, however, she needs to make the actions of Sutpen, and especially those of herself and her community, seem necessary and inevitable.

This use of many logical connectors in the text can be related to the use of attributive clauses, especially the abundant use of the that-clause. That-clauses with the attributive verb *know* are found in great multitude and form a characteristic aspect of Miss Rosa's mind-style:

our neighbors and the people we lived among knew that we knew and we

---

122 The opposition between tradition and freedom serves as a metaphor for all sorts of contradictions in Quentin's mental life. The need for a tradition within which to live is connected with early childhood, when the world is experienced as a natural part of the self, a feeling that is lost when one becomes an independent individual. The loss is revived in case of a move to different surroundings, such as Quentin's move to Harvard. The pain caused by this loss is a universal problem of growing up; for Quentin, however, the paradox is that the tradition connecting him to childhood at the same time makes him old—a ghost—because it confronts him with a tragedy for which he feels he is too young. Quentin seems to recognize this problem in Miss Rosa; and he projects it onto Henry and Bon when he imagines them at the gate of the Sutpen mansion: 'two men, young, not yet in the world, not yet breathed over long enough, to be old but with old eyes' (165).

knew [that] they knew we knew and we knew that they would have believed
us... just as anyone could have looked at him once and known that he
would be lying
(15)
I knew at once that he was absent without knowing that he would now be in
the scuppernong arbor drinking with Wash Jones. I only knew, as soon as
papa and I crossed the threshold, that he was not there
(27)

The that-clause, as I have argued in Chapter 1, conveys an experiencer's conclusion
regarding certain events in the appended clause, and may combine this conclusion with
an added judgment of the speaker in the main clause. This judgment, where the attributive verb *know* is used, is normally one of consent. The use of the first-person
pronoun with the past tense entails a positive judgment of the speaker on a conclusion
reached by this speaker's 'younger self.' Miss Rosa, as an older speaker, still holds
that the conclusions she made about the experience she had as a young experiencer are
'the truth.'

A smaller number of that-clauses, in addition, make use of the attributive verb
realise, which has the same effect as *know*:

this town finally realised that he had turned that road from Sutpen's
Hundred in to the church into a race track.
(23)
since we would all realise now that we were faced by more than a child's
tantrum or even hysteria: [realise] that his face had been in that carriage all
the time; [realise] that it had been Judith
(26)

The text presents the noun phrase 'this town' and the pronoun *we* here, as in many of
its that-clauses, explicitly linking Miss Rosa's own conclusions with those held by the
community at large: Miss Rosa is still sure 'now' that her own conclusions at a time
when she was little more than a baby aligned with those around her. Only once does
the text present a that-clause with the attributive verb *believe*, which is neutral with
regard to the truth of the embedded conclusion. This is one of the rare occasions where
Miss Rosa needs to correct herself:

Perhaps once a year papa and I would go out there and have dinner, and
maybe four times a year Ellen and the children would come in and spend
the day with us. Not he... I was young then; I was even young enough to
believe that this was due to some stubborn coal of conscience, if not
remorse, even in him. But I know better now.
(29)

However, even in this episode, in which the text attributes to the young Miss Rosa a
certain childish misjudgment, one is struck by its decisiveness and control: 'But I know
better now.'

A very conspicuous feature connected with this decisiveness and control is the use
of complex sentences. The first section of Miss Rosa's text contains not a single simple
sentence. Each of her sentences contains at least one subordinate clause and most of
them contain more than one, in addition to one or more coordinate clauses. One good
example is the sentence that expresses Miss Rosa's hope of being remembered by

Quentin, which consists of four subordinate clauses:

Perhaps you will even remember kindly then the old woman who made you spend a whole afternoon sitting indoors and listening while she talked about people and events you were fortunate enough to escape yourself when you wanted to be out among young friends of your own age.
(6)

Subordinate clauses, in particular, demand a large degree of mental organization on the speaker's part—the holding in the mind of many different ideas and their relations to each other—and so require a degree of control beyond that of simple sentences and coordinate clauses. This same decisiveness and control shows itself through the ostentatious repetition of its thematization, the organization of the text in such a way that it draws attention to its most important themes: 'That is what I expected. This is what I saw as I stood there before the church between papa and our aunt... this is the vision of my first sight of them which I shall carry to my grave' (24).

Here, as in other passages, the text presents Miss Roa in the role of 'seer.' Often these passages seem to have an almost hallucinatory quality:

I saw what had happened to Ellen, my sister. I saw her almost a recluse, watching those two doomed children... I saw the price which she had paid... I saw Judith's marriage forbidden... I saw Ellen die with only me, a child, to turn to and ask to protect her remaining child; I saw Henry repudiate his home and birthright... I saw that man return
(17f.)

Notice the sudden occurrence here of a great number of small-clauses:

I saw her... watching
I saw Judith's marriage forbidden
I saw Ellen die
I saw Henry repudiate
I saw that man return

These small-clauses convey Miss Rosa's experience 'raw,' without any conscious consideration of truth. Here she simply steps back into the shoes of her 'younger self' and relives a very personal experience. Because of this, her text is not open to criticism; her listener Quentin must take it at face value.

This part of the text concerns a date shortly before Miss Rosa herself became involved with Thomas Sutpen, after he returned from the war. What is especially clear in this episode is the ambivalence of Miss Rosa's feelings for this man who 'had fought for four honorable years for the soil and traditions of the land where she had been born... emerging from the same holocaust in which she had suffered, with nothing to face what the future held for the South but his bare hands and the sword which he at least had never surrendered' (19).[123] Throughout the more emotional part of the text to which the episode above belongs, the text displays, however, a form of viewpoint shift with which Miss Rosa distances herself from her own experience:

a young woman without resources
a young woman emerging from a holocaust

---

123 Mr. Compson pinpoints the paradox when he presents her as 'writing heroic poetry about the very men from whom her father was hiding... and incidentally of whom the ogre of her childhood made one' (81).

a young woman... thrown into daily and hourly contact with one of these
men
(18,18,19)

By thus distancing herself from her own experience at the same time as she lets it come
through, Miss Rosa relinquishes one form of control—the power of reason over
emotion—in favor of another—the power of distancing. It is clear, then, that Miss
Rosa is intent on keeping distance and control, on finding certainty and strength in
'logical' explanations, and on creating a dependable world of action and necessary
reaction, of cause and effect. The sheer energy she puts into this effort, however,
should direct her listener's attention to the fears—of chaos, of the inexplicable, of loss
of control—that lurk just under the surface of Miss Rosa's consciousness, and ultimately to her fear of spontaneous feeling, of emotion itself. Her text is moreover pervaded
by a sense of breathlessness caused by the extreme length of her syntactic units.[124]

Although the text presents several types of attributive discourse—small-clauses and
various kinds of that-clauses—Miss Rosa attributes only two direct quotes to herself
in this first chapter:

A child, yet whose child's vouchsafed instinct could make that reply which
the mature wisdom of her elders apparently could not make: 'Protect her?
From whom and from what? He has already given them life: he does not
need to harm them further. It is from themselves that they need protection.'
(22)

No, not asking even then, but just looking at that huge quiet house, saying
'What room is Judith sick in, papa?'
(27)

Both of the attributive clauses are incomplete. The first contains no attributive verb.
Moreover, it refers to the experiencer—'a child'—in an impersonal way. The second
lacks a subject altogether. It does not refer to Miss Rosa herself, nor to an addressee,
again as if to Miss Rosa taking a certain distance from her experience were essential
to telling her story. Although there are three verbs in this last example: *asking, looking*, and *saying*—progressives that stress the simultaneity of the actions—the obvious
attributive verb in view of the question mark after the quote—*asking*—is negated. Even
though Miss Rosa remembers pronouncing a question, it obviously is not the one that
might have been asked; what she might or should have asked remains unarticulated:
an ellipsis in the text. Another important aspect of the attributive clause of Miss Rosa's
self-quotation is found in the indication of the tone of the question, which was 'said'
'with that quiet aptitude of a child for accepting the inexplicable' (27). Here the text
makes a generalization about children, while the use of the demonstrative *that* seems
to convey the certainty that Miss Rosa's addressee, Quentin, will agree with her. However, neither Miss Rosa's text, nor in fact Quentin's own, shows a readiness to accept
'the inexplicable.'

---

124 Readers of *The Sound and the Fury* may remember a similar defense mechanism in Quentin himself,
who is perhaps able to identify the defenses and gaps in the texts of others if not in his own text. It is
interesting to notice, in connection with this, that in spite of Miss Rosa's attempts at reason, logic and control, to Quentin 'it (the talking, the telling) seemed... to partake of that logic- and reason-flouting quality
of a dream' (22).

We have seen already how Miss Rosa often uses that-clauses to attribute mental activities to herself as a member of a group. In addition to these instances, she occasionally uses a that-clause to attribute mental activity to others, suggesting that she is able to know the conclusions of these others: 'Ellen running down the hill from the house, bareheaded, in time to hear the sound, the screaming, hearing it... before the spectators knew that she was there' (31). With a that-clause that uses the attributive verb *knew*, the text not only makes it clear that Miss Rosa knows which conclusion was reached by 'the spectators' ('Ellen is here') but also that she believes it was the right conclusion. This is curious because she was not even present at the time: 'But I was not there' (33). In this way, Miss Rosa maintains control over aspects of a world from which she is nevertheless absent.

Miss Rosa also quotes others directly, especially towards the end of the chapter. The attributive clauses introducing these quotes consistently use the attributive verb *said*, which is neutral with regard to truth and merely introduces the speaker: 'the negro,' 'my aunt,' 'papa,' 'Ellen,' 'one spectator,' and 'he.' She uses a form of empathetic projection when she attributes a quote to her father, calling him by the name she would have used as a child. In contrast, the reference to Thomas Sutpen is a very impersonal 'he.' Only one quotation, the first one, has a more complex attributive clause. Apart from introducing the verb *said* and the speaker, 'the negro,' it also mentions the gestures of this speaker, interpreted as violent, since he speaks · 'with the stick lifted and his teeth showing a little' (25).

It is clear that Miss Rosa's quotes cannot be taken as authentic, since the speech acts they convey happened long ago and often under very emotional circumstances. Apart from this, Miss Rosa often quotes speech that she could never have heard first-hand simply because she was not present. This happens especially where she quotes her sister Ellen, for instance when the latter presumably discovers her children watching their father fight his 'wild negroes' (30).[125] A consideration of the content of the quotations she cites—of why she cites these particular words from among all the words she has heard—provides an indication of the themes that occupy Miss Rosa most: youth, responsibility, power and powerlessness, and most of all, the disruption of her family's life caused by Thomas Sutpen.

Repetitions in Miss Rosa's Text

Repetitions in Miss Rosa's text form the most important route to the 'sore spots' her story both hides and reveals.[126] One of these repetitions concerns the status of the man her sister Ellen marries, and whom she herself, suffering the effects of a war that

---

125 The outrage that this causes in Miss Rosa can be understood from a behavioral code that demanded from children that 'if they wished, for any reason, to leave the room, permission to do so had to be obtained from the elders,' and that demanded that when an older person entered the room, they 'rose and remained standing until their elders had seated themselves or had retired' (Jobe 1930:28).
126 'Narration-as-repetition,' Rimmon-Kenan argues, 'may lead to a working through and an overcoming, but it may also imprison the narrative in a kind of textual neurosis, an issueless re-enactment of the traumatic events it narrates and conceals,' causing 'the entrapment of narration in the story it tells' (1987:178). Although Rosa's narration at this point in *Absalom, Absalom!* is not 'issueless,' it does not (yet) seem to constitute a 'working through' or 'overcoming,' lacking in what Rimmon-Kenan calls 'the proportion of difference within the repetition' (1987:178; cf. Kubie 1961). Compare the 'working through' of Vardaman Bundren in *As I Lay Dying*, which does show this difference.

killed her father and made her an orphan, would eventually plan to marry as well:

He wasn't a gentleman.

He wasn't even a gentleman.

No: not even a gentleman.

(13,13,15)

These sentences are also the first simple sentences of Miss Rosa's text, which fore-grounds them and increases their impact. Sutpen's activities before the war, and even before Miss Rosa's birth, are especially important here. Miss Rosa's text presents him as a man who 'fled,' 'hid,' 'concealed himself,' and 'took.' To her, he is both a coward and an usurper; a man who came 'seeking some place to hide himself' (13); who 'fled here and hid, concealed himself behind respectability' (14f.); who 'had had to choose respectability to hide behind' (16); and who even found 'the protection he sought' (15) from the men in Jefferson, her own home town. The extent to which everyone in Jefferson was intoxicated by this man, at least in Miss Rosa's eyes, is conveyed through the hallucinatory parallelisms of her text:

and Yoknapatawpha County supplied him with it.

and Jefferson gave him that.

and it was mine and Ellen's father who gave him that.

(13,13,13)

Notice the narrowing scope of the sentences—from the county to the town to her family—the emotional impact of which threatens Miss Rosa's attempts at control.[127]

A second instance of repetition concerns her sister Ellen, that 'blind romantic fool'; 'blind romantic fool, then later blind woman mother fool' (13); 'Yes, blind romantic fool' (14). This is the only instance where Miss Rosa's text in this chapter shows a multitude of adjectives, conveying the intensity of her feelings, her 'Faulknerian' need to 'say it all.' Thirdly, there is repetition in the account of Ellen's daughter Judith, 'who was already the same as a widow without ever having been a bride' (13); 'a widow sure enough without having been anything at all' (14); 'doomed to be a widow before she had even been a bride' (22).

Another important theme involves the position of Miss Rosa's father, and especial-ly the nature of his involvement with Sutpen. Here Miss Rosa's tone is more openly emotional, as can be heard from the exclamatory nature of her discourse:

the father who was to give him a daughter in marriage

But that it should have been our father, mine and Ellen's father

That it should have been our father.

How he could have approached papa

what there could have been beside the common civility of two men

what there could have been between a man like that and papa

what there could have been

(14,19,19,19,20,20,20)

Notice the suffocating narrowing scope in the progression from 'the father' to 'our father' to 'papa,' showing the increasing emotional involvement. Miss Rosa's world

---

127 It is important to realize that this happened before Miss Rosa was born. In Chapter II of *Absalom, Absalom!* it will become clear that Mr. Compson blames 'the aunt' for teaching the young Rosa to see Sutpen as a 'Bluebeard' (71,74,84).

seems to boil down to this one unanswerable question: 'why papa, why us, why me?'

Two themes most directly concern Miss Rosa's own position and her role in the events that happened. The first is connected with the responsibility she feels now at the time of narration and as an adult, and shows clearly the surface decisiveness and self-righteousness identified before:[128]

Oh, I hold no brief for Ellen
No. I hold no more brief for Ellen than I do for myself. I hold even less for myself
No. I hold no brief for myself.
I dont plead youth
I dont plead propinquity
I dont plead material necessity
And most of all, I do not plead myself
(13,17,18,18,18,18,18)

Again, one sees clearly how the succession of repetitions claustrophobically closes in on Miss Rosa herself. The second passage concerns the responsibilities laid upon her as a child:[129]

only I, a child, a child, mind you
only me, a child
I, a child still too young
I... a child
A child, yet
I was a child
Because I was born too late.
Yes. I was born too late.
(14,17,21,22,22,23,22,23)

The utterances of Miss Rosa looking back with pity upon herself as a child who had to take up adult responsibilities too soon resemble Quentin's awareness that he himself is 'still too young to deserve yet to be a ghost but nevertheless having to be one' (5).[130] The awareness may explain Quentin's own growing interest.

One of the 'sore spots' that Miss Rosa's text both hides and reveals is the ambivalence of her feelings towards Thomas Sutpen. From her repetitions it is obvious that she projects these feelings unto others. Unable to realize the degree to which she herself needed protection from her feelings towards Sutpen, her text focuses again and again on a need that she assumes in others:

It is from themselves that they need protection.
Yes. From them; from themselves.
Yes. From themselves.
(22,25,29)

---

128 The narrator, going beyond Quentin's point of view in a rare intrusion, characterizes Miss Rosa's handwriting as 'revealing a character cold, implacable, and even ruthless' (7), which Quentin cannot recognize, perhaps, as the narrator puts it, because he is only twenty years old.

129 Mr. Compson describes Miss Rosa's childhood as 'that aged and ancient and timeless absence of youth which consisted of a Cassandra-like listening beyond closed doors' (72).

130 Both Dewey Dell and Vardaman Bundren in *As I Lay Dying* express the same sentiment. The theme must have been important to Faulkner.

A similar projection is evident in the name Miss Rosa gives her sister: 'romantic fool' (a name she might well apply to herself), and from her concentration on Judith, who, like herself, had lost a husband before she even had one. Other 'sore spots' seem to need displacement as well; for instance, the text repeats Sutpen's act of hiding or concealing himself many times but does not mention her own father's behavior during the war (who concealed himself in his store, where he finally died of starvation). Her mother, finally, is completely absent from her story. Once more the reader is confronted in Miss Rosa with a 'Faulknerian' victim of an absent mother and an embittered father.

The text presents Miss Rosa as a victim of circumstances beyond her control: tragedies she was forced to watch and endure because she was 'too young' to act. As she presents it, life before the fall was not the traditional 'life before the War' but 'life before Thomas Sutpen,' before 'he could have approached papa.' She seems to offer her story to the young Quentin—as a relative of the only friend that Sutpen ever had—in order to find the 'logic' behind this inexplicable event in the past. Her story seeks in vain to answer the one claustrophobic question that haunts Miss Rosa: Why papa... why us... why me? This unsolved personal enigma has made Miss Rosa into one of the 'garrulous ghosts,' not of the Civil War but of the remembrance of Thomas Sutpen.

Mr. Compson

It's just incredible. It just does not explain. Or perhaps that's it: they dont
explain and we are not supposed to know.
In Chapter II the narrator again focuses on Quentin's mental activity: 'It was a day of listening too—the listening, the hearing in 1909 even yet mostly that which he already knew since he had been born in and still breathed the same air in which the church bells had rung on that Sunday morning in 1833' (34). This section contains an almost verbatim repetition of a part of Chapter I: 'this first part of it, Quentin already knew. It was part of his twenty years' heritage of breathing the same air... which the man himself had breathed between this September afternoon in 1909 and that Sunday morning in June in 1833 when he first rode into town' (9). Again and again the text stresses that Quentin is 'hearing' or 'listening,' and that what he hears or listens to are stories that he has heard many times over. As in Chapter I, the text presents the narrator's empathetic deictic projection, conveying the family relations in terms of their relation to Quentin, naming the characters 'Quentin's father' and 'Quentin's grandfather.' Even more than in Chapter I, however, the community's knowledge, or lack of knowledge, is stressed: 'the town learned...'; 'the town likewise failed to learn...'; 'there were men as well as women who believed...'

Mr. Compson's Mind-Style
Eventually, the narrator focuses on Mr. Compson's discourse, as it is received by Quentin. This discourse shows a somewhat greater awareness of Quentin's presence than Miss Rosa Coldfield's, apart from her first few paragraphs. Through the force of her logic, her thematization, her use of the attributive verb *know*, and her small-clauses with the verb *see*, Miss Rosa's speech acts almost seem to defy Quentin's very

presence. Mr. Compson, on the other hand, does refer to his listener from time to time, as his adverbial clauses show: 'his position had subtly changed, as you will see' (49); 'Because, you see, they had been too busy speculating' (53); 'in fact, you will notice' (57).

Like Miss Rosa, Mr. Compson is intent on establishing logical connections in his story of Thomas Sutpen:

Because when he came back this time, he was in a sense a public enemy.
(49f.)
because when... four wagons left Jefferson... it was known that Mr
Coldfield was the man who hired and dispatched them.
(50)
Because there was still no warrant for him... so that there was quite a posse
waiting
(53)
He wore a new hat now, and a new broadcloth coat, so they knew what the
portmanteau had contained.
(53)

However, his use of the connector *so* often has the summarizing effect of *thus* rather than the logical effect of *therefore*, for instance: 'So at last civic virtue came to a boil' (51). Thus, the logic of Mr. Compson's story is not quite as coercive as Miss Rosa's.

In Mr. Compson's text, as in Miss Rosa's, one finds a majority of complex sentences, with hypotaxis as well as parataxis. However, it contains significantly more simple sentences than Miss Rosa's text, and does not have the feverish forward-thrusting movement that characterizes hers. When Mr. Compson's text uses subordinate clauses, they are often modifying, as in: 'public opinion... had swallowed him even though he never had quite ever lain quiet on its stomach' (60). Such modifying clauses create different shades of the truth, whereas Miss Rosa's subordinate clauses are mainly specifying, creating a detailed and much more decisive, one-sided view of the world.

Miss Rosa's text contains very few modal auxiliaries and adverbs; the few that she uses are almost all in the first section of her text and concern Quentin's future life, a life that she imagines for him:

So maybe you will enter the literary profession
maybe some day you will remember this
perhaps your wife will want a new gown
(6,6,6)

These modals show the confidence with which she pictures Quentin's future rather than any uncertainty. It is interesting in this respect that she claims for herself 'almost omniscient conviction,' 'instinctive knowledge' (27), while Quentin thinks of the 'sternly prophetic' way (22) she had as a child. Mr. Compson's story, however, contains significantly more modals than Miss Rosa's. They indicate different degrees of certainty:

Perhaps this was because of what he brought back
Doubtless something more than this transpired at the time
He seems to have intended to use the church
perhaps it was some innate sense of delicacy and fitness
she probably looked upon it as the one chance to thrust him back

her own position... apparently sanctioned and permitted the wedding
(50,52,58,58,61,61)

The same effect can be observed in the that-clauses in the text, which use the verbs *think* or *suppose* that are not decisive but neutral with regard to the truth of the embedded clause, in contrast to Miss Rosa's almost consistent use of the verb *know*:

I think [that] it was a little more involved than the sheer value of his chandeliers and mahogany and rugs.
(50)

I think that the affront was born of the town's realization that he was getting it involved with himself; that... he was forcing the town to compound it.
(50)

I suppose [that] they knew that he would have to come out sometime
(53)

I suppose [that] they sat there and thought about those two pistols.
(53)

The text also presents attributive clauses that feature the connector *how*:

All I ever heard is how the town... saw Sutpen... ride onto the square
(52)

I heard how he turned there and looked at them again
(52)

I have heard how during none of his three passages that day through that street did his bearing alter
(55)

These how-clauses are like to-infinitives in their concentration on the state of mind of the experiencer (the 'hearer') as a process rather than in terms of a conclusion this experiencer might have reached. Such forms never appear in Miss Rosa's text, which sticks to final, impermeable conclusions. The first example also contains, on an embedded level, the small-clause 'the town saw Sutpen ride onto the square.' With it, Mr. Compson's text conveys the 'raw' or unassessed mental activity of the experiencers (the town) and conveys pure sense experience.

All in all, we can say that Mr. Compson's discourse shows a greater willingness or ability to admit uncertainty than Miss Rosa's. Naturally, Mr. Compson is much less personally involved than Rosa with the events themselves. His text infuses Miss Rosa's experience with subtlety precisely because he is less emotionally involved. Nevertheless, the specific characteristics of the text reveal aspects of the story that Mr. Compson wants to emphasize or about which he feels strongly. These can lead us to the themes that are important to him personally.

Personality Themes in Mr. Compson's Text

One of these aspects is deictic projection with regard to time adverbials, as in the sentence 'Yes, she was weeping again *now*' (69; my emphasis). Another aspect is thematization, as in:

It was the wedding which caused the tears: not marrying Sutpen.

It was the aunt who persuaded or cajoled Mr Coldfield into the big wedding
(56,59)

Mr. Compson's universal attributions, or generalizations, seem to touch on the same subject:

> Being a woman, she was doubtless one of that league of Jefferson women who... had agreed never to forgive him for not having any past
> (61)
> Or maybe women are even less complex than that and to them any wedding is better than no wedding
> (61)
> the fact that women never plead nor claim loneliness until impenetrable and insurmountable circumstance forces them to give up all hope of attaining the particular bauble which at the moment they happen to want.
> (63)
> one of the Coldfield negroes... following her, perhaps for protection, perhaps just sucked along like a leaf in the wake of that grim virago fury of female affront
> (64)

His text evokes the power that women have over men, involving the weapons they use, tears, and also the shallowness of their goals and emotions. Thus, the actions attributed to women are 'persuade,' 'cajole,' 'force,' 'nag,' and 'weeping.'

Mr. Compson's one long digression away from the story itself is illustrative in this respect: 'I dont speak of Ellen, of course; in fact, you will notice that most divorces occur with women who were married by tobacco-chewing j.p.'s in country courthouses or by ministers waked after midnight, with their suspenders showing' (57). One wonders why Mr. Compson starts on this subject at all, since divorce is not a part of the history of the Coldfields, the Sutpens or the Compsons. As it turns out, the digression here serves as an introduction to the same theme of female shallowness and coldness:

> regardless of the breathing evidence of children and all else, they [women] still have in their minds even yet the image of themselves walking to music and turning heads, in all the symbolical trappings and circumstances of ceremonial surrender of that which they no longer possess? and why not, since to them the actual and authentic surrender can only be (and have been) a ceremony like the breaking of a banknote to buy a ticket for the train
> (57)

The sarcastic tone of Mr. Compson's rhetorical question 'and why not?' is illustrative, as is his comparison of the two marriage partners: 'Sutpen wanted the big wedding more than Ellen did, or for a deeper reason than she did' (63); 'He did not forget that night, even though Ellen, I think, did, since she washed it out of her remembering with tears' (69). Thus he stresses what seems to him the more genuine nature of Sutpen's emotions.

Mr. Compson's text shows a certain compassion for Sutpen's plight. He was a man who 'set out into a world which even in theory, the average geographical schooling of the normal boy of fourteen, he knew nothing about' (62); a young man who had to weigh 'circumstance against human nature, his own fallible judgment and mortal clay against not only human but natural forces, choosing and discarding, compromising with his dream and his ambition like you must' (62). With the use of the pronoun *you*, Mr. Compson draws the experience very near and explicitly includes himself as well as Quentin. At the same time he creates an opposition here between the son, Henry, who at fourteen 'could not quite stand up to' watching his father fight his 'wild negroes' and the father, Thomas, who, being 'just fourteen,' decided to 'turn his back on all that he knew' with 'a fixed goal in his mind' (62).[131] Sutpen's nonverbal behavior is presented with respect and even with admiration:

> He just walked on, erect
> still without once looking back
> he standing there, not moving
> standing there motionless
> He... shielding the two women with his body
> (54,54,67,67,68)

Notice that Mr. Compson discusses with Quentin the fact that Miss Rosa 'admitted... that he was brave' (60). With its that-clause featuring the attributive verb *admitted*, the text indicates agreement with Miss Rosa's conclusion: to him, also, Sutpen is a brave man. It is clear, however, that Mr. Compson tells a different story than Miss Rosa, even if they both focus on the same events, as each claims they once happened. Whereas her focus is on the lack of respectability and humanity of the man she believes ruined her life, Mr. Compson focuses on the lack of compassion he received and the willpower he showed.[132]

Mr. Compson's Story Continued

Chapter III is not a straightforward continuation of Mr. Compson's story in Chapter II. It is clear that there is an information gap here between Mr. Compson's ending with a general statement about Ellen's wedding ('Yes, she was weeping again now; it did, indeed, rain on that marriage' [69]) and Quentin's beginning with an unrelated remark about Miss Rosa ('If he threw her over, I wouldn't think she would want to tell anybody about it' [70]). Though the text in addition contains the attributive clauses *Quentin said*; *Mr Compson said again*, and later once more *Quentin said* (73), it no longer uses quotation marks as in Chapter II. Strangely, the attributive clauses are printed in italics (just as here in my text). These formal changes make it unlikely that the text of Chapter III is a simple continuation of Chapter II, in which the narrator quotes what 'Mr Compson told Quentin' (49).

It has been argued that all of Chapter III of *Absalom, Absalom!* conveys the musings inside Quentin's mind that recapitulate the story his father told him earlier. If so, the attributive clauses must be excluded, since one is confronted there with the narrator's name for his father, Mr. Compson, a name that neither Quentin nor his father would use. Yet, even though the chapter's exact status is hard to determine, it

---

131 Notice, especially, the emphatic 'just.' Would Quentin hear the irony of the adverb *quite* versus the admiration in the adverb *just*? One might speculate what hearing this may mean to Quentin, whose verbal powerlessness in front of his father, as we know from *The Sound and the Fury*, is so deeply felt.

132 Mr. Compson's text is more in accordance with what Faulkner himself said about Sutpen: 'the old man was himself a little too big for people no greater in stature than Quentin and Miss Rosa and Mr. Compson to see all at once. It would have taken perhaps a wiser or more tolerant or more sensitive or more thoughtful person to see him as he was' (Gwynn and Blotner 1959:274).

seems to form part of Mr. Compson's mind-style, presenting the names that he uses to refer to people: 'Mr Coldfield,' 'Miss Rosa,' and the objective 'the aunt' (never 'her aunt'). One also finds the same profusion of modal auxiliaries and adverbs and the same use of logical connectors as in Chapter II, and there is the same deictic projection with regard to adverbs of time:

Now the period began which ended in the catastrophe

the same woman who had been that child now watched him

(81,82)

There is in addition the same empathetic projection of social deictics as in Chapter II, where Mr. Compson named people with the social terms that Quentin would use: 'your grandfather' instead of 'my father,' and 'your grandmother' instead of 'my mother.' When Mr. Compson suddenly breaks this deictic projection and changes to 'Father' and 'Mother' at the end of the chapter, one can sense how his personal involvement has increased. Again, there is much reference to the community: 'so the town believed' (80); 'the tale came through the negroes' (96); 'so the neighbors said' (99). These references are not, however, inclusive of the speaker, as in Miss Rosa's text.

Occasionally, the text refers to Mr. Compson's speech partner, Quentin, directly: 'Miss Rosa didn't tell you that two of the niggers in the wagon that day were women?' (73); 'this creature, this face which hardly ever spoke during the meal, with eyes like (as you put it) pieces of coal pressed into soft dough' (78). In general there is very little reference to the speaker himself. A few instances of self-attribution of mental activity show that-clauses, presenting the conclusion of the experiencer, who in first-person and present-tense discourse is the speaker himself. However, they show the attributive verb phrases: *believe, like to think* and *like to believe*, which remain neutral with regard to the truth of the embedded conclusion.

I have always liked to believe that he intended to name her Cassandra

So I believe [that] she stole it.

so I would like to think... that its very simplicity fooled him.

(74,94,94)

What makes the first example of self-attribution of mental activity more complex than the others is the existence of a second, more embedded level containing a to-infinitive construction ('he intended to name her Cassandra'), which refers to the state of mind of an experiencer other than the speaker (Sutpen). But because this clause is embedded in a 'believe-clause,' no truth about the conclusion is asserted. In addition to this to-infinitive attributed to Thomas Sutpen, the text uses a to-infinitive to refer to Ellen Sutpen's state of mind, albeit in a negative and stipulative way: 'it may not have occurred to Ellen... to tell her sister' (106). A small-clause is used only once, when Miss Rosa's 'raw,' unassessed, mental activity is conveyed: 'She just saw Ellen depart' (92). Compare this to the series of small-clauses with the attributive verb *saw* that Miss Rosa attributes to herself. Here Mr. Compson's text adopts some of the hallucinatory aspects of Miss Rosa's text. On the whole, when Mr. Compson attributes mental activity to others, he characteristically uses a that-clause and the neutral attributive verb *believe*, with which he abstains from passing judgment on the conclusions of these others:

there were some among his fellow citizens who believed even yet that there

was a nigger in the woodpile somewhere, ranging from the ones who

believed that the plantation was just a blind to his actual dark avocation,
through the ones who believed that he had found some way to juggle the
cotton market itself... to the ones who believed apparently that the wild
niggers which he had brought there had the power to actually conjure more
cotton per acre from the soil than any tame ones had ever done.
(87)

However, even though the attributive verb does not entail judgment, other aspects of
the text may do so, for instance the adverbial *even yet* in the first line. This pretending
not to judge while doing so nevertheless, is perhaps responsible for the slightly
sarcastic and insincere tone of the utterance.[133]

Only on a few occasions does the text present a form of attribution that shows an
attributive verb conveying a positive judgment; these are *know, admit, learn* and *discover*. The attributive clauses 'they knew even better than she that...' (88), 'doubtless
she did not ask... perhaps knowing [that]...' (97) and 'Ellen did not before she died
know that...' (107) convey the positive judgment of the speaker concerning the truth
of the embedded clause, which conveys the conclusion of the experiencer(s) in each
case ('they,' 'she,' and 'Ellen'). The same can be said of the attributive clause with the
verb *admit* ('Mr Coldfield probably admitted that...' [89]), which seems to indicate that
Mr. Compson agrees with Mr. Coldfield's likely conclusion that 'war was unavoidable.' Similarly, the verb *learn* indicates agreement with Mr. Coldfield's conclusion
that 'his store had been broken into and looted' (100), and the verb *discover*, indicates
agreement with Miss Rosa's conclusion that 'Ellen had been dyeing her hair evidently
for years' (104). It is important, however, to notice the large number of modals in
these utterances. This clearly is a sign of Mr. Compson's caution with regard to
opinions, and thus contrasts strongly with Miss Rosa's discourse. In a sense this is
normal, since he was not present when the events took place. But one cannot help
remembering Mr. Compson's nihilism and sarcasm, and his general lack of conviction,
which filled the mind of Quentin in *The Sound and the Fury* on the day of his suicide.
Yet, Mr. Compson occasionally attributes mental activities to others by quoting them
directly. The attributive clauses identify Quentin's grandmother, Miss Rosa and Ellen
Sutpen. Just a few times the text specifies the speaker's tone of voice—Ellen, for
instance, 'shrieked'—but usually quotes are introduced neutrally by the attributive verb
say.

All the aspects mentioned so far would seem to show that the text of Chapter III
is not very different from that of Chapter II. There are, however, gradual differences
that have as their result an important increase in the irregularity of sentence length.
One is the occurrence of more embedded levels of attribution, which was mentioned
already. Another is the much more frequent occurrence of appended groups, or 'quasi
clauses' (Kaluza 1967). For example:

He probably did not even look at her twice as compared with, weighed
against, his own family and children—the small slight child whose feet,
even when she would be grown, would never quite reach the floor even
from her own chairs, the ones which she would inherit nor the ones—the

---

133 This is an aspect of his father's text to which Quentin, as we have seen in *The Sound and the Fury*,
is very sensitive.

objects—which she would accumulate as complement to and expression of individual character, as people do, as against Ellen who, though small-boned also, was what is known as fullbodied (and who would have been, if her life had not declined into a time when even men found little enough to eat and the end of her days had been without trouble, fullbodied indeed. Not fat: just rounded and complete, the hair white, the eyes still even young, even a faint bloom yet on what would be dewlaps and not cheeks any longer, the small plump ringed unscarified hands folded in tranquil anticipation of the food, on the damask before the Haviland beneath the candelabra which he had fetched to town years and years ago in wagons, to the astonished and affronted outrage of his fellow citizens), and against Judith already taller than Ellen, and Henry though not as tall for sixteen as Judith was for fourteen, yet giving promise of someday standing eye to eye with his father

(77f.)

Mr. Compson's language here is highly complex, both syntactically and semantically. One finds an accumulation of clause-like structures, all following the simple clause 'he probably did not even look at her twice.' Some of these structures are complete clauses in that they contain both subject and verb, but most are 'quasi-clauses,' missing either subject or verb or both. They all maintain a certain degree of internal structure, which shows their basic verbal ('weighed against') or adverbial ('fullbodied indeed') nature, but because of their varying degree of incompleteness, they can be ambiguous.[134] This ambiguity tends to increase towards the end of the sentence, as the relation of the 'quasi-clause' to the main clause becomes increasingly unclear. Such long sentences suggest fluid associative thinking. Framed between much shorter, more straightforward sentences, they again suggest aspects of the story that, for personal reasons, stir Mr. Compson's imagination and his emotions.

The accumulation of adjectives also contributes to the extreme length of sentences here. Usually, these long strings of adjectives are applied to women, for instance: 'that strong vindictive consistent woman' (75); 'the foolish unreal voluble preserved woman' (83). Mr. Compson is at pains to describe women in a detailed way, so as to convey his paradoxical and negative feelings about them. These series of adjectives occur without punctuation, presenting his urgency, his 'compulsive need to say everything' (Bleikasten 1973:29). Very often the adjectives occur in pairs. These paired ones tend to refer to abstract entities and show the rhetoric of 'hypallage,' weighing the abstract down with material qualities on the one hand and causing the concrete to lose substance, to evaporate into abstractions on the other (Bleikasten 1973:27):

living and walking reproach
passive and hopeless grief
irrevocable and incalculable damage
lugubrious and vindictive anticipation
sardonic and watchful triumph

134 Appended groups, as Irena Kaluza (1967) has argued, form a very characteristic aspect of Quentin's text in *The Sound and the Fury*. There many appended groups have no internal structure at all, with the result that the ambiguity of Quentin's discourse is much greater than his father's here.

curious and paradoxical awkwardness
impossible and foundationless advice
final and complete abnegation
(71,71,72,72,76,78,89,92)

Most other nouns that are accompanied by adjectives also refer to abstract entities: 'breathing indictment' (71); 'irrational fury' (71); 'jeering suspension' (71); 'pearly lambence' (80); 'nebulous suspension' (80); 'peaceful despair' (92); 'fateful mischance' (94); 'tranquil disregard' (105). This feverish association of ideas often shows aspects of personification and more or less violent juxtaposition. Walter Slatoff has argued that such pairs do not 'so much explore or analyze a condition as render it forcefully.' Traditionally, he points out, they have been used to reflect 'desperately divided states of mind' (1961:187).

Mr. Compson's powers of association also show themselves in the similes and metaphors of his text. Chapter II shows a few similes, some of which originated presumably with his own father: 'eyes... like pieces of a broken plate'; 'beard... strong as a curry-comb' (51), or with Quentin: 'eyes like (as you put it) pieces of coal pressed into soft dough' (78). Here in Chapter III, however, the similes become more frequent and much more elaborate:

this small body... like a costume borrowed at the last moment and of
necessity for a masquerade which she did not want to attend
(78)
the destiny of Sutpen's family... like a lake welling from quiet springs into
a quiet valley and spreading, rising almost imperceptibly and in which the
four members of it floated in sunny suspension
(89)

One combination of simile and metaphor, especially, is extended throughout the chapter:

the woman... rose like the swamp-hatched butterfly, unimpeded by weight
of stomach and all the heavy organs of suffering and experience, into a
perennial bright vacuum of arrested sun
(83f.)
Apparently Ellen had now served her purpose, completed the bright
pointless noon and afternoon of the butterfly's summer and vanished
(94)
Ellen was dead two years now—the butterfly, the moth caught in a gale and
blown against a wall and clinging there beating feebly, not with any
particular stubborn clinging to life, not in particular pain since it was too
light to have struck hard, nor even with very much remembrance of the
bright vacuum before the gale, but just in bewildered and uncomprehending
amazement
(103)
Ellen preened and fluttered out her unwitting butterfly's Indian summer
(119)

This repetition of images emphasizes the 'emptiness' of Ellen Sutpen, and illustrates the generalizations about women in Chapter II. Ellen, then, exemplifies Mr. Compson's characteristically negative view of women.[135]

Other repetitions in Mr. Compson's text in Chapter III include his account of Miss Rosa's feelings for her own father, 'whom she hated without knowing it' (71); 'the man whom she hated' (101). Mr. Compson also explains why, in his opinion, this is so: she never forgave him for the death of her mother at her own birth. Thus, a different light is cast upon Miss Rosa's complaint about Sutpen's behavior towards her own father. Another repetition is concerned with Sutpen, 'who did not even know that he was an embattled foe' (75); 'a foe who did not know that he was at war' (77); 'the foe who was not even aware that he sat there not as host and brother-in-law but as the second party to an armistice' (77). Both sets of repetitions stress an important lack of knowledge on the part of a character, and present Miss Rosa as unconscious 'hater' and Thomas Sutpen as unconscious 'victim.' The most intriguing repetition, perhaps, concerns the statement that Miss Rosa 'was not at home'; 'actually was not at home' when Henry took Judith's fiancé Charles Bon to visit her (86), and that, in fact, she never saw Bon alive at all:

So Miss Rosa did not see any of them, who had never seen (and was never to see alive) Charles Bon at all
(89)
Miss Rosa never saw him; this was a picture, an image.
(90)
a man whom she was not even to see alive.
(95)

The 'fact' that Miss Rosa never met Bon is essential to Mr. Compson's story, because it stresses the irrational aspects of her behavior. The text repeats that Miss Rosa was not jealous of Judith, that she felt 'not one whit of jealousy' towards her (85), but that she projected upon Judith 'all the abortive dreams and delusions of her own doomed and frustrated youth' (85).

Mr. Compson's 'Necessary' Worlds

When in Chapter IV Mr. Compson shifts the focus of his story from Thomas and Ellen Sutpen to their children, Henry and Judith, and to Judith's 'sweetheart' Charles Bon, bringing out a letter that Bon presumably wrote to Judith during the war,[136] an important change has taken place. His text now presents his version not as a careful conjecture but as a necessity. The modals *might* and *may* are replaced by *must*, with which Mr. Compson's 'possible world' is forced upon his listener Quentin:

he [Henry] must have realised that his father could not and would not have made [the statement about Bon's bigamy] without foundation and proof...
he must have known that what his father told him about the woman and the child was true.
(110)

---

135 As William Alexander Percy wrote in his autobiography, 'the lily-of-the-field life of the Southern gentlewoman existed only in the imagination of Northern critics and Southern sentimentalists, one about as untrustworthy as the other. They had too many duties even in slavery days to be idle' (1990:10). The mind-style of Mr. Compson, neither Northern critic nor sentimentalist, is basically cynical.
136 The letter is 'without date or salutation or signature' (160).

> He must have known that it would be vain... not to speak of what he
> learned
> (111)
> he must have known, as he knew that what his father had told him was
> true, that he was doomed and destined to kill. He must have known that just
> as he knew that his hope was vain
> (112)

Thus Mr. Compson paints a forceful picture of Henry's plight and shows clearly how he creates his 'possible world.' What he felt 'must' be true in the first two quotes above (that Henry knew his father's accusation of Bon was true) is already posited as a certainty in the third passage: Henry knew that his father was right. Subsequently, the 'necessary world' is extended one step further: Henry knew that his father was right in accusing his sister's 'sweetheart' of bigamy, therefore Henry 'must have known' that he would finally kill Bon. In addition, Mr. Compson's use of the attributive verbs *realise* and *know*, verbs he seldom uses, serves here to convince his listener in a subtle way that he agrees with the conclusions of the matrix subject Henry. As the text presents it, not only was Henry convinced of these 'truths' at the time but Mr. Compson is also convinced of them at the moment of his narration.

How much Mr. Compson identifies with Henry is shown by the observations he makes, culminating in the 'quotation' of an imagined utterance of Henry. With this, Mr. Compson actually 'moves into' the experience of Henry:

> He must have said to himself, must have said when he closed the library
> door for the last time behind himself that Christmas eve and must have
> repeated while he and Bon rode side by side through the iron dark of that
> Christmas morning, away from the house where he had been born and
> which he would see but one time more and that with the fresh blood of the
> man who now rode beside him, on his hands: *I will believe; I will. I will.*
> *Even if it is so, even if what my father told me is true and which, in spite of*
> *myself, I cannot keep from knowing is true, I will still believe.*
> (110f.)

The pseudo-quote 'I will believe; I will. I will' is repeated throughout Mr. Compson's text:

> the man, the struggling and suffocating heart behind it saying *I will believe!*
> *I will! I will! Whether it is true or not, I will believe!*
> (137)
> Henry... suppressing still that first cry of terror and grief, *I will believe! I*
> *will! I will!*
> (139)

These almost hallucinatory 'conjectures of necessity' show how Mr. Compson feels a need to create in Henry an ability to hold on to a conviction. It is the loyalty to a chosen point of view that Mr. Compson admires. But one must not forget that this desperate adherence to an untenable conviction involves a certain measure of 'schizoid splitting,' which Mr. Compson projects unto his subject Henry, as well as unto his listener Quentin.[137]

Mr. Compson's technique of creating a world thus conveys clearly and forcefully his power to convince his listener. The 'possible world' that 'must' exist is, moreover, visualized in great detail, for instance where it concerns the 'womanlike' qualities of Charles Bon, his 'flowered, almost feminised gown' (117), the 'outlandish and almost feminine garments of his sybaritic privacy' (118), his behavior of 'elegant and indolent esoteric hothouse bloom' (119). It is true that Mr. Compson's text sometimes displays more modest attributive clauses: *I can believe, I like to think, I believe*, but these introduce details of this world rather than the world itself. If Mr. Compson thus implicitly forces his personal imagery on Quentin, he does so explicitly as well:

> You can not even imagine him and Judith alone together. Try to do it
> (120)
> You see? there they are: this girl, this young countrybred girl who sees a
> man for an average of one hour a day for twelve days during his life and
> that over a period of a year and a half, yet is bent on marrying him to the
> extent of forcing her brother to the last resort of homicide, even if not
> murder, to prevent it
> (122f.)

One unquestioned observation stands at the heart of Mr. Compson's 'necessary world': 'that Henry had formally abjured his father and renounced his birthright and the roof under which he had been born' (96). This observation possesses some collateral support, because Miss Rosa had earlier told Quentin: 'I saw Henry repudiate his home and birthright' (17f.). Yet, while Miss Rosa claims that she 'saw' Henry take the decisive step, according to Mr. Compson it was a tale that came 'through the negroes' (96); and he argues that no one ever knew 'just why or just what happened between Henry and his father' (130).

Even if the 'news that Henry and Bon had ridden away in the dark and that Henry had formally abjured his home and birthright' (130f.) was, as Mr. Compson puts it, based on 'cabin-to-cabin whispering,' this does not keep him from repeating it again and again as if it were the truth:

> He repudiated blood birthright and material security for his sake, for the
> sake of this man who was at least an intending bigamist even if not an out
> and out blackguard
> (110)
> as witness Henry's violent repudiation of his father and his birthright when
> Sutpen forbade the marriage.
> (118)
> Henry... going fast now and his back rigid and irrevocably turned upon the
> house, his birthplace and all the familiar scenes of his childhood and youth
> which he had repudiated for the sake of that friend
> (131)

---

137 Readers of *The Sound and the Fury* will remember how much Quentin dislikes the creation of such 'necessary worlds': 'They all talked at once, their voices insistent and contradictory and impatient, making of unreality a possibility, then a probability, then an incontrovertible fact, as people will when their desires become words' (134). He does not, however, confront his father with his feelings.

the man for whose sake he had repudiated not only blood and kin but food
and shelter and clothing too
(136)

The use of the same words, 'repudiation' and 'birthright,' may indeed suggest that the story is more or less a 'set piece,' repeated again and again in the community. But although Mr. Compson's and Miss Rosa's texts use the same words, they endow them with their own preoccupations and their own significance.

Mr. Compson tries almost desperately to assign a cause-effect relationship to Henry's behavior: 'Because Henry loved Bon... So much so that he (Henry) could give his father the lie' (110). Throughout the text the attribution is repeated, often in a sudden simple sentence, always forceful and with remarkable conviction:

Because Henry loved Bon.
Because he loved Bon.
Yes, he loved Bon
he loved grieved and killed, still grieving and, I believe, still loving Bon
(110,111,118,119)

Mr. Compson is certain of this love, and the attributive clause *I believe*, here, modalizes not his conviction that Henry loved Bon, but rather his view that he still loved him even when he killed him. One notices here again the admiration that Mr. Compson feels for Henry's fidelity to a chosen point of view and the honesty of his emotions. For four years, while they were in the army, Henry presumably tried to get Bon to renounce his wife and child, so 'his (Henry's) sister' would not become 'a sort of junior partner in a harem' (147), all the while holding on to his devotion.[138] Yet Compson cannot fully understand why Henry killed his friend.[139]

If Mr. Compson is certain about Henry's feelings for Bon, he is also certain of the reciprocity of their feelings, and of Judith's role in them:

She must have seen him in fact with exactly the same eyes that Henry saw
him with. And it would be hard to say to which of them he appeared the
more splendid—to the one with hope, even though unconscious, of making
the image hers through possession; to the other with the knowledge, even
though subconscious to the desire, of the insurmountable barrier which the
similarity of gender hopelessly intervened[140]
(117)

---

138 The admiration that Mr. Compson feels for such an act also speaks from the 'pseudo-quotation' with which he enters Henry's sister Judith's mind, and discovers there a 'true pride which can say to itself without abasement *I love, I will accept no substitute... if happy I can be I will, if suffer I must I can*' (150). This, in fact, throws a different light on his 'conviction' in *The Sound and the Fury* that no emotions spent on love are worthwhile, and provides further illustration of the double bind that Quentin finds himself in.

139 As Estella Schoenberg puts it, 'the prior marriage [of Charles Bon], involving miscegenation, was not legally binding in either Louisiana or Mississippi' (1977:44). This is why Mr. Compson, as a lawyer, cannot fully explain the murder as the result of bigamy. The idea that Bon was black, and that he was Judith and Henry's half-brother, as Quentin's text will argue, is not part of father's story, except for one small hint that may have inspired Quentin: that Sutpen named all his children himself, even Clytie (the black half-sister), and even 'the one before Clytie and Henry and Judith' (73). There is no indication, however, that Quentin's father was aware that this unknown child might be Charles Bon.

140 Notice the subtle difference between Mr. Compson's use of 'unconscious' for Judith's hope (suggesting that she could not know it) and 'subconscious' for Henry's knowledge (suggesting that he might know it but pushes it out of his awareness).

It was because Bon not only loved Judith after his fashion but he loved
Henry too and I believe in a deeper sense than merely after his fashion.
Perhaps in his fatalism he loved Henry the better of the two, seeing perhaps
in the sister merely the shadow, the woman vessel with which to
consummate the love whose actual object was the youth
(133)

as I said before, it was not Judith who was the object of Bon's love or of
Henry's solicitude. She was just the blank shape, the empty vessel
(148)

Step by step, and almost imperceptibly, Mr. Compson's text extends his 'necessary
world' into a 'real' one. While Judith is at first 'perhaps' the 'woman vessel' to serve
the love of the men, in the last quote she is already unquestionably 'just the blank
shape, the empty vessel' that exists to hold their love. The forceful associations present
in the 'empty vessel' image must suggest something of Mr. Compson's own prefer-
ences. These link up with his generalization concerning 'that complete and abnegant
devotion which only a youth, never a woman, gives to another youth or a man' (132).

In Mr. Compson's eyes Bon's love for Judith can only be explained in terms of
Bon's love for Henry ('it was Henry, because at that time Bon had not even seen
Judith' [121]), that is, as the result of the closeness of Judith and Henry: 'that relationship between them—that single personality with two bodies both of which had been
seduced almost simultaneously' (113). We see that Mr. Compson's preoccupations, as
in *The Sound and the Fury*, lead directly to Quentin's problems. The explicitly incestuous atmosphere that his father chooses to create cannot but trouble Quentin, who is
struggling with such feelings for his own sister Caddy. Mr. Compson maintains this
incestuous atmosphere, without hesitation, as part of his 'necessary world':

So it must have been Henry who seduced Judith, not Bon: seduced her
along with himself... as though by means of that telepathy with which as
children they seemed at times to anticipate one another's actions as two
birds leave a limb at the same instant; that rapport not like the conventional
delusion of that between twins but rather such as might exist between two
people who, regardless of sex or age or heritage or race or tongue, had
been marooned at birth on a desert island[141]
(122)

Mr. Compson's disturbing version of the story is hopelessly upsetting to Quentin, who
readily identifies with Henry, 'this brother in whose eyes that sister's and daughter's
honor and happiness, granted that curious and unusual relationship which existed
between them, should have been more jealous and precious than to the father even'
(123). Here, in Mr. Compson's plottings, one finds the background to Quentin's

---

141 This passage, focusing on the desperate loneliness underlying the closeness of the brother and the sister,
touches Quentin forcefully. As readers of *The Sound and the Fury* know, he was to voice a similar emotion
and a similar image not much later, on the day of his suicide: 'When I was little there was a picture in one
of our books, a dark place into which a single weak ray of light came slanting upon two faces lifted out of
the shadow... It was torn out, jagged out. I was glad. I'd have to turn back to it until the dungeon was
Mother herself she and Father upward into weak light holding hands and us lost somewhere below even them
without even a ray of light' (198).

questions about incest in *The Sound and the Fury*.[142] Mr. Compson clearly refused to face such questions. Apparently it is easier for him to deal with events that might have happened years ago, with figments of his strained imagination, than with the immediate problems of his son.

Dirk Kuyk has argued that Quentin's concern in *Absalom, Absalom!* is not with his sister. As he puts it: 'if Faulkner means to make *Absalom* congruent with *The Sound and the Fury*, then Mr. Compson's discussion of Henry's possibly incestuous feelings is tactless and peculiar' (1990:93f.). But, of course, this is precisely what it is. As an answer to the question of how much the reader can 'feel that this is the Quentin, the same Quentin, who appeared in *The Sound and the Fury*—that is, a man thinking about his own Compson family, his own sister,' Faulkner himself said in any case: 'To me he's consistent. That he approached the Sutpen family with the same ophthalmia that he approached his own troubles' (Gwynn and Blotner 1959:274), and he stated that he told the story through Quentin because 'it is just before he is to commit suicide because of his sister.'[143]

Estella Schoenberg (1977) has provided a time-table that convincingly shows the interlocking of the novels. The shared chronology of *The Sound and the Fury* and *Absalom, Absalom!* and the closeness in time of the important events of the two novels have also been noted by Cleanth Brooks (1979) and Paul Ragan (1986). [144] After all, it is in the summer of 1909, in *The Sound and the Fury*, that Quentin tries unsuccessfully to face up to his sister's lover Dalton Ames. His father tries to convince him that the whole issue of Caddie's behavior is not worthy of his despair, and advises him to go up to Harvard, leaving Quentin in a state of threatening ego-fragmentation: 'but if it was that simple to do it wouldn't be anything and if it wasn't anything, what was I' (169). It is only about a month later, in September of that same year, and on the eve of his departure for Harvard, that Quentin listens to Miss Rosa's story and talks to his father afterwards.[145] His father, however, seems unaware of the implications of the story for his son, and continues to pursue his own obsessions.

Mr. Compson's whole story, it seems, forms an introduction to the letter that he brings out for Quentin to read, a letter that to him is proof that Bon did love Judith and that was preserved because Judith brought it to Quentin's grandmother after Bon's death, to save it or not save it as she wished. Judith's explanation of her action is presented by Mr. Compson in the form of a lengthy direct quote, which cannot pos-

---

142 His father's text uses a phrase that seems straight from *The Sound and the Fury:* 'that Henry had a sister' (121).

143 Naturally, one can choose to read the books as separate stories. Linking them, however, does add extra meaning with regard to characterization, and does not have to result in misreadings.

144 This does not mean that there are no inconsistencies between the two texts. Schoenberg mentions, for instance, that 'in August Caddy introduced Quentin to Dalton Ames in a drizzling rain, but when Quentin accompanies Rosa through the hot dusty night to Sutpen's Hundred about a month later it has not rained for sixty days' (1977:78).

145 This same night Quentin accompanies Rosa to Sutpen's Hundred (*Absalom, Absalom!*). Quentin spends the following Christmas and New Year at home with his family (*The Sound and the Fury*), so that he has only just returned to Harvard when his father's letter, dated January 10 (*Absalom, Absalom!*) arrives, informing him of Miss Rosa's death. He spends this night talking about the Sutpens with his roommate Shreve (*Absalom, Absalom!*). All this is before Quentin learns, also in January, that Caddy is pregnant and has become engaged to Sidney Herbert Head (*The Sound and the Fury*).

sibly be authentic, and which therefore naturally 'sounds like Father': 'it would be at least a scratch, something, something that might make a mark on something that *was* once for the reason that it can die someday, while the block of stone cant be *is* because it never can become *was* because it cant ever die or perish' (158). With its emphasis on states of being, however, it also sounds like Quentin, through whose mind the story is filtered.[146] The explanation, whatever its authentic form may have been, is explicitly linked with an act of suicide through his grandmother's presumed reaction to it: 'No! No! Not that! Think of your—' (158). At this moment, as the subject of a self-chosen death enters the text, both Mr. Compson and Quentin feel the need to move suddenly; perhaps they are moved by the story itself. As if to shake off associations that connect the two men all too tangibly, albeit implicitly, their behavior is suddenly nonverbal. His father 'half rising' (159), Quentin takes the letter out of his hands and starts to read it. And while Mr. Compson hears in his mind the last conversation of the two young friends: 'Henry saying to the other *Do you renounce then? Do you renounce?* and the other saying *I do not renounce*' (164), Quentin visualizes the scene, finally focusing on his own 'sore spot':

> It seemed to Quentin that he could actually see them, facing one another at the gate... two men, young, not yet in the world, not yet breathed over long enough, to be old but with old eyes.[147]
> (164f.)

Finally, Quentin imaginatively enters their minds and reads there the all too familiar tragedy of the brother facing the lover: 'the two faces calm, the voices not even raised: *Dont you pass the shadow of this post, this branch, Charles*; and *I am going to pass it, Henry*' (165). It is as if Quentin faces Caddy's lover Dalton Ames again. Although he longs to free himself from the ghosts of the past, Quentin clearly needs a cause with which his personality can be merged in order to lessen his confusion, his loneliness, and his fears.

Mr. Compson's story, throughout his text one question especially seems to occupy his mind: the question of why Henry Sutpen repudiated his birthright. To answer this question, Mr. Compson's text creates a 'necessary world' of love and devotion between two males and between brother and sister. We have clearly seen the power of persuasion that his 'necessary world' possesses on a linguistic level. An analysis of the complexities of Mr. Compson's style of attribution has shown how, largely invisibly to himself as well as to others, he advances this world step by step and thereby converts it into a 'real' one. In this way, he persuades not only Quentin but also himself of its 'truths.' The configuration of his world becomes such that it conforms to the basic preoccupations of Mr. Compson himself. He is clearly disappointed in women and hopes, or rather needs, to find a more honest and trustworthy dedication in men. He admires the honest emotions and the bravery of those who value and preserve these emotions. Yet at the same time, here and in *The Sound and the Fury*, his rationalizations seem to deny the existence of any such honest emotions in himself. From *The*

---

146 But most of all, the quote, with its hope of locating meaning in the living mind, sounds like Darl Bundren in *As I Lay Dying*.

147 The expression 'breathed over,' with its sexual connotations, is found in *The Sound and the Fury*. Quentin, there, imagines his sister Caddy and her lover.

Sound and the Fury, however, the reader knows that his behavior reveals an unbearable grief over his daughter Caddy's predicament, which belies his cynical words.

Miss Rosa Revisited

that Why? Why? and Why? that I have asked and listened to for almost fifty years

While Miss Rosa's story in Chapter I is introduced by an external narrator who introduces the setting and makes clear Quentin's position as listener, Chapter V has no such introduction. Moreover, it is rendered almost completely in italics. Although Faulkner's consistency in the use of italics has not remained unquestioned, it is clear from my discussions of *The Sound and the Fury*, *As I Lay Dying* and *Light in August* that italics always introduce a change in level of experience. In these novels, the reader enters the sub- and unconscious levels of the minds of different speakers: Quentin and Benjy Compson, most of the Bundren children, and Joe Christmas.

In *Absalom, Absalom!* the italics do not always lead to deeper levels of mental functioning of the speaker, but often to those of the addressee, Quentin Compson. In Chapter I this is immediately made explicit:

> the two separate Quentins now talking to one another in the long silence of notpeople in notlanguage, like this: *It seems that this demon—his name was Sutpen—(Colonel Sutpen)—Colonel Sutpen. Who came out of nowhere and without warning upon the land with a band of strange niggers and built a plantation—(Tore violently a plantation, Miss Rosa Coldfield says)—tore violently. And married her sister Ellen and begot a son and a daughter which—(Without gentleness begot, Miss Rosa Coldfield says)—without gentleness. Which should have been the jewels of his pride and the shield and comfort of his old age, only—(Only they destroyed him or something or he destroyed them or something. And died)—and died. Without regret, Miss Rosa Coldfield says—(Save by her) Yes, save by her. (And by Quentin Compson) Yes. And by Quentin Compson.*
> (5f.)

It is clear that the italics here convey a 'discussion' on a deeper level of mental functioning between two 'voices' that belong to Quentin, while he is listening to Miss Rosa Coldfield. These voices seem to combine the legend that Quentin already knows with the effects of the story that Miss Rosa is telling. They encompass, in a nutshell, the whole story of *Absalom, Absalom!* Such episodes in italics characteristically do not require quotation marks to introduce them because they are not 'realized' on the surface level of mental functioning, not being conscious speech or thought. Thus Chapter V may be read as one long 'pre-thought act' experienced by Quentin. This is especially clear at the end of the chapter, where the sentence 'but Quentin was not listening' (215) brings the reader back to his image of the crucial scene in the previous chapter, where Henry Sutpen faced his sister's 'sweetheart' Charles Bon.[148]

---

148 This does not mean, as Estella Schoenberg has argued, that 'Rosa's whole diatribe is wiped out' (1977:103), but that it never reaches Quentin's conscious mind, so that its effects are hidden from his own awareness.

Readers of *The Sound and the Fury* have already seen how Quentin is trapped within the paradoxical qualities of his father's behavior, the incompatibility of the latter's verbal and nonverbal acts. These behavioral qualities are also found in Chapters II, III and IV of *Absalom, Absalom!* Mr. Compson's story, in these chapters, both creates Quentin's present preoccupations and confirms his prior obsessions. No wonder, then, that the story as it floats through Quentin's mind becomes more and more his own, and that all of it starts to sound more and more 'like Father.'[149] Although he answers 'yessum' to Miss Rosa in a docile way he is still able to think critically about her text, as his thought '*only she dont mean that*' (7) shows. To his father's story, however, Quentin listens quite passively.

The consequences of this passivity remain apparent in Chapter V, which shifts again to Miss Rosa's discourse. The story, as she tells it to Quentin later that night while they drive out to Sutpen's Hundred together, undergoes certain changes in Quentin's mind that make it more like Mr. Compson's. It seems as if, at this stage, Miss Rosa's text is received through the matrix that his father's text has already laid down. This would explain its 'Compsonesque' adjectives, such as: '*brooding house*' (169); '*ancient young delusions of pride and hope and ambition (ay, and love too)*' (170); '*furious yet absolutely rocklike and immobile antagonism*' (170); '*bold blank naked and outrageous words*' (208); and its preoccupation with time: '*the Sutpen face... antedating time and house and doom*' (169), all of which are not characteristic of Miss Rosa's earlier text. Quentin seems to be overcome by the stories that he has somehow to digest; no wonder he experiences himself as 'an empty hall echoing with sonorous defeated names... not a being, an entity' (9).

In this fifth chapter, then, the stories of Miss Rosa and Mr. Compson are superimposed in the 'empty hall' of Quentin's mind. Here, in this imaginative space, Miss Rosa, the '*neglected root... planted warped*' (179), unable to come to terms with her awakening sexuality, her loneliness and her need for love, appears as Judith's double, watching her and waiting, as she imagines Judith to wait, for the beloved Bon:

> *I dreamed in the lurking harborage of my own shrub or vine as I believed*
> *she dreamed upon the nooky seat which held invisible imprint of his absent*
> *thighs just as the obliterating sand, the million finger-nerves of frond and*
> *leaf, the very sun and moony constellations which had looked down at him,*
> *the circumambient air, held somewhere yet his foot, his passing shape, his*
> *face, his speaking voice, his name: Charles Bon, Charles Good, Charles*
> *Husband-soon-to-be.*
> (184)

Henry's college friend Charles Bon has already left Sutpen's Hundred by this time. Just as the story of Miss Rosa's own behavior in the past is a story of negations ('*I never saw him. I never even saw him dead. I heard an echo, but not the shot; I saw a closed door but did not enter it*' [187]), so Miss Rosa's story of Charles Bon is a story of negations: '*three women put something into the earth and covered it, and he had never been*' (190). Nevertheless, the text that returns to the fourteen-year-old Miss Rosa, who never did see Charles Bon, makes an 'absence' into a person and invests it with

---

149 Quentin's section in *The Sound and the Fury*, as we have seen, also sounds 'like Father' to a large degree.

adolescent devotion. Yet, while she does so, she again and again denies both love and jealousy: '*it was not jealousy, because I did not love him. (How could I have, when I had never seen him?)*' (182). While Miss Rosa presents herself as Judith's double, placing herself in the role of Bon's beloved and then displacing herself again, she also, however circumferentially, envisions embracing the role of Judith's lover: '*That was the miscast summer of my barren youth which... I lived out not as a woman, a girl, but rather as the man which I perhaps should have been*' (179), and elaborates on '*the jealousy of the lover... who spies to watch, taste, touch that maiden revery of solitude which is the first thinning of that veil we call virginity*' (183f.).

Although these imaginings are negated as soon as they are formed ('*No, it was not that; I was not spying*' [184]), they still evoke the dream in which Miss Rosa dwells, infusing her with unexperienced identity, so that, for a time, she can escape '*that non-descript too long a child yet too short a woman*' (185). As the adolescent infatuation of a lonely child, Miss Rosa's dreamworld is perhaps not unusual. It is not this experience, however, but her abortive 'love affair' with Sutpen a number of years later that retrospectively forms the motif of the summer of '*root bloom and urge*' that Miss Rosa's text presents here. Her story to Quentin, as a sequel to both experiences, necessarily bears the stamp of the disappointments and outrage of the experience with Sutpen. If it is this 'summer of wistaria' when her sexuality awakens that prepares her for Sutpen, a man she believes her sister and cousin, not herself, 'needed protection from,' it is her outrage that prepares her for the story she tells Quentin. The text presents alternative worlds only to deny them, and foregrounds its different aspects through its 'Compsonesque' accumulations of adjectives: '*electric furious immobile urgency and awareness of short time*' (200); '*the same aghast and outraged unbelief*' (208); '*the old outraged and aghast unbelieving*' (210).

Miss Rosa's text conjures differences: between the knowledge of the community (that which '*they will have told you doubtless*' [166]) and the experience of Miss Rosa herself (that which '*they cannot tell you*' [168]), differences between her personality as seen by the community and as felt by herself.[150] She does not deny the social image of her personality, but she implies that some of it is wrong and that there is more. She explicitly addresses Quentin here as well:

> *Yes. You will say (or believe) that I waited even then to become engaged to him; if I said I did not, you would believe I lied. But I do say I did not. I waited for him exactly as Judith and Clytie waited for him: because now he was all we had, all that gave us any reason for continuing to exist, to eat food and sleep and wake and rise again: knowing that he would need us (191f.)*

Thus Miss Rosa forcefully implicates Quentin in her story, making him one of the community and attributing to him the judgments that her story demands. He should learn here what the insult to her really was: not that Sutpen offended her with his

---

150 Rosemary Coleman calls this community knowledge about Rosa 'the very stuff of the Southern collective memory, those stories which confirm the community mind and values: frustrated female sexuality; insulted female priggishness; an ugly woman's veneer of rigid morality designed to hide her unadmitted lusts' (1988:424n.). Coleman argues that critics also follow these communal myths by denigrating Rosa and dismissing her as irrelevant, instead of taking her seriously.

proposal, not that he jilted her, '*that was not even the nub of the insult*' (214), but that he was unable to attach himself emotionally to any woman, and thus used them all for his own purpose.[151]

Quentin's mind, however, is elsewhere, stuck where Miss Rosa, with her need to belong to something larger than herself, merges with both lover and beloved: with Bon and with Judith. This story, which superimposes itself on his father's, in which it is Henry who merges with lover and beloved (Bon and Judith), cannot but sharpen again Quentin's own obsession, calling up the image of

> the two of them, brother and sister… speaking to one another in short brief
> staccato sentences like slaps, as if they stood breast to breast striking one
> another in turn, neither making any attempt to guard against the blows:
> *Now you cant marry him.*
> *Why cant I marry him?*
> *Because he's dead.*
> *Dead?*
> *Yes. I killed him.*
> (215)

Quentin is left with a heritage of obsessions revolving around a brother and sister, alone in a chaotic world. 'He too,' as Deborah Robbins has put it, 'is brother to a beloved sister whose choice of men has challenged his personal code' (1981:322), and he too is alone in a chaotic world. Thus Miss Rosa's story, as it floats through his mind, reflects obsessions that characterize Quentin's own mind-style. He will need to externalize some of these obsessions if he is to keep his sanity.

Miss Rosa's outrage over Thomas Sutpen's behavior, and especially over the enigma of her father's implication in it, is complemented here by self-attributions through which she constructs causal relations between the outrageous behavior of the two men in her life—her father and Thomas Sutpen—and her own behavior. But she is aware of her position as public figure; she feels she has to contend with the characterizations that others have made of her, and that have become public property. That these public accounts of her personality, as Miss Rosa understands them, are extremely stereotypical is clear from the children's song she repeats several times with slight alterations:

> *Rosie Coldfield, lose him, weep him; caught a man but couldn't keep him*
> *Rosie Coldfield, lose him, weep him; found a man but failed to keep him*
> *Rosie Coldfield, lose him, weep him; caught a beau but couldn't keep him*
> (210,212,213)

Quentin and Shreve

> *the two of them not moving except to breathe, both young, both born within*
> *the same year: the one in Alberta, the other in Mississippi*

Throughout five chapters, now, we have seen that Quentin has been forced to internalize the obsessions of Miss Rosa Coldfield and his father (her outrage and his neces-

---

151 The insubstantial lightness of the man, in Miss Rosa's image, curiously parallels the butterfly-image that Mr. Compson created of Sutpen's wife: '*He was the light-blinded bat-like image of his own torment cast by the fierce demoniac lantern up from beneath the earth's crust*' (214).

sities). He has had to experience for himself the tragic moments of Miss Rosa's life, and of the Sutpens, and he has been persuaded to identify with Henry, the tragic fratricide. Several times it seems that Quentin cannot listen any longer, that the story has brought to life 'something which he too could not pass' (215). At last he actually has to walk 'out of his father's talking,' suggesting the fervor with which the un- stoppable story goes on and on (218). It seems as if Quentin will also need to tell his own story, and externalize some of the obsessions that have been revitalized in him, to keep his sanity. But in order to accomplish this, Quentin needs first of all to create a distance between himself and the stories he has heard. He does this by insisting that Miss Rosa, and the whole Sutpen family, are no kin to him: 'No, neither aunt cousin nor uncle Rosa. Miss Rosa' (218). The necessity of this distancing and the energy behind it are impressive, as is clear from his discussion with his friend Shreve:

'Miss Rosa,' Quentin said.
'All right all right.—that this old dame, this Aunt Rosa—'
'Miss Rosa, I tell you.'
'All right all right all right.—that this old—this Aunt R—All right all right all right all right.'
(221)

At the beginning of Chapter VI, some aspects of the text, for instance its appended groups, may remind the reader of Quentin's mind-style in *The Sound and the Fury*: 'There was snow on Shreve's overcoat sleeve, his ungloved blond square hand red and raw with cold, vanishing' (217), whereby it is unclear what is vanishing. Through heightened voice the narrator presents Quentin's 'dim and blurred impressions,' experienced as if in a 'dreamlike state of mind' (Kaluza 1967:67). Notice the eerie quality of Quentin's logic, evoked by the causal connector *so that*, and familiar from *The Sound and the Fury*: 'the white oblong of envelope, the familiar blurred mechan- ical *Jefferson Jan 10 1910 Miss* and then, opened, the *My dear son* in his father's sloped fine hand out of that dead dusty summer where he had prepared for Harvard so that his father's hand could lie on a strange lamplit table in Cambridge' (217). One also finds a reprise of Quentin's obsessions, foreshadowing the scene of his psychosis a few months later:

something which he still was unable to pass: that door, that gaunt tragic dramatic self-hypnotised youthful face... the sister facing him across the wedding dress which she was not to use, not even to finish, the two of them slashing at one another with twelve or fourteen words and most of these the same words repeated two or three times so that when you boiled it down they did it with eight or ten.
(218f.)

The universal implications of the definite articles in the phrase '*the* sister facing him across *the* wedding dress' (my emphasis) suggest a reference to all sisters, including Quentin's own.

Quentin obviously has told some of the ancient stories to his roommate, as the text seems to indicate not so much out of his own need but in answer to questions like: '*Tell about the South. What's it like there. What do they do there. Why do they live there.*

Why do they live at all' (218).[152] Especially the last of these questions may be seen
to present also Quentin's own preoccupations. Quentin has apparently been speaking
of the South, but it seems that he has not been able to discuss his own obsessions. On
the evening of their conversation in January of 1910, again, Quentin does not seem to
have a chance to externalize his own preoccupations. Instead, he must *'hear it all over
again'* (264) while his friend Shreve—who is later to become a surgeon—'dissects' the
situation and confronts Quentin with his own conclusions. As Faulkner had done only
briefly in *As I Lay Dying*, where Cash Bundren addresses an external audience to find
understanding for his brother Darl, and in *Light in August*, where Gavin Stevens speaks
to his old college friend from Harvard about Joe Christmas's fate, a speech partner is
created who can view the problems of the South from the outside. Here, however, the
external viewpoint is not just evoked as a silent 'appellative element' in the text
(Martínez-Bonati 1981:85), but as an important world-creating technique with which
the author tries to step outside his own worldview. Faulkner said about this outside
voice, embodied by the Canadian student Shreve: 'Probably his friend McCannon had
a much truer picture of Sutpen from what Quentin told him than Quentin himself did'
(Gwynn and Blotner 1959:274).

Faulkner creates much room for this voice here. The whole of Chapter VI, in fact,
might be considered one long appended clause to the outsider's attributive clause 'you
mean that this old gal, this Aunt Rosa—?' (221), interrupted only by Quentin's musings
and an occasional 'yes.' Quentin must once again cope with his own memories, his
imaginings, his emotions. It is Shreve who does the talking, and who tries to put the
characters into perspective, blowing them up beyond a specific time and place, labeling
Sutpen 'an ancient stiff-jointed Pyramus,' 'this Faustus' and 'this Beelzebub,' and Miss
Rosa 'eager though untried Thisbe' (222). It is Shreve, also, who gives the most down-
to-earth explanation for Sutpen's treatment of Miss Rosa: 'he approached her and
suggested they breed like a couple of dogs together, inventing with fiendish cunning
the thing which husbands and fiancés have been trying to invent for ten million years...
who said it and was free now' (226). It is this subject, man's struggle to regain his
freedom from women in general and Sutpen's 'escaping it' and 'getting back into it'
in particular, that makes Quentin think: *'He sounds just like Father.'*[153] Indeed,
Shreve's text echoes Mr. Compson's words such as: 'Yes. They lead beautiful
lives—women. Lives not only divorced from, but irrevocably excommunicated from,
all reality' (240).

As in Chapter II, the text presents a familiar type of digression originating with
Mr. Compson: 'You had an aunt once (you do not remember her because I never saw
her myself but only heard the tale)' (240). The digression is meant to convince Quentin
of the 'truth' of his father's typical generalizations about women. Not much later,
Quentin's musings elaborate the same view:

152 Dirk Kuyk has commented on the lack of question marks here. As he puts it: 'Despite the sentences'
interrogative form, Shreve isn't asking questions. He's giving commands because he thinks he knows "about
the South." He expects a story that will confirm his notions' (1990:88). I think, rather, that the quotation
marks are lacking because the questions are presented not as Shreve's utterances but as Quentin's thought
acts, as the italics indicate.
153 This is not so much Quentin mentally dismissing Shreve's account, as Kuyk argues (1990:90), but
rather a sign of Quentin's desperation, to be gathered from his repeated 'too much'; 'too long.'

*Beautiful lives—women do. In very breathing they draw meat and drink
from some beautiful attenuation of unreality in which the shades and shapes
of facts—of birth and bereavement, of suffering and bewilderment and
despair—move with the substanceless decorum of lawn party charades,
perfect in gesture and without significance or any ability to hurt.*
(264)

If this is still Mr. Compson's general outlook on life, we find in it Quentin's characteristic linguistic choice *unreality*, where his father has used 'divorced from' and
'irrevocably excommunicated from reality.' While in his father's mind, then, reality
exists but does not allow for women, in Quentin's mind one finds the world of women
as an 'unrealized' state. From Quentin's mind-style, however, one knows also that this
unrealized state reflect not just the female world; it is Quentin's own 'unworld' of 'not-
husband' (3), 'unamaze' (5), 'notpeople' (5), 'notlanguage' (5); 'unregret' and 'unforgiving' (13) that one is confronted with.[154] Mr. Compson's text, here, also
contains the paired, often oxymoronic and personifying adjectives of Chapter III, with
which he tends to weigh down abstract qualities and invest them with all the depressive
stasis of the human flesh: 'furious and indomitable desperation' (254); 'terrific and
incredulous excretion' (257); 'curious and outrageous exaggeration' (259). One may
recognize here also Mr. Compson's nihilism, familiar from *The Sound and the
Fury*—'all the old accumulated rubbish-years which we call memory, the recognisable
I' (245f.)—now dangerously applied to identity itself. Quentin is very sensitive to his
father's point of view and tends to adopt it without question, as one can see when his
own musings present Judith as a woman '*filled with that seduction, that celestial
promise which is the female's weapon*' (261). While his father stresses 'tears' as
'female weapons,' Quentin fears 'seduction,' bringing back to mind his complaint in
The Sound and the Fury: 'I could not be a virgin, with so many of them walking along
in the shadows and whispering with their soft girlvoices' (169).

So far, then, Quentin's mind has been filled with Miss Rosa's text, with his
father's text, and with his grandfather's text. His own text has shown a form of deictic
projection familiar from *The Sound and the Fury*, whereby 'I' stands for Miss Rosa or
for his father but never for Quentin himself. In this chapter, however, it is possible for
the first time to analyze a long stretch of Quentin's text in which his deictics are
anchored to his own position as speaker. Here we may finally expect the pronoun *I* and
its related forms to refer to Quentin. It is a curious fact, however, that this stretch of
text avoids the first-person pronoun almost completely. While Mr. Compson's text,
which also conveys events in which he did not himself participate, shows the first-
person pronoun—'I can imagine him' (111); 'I don't think she ever did' (112); 'He is
the curious one to me' (114); 'I like to think this' (117)—Quentin's use of 'I' is
restricted to his very first sentence: '*Just exactly like Father if Father had known as
much about it the night before I went out there as he did the day after I came back*'
(227). Quentin presents himself here as the actor of a simple, circular action: 'I went
out... I came back,' as he did in *The Sound and the Fury*.

Although the text does not refer to Quentin directly in this first stretch in italics,

---

154 Soon, as readers of *The Sound and the Fury* know, Quentin will have to flee this 'unworld' because,
as an unrealized state, it cannot sustain him.

it does refer to him indirectly, for instance through his use of modals and attributive verbs. From the auxilliary *must* and the attributive verb *realise* it is clear that his text, like his father's, creates a 'necessary world.' Twice the text displays the modal adverb *perhaps* and the attributive verb *believe*, where Quentin is talking of 'fear' (229) and of 'the lie' (231), subjects he approaches cautiously. At one point the text uses the modal adverb *apparently*; here Quentin is careful to limit his information to what can be observed from the outside, but shows at the same time a certain measure of identification with the person observed, since he feels he can deduce from the observed behavior a certain motivation. The attributive clauses most often use a that-clause, indicating that Quentin is interested in the conclusions of the experiencer in the matrix clause; for instance, the *'mad impotent old man who realised at last that there must be some limit even to the capabilities of a demon for doing harm'* (227). Here the speaker 'creates' the conclusion of the matrix subject—the mad impotent man—but also distances himself from it by looking at it and pronouncing judgment on it. The attributive verb *realise* indicates that he agrees with this conclusion. A few times, however, Quentin uses a small-clause, relinquishing this judging faculty and entering into the experience itself, identifying himself with it:

the old wornout cannon... saw son gone, vanished, more insuperable to him
now than if the son were dead
(228)
the two daughters watched... the old demon, the ancient varicose and
despairing Faustus fling his final main now
(229)

Quentin has taken over and elaborated upon Shreve's label for Thomas Sutpen: 'Faustus'; in fact, the sentence seems to combine Shreve's label with his father's construction of paired adjectives. Another characteristic of the text is its large number of progressives, stressing the simultaneity of the images in Quentin's mind: 'the demon lying in the hammock while Jones squatted against a post, rising from time to time... squatting again, chortling and chuckling and saying... the two of them drinking turn and turn about from the jug and the demon not lying down now nor even sitting but reaching after the third or second drink that old man's state of impotent and furious undefeat in which he would rise, swaying and plunging and shouting for his horse and pistols' (230).[155] Again, the use of the paired, often personifying adjectives ('impotent and furious') remind one of his father's text. They are combined here with Quentin's characteristic unrealized state: 'undefeat.'

The whole first part of these musings, until Quentin interrupts himself with a 'yes' to Shreve, consists of one long sentence, taking up more than five pages. This sentence includes direct quotes and contains many appended groups or 'quasi clauses' with various degrees of ambiguity. In contrast, the second part of the musings, after the

---

155 Quentin charges Sutpen with the same kind of self-destructive, degenerate behavior that the Compson children in *The Sound and the Fury* attribute to their father: '*Father will be dead in a year they say if he doesn't stop drinking and he wont stop he cant stop since I since last summer*' (142); 'Father wouldn't even come down town anymore but just sat there all day with the decanter I could see the bottom of his nightshirt and his bare legs' (268).

'yes' and starting with a summarizing 'so' (232), consists of a number of shorter sentences, slowing down the feverish pace of the first part. Quentin's views concerning Judith's coldness, very much an internalization of Mr. Compson's general idea about women, are repeated twice here. When Sutpen is killed by Wash Jones for taking advantage of his granddaughter, and his body is taken 'in the light of the lanterns and the pine torches' up the steps to the house, Judith, 'the tearless and stonefaced daughter' holds the door open 'for him too' (232). She, in Quentin's words, shows 'no tears, no bereavement this time too' (233). That Quentin reminds himself again of the other killing—Bon's death through Henry's bullet—is clear from the twice-repeated 'too' at the end of a phrase, where it receives much emphasis. A second stretch of Quentin's own text in italics, starting with the pronoun *I* referring to Quentin himself, repeats his earlier complaint: '*Yes. I have heard too much, I have been told too much; I have had to listen to too much, too long*' (259f.). A third episode again repeats: '*Yes, to too much, too long. I didn't need to listen then but I had to hear it and now I am having to hear it all over again because he sounds just like Father*' (264).

Neither passage shows the first-person pronoun, except for the sentences quoted here. In the middle of this last section, however, a curious change takes place: the text starts referring to Quentin with the second-person pronoun *you*. Whether these words are understood as Quentin's own, in unanchored deictic projection, or whether they are Shreve's, reflected in Quentin's mind, one is struck by the sudden and enormous proliferation of this pronoun and its corresponding forms. The passage is the first to be concerned with Quentin's own experience. In this respect the replacement of the wistaria smell of Miss Rosa's summer of 'root and urge' with Quentin's 'jungle of... honeysuckle' (268) is very suggestive, and seems to link the image of Miss Rosa as an adolescent girl with the image of Quentin's sister Caddy. The passage describes Quentin's personal involvement with the history of the Sutpens, beginning with his first introduction as a little boy to the remnants of the Sutpen dynasty: Judith's very old mulatto half-sister Clytie and an imbecile young boy, introduced as the great-grandchild of Sutpen, the grandchild of Charles Bon: 'the Jim Bond' (268).

A Story about Thomas Sutpen

At the start of Chapter VII, one is again confronted immediately with Quentin's mental activity: his somewhat fragmented view of his friend Shreve's appearance and actions: 'There was no snow on Shreve's arm now, no sleeve on his arm at all now: only the smooth cupid-fleshed forearm and hand coming back into the lamp and taking a pipe from the empty coffee can where he kept them, filling it and lighting it' (271). The text focuses on Quentin's nonverbal, and especially his paraverbal behavior:

Quentin did not answer. He sat quite still, facing the table
(271)
his voice level, curious, a little dreamy yet still with that overtone of sullen bemusement, of smoldering outrage: so that Shreve, still too... watched him with thoughtful and intent curiosity.
(272)

Again and again, his 'curious repressed calm voice' (273); this 'flat, curiously dead voice' (322) is referred to, talking

as though to the table before him or the book upon it or the letter upon the

book or his hands lying on either side of the book.
(273)
apparently (if to anything) to the letter lying on the open book on the table between his hands.
(318)
still in that curious, that almost sullen flat tone which had caused Shreve to watch him from the beginning with intent detached speculation and curiosity
(319)

Estella Schoenberg has characterized Quentin as a 'reluctant narrator' (1977:69). Perhaps his way of talking is a protective measure, guarding him from too much emotion. Yet, in any case, he finally speaks.

The story that Quentin tells to Shreve is one that he has heard from his father, who heard it from his, who presumably heard it from Sutpen himself. This is the story of the ten-year-old Thomas Sutpen, traveling with brothers and sisters and a drunken father to find a new place to live. As the story goes, the mother almost immediately dies: 'he said something to Grandfather about his mother dying about that time and how his pap said she was a fine wearying woman and that he would miss her' (278). Notice the matter-of-fact tone of this sentence, presumably bearing the stamp of Sutpen's father and of Sutpen himself, but also of General Compson, of Mr. Compson and of Quentin. An entire orchestration of male voices thus presents the woman as an insubstantial being.

Quentin's text puts great emphasis on the way the family traveled: 'sliding back down out of the mountains and skating in a kind of accelerating and sloven and inert coherence like a useless collection of flotsam on a flooded river moving by some perverse automotivation such as inanimate objects sometimes show, backward against the very current of the stream, across the Virginia plateau and into the slack lowlands about the mouth of the James River' (278). With its elaborate simile, the text creates for the Sutpen family a sort of grotesque stubbornness reminiscent of the Bundren family in *As I Lay Dying*. With the Bundrens, the Sutpens belong to the large and various group of non-slaveholding white people that populated the hill country of different Southern States. Displaced time and again into less profitable mountainous areas by 'more prosperous yeomen and small slaveholders,' who, as James Oakes has argued, 'together established the community's all-important ties to the market' (1990:104), the Sutpens seem over the years to have gathered a momentum that makes them finally slide down again with the same volitionlessness that characterizes the movements of Anse Bundren in *As I Lay Dying*.

But one may also recognize Quentin's own feelings of stasis here. The adjectives used again have a personifying quality: 'furious inertness and patient immobility' (280). They come in pairs ('dreamy and destinationless locomotion' ([280]) or in strings ('sober static country astonishment' [281]). One is reminded at once of Mr. Compson's text and of Quentin's desperate and unbearable feelings of stasis in *The Sound and the Fury*. In the same way, something of Quentin's own mind-style shows itself in the confused sense of time that he attributes to Sutpen: 'He didn't remember if it was weeks or months or a year they traveled... whether it was that winter and then spring and then summer overtook and passed them on the road or whether they overtook and passed in slow succession the seasons as they descended or whether it was the descent itself that did it' (280). But the text still does not refer directly to Quentin himself here. Indirectly, however, its modals and attributive verbs show the pattern of his father, creating 'necessary worlds' ('they must have realised, believed at last that they were no longer traveling' [282]) and 'possible worlds' ('maybe he even realised, understood the pleasure it would have given his sisters' [285]) that reflect his own need for structure and sequence.

The story that Quentin's text creates seems basically directed at the exploration of one characteristic of Sutpen: 'His trouble was innocence' (274). Throughout the text this complicated concept is repeated in different contexts, which reveals much about Quentin's own mind-style. In the beginning, as Quentin's text presents it, the experience of innocence is so natural that Sutpen is not consciously aware of it:

he had not only not lost the innocence yet, he had not yet discovered that he possessed it.
(285)
He didn't even know he was innocent that day when his father sent him to the big house with the message.
(286)
he was still innocent. He knew it without being aware that he did
(286)

To convey the painful experience that made Sutpen aware of his 'innocence,' Quentin starts by using a how-clause concentrating on the mental process that Sutpen went through: 'he never even remembered what the nigger said, how it was the nigger told him, even before he had had time to say what he came for, never to come to that front door again but to go around to the back' (290). What Sutpen, in his 'innocence,' had never realized is that he is a part of a white underclass that does not share in the slaveholder's white supremacy, and that, lacking white loyalty, can be forced to take commands even from blacks. But the negation in Quentin's text evokes Sutpen's mental processes at the same time as it negates his memories of these processes. Their influence is thus unassessed, and aptly the text switches to small-clauses that enter the 'raw' experience of Sutpen: 'He didn't even remember leaving. All of a sudden he found himself running' (290). Finally, Quentin's text focuses on the depersonalization that this devastating experience causes: 'He went into the woods. He says he did not tell himself where to go: that his body, his feet, just went there' (290). Notice the sudden use of deictic projection of tense, the verb *says* making clear the extent of Quentin's involvement and anticipating the similar splittings of Quentin himself in *The Sound and the Fury*.[156]

Quentin's text here conveys the experiences that Thomas Sutpen had to go through before he even realized that he possessed 'the innocence'; when 'he couldn't even realise yet that this trouble, his impediment, was innocence because he would not be able to realise that until he got it straight' (290f.). The to-infinitives and that-clauses of the text give Quentin the chance to evoke Sutpen's thinking processes and conclusions:

he had actually come on business, in the good faith of business which he

---

156 Quentin himself must have felt subconsciously that he needed to accomplish and maintain a split between his thinking processes and his feeling processes. He, in any case, presents the same kind of split in Sutpen at this decisive moment of his life.

had believed that all men accepted. Of course he had not expected to be
invited in to eat a meal... perhaps he had not expected to be asked into the
house at all. But he did expect to be listened to

(291)

With his choice of the attributive verbs *believed* and *expected*, Quentin refrains from
passing judgments on the mental activities of his subject, the young Thomas Sutpen,
who came to deliver his father's message. However, Thomas Sutpen 'knew,' Quentin
argues, 'that something would have to be done' about the insult of being sent away
from the door by a negro servant, 'in order to live with himself for the rest of his life'
(292). With the choice of his attributive verb *knew*, here, Quentin not only evokes
Sutpen's conclusion but also indicates that he agrees with this conclusion. Perhaps the
need to do something to restore one's sense of self-worth strikes a note in Quentin,
who himself had felt the need to confront his sister's lover Dalton Ames with the
disastrous results that would set the scene for his psychosis in *The Sound and the Fury*.

No single piece of information that Quentin gives is completely reliable with regard
to the 'truth' about Thomas Sutpen. Too many years have passed, too many minds have
filtered a story that is complicated to begin with. In addition, as I have shown, Quentin
himself is too much involved, if not with its people, who are no relatives of his, then
with its themes.[157] Yet, if the story is not reliable with regard to the 'truth' about
Sutpen, it *is* reliable with regard to the state of mind of Quentin, the speaker, as
conveyed through his mind-style. In stating that Thomas Sutpen said a certain thing,
or that his (Quentin's) grandfather said he did a certain thing, the text conveys
Quentin's choices, *his* emphasis, *his* obsessions. It shows the mind that conveys, or,
rather, 'creates,' Sutpen's experience of 'arguing with himself' (292), no matter how
much this mind is influenced by other minds:

> But I can shoot him: and the other: No. That wouldn't do no good: and the
> first: What shall we do then? and the other: I dont know: and the first: But I
> can shoot him. I could slip right up there through them bushes and lay there
> until he come out to lay in the hammock and shoot him: and the other: No.
> That wouldn't do no good: and the first: Then what shall we do? and the
> other: I dont know.

(293f.)

One almost hears Quentin try to decide what to do about the despised Dalton Ames.
Quentin has again come dangerously close to his own obsession, the same 'sore spot'
that Henry's killing of Bon had brought him to. With his pseudo-quote (*'But I can
shoot him... No. That wouldn't do no good'* [293]) Quentin creates both voices out of
his own tendency towards splitting, and enters thereby two sides of the young Thomas
Sutpen's mind—the rational and the feeling side—sides that he desperately tries to keep
separate in himself.

That Quentin identifies with the young Sutpen is clear from the deictic projection
of time adverbials: '*Now* he was hungry' (294; emphasis added), and from the sense

---

157 Estella Schoenberg has wondered about Quentin's compliance in listening to the story Rosa tells, and
she argues: 'Quentin is helpless to resist for two reasons: first, he is a polite young man easily drafted to
the service of a little old lady poet; and second, he sees in the stories of Judith and Henry Sutpen a situation
with which he is personally familiar but which he has been unable to resolve' (1977:27).

of depersonalization that foreshadows his own last day: 'now there was no sun at all where he crouched though he could still see sun in the tops of the trees around him. But his stomach had already told him it was late and that it would be later still when he reached home. And then he said he began to think *Home. Home* and that he thought at first that he was trying to laugh and that he kept telling himself it was laughing even after he knew better' (294).[158] As Quentin's text conveys it, Thomas Sutpen's splitting continues when he is at home in bed:

> Because he said how the terrible part of it had not occurred to him yet, he
> just lay there while the two of them argued inside of him, speaking in
> orderly turn, both calm, even leaning backward to be calm and reasonable
> and unrancorous: *But I can kill him—No. That wouldn't do no good—Then
> what shall we do about it?—I dont know*
> (295f.)

This 'terrible part': the terrific loneliness created by the parental neglect on which the text focuses here as in *The Sound and the Fury* is an experience that, in Quentin's conceptualization, totally defeats Thomas Sutpen.

According to Quentin, the young Thomas Sutpen realizes here that he need not even worry 'if he was going to lie or not' to his father about why he had not given the message to the planter, because his father did not even care to ask him if he did. As he puts it:

> *Pap never asked me if I told him or not and so he cant even know that Pap
> sent him any message and so whether he got it or not cant even matter, not
> even to Pap*
> (296).

In Quentin's story, Sutpen's relation to his father is certainly not as relaxed as Kuyk considers it, who argues that 'Sutpen recalls his father clearly without being either fixated on him or fixated on ignoring him' (1990:105). The terrible experience is Sutpen's first defeat. Quentin, who could not get his own father to attach any importance to his actions—not even his (pretended) incest with Caddy—puts great emphasis on the agony over such suffering, and he recognizes, subconsciously, the threat it can pose to a sense of self. Quentin tries to externalize his own desperation over senseless suffering via the story of Thomas Sutpen. But with conceptualizations like these, as Estella Schoenberg has argued, he only 'brings himself, Caddy's brother, to the point of no return on his path towards self-destruction' (1977:70).

When the young Sutpen realizes, 'like an explosion,' *'there aint any good or harm either in the living world'* (297) that he can do, he sees 'the severe shape of his intact innocence rising,' as Quentin puts it, from the 'limitless flat plain' of his ruined world. The small-clause form of the attribution—'he sees it rising'—clearly conveys Quentin's

---

158 An observation on the relentless needs of the body—'his stomach had already told him it was late'—is also found in Quentin's text on the last day of his life, in *The Sound and the Fury*, as is the concentration on trees and sunlight that the text attributes to Sutpen at this time of great emotional stress. A similar concentration occurs in Quentin's section in *The Sound and the Fury*, where Quentin faces his sister Caddy: 'her face looked off into the trees where the sun slanted' (187). In addition, an inappropriate, 'crazy' laughter marks the onset of Quentin's psychosis in *The Sound and the Fury*: 'I began to laugh again. I could feel it in my throat and I looked off into the trees...,. But I still couldn't stop it and then I knew that if I tried too hard to stop it I'd be crying' (169).

identification with his subject. Thomas Sutpen's loss of innocence thus amounts to the loss of the sense of 'we' that he had always innocently assumed. This loss occurs simultaneously both in the family, where his father obviously does not care, and in the world at large, where there obviously is no loyalty between whites. He sees the source of his insult: it was not the negro, nor even the planter, but 'them,' and his situation becomes clear to him. Both parts of him now agree, allowing him to act:

> 'If you were fixing to combat them that had the fine rifles, the first thing
> you would do would be to get yourself the nearest thing to a fine rifle you
> could borrow or steal or make, wouldn't it?' and he said Yes. 'But this aint
> a question of rifles. So to combat them you have got to have what they have
> that made them do what he did. You got to have land and niggers and a
> fine house to combat them with. You see?' and he said Yes again.
> (297)

Thus Sutpen's innocence turns into a 'design.' This entails leaving his former life behind. As Quentin tells it, 'He left that night... He never saw any of his family again' (297).

Dirk Kuyk has tackled the question of the nature of Sutpen's 'design.' Although many critics have argued otherwise (cf. Kuyk 1990:6f.), to Kuyk it seems clear that 'having land and niggers and a fine house' is not the design itself but the weapon to 'combat them with.' The design is what can be accomplished with this weapon. As he puts it: 'Sutpen is establishing his dynasty in preparation for the moment when "his turn" will come for a little boy to knock on his door. When the boy knocks, the butler will go to the door to do whatever Sutpen has trained him to do. Sutpen may seem to be preparing to reenact his own rejection by inflicting it on a boy who symbolizes the young Sutpen.'[159] But Kuyk notices 'that Quentin tells a different story' (1990:18). What Quentin's text conveys instead is that Sutpen 'would take that boy in where he would never again need to stand on the outside of a white door and knock at it: and not at all for mere shelter but so that that boy, that whatever nameless stranger, could shut that door himself forever behind him... forever free from brutehood just as his own (Sutpen's) children were' (326). Sutpen intended to teach society a lesson: 'that those lucky enough to have risen above brutehood should at least care about the feelings of the unlucky' (1990:21).[160] Even though Kuyk identifies the above clearly as Quentin's story, he nevertheless concludes: 'that is Sutpen's design.'

Kuyk can do this because he considers Sutpen one of *Absalom, Absalom!*'s narrators. As he puts it: 'Of course we hear Sutpen's words indirectly: he had spoken them to General Compson, who passed them on either to Mr. Compson or directly to Quentin. Nevertheless, since nothing suggests that this mediation has distorted what Sutpen said, I certainly count him as a narrator although his words do reach us through a line of Compsons' (1990:34).[161] One may wonder, however, how this mediation

---

159 This would be the defense mechanism of turning passive into active.

160 Faulkner himself did not mention such a goal, but argued: 'He'd have to have a male descendant. He would have to establish a dukedom which would be his revenge on the white Virginian who told him to go to the back door' (Gwynn and Blotner 1959:272).

161 Kuyk argues: 'If we were to count as narrators only those whose words are unmediated, then Rosa, Mr. Compson, Shreve and Quentin would themselves cease to be narrators. There is, after all, a third-person narrator' (1990:35). Kuyk forgets, however, that the mediation of voice through an external narrator is

could have avoided distorting what Sutpen originally said if the different speakers were emotionally involved with Sutpen and with his theme. (My discussion has focused on the different levels of involvement of the various speakers as this shows in their stylistic choices). In addition, Sutpen himself presented his story a full thirty years after the event that caused him to create the design under highly emotional circumstances. According to Quentin, even Sutpen's own first-hand version was 'a story' to begin with: 'He was telling a story. He was not bragging about something he had done; he was just telling a story about something a man named Thomas Sutpen had experienced, which would still have been the same story if the man had had no name at all, if it had been told about any man or no man over whiskey at night' (308f.).

One may imagine that Sutpen was very much concerned with class, and with the disappointing lack of loyalty between whites that are planters and whites that are poor. The way Quentin presents the details of the story of Thomas Sutpen, however, also creates many points of contact with his own history and fate. In this conceptualization, the wealth that was important to Sutpen was not the wealth of money but the wealth of belonging to a caring, close-knit family. As Quentin presents it, Sutpen envisioned trying to heal his own wound by making it up to some nameless little boy. This means especially acquiring a more adequate father, one who could save him by closing the door between him and the 'brutehood' of the world, just the sort of father that both Thomas Sutpen and Quentin Compson had to do without.

Quentin's story reveals a certain degree of admiration for Thomas Sutpen. But he, desperately looking for a model of manhood—unable either to follow or to cast away his father's nihilism—cannot leave his family behind like Sutpen did, even if physically he has gone away, to Harvard. He cannot follow the example of a man who 'could unify the various impulses in himself and that inexorable drive towards fulfillment, however bizarre and distorted the result' (Karl 1989:25). Unlike Sutpen, Quentin's ambivalence is so strong that it will never allow him to unify his impulses. Yet, something of his admiration shows itself from the text's repetition and thematization: 'That was how he said it'; 'That's how he said it'; 'He just said, "So I went to the West Indies"' (298f.). It is this hidden sense of admiration, perhaps, that makes Quentin enter a long stretch of deictic projection that is only barely anchored. The passage shows a tremendous proliferation of the pronoun *I*, referring not to Quentin but to Sutpen. It is amazing how Quentin manages to speak without referring to himself, either by using *I* where this pronoun refers to someone else, or by using *you* where it refers to himself.

Within a little more than two pages (302ff.), the pronoun *I* is encountered 46 times, not counting the related forms *myself* and *us*. The most frequent roles that are associated with this 'I' are those of knower and learner; other cognitive verbs include *listen, realise, design, believe, grasp, doubt, need, remember, recall, ask* and *say*. The majority of these mental verbs occur with that-clauses. Thus, a wide variety of mental activities leading to various conclusions is attributed to Sutpen. They evoke Sutpen as a thinker, an image that is completely at odds with those evoked by Miss Rosa and by Mr. Compson. In addition to these mental activities, Sutpen is also associated with

different from the mediation through a fellow character's voice. My discussion in Chapter 4 has made this clear.

physical activities, as the verbs *attend, enter, take, hold* and *went* show. Although a number of these verbs are negated or stipulative, they all associate physical activity, or the expectation of physical activity, with Sutpen. Remember, with respect to this, that the only role the text attributes to Quentin himself is that of a performer of a simple circular motion ('I went... I came back') and of a passive, forced experiencer of an internal process ('having to hear'). This is consonant with his roles in *The Sound and the Fury*. Quentin's need to involve himself with someone more active and powerful than himself is revealed clearly in these pages.

Thirty years later, Sutpen finally confronts with the problems in his 'design' the 'someone else, some older and smarter person' (292) for whom he had yearned after his hurtful experience, Quentin's grandfather, and he tells him: 'You see, I had a design in my mind. Whether it was a good or a bad design is beside the point; the question is, Where did I make the mistake in it, what did I do or misdo in it, whom or what injure by it to the extent which this would indicate' (329). The mistake in the 'design' returns again and again in the story:

he came to Grandfather, not to excuse but just to review the facts
(334)
he... came in to see Grandfather, trying to explain it, seeing if Grandfather could discover that mistake which he believed was the sole cause of his problem
(338)
hoping maybe (if he hoped at all, if he were doing anything but just thinking out loud at all) that the legal mind might perceive and clarify that initial mistake which he still insisted on, which he himself had not been able to find
(341)

Once more, Quentin's text presents a proliferation of the pronoun *I*, thereby entering into Sutpen's experience and making him speak with tremendous awareness of self, explaining how he first set out to accomplish this 'design': 'I should require money, a house, a plantation, slaves, a family—incidentally of course, a wife' (329).

Sutpen's text, as presented by Quentin, also touches on the reason for his repudiation of his first wife: 'they deliberately withheld from me the one fact which I have reason to know they were aware would have caused me to decline the entire matter, otherwise they would not have withheld it from me—a fact which I did not learn until after my son was born' (329). But what this 'one fact' actually is remains a mystery. Kuyk explains the mystery as follows: 'If Sutpen's wife is partly black, society would... judge their union to be illegal and taboo. To open the door to a white boy and invite him into such a household would, in the eyes of society, be to besmirch the status of even a nameless stranger' (1990:20). Sutpen certainly could not teach society a lesson that way. Whether or not this is so, Sutpen is defensive about his reasoning, as shown by his repeated 'I told you' and his many negations:

I did not undertake this risk purely and simply to gain a wife
I did not even demand
I did not demand
a fact which I did not learn until after my son was born.
I did not act hastily

I did not.
I made no attempt
(329,329,329,329,329,330,330)

And he concludes: 'if I had done an injustice, I had done what I could to rectify it' (330). In Quentin's conceptualization, Sutpen is faced with an unsolvable dilemma as soon as he sees Charles Bon: 'Henry said, "Father, this is Charles" and he... saw the face and knew' (333). The only choice left him is to destroy the design with his own hand or 'do nothing, let matters take the course... they will take.' Whether he forces Henry to kill Bon or allows Bon to marry Judith, the result will be the same: the 'weapon' with which to realize his 'design' will fall to dust.

The text, here, evokes the confrontation between Sutpen and Henry that makes Henry decide to repudiate his birthright. This is a scene that Quentin's father had already envisioned in Chapter III, but now the text incorporates the information that Quentin himself supposedly brought back from his visit to the dilapidated Sutpen mansion with Miss Rosa Coldfield, and that he presumably offered to his father at that time. The revised story serves as a solution to the question his father could not answer: the question of why Bon could not be accepted as Judith's husband. Curiously enough, however, although Quentin himself is the only one with first-hand information here, he still does not tell *his* story to Shreve, but conveys his own information as if it were his father's. It is Shreve who has to press on to get to the actual source:

'Your father,' Shreve said. 'He seems to have got an awful lot of delayed information awful quick, after having waited forty-five years. If he knew all this, what was his reason for telling you that the trouble between Henry and Bon was the octoroon woman?'
'He didn't know it then.'...
'Then who did tell him?'
'I did.' Quentin did not move, did not look up while Shreve watched him.
'The day after we—after that night when we—'
'Oh,' Shreve said. 'After you and the old aunt. I see. Go on.'
(332)

Afterwards, Quentin still refuses to take responsibility for the story. As in *The Sound and the Fury*, he quickly returns to the things 'Father said,' this time with the help of Shreve, hiding, as it were, behind them.

The story is laced with the attributive verb *know*, much like Miss Rosa's, making for a very opiniated stretch of text. 'Under the umbrella' of his father's text, Quentin makes positive judgments on the truths of the statements that he has Sutpen utter. These statements culminate in nihilistic generalizations, creating the type of 'necessary world' found in his father's text, only slightly weakened by *maybe*, which modalizes Sutpen's knowledge but not the 'truth' of the conclusion itself:

Sutpen must have known... what Henry was doing now... maybe even turned fatalist like Bon now and giving the war a chance to settle the whole business by killing him or Bon or both of them... or maybe he knew that the South would be whipped and then there wouldn't be anything left that mattered that much, worth getting heated over, worth protesting against or suffering for or dying for or even living for.
(337)

Finally, Quentin briefly reaches a point where he can refer to himself as story-teller; the first-person pronoun referring to Quentin himself occurs only three times:

I reckon he looked at her and she looked at him

I reckon Wash answering like it used to be

I reckon this was for more reason than because he just had one arm

(338,344,344)

With the attributive verb *reckon*, Quentin characteristically refrains from taking responsibility for the truth of what is contended. Yet the subjects here are important to Quentin: marriage, drunkenness and bravery. But after this, all the references to older voices return again, as Quentin keeps careful track of the stories of his father and his paternal grandparents. He is only briefly interrupted by Shreve, who protests: 'No... you wait. Let me play a while now' (349), showing that he underestimates, here, how serious the endeavor of story-telling is for Quentin.

A Story of Charles Bon

In Chapter VIII, the text suggests that it is Shreve again who speaks, voicing as one what both young men are thinking or imagining: 'it might have been either of them and was in a sense both: both thinking as one' (378). One cannot take this for granted completely, however, and simply consider both of them as the narrators of this last version of the story, because of the modal construction *might have been*, the adverbial *in a sense*, and the necessity of statements such as: 'never at any time did there seem to be any confusion between them as to whom Shreve meant by "he"' (388), and 'yet again Quentin seemed to comprehend without difficulty or effort whom he meant' (392). Indeed, Quentin is characterized in that he does *not* speak, that he does *not* take the chance to externalize his obsessions.[162] While Shreve speaks, then, only Quentin's nonverbal behavior is presented:

Quentin... sat hunched in his chair, his hands thrust into his pockets as if he
were trying to hug himself warm between his arms, looking somehow
fragile and even wan in the lamplight
(367)

He just sat as before, his hands in his trousers pockets, his shoulders
hugged inward and hunched, his face lowered
(405)

The distress that Quentin has shown earlier seems to increase gradually. This, as I have argued, may be explained by reference to *The Sound and the Fury*. As Estella Schoenberg has argued, unless the reader knows of his mental state in *The Sound and the Fury* and the reasons for it, 'Quentin's dejection and psychic withdrawal throughout the last half of the novel are not adequately explained' (1977:4).

Here Shreve's text starts by elaborating upon Quentin's speculations regarding Charles Bon's parentage, by imagining how Thomas Sutpen tells his son Henry that Judith and Bon cannot marry each other. The reason now is that Bon is their half-brother ('And Henry came in and the old man said "They cannot marry because he is your brother"' [366]), and not that Bon is already married, as in Mr. Compson's text.

---

162 Schoenberg (1977:74) notices that the other character who says very little is, significantly, the one with whom Quentin chiefly identifies: Henry Sutpen.

Thus Shreve's text inscribes the incest-motif that Quentin has implied but refuses to voice, and thereby presents a solution to Mr. Compson's difficulties in understanding why the tragic murder took place. But by helping Quentin set in motion again his father's halted process of attribution, Shreve also unwittingly increases Quentin's identification with the Henry-Judith-Bon triad.

Yet Shreve's own interest clearly lies somewhere else. His version of the story initially focuses on the revenge of the mother, which Bon is to effectuate: 'He is your father. He cast you and me aside and denied you his name. Now go' (371). Shreve's text attributes attitudes to Bon's mother by using a number of adjectives that are similar to Quentin's lexical choices ('unsleeping'; 'unforgetting' [370]; 'unforgiving' [372]), the last one combined with the paired adjectives associated with Quentin's father's text: 'furious and almost unbearable.' In addition, one finds the generalizations about women originating with Mr. Compson: 'your father said how being a woman she probably wasn't even surprised' (370f.). The material about Bon's mother and the 'hired lawyer' that Shreve invents was 'just so much that had to be overpassed' to reach the real subject—love: '"And now," Shreve said, "we're going to talk about love"' (395).

Shreve's story, after this point, is actually built around the idea that Bon comes to know he is Sutpen's son, and needs desperately to get his father to recognize him as his son: 'Because he knew exactly what he wanted; it was just the saying of it—the physical touch even though in secret, hidden' (399). As Shreve's text presents it, the sign might be a bodily sign: 'the living touch of that flesh' (399); 'hot communicated flesh that speech would have been too slow even to impede' (400). Shreve's text repeats again and again how all of Charles Bon's actions are dedicated to catching Sutpen's 'sign,' or secret 'signal,' or giving Sutpen the opportunity to communicate:

That's all I want. He need not even acknowledge me; I will let him
understand just as quickly that he need not do that, that I do not expect
that, will not be hurt by that, just as he will let me know that quickly that I
am his son
(398)

And the day came to depart and no sign yet; he and Henry rode away and still no sign, no more sign at parting than when he had seen it first
(400)

since he wanted so little, could have understood if the other had wanted the signal to be in secret, would have been quick and glad to let it be in secret even if he could not have understood why
(401)

Bon, presumably, might go as far as necessary to force Sutpen to give him a sign, even so far as to commit incest with Judith.

Thus, in Shreve's text Charles Bon uses the issue of incest to force the father into action in precisely the same way as Quentin did only one month earlier (and Quentin's text, of course, created this possibility by introducing the information on Bon's parentage). But Quentin does not yet seem to see it, fixated as he is on the triad Bon-Henry-Judith. Throughout all of this, Quentin almost does not speak at all. Apart from his protests ('it's not love'; 'that's still not love') one finds only his repeated 'I dont know' (405) as an answer to Shreve's negative tirade about love as 'the vain evanescence of the fleshly encounter' (404). The situation therefore seems a reprise of Mr. Compson's discussion with his son that same summer, when Quentin tried in vain to voice his despair over his sister Caddy in *The Sound and the Fury*. Yet, as Shreve's text presents them, all of Bon's actions, stipulative or actual, are in fact nothing but a way to obtain the recognition without which he cannot live:

> he stopped and said, right quiet: *All right. I want to go to bed with who might be my sister. All right* and then forgot that too. Because he didn't have time. That is, he didn't have anything else but time, because he had to wait. But not for her. That was all fixed. It was the other
> (407)

In Shreve's story, then, the primary referent of 'love' is not the incestuous love of a brother for his sister, but the love a father should have for his son. This is sufficiently clear when Shreve imagines how Bon, talking to Judith 'gallant and elegant and automatic,' takes the girl 'by the elbows,' turning her around 'easy and gentle' until she faces the house, and tells her: 'Go. I wish to be alone to think about love' (416).

As Shreve imagines it, Henry does not realize that Bon's need of his sister is secondary to his need of a father:

> Henry believing it was the letter from her that he was waiting for when what he was thinking was *Maybe he will write it then. He would just have to write 'I am your father. Burn this' and I would do it. Or if not that, a sheet a scrap of paper with the one word 'Charles' in his hand, and I would know what he meant and he would not even have to ask me to burn it. Or a lock of his hair or a paring from his finger nail and I would know them*
> (407f.)

The same sort of misunderstanding that exists between Henry and Bon, however, seems at this point to exist between Shreve and Quentin. While Shreve clearly focuses on Bon's need to be recognized by his father, even if it would take incest to accomplish this, Quentin still focuses on the incestuous love itself, protesting at the way Shreve presents Bon's feelings for Judith:

> But it's not love
> That's still not love
> (402,410)

It is this initial difference in understanding, I believe, that in part explains the parallel Shreve-Charles and Quentin-Henry (417). While Shreve identifies with Bon's need for recognition, Quentin identifies with Henry's need to defend his sister's honor. Thus it is the four of them—Shreve-Charles and Quentin-Henry—who travel to New Orleans to find out about Bon's parentage, still concentrating on different aspects of the situation that Shreve creates: Henry-Quentin asking Bon: 'But must you marry her? Do you have to do it?' and Bon-Shreve answering: 'He should have told me. He should have told me, myself, himself. I was fair and honorable with him. I waited... I gave him every chance to tell me himself. But he didn't do it. If he had, I would have agreed and promised never to see her or you or him again. But he didn't tell me' (426).

Once all three men—Henry, Bon and Sutpen—have gone to war, Bon still waits for Sutpen's recognition: '*what I believe probably is that war, suffering.... will have changed him (which I know that it does not do) to where he will say to me not: Forgive me: but: You are my oldest son. Protect your sister; never see either of us again*' (433).

Nothing is important to Bon, not even the Southern defeat, except '*the space between him and the other regiment, between him and the hour, the moment: "He will not even have to ask me; I will just touch flesh with him and I will say it myself: You will not need to worry; she shall never see me again"*' (434f.). But when Bon finally sees Sutpen again, he looks '*at the expressionless and rocklike face, at the pale boring eyes*' in which there is '*no flicker, nothing*' (435), thinking briefly '*I could force him. I could go to him and force him,*' but soon concluding: '*That was all, there was nothing further now... it was all finished now, that was all of it now and at last*' (435). Yet, Bon's now futureless longing is voiced once more, when Henry tells him that he has received from his father the final piece of information that Bon is black:

> *And he sent me no word? He did not ask you to send me to him? No word to me, no word at all? That was all he had to do, now, today; four years ago or at any time during the four years. That was all. He would not have needed to ask it, require it, of me. I would have offered it. I would have said, I will never see her again before he could have asked it of me. He did not have to do this, Henry. He didn't need to tell you I am a nigger to stop me. He could have stopped me without that, Henry.*
> (445)

During this part of the story, as the narrator-text presents it, neither Shreve nor Quentin is speaking. Both are actually 'living' the situation, first as Shreve has created it, but then, when they smell 'the very smoke which had blown and faded away forty-six years ago from the *bivouac fires burning in a pine grove, the gaunt and ragged men sitting or lying about them, talking not about the war yet all curiously enough (or perhaps not curiously at all) facing the South*' (439), as it once happened. Thus the narrator's account here finally grounds the story of Sutpen and his sons in historical truth. As Kuyk has put it: 'The account in italics, which run unbroken from page 439 to 447, does not depend on any character's experience, observation, or inference but comes directly from the third-person narrator. Therefore, no other passage in the book can attain greater reliability than this account' (1990:42). Seen in this way, *Absalom, Absalom!* is not the postmodern novel without any resolution that it is sometimes made out to be.

From this section it is clear that Bon did indeed write a letter to Judith, presumably the one Mr. Compson showed his son on the night of his visit to Miss Rosa's, which bore no date, salutation or signature (160). The passage does provide some proof that Charles Bon once felt love or desire for Judith, when it goes further into the past and presents Judith and Bon strolling '*in that slow rhythm where the heart matches the footsteps and the eyes need only look at one another*' (442). It mentions the decision that Bon and Henry finally reached—that Bon will marry Judith—but neither it nor the letter founds this decision on love. By conveying that Henry has put aside his objection, it makes clear that this objection was indeed originally founded on the fact that Bon and Judith were brother and sister: '*Brother or not, I have decided. I will. I will*' (443). It also makes clear that Henry overcomes his objection out of despair over the situation of the South: '*when you dont have God and honor and pride, nothing matters except that there is the old mindless meat that dont even care if it was defeat or victory*' (442).

The passage makes clear that Sutpen's objection to his Haitian wife was indeed that, according to him, she 'was part negro' (443). If the woman was indeed 'part negro,' but so light in color that Sutpen was not aware of it, she would in Haitian terms be a high status mulatto, a social category completely different from the 'part nigger' of the American South. As H. Hoetink has argued: 'In all but one of the Afro-American multiracial societies, a group of coloreds with its own internal social differentiation came to occupy an intermediate rank between blacks and whites in the socioracial structure,' based among other things upon 'the general notion of greater physical proximity between mulatto and white as compared to black and white' (1973:36). In the United States, except for New Orleans and a few other places, this 'three-tier socioracial structure' did not evolve, mainly because of what Hoetink calls 'the socially downgrading influence always exerted by the numerous groups of poor whites, who had been impoverished in the South since the end of the eighteenth century, and to whom were added the influx of poor white immigrants after the middle of the nineteenth century' (1973:37). This, Hoetink believes, also explains the 'formal disapproval of interracial sexual relations,' which, in contrast to other racially diverse societies, only intensified and expanded with time in the South. With his origin in the social class of poor whites, Sutpen is clearly unable to see the distinctions of the foreign culture. Naturally, this inability determines his attitude towards Bon, and it also influences his son Henry.

It is indeed the racial information about Charles Bon's mother, Sutpen's last trump card, that forces Henry into action: *'he knew what he would do; it now depended on what Bon would do, would force him to do, since he knew that he would do it'* (444). And yet, unlike what Kuyk has argued, the passage does not give evidence of Sutpen's wife having black blood; it only conveys that Sutpen thinks she has. Bon, guessing from Henry's behavior what their father has told him, confronts Henry with his conclusion: *'So it's the miscegenation, not the incest, which you cant bear'* (445). This shows that Sutpen, even if he was forced to divulge his secret, still refuses to recognize his son, and it validates what Shreve had imagined as Bon's need for a sign from Sutpen, a sign that would have set all of them free. The text makes clear that Bon knows Henry is planning to kill him: *'His hand vanishes beneath the blanket and reappears, holding his pistol by the barrel, the butt extended towards Henry.—Then do it now, he says'* (446). One fully understands now why Bon needed to marry Judith and why this is impossible. One may wonder, however, what Bon stands to gain by letting himself be killed at this point, when he might just as well have disappeared.[163]

If the letter that Judith received was actually written by Charles Bon, one might return to it as one of the few sources of Bon's mind-style. The letter, clearly, is no ordinary love-letter as they are sent from wars. It contains no terms of endearment and it creates no shared expectations or desires concerning the future for writer and addressee, except that both are 'doomed to live' (163). The letter-writer starts by focusing on the physical aspects of the letter: the paper, with its 'French watermarks dated seventy years ago' as 'the best... of the old South which is dead,' and that which functioned as ink, 'manufactured not twelve months ago' in New England as 'the best... of the new North.' Together they provide the image of a new material from the

---

163 The same can be said about Joe Christmas in *Light in August*. Both he and Charles Bon choose to present themselves in front of their executioners.

North imposing itself on the old surface of the South. The visual image merges with a mental configuration, which is echoed later in the letter:

Because what WAS *is one thing, and now it is not because it is dead, it died in 1861, and therefore what IS—*
(162)
Because what IS is something else again because it was not even alive then.
(163)

On one level, the stove-polish 'ink' may well inscribe life in the South after the defeat (although, as we have seen, this defeat did not matter much to Bon), on another, it certainly inscribes Bon's and Judith's relationship after the war. Whatever made the two of them stroll 'to the rhythm of their hearts,' this WAS is now dead. Whatever it was that made Bon start to court Judith, it is not the IS of his letter or the reason for letting himself be killed. What, then, is this IS? The context of the letter can provide certain suggestions. Quentin takes the letter from his father immediately after the latter has 'quoted' Judith's explanation for bringing it to his mother, which was to 'make a mark on something that *was* once for the reason that it can die someday' (158). Perhaps letting himself be killed is Bon's way to 'make that scratch, that undying mark' on those that *are* because they can become *was* (159). Shreve and Quentin's story of Charles Bon, in any case, proves that he has made his scratch on *them*.

The fact that Quentin has now 'become' both Henry and Bon allows him to see the links between his (unvoiced) story of incest and Shreve's (voiced) story of recognition. The connection is formed by the imagined fate of Bon, whose incestuous intentions served as a last, doomed endeavor to shock his father into recognizing his needs. When Shreve's text makes clear how Charles Bon feels 'that same despair and shame like when you have to watch your father fail in physical courage,' and conveys how he thinks '*It should have been me that failed; me, I, not he*' (401), Quentin is forced to identify with Bon as well as with Henry. His nonverbal behavior indicates this in a subtle way; his 'still laxed and hunched figure' suddenly shows 'some quality, some gathering... which presaged speech' (401). Thus, as Quentin finally sees the direction and the impact of Bon's love, and as he finally understands the image of the failing father, his own lack of an adequate father-figure must become painfully apparent.

The Story of Quentin Compson

Quentin, not Faulkner is the correct yardstick here. I was writing the story, but he not I was brooding over a situation... he grieved

Chapter IX shows an increased emphasis on the importance of the body, as the two friends in their dormitory room at Harvard breathe together 'in the darkness' (451). As in the previous chapters, Quentin hardly speaks at all, except to inform Shreve of his physical state: 'No... I'm not cold. I'm all right. I feel fine' (450). Quentin is confronted with a past that haunts him imaginatively through his body:

He could taste the dust. Even now, with the chill pure weight of the snow-breathed New England air on his face, he could taste and feel the dust of that breathless (rather, furnace-breathed) Mississippi September night. He could even smell the old woman in the buggy beside him, smell the fusty camphor-reeking shawl and even the airless black cotton umbrella... He

could smell the horse; he could hear the dry plaint of the light wheels in the
weightless permeant dust and he seemed to feel the dust itself move
sluggish and dry across his sweating flesh
(451f.)
Through these physical experiences, Quentin enters the final stage in the story of the
Sutpen dynasty. While he returns to the evening of his visit with Miss Rosa to what is
left of the Sutpen mansion, his bodily experiences move him still further back, to
where he might, 'if he stopped the buggy and listened... even hear the galloping
hooves; might even see at any moment now the black stallion and the rider rush across
the road before them' (452f.). The experience itself attributes to Sutpen what seems an
ultimate emphasis on the alive body as a sign of personality: even if all else has been
lost, the text seems to say, at least there is 'breathing left' (453). Having come to this
imaginative construction of Sutpen's fate, Quentin himself, 'peaceful for a time in the
warm bed,' starts 'to breathe hard again... breathing hard the heady pure snowborn
darkness' (453), and returns to the events of that September night twelve miles out of
Jefferson, Mississippi. Retracing the steps of Henry Sutpen, he must himself pass the
gateless posts of the Sutpen drive, wondering which objects once cast the shadows that
Henry forbade Bon to pass. Quentin's physical desperation clearly shows itself when
'all his organs' seem to lift 'sickeningly' (459).

All these bodily sensations culminate when Quentin has returned home to his own
room and lies on his bed 'sweating, breathing fast... naked, swabbing his body steadily
with the discarded shirt, sweating still, panting' (464). In his Harvard dormitory room
in January, Quentin relives the experience of having to face the impact of the encounter
with Henry Sutpen in the dark house of his parents, reconstructed in chiasmic form:
And you are—?
Henry Sutpen.
And you have been here—?
Four years.
And you came home—?
To die. Yes.
To die?
Yes. To die.
And you have been here—?
Four years.
And you are—?
Henry Sutpen.
(464f.)
The image of the 'wasted yellow face with closed, almost transparent eyelids on the
pillow, the wasted hands crossed on the breast as if he were already a corpse' (464)
is an image that Quentin is sure will 'be the same forever,' as long as he lives, causing
him, in desperation, to think:
Nevermore of peace. Nevermore of peace. Nevermore. Nevermore.
Nevermore.
(465).
Many critics have speculated about the reasons for this extreme reaction on Quentin's
part. Some center on the discovery of Charles Bon's supposed black blood, arguing

that Quentin learns from Henry that Bon is a mulatto, and that this is the reason for his despair. Quentin's earlier text, indeed, seems to contain some indication that he learned something from this visit that alters his view of his father's story of the reasons for Sutpen's repudiation of Charles Bon. The text here, however, does not include any such message.

The external narrator does not, as Kuyk would have it (1990:105), authenticate 'Bon's status.' He only authenticates Sutpen's statement to that effect, and one cannot automatically conflate the two. Thus Charles Bon's racial status, like Joe Christmas's in *Light in August*, remains a 'shape to fill a lack,' even if Faulkner wrote in the appendix to the novel that in 1831 'Sutpen learns his wife has negro blood, repudiates her and child' (1987:473). The status of such a chronology is necessarily problematic, and even if, as Shlomith Rimmon-Kenan has argued, 'one... agrees to grant the chronology the same status as the text itself... the question still remains as to how Quentin and Shreve obtained this information without reading the chronology at the end of the novel in which they appear' (1978:10f.).[164] No matter how Quentin receives the information that Bon has black blood, it cannot in itself explain why he would react with such violence to Henry's situation.

Quentin's Defeat

Faulkner himself stated that Quentin commits suicide 'because of his sister.' But in *The Sound and the Fury* it is in the last instance the loss of hope reflected in his father's text that leads to Quentin's failure to save himself. Now that we know from *Absalom, Absalom!* what happens to Quentin during the time after he leaves for Harvard in the summer of 1909 and before he learns about his sister's wedding in the spring of 1910 in *The Sound and the Fury*, the motivation for his suicide becomes even clearer. As David Ragan has put it, 'Quentin searches in *Absalom* for evidence of significant action to combat his father's denial of meaning in human relations' (1986:339). In other words, Quentin, who cannot find hope in the text of his father, tries to find hope in the texts of others. But these stories, both old and new, cannot in the end create such hope. Instead, the story of his friend Shreve unwittingly evokes the very loss of hope that Quentin has been trying to overcome in his concentration on Charles Bon, Judith and Henry.

Miss Rosa Coldfield's text introduces the story of the son who leaves his degenerate father, 'repudiating his birthright' for the sake of a friend. Even if the world evoked by Miss Rosa's text seems beyond redemption, Henry's resolute action creates hope for the individual who is capable of escaping his father's negative influence. Why exactly Henry had to leave remains a mystery; for Miss Rosa it is enough that it illustrates Sutpen's bestiality. Mr. Compson, however, needs to fill the gap in the text by creating for Bon an octoroon wife, which causes Henry to be pulled back towards home to guard his sister from becoming the 'junior partner' in Bon's marriage. The story explains nothing except Mr. Compson's general defeatism, and his

---

164 The same can be argued about the map of Jefferson, in which Faulkner indicated the place 'where Christmas killed Miss Burden.' Even if one grants the map sufficient status to complement the story of *Light in August*, how can the inhabitants of Jefferson decide that Christmas killed Joanna Burden on the authority of a map that the author provided for a different novel?

disregard of women, with their inability to maintain a grip on reality. In this respect, the story also works to deconstruct Miss Rosa's story. Quentin's memory of his second encounter with her already bears the stamp of his father's mind-style.

From the only section that is actually narrated by Quentin, which describes Sutpen's boyhood and young adulthood as derived from the stories of his grandfather, Quentin's own needs are clear. As we have seen, a hidden admiration for the decisive actions that Sutpen undertakes shows itself in Quentin's mind-style, but this admiration cannot ultimately survive the degeneration that overtakes Sutpen's life when he does not understand what the mistake in his design is. Desperately, Quentin tries to hold on, then, to the two things for which he can admire Sutpen's son Henry: first his power to leave his home and give up his birthright for the sake of a friend, and second to defend his sister against this same friend. However, an admiration for Henry brings with it Quentin's self-loathing over his encounter with his own sister's lover, Dalton Ames, when he passed out in front of his rival. This incident, we remember, occurred only one month before his visit to the remains of Sutpen's Hundred with Miss Rosa. When Quentin finally meets Henry Sutpen, the man is, as Deborah Robbins puts it, 'an appalling spectacle of human waste; he is not the champion of human value asserted and preserved' (1981:323). What Quentin had wanted to distill from the stories of Henry is a new meaning for the concept of *honor*, not as the defeated 'public, social, collective matter' (cf. Wyatt-Brown 1988:117), but as a highly personal decision to act.

Stories of the South

God could not let us win the war because we were wrong, but he did give us the best soldiers

When Faulkner's first-grade schoolteacher presented her children with the above explanation of why 'Heaven saw fit' for the South to lose the War between the States,[165] she explicitly linked, through contrast, those aspects of Southern experience—a nostalgic return to a glorious past; a belief in the South's special status before God; a sense of defeat; and feelings of guilt—that were the subjects of W.J. Cash's famous and influential *The Mind of the South*.[166] The sentence would seem to capture in a nutshell, then, the influence of the past on the lives of people during the first decade of the twentieth century in the South (when both Faulkner and Cash, who was three years younger than Faulkner, were in grade school). In *Absalom, Absalom!* Faulkner accomplished a fictional return to this time: the summer of 1909, when Quentin has his crucial encounters with Miss Rosa Coldfield, and the winter of 1910, when he tells his friend Shreve about them. In *The Mind of the South*, Cash does something that is not so different as one might think.

As his biographer Bruce Clayton makes clear, 'Cash, a down-at-the-heels news-paperman when the book appeared in 1941, wrote out of his heart, his soul. He borrowed here and there from historians and others, but the book is uniquely his own

165 Personal information by Mrs. Bessie Sumners of Oxford, Mississippi.
166 Recently three symposia were held in the South to commemorate the fact that Cash's book was published fifty years ago: at Wake Forest College (February 1991); at the University of Mississippi at Oxford (October 1991); and at a special session of the Southern Historical Association (November 1991).

in the same way a William Faulkner or a Thomas Wolfe novel is their own' (1992:3). C. Vann Woodward calls the approach of *The Mind of the South* 'literary and imaginative' rather than 'scholarly.' Cash himself wrote in 1936, in a biographical sketch for his publisher, Knopf: 'I want above everything to be a novelist' (quoted in Hobson 1983:260). Like Faulkner's, Cash's life was 'in great part' what Clayton calls a 'complex coming to terms with being a white, male, Christian southerner and a simultaneous attempt to free himself from all that that meant' (1992:4). Cash's narration, like those of Faulkner and many of his characters, amounted to 'an act of self-discovery, of exorcising demons, of settling old scores, of trying desperately to say that southern history had to be confronted—and escaped' (Clayton 1992:4).

Southern history, or as C. Vann Woodward called it: 'the collective experience of the Southern people' (1989:16), opposes the American myths of abundance, innocence and success. It includes, first of all, 'a long and quite un-American experience with poverty,' 'a continuous and conspicuous feature of Southern experience since the early years of the Civil War' (1989:17). As Woodward put it: 'Generations of scarcity and want constitute one of the distinctive historical experiences of the Southern people,' uniting them as 'a "People of Poverty" in a land of plenty' (1989:17f.).[167] The experience of poverty, opposing the myth of American abundance, connects with another distinctive feature of Southern history: the experience of defeat. The experience opposes the American myth of success, which Woodward called 'a legend with a foundation in fact,' because in America, as he saw it at the time (1958), 'almost every major collective effort, even those thwarted temporarily, succeeded in the end,' so that 'success and victory' were 'still national habits of mind.' Southern history, in this view, stands out by recording a degree of 'frustration, failure and defeat,' not just military but also political, social, and economic, that is unknown in the North (Woodward 1989:18f.).

In the mind-styles of his different narrators, Faulkner has personified these feelings of frustration, failure and defeat caused by the Civil War and its aftermath. In Miss Rosa Coldfield's text, for instance, there is ample evidence that poverty shaped her fate; as she puts it: 'an orphan a woman and a pauper, I turned naturally not for protection but for actual food to my only kin: my dead sister's family' (18). Her frustration at being used by Sutpen—to be swept 'into his design, even though she doesn't know what it is' (Kuyk 1990:65)—is a direct result of her being around for him to notice her when he returns from the War. It was her father's defeat—locking himself into an attic, where he finally died of starvation—that made her an orphan in the first place, and that forces her to turn to her 'dead sister's family.' Miss Rosa's life is shaped by failures: a failure to save her father, whom she tried to feed; a failure to help her sister Ellen; a failure to save her niece Judith; a failure to keep Sutpen; a failure, ultimately, to have a life of her own. But her refusal to be defeated causes her to call upon Quentin Compson, shortly before her death, to help her finish *her* design. Fred Hobson has

---

167   Of course, the myth, as all myths do, ignores many aspects of experience, such as the existence of poverty, long before the early years of the Civil War, among the poor whites, who 'without slave labor... tended to isolate themselves on the least expensive tracts, generally those areas with the most restricted access to water and transport facilities, further limiting their ability to produce for the market' (Oakes 1990:105). To these population groups the Bundrens and the Sutpens belong.

written about the Southerner who wears his 'heritage of failure as his badge of honor' (1983:12). One may sense something of this pride from Rosa's repetitions, as in the following: 'I dont plead youth': 'I dont plead propinquity': 'I dont plead material necessity': 'and most of all, I do not plead myself' (18).

Mr. Compson's material poverty is clear from his having had to sell his pasture to send his son Quentin to Harvard, and from the general state of his home and 'shaggy lawn' (34). If he seems untouched by this, it is because he hides his feelings behind a pretended lack of involvement and through the detachment of irony. He is a 'Southern stoic' without hope, whose 'finest hour is,' to use Walker Percy's words, 'to sit tight-lipped and ironic while the world comes crashing down around him' (1956:xiii; quoted in Hobson 1983:290). But, in fact, his defeat shows itself through his every action, both the pathetic nonverbal and the ironic verbal. His definition of personality as 'all the old accumulated rubbish-years which we call memory' (245) is only one example of the mind-style of defeat with which he burdens his son Quentin.

Before Woodward published his work on the Southern experience of frustration, failure, poverty and defeat, which, he argued, alienated it from the prevalent American myths of abundance and success, Cash had already written: 'the peculiar history of the South has so greatly modified it from the general American norm that, when viewed as a whole, it decisively justifies the notion that the country is—not quite a nation within a nation, but the next thing to it.' He spoke of 'a fairly definite mental pattern, associated with a fairly definite social pattern—a complex of established relationships and habits of thought, sentiments, prejudices, standards and values, and associations of ideas' (1969:viii) that went beyond feelings of defeat to the sentiments that could cover them up. During his youth, after the Civil War and Reconstruction, Cash felt that the South, 'like many another people come upon evil days,' was filled 'in its entirety'[168] with 'an immense regret and nostalgia,' yearning backwards 'towards its past with passionate longing':

> With the antebellum world removed to the realm of retrospect, the shackles
> of reality, as so often happens in such cases, fell away from it altogether.
> Perpetually suspended in the great haze of memory, it hung, as it were,
> poised, somewhere between earth and sky, colossal, shining, and
> incomparably lovely
> (1969:127)

This nostalgic return to the past implies, first of all, a return to the antebellum Cavalier myth.[169] According to this myth, the wealthy planter families of the South sprang

168 One has to criticize Cash here for speaking of the South 'in its entirety.' Trying to deconstruct a set of myths into which he himself was born, Cash did not always succeed in going beyond his own white, male perspective. Many have criticized Cash for lapses such as this. When Cash writes about the importance for 'every Southerner' of the 'boast, voiced or not,' that he would 'knock hell out of whoever dared to cross him,' John Shelton Reed argues, 'plainly, Cash did not mean "every Southerner" to include Southern blacks and Southern women. For a woman to reveal that attitude would have been unladylike; for a black to display it could have been fatal' (1992:147). Reed's own lapse, meanwhile, is that he forgets about the individual who is both black *and* a woman.

169 Actually, Woodward and Cash differ considerably in their opinions on the degree of continuity in the South. While Woodward argued that southern myth—the 'Cavalier legend,' 'the plantation legend of antebellum grace and elegance' and the 'pleasant image of a benevolent and paternalistic slavery system as

from noble Virginian families, who had been the most adventurous of the English Cavaliers. According to Cash, however, less than 500 planters were actually descendants of English aristocrats.[170]

As Daniel Singal presents it, the South, ever since the seventeenth century, had had to defend itself against charges of 'frontier crudeness.' The myth came into existence, he argues, to 'mask the apparent deficiencies' in southern society, and created at the same time the necessary 'organizing framework for the society's shared emotions' (1982:17). Due in part to the popularity of the novels of Sir Walter Scott, with their knights and lords and feudal splendor—William Alexander Percy's father read *Ivanhoe* once every year—the myth bloomed in the 1830s, when cotton boomed, and consequently slavery as well. As Singal puts it: 'By setting forth the heroic figure of the southern gentleman, with his heroic ability to bring order and culture to all he surveyed, it enabled southerners to convince themselves and others that the South enjoyed the *most* stable and civilized society in America' (1982:17f.). Cash speaks of the cult of the 'Great Southern Heart' (1969:131), which stresses the tender feelings of the white planter towards his black slaves:

> The lash? A lie, sir; it had never existed. The only bonds were those of tender understanding, trust, and loyalty. And to prove it, here about us in this very hour of new freedom and bitter strife are hundreds of worn-out Uncle Toms and black mammies still clinging stubbornly to the old masters who can no longer feed them, ten thousand Jim Crows still kicking their heels and whooping for the smile of a white man. Such is the Negro, sir, when he is not corrupted by meddling fools. Hate him? My good friend, we love him dearly—and we alone, for we alone know him.
> (1969:131)

Indeed, Sergeant S. Prentiss, one of the state's most eloquent orators, argued in 1836: 'People of the state of Mississippi look upon domestic slavery as it exists among them, not as a curse, but as a blessing, as the legitimate condition of the African race, as authorized both by the laws of God and the dictates of reason and philantrophy.' He added that his generation of Mississippians would 'transmit this situation to their posterity, as the best part of their inheritance' (quoted in Sansing 1986:3f.). The planter

---

a school for civilizing savages"—was increasingly being deconstructed (see also McPherson 1988), Cash believed that 'the extent of the change and the break' between the Old South and his own time was 'vastly exaggerated' (1969:x). As he put it: 'the foolish meddling of Reconstruction' only succeeded in making the Southern mind 'one of the most solidly established, one of the least reconstructible ever developed.' Lacy K. Ford has argued recently: 'the wise and expert teachings of C. Vann Woodward not withstanding, most southerners have not, despite the burden of their history, distanced themselves that much from the prevailing myth of American innocence' (1992:110). One might argue that it is not 'despite the burden of their history' but rather *because of* this burden that the South has not relinquished some of its myths.

170   Presumably William Alexander Percy of Greenville, Mississippi, whose *Lanterns on the Levee: Recollections of a Planter's Son* was published in the same year as Cash's *The Mind of the South*, was one of them. Comparing the two, the novelist Walker Percy writes in his introduction to his uncle's work: 'Both books are classics in their own right, yet they couldn't be more different; their separate validities surely testify to the diversity and complexity of this mysterious region. Yet in this case, I would suppose that Will Percy would today find himself closer to Cash in sorting out his heroes and villains": 'Will Percy had no more use than Cash for genealogical games, the old Southern itch for coats of arms and tracing back connections to the English squirearchy... His own aristocracy was a meritocracy of character, talent, performance, courage, and quality of life' (1990:xviif.).

himself, in the meantime, did not need to be controlled; he was, in the best Victorian tradition, 'a paragon of temperance' (Sansing 1982:18), guided only by one law: the common good.

The complementary myth was, of course, that of a 'Yankee' society in which self-love was the only law. Not surprisingly, then, as tensions between the North and the South increased, the need for southern higher education rose as an alternative to the 'Yankee' universities. As Mississippi's Governor Brown put it in 1844, they were to keep young people from growing up 'with false prejudices against home institutions and laws' (quoted in Bailey 1986:4). In *Absalom, Absalom!* this explains why Thomas Sutpen, who could have afforded to send his son to Harvard, can settle for Oxford. The preoccupation with an honest southern education for southern youth is clear in Governor McNutt's 1939 address: 'Patriotism, no less than economy, urges upon us the duty of educating our children at home. In early life the strongest impressions are made. Those opposed to us in principle, and alienated in interest, cannot safely be entrusted with the education of our sons and daughters' (quoted in Bailey 1986:4). Centenary College, opened in 1841, stated its goal in its prospective: 'to sustain and control—the uncongeniality in the climate, politics, and institutions of the North and Northwest; the evils resulting from estrangement from home, parental control and affection with their moral and religious influences' (quoted in Bailey 1986:4).

In *Absalom, Absalom!* Mr. Compson's story makes explicit how a sense of defeat may lead to a nostalgic longing for a more glorious past. He sees his antebellum ancestors as 'larger, more heroic and the figures therefore more heroic too, not dwarfed and involved but distinct, uncomplex who had the gift of loving once or dying once instead of being diffused and scattered creatures drawn blindly limb from limb from a grab bag and assembled' (109f.). In his disgust over compromise and lack of conviction, Mr. Compson seems to idealize 'the gallant mimic marching and counter-marching of the sons and the brothers': 'young men, the light quick bones, the bright gallant deluded blood and flesh dressed in a martial glitter of brass and plumes, marching away to a battle' (151f.). Underneath, however, one can still sense the defeat, for instance from the adjectives *deluded* and *mimic*. As we have seen, Mr. Compson attributes to Henry Sutpen a heroic capacity for conviction, for sacrifice and for love, and he admires him for it. In the same way, he attributes to Judith Sutpen the heroic ability to love and to suffer, and he admires her for it as well. But one senses, also, the strain underlying his 'necessary worlds.'

The Cavalier myth is present in Miss Rosa Coldfield's text as well. The imaginative recreations of Thomas Sutpen's life that Miss Rosa engages in—herself a part of the 'grimly middle class' and 'the perfect defender of the idols of the South' (Vickery 1959:101)—attempt to exclude Sutpen from antebellum society. As Miss Rosa sees it, Sutpen's apparent rootlessness and his life style were an outrage to the 'genteel' community. Many have argued, however, that the South in the 1830s, 40s and 50s, was not 'more than a few steps removed from the frontier stage' (Cash 1969:11); by 1860 most of northern Mississippi had been settled for less than twenty years.[171] In Faulk-

---

171 Cash, as his biographer Bruce Clayton argues, 'found support for many of his ideas about the Old South in William E. Dodd's *The Cotton Kingdom: A Chronicle of the Old South*,' who insisted 'that the typical planter was a product of the wilderness' (Clayton 1992:12; Dodd 1921:24).

ner's fictional adaptation, in any case, when Sutpen arrives in Jefferson the people there are obviously familiar with his type. Much to Miss Rosa's regret, the men do not seem nearly as upset by Sutpen's behavior as she is in remembering it and telling about it. They, in any case, readily join him in his pastimes. 'Vulgarity—ignorance—fuzzy and arrogant pretension—unmitigated rowdyism—bullying insolence,' as the Alabama judge Baldwin, himself a Southerner and a patriot, argued, belonged to the behavioral repertoire of all successful men (quoted in Cash 1969:19). 'Men on the make with sharp wits, few scruples, and no pedigree,' Singal explains, 'flocked to the booming cotton lands of Alabama, Mississippi, and Georgia in search of instant fortunes; with a few years of hard work and a little luck at marketing their crops (or at real-estate manipulation or card-dealing), they could soon elevate themselves to the stature of "gentlemen"' (1982:13).

In antebellum society, supposedly, all shared these goals. As an editorial in a Vicksburg newspaper expressed it on the eve of the Civil War:

A large plantation and negroes are the *ultima thule* of every gentlemen's [sic] ambition. For this the lawyer pores over his dusty tomes, the merchant measures his tape, the doctor rolls his pills, the editor drives his quill, and the mechanic his plane-all, all who dare aspire at all, look to this as the goal of their ambition. The mind is used, from childhood, to contemplate it, and the first efforts are all lost if the objects in life should be changed. The mind is thus trained from infancy to think of and prepare for the attainment of this end.

(quoted in Sansing 1986:4)

While Miss Rosa's story thus argues Sutpen's excommunication, the stories of Mr. Compson and his son Quentin attempt his inclusion into a frontier myth of self-reliance, mobility, ruggedness and independence, showing a genuine admiration for the 'young boy' of 'just fourteen' from the Virginia mountains, who had to build his life from scrap with his own bare hands.[172] Sutpen's background of belonging to one of these poor white farming families, who generally 'eked out,' as Oakes puts it, 'a meagre subsistence on the poorest soils and in conditions of more or less permanent destitution' (1990:106), indeed provides the connection with frontier existence. As Oakes explains: 'Settled and resettled relatively late in southern history, the upcountry assumed much of its character from the exigencies of frontier life' (1990:107). 'Isolated by distance and terrain from the major marketing centers,' the poor whites produced mainly to meet their own, and their community's needs. Owning no slaves and having no opportunity to idealize their women, whose farm labor was essential, they fell outside the territory of the Cavalier myth altogether. We have seen this clearly in Faulkner's portrayal of the Bundren family. By 'usurping' his place in society, however, Sutpen makes it impossible for the Jeffersonians to keep the clear distinction between Cavalier and frontier phenomena that tradition required. Both Miss Rosa and Mr. Compson, in their different stories, are forced to draw their own lines and review their conceptualizations.

Quentin's involvement with the Cavalier myth is still more complex, however, than

---

172 In this Thomas Sutpen is like the author's grandfather, who 'came into Mississippi on foot when he was fourteen years old,' after having run away from home in Virginia (Fant and Ashley 1964:108).

either that of Miss Rosa or that of his father. On the one hand, Quentin's pathological concentration on his sister Caddy, and on Henry Sutpen's plight, can be seen in terms of the Cavalier myth, and more specifically of the cult of the adoration of the Southern woman, which, as Cash put it, only increased after the Civil War and thus produced 'yet more precious notions of modesty and decorous behavior for the Southern female to live up to' (1969:131). Climbing a pear tree and showing one's dirty underwear clearly does not belong to this behavior; even at Caddy's tender age it would certainly worry a brother. Paradoxically, perhaps, the more women are idealized and 'purified,' the more they are robbed of their personalities, and the more empty and weightless, like angels, they become. One of Mississippi's politicians went as far as to state, as late as 1948:

Now what of the ladies? When God made the Southern woman he summoned His angel messengers and He commanded them to go through all the star-strewn vicissitudes of space and gather all there was of beauty, of brightness and sweetness, of enchantment and glamor, and when they returned and laid the golden harvest at His feet He began in their wondering presence the work of fashioning the Southern girl
(quoted in Smith 1978:169).

Mr. Compson's complaints on the insubstantiality of women seem to be based on this paradox; his narration itself turns into an act of aggressive depletion of the mother and the wife. Yet, Quentin, who hears and internalizes his father's generalized views on women, cannot bring himself to apply these views to his sister Caddy. As is clear in *The Sound and the Fury*, she remains earthly to him: a threat to his Victorian innocence, no matter how he—the 'half-baked Galahad'—tries to elevate her to the sphere of purity.

On the other hand, in Quentin's narration the deconstruction of what Cash has called 'the development of Southern unreality' (1969:126) surfaces most clearly. As Cash uses the term *unreality*, it comes to designate and evaluate what he called 'the glorification of the Southern heritage,' involving the growing tendency in the early 1900s to attribute 'the noblest motives' to every Southern action (1969:128f.) As Singal has explained: 'Whatever proof might once have existed either to substantiate or refute the myth was now safely buried in the past, and the only limits placed on the Cavalier's splendor lay in the ample capacities of the southern imagination and in the requirements of the region's wounded pride' (1982:21). Yet the 'increasing rift' between such representations and what people deep-down knew to be the case, Cash argued, greatly increased already existing feelings of inadequacy. Those who seemed to question or doubt the South and its causes, or 'merely to stand aloof a little' (1969:139), could find themselves under serious attack. Moved by the death, in 1935, of Clarence Cason, who had ventured only into 'mild criticism' (Hobson 1983:256), Cash wrote in his manuscript: 'poor Clarence Cason, who taught journalism at Alabama, felt compelled to commit suicide, in part at least because of his fear of the fiercely hostile attitude which he knew that both the school authorities and his fellow faculty members would take towards his criticism of the South in his *90° in the Shade*' (1969:334; quoted in Hobson 1983:256). Cash was anticipating criticism that he himself would have to endure.[173]

Cash's term *unreality* is one of the words that Quentin uses to describe the world of the Sutpens and the Coldfields. Despite his Victorian innocence and his Cavalier romanticism, Quentin cannot but see right through the 'unreality' of the South into its paradoxical 'undefeat': a defeat desperately trying to be glorious. In Cash's summary: 'the memory of defeat in arms after a struggle so genuinely heroic as to have deserved a better end, the sense of suffering intolerable wrong under the pressure of overwhelming odds' (1969:130). As we have seen, there is no sense of a glorious defeat in Quentin's text; no sense of God having given the South 'the best soldiers.' Forced to deconstruct the 'Cult of the Lost Cause' (Sansing 1986:4), Quentin sees soldiers returning with their 'gaunt powder-blackened faces looking backward over tattered shoulders, the glaring eyes in which burned some indomitable desperation of undefeat' (237), while Shreve mentions 'the spurious bronze medals that never meant anything to begin with' (409). But in contrast to the Canadian Shreve, Quentin's history of having 'breathed the same air' (34) makes it impossible for him to stand more than a little aloof. For all his awareness, he cannot escape the 'unrealities' of the South. It is this inescapable world that makes Quentin 'an empty hall echoing with sonorous defeated names': 'a barracks filled with stubborn back-looking ghosts' (9). One can now see that Quentin's personality weaknesses, as evidenced in *The Sound and the Fury*, may be related not only to his genetic disposition and family situation, but also to specific historical influences: the South's 'peculiar history.'

Quentin's precarious sense of self also proves to be an embodiment of the times' taboo on criticism, analysis and inquiry (Cash 1969:101). Southern culture, as Lillian Smith argued, 'was a culture that lacked almost completely the self-changing power that comes from honest criticism, because in the past it forced out its children who saw dangers and tried to avert them, who had insight and talents that could have contributed so richly to the South's recovery; because it bruised those who grimly stayed, un-welcomed, until their energies were depleted' (1978:152). Precisely because he cannot create his own world through questioning and 'honest criticism,' Quentin has become 'not a being, an entity' but 'a commonwealth' (9). Quentin is defeated not by the war, but by the 'unreality' of the Southern people.

Where within this mesh of myth and defeat, one might ask, stand characters like Thomas Sutpen and his wife Ellen, their children Henry and Judith, Sutpen's daughter Clytie, his son Charles Bon, and the descendants of Charles Bon?

Those critics who have read Sutpen's design as a quest only for status and wealth naturally believe him to be defeated by the war, as Miss Rosa Coldfield and Mr. Compson do. For her, as Quentin understands it, it is true that God used '*the blood of our men and the tears of our women*' to '*stay this demon and efface his name and lineage from the earth*' (8); for him 'the destiny of Sutpen's family' was at the same

---

173 From the use of his attributive verb *knew*, one can see that Cash believed Cason's fear to be justified. Chillingly, Cash himself committed suicide in 1941, not shortly before his work came out, as Cason did, but roughly five months after it was published, and in a near-hallucinatory paranoid state of mind (Clayton 1992). It is a curious thought that in Faulkner's fictional treatment of the South, one of the main characters also commits suicide roughly five months after he tells about the South, and in a similar state of mind.

time 'the land's catastrophe' (89). But if one accepts Quentin's reading, validated in part by the external narrator, both Miss Rosa and Mr. Compson are wrong about Thomas Sutpen. If one understands Sutpen's design as Quentin does, one knows that the war served to postpone rather than to cause the defeat of Sutpen, and with it the defeat of his sons. From the one section of the text that can be considered reliable narration, it is clear that Sutpen has been forced to play his last trump card in front of Henry at the final stage of the War, when he tells Henry: 'his [Bon's] mother was part negro' (443). But for the War, he might have been forced to do so much earlier. Of the two alternatives that Quentin had imagined—to destroy the design with his own hands, or to 'do nothing, let matters take the course... they will take' (342)—Sutpen chose the former.

The section of historical truth also provides reliable information on Henry. Like Quentin, who identifies with him, Henry speaks very little. One can see his defeat most clearly, then, in his nonverbal behavior, when Charles Bon finally accuses their father in front of him: '*He didn't need to tell you I am a nigger to stop me. He could have stopped me without that, Henry*' (445). As Henry, perplexed, inquires how, and perhaps for the first time understands what Bon really wanted, the narrator-text conveys how his '*face is working*'; how '*Bon can see his teeth within the soft beard which covers his sunken cheeks*'; how his eyeballs seem to struggle '*in their sockets*'[174], and especially how he looks at the pistol '*not only panting*' but also '*trembling*'; how he grasps the pistol '*panting and panting*,' and how he grips Bon '*by both shoulders, panting*' (445f.). It is this last form of behavior, the forced breathing, that finally ties Henry's defeat most clearly to Quentin in his Harvard dormitory, first shaking 'faintly and steadily,' then beginning to 'jerk all over, violently and uncontrollably' (449f.);

> breathing hard the heady pure snowborn darkness.
> in the Massachusetts bed and breathing fast now
> breathing hard but slow
> panting in the cold air, the iron New England dark
> (453,459,465,471)

Quentin, the 'empty hall' (9), has become filled with the defeat of the son who was unable both to defend his brother *and* his sister at the same time, and had to choose the sister above the brother.

Although Charles Bon is given voice in the stories of others, virtually nothing about him is known with certainty by the other characters, or for that matter by readers. Everyone is free to invest him with physical and mental characteristics and personal motivations, needs and emotions, with Judith and Henry merely as pawns. Thus Miss Rosa uses all Bon's potential as the mysterious lover, yearned-for by Judith as well as by herself, even if she will not admit it. Thus Mr. Compson invests him with all the effeminate attractiveness and worldliness that he believes inspired Henry to 'that complete and abnegant devotion which only a youth, never a woman, gives to another youth or a man' (132). Thus Shreve, the outsider, of whose motivations we

---

174 Kuyk has called these 'Sutpen gestures' (1990:75) because the same behavior is shown by Sutpen at the final stage of his defeat. When he discovers that Milly Jones has borne him not the necessary son but a daughter, the midwife sees 'his eyes and then his teeth inside his beard' (356).

also know very little, creates in Bon the need to be recognized by a father. This 'invention,' finally validated in the historic passage, in fact, is the most universally human one; and although Quentin first misunderstands his friend, this story is the version that ultimately touches Quentin most. It is the story of Bon's ultimate defeat. When Quentin comes to 'see' the tragedy of Charles Bon, he has finally come full circle to his own unfulfilled need for a sustaining father figure, and to his own defeat.

As was the case with Joe Christmas in *Light in August*, Bon's defeat is ultimately caused by the fact that he is *believed* to be black. As I have argued before, one cannot conclude from the reliable narrator's quotation of what Sutpen said that Sutpen is right about Bon's racial status. Although the quote 'his mother was part negro' (443) is authentic, it does not necessarily contain 'the truth.' Sutpen may have been lying to Henry—his trump card may after all be a false one—or he may himself have been misled. If Bon's mother indeed had some black blood, this would make him a 'negro' in Mississippi (even though he would have been a high status colored in New Orleans); but the thought that Bon was black never crossed the minds of either Miss Rosa or Mr. Compson. If it had ever come up at the time, Miss Rosa or Mr. Compson would certainly have heard about it. Mr. Compson, in any case, has Bon say of himself 'we... the white men' (142). All one can conclude, then, is that Sutpen believed Bon to be black.[175] Still, in Quentin and Shreve's story Charles Bon bears the burden of this belief.

Is it possible that Quentin and Shreve, reliving the past brought back to life, have 'heard' Sutpen's remark to Henry, or does their intuition make them conclude that Bon is black from the problems that Mr. Compson had in accounting for Bon's rejection? In either case, Shreve and Quentin have understood too well that most white fathers in Mississippi would be reluctant to acknowledge their 'black' children, even if they occasionally provided for them, as Sutpen presumably did. 'The stark ugly fact is,' as Lillian Smith wrote, 'that millions of children have been rejected by their white fathers and white kin and left to battle alone the giants that stalk our culture' (1978:125). Smith attributes great and long-lasting consequences to the rejection of children of mixed race:

> This mass rejection of children has been a heavy thing on our region's conscience. Like a dead weight dropped in water it lies deep in the ooze of the old and forgotten, but when talk of change is heard, it stirs restlessly as if still alive in its hiding place and is felt by minds innocent of participating in the original sin but who for involved reasons have identified themselves with it.
> (1978:25)

We have touched here on the feelings of guilt that certain authors see lurking behind the cult of 'the Great Southern Heart,' and that would influence the South, as Lillian Smith put it, 'unto the third and fourth generation' (1978:57).

One must mention, in this respect, the third national myth that C. Vann Woodward identified: the myth of American innocence, or the supposed absence of injustice,

---

175 Bon's remark to Henry, '*he didn't need to tell you I am a nigger*,' cannot be read as a validation of Sutpen's belief.

corruption and oppression throughout the United States. Woodward has wondered: 'How much room was there in the tortured conscience of the South for this national self-image of innocence and moral complacency?' As he put it:

> Southerners have repeated the American rhetoric of self admiration and sung the perfection of American institutions ever since the Declaration of Independence. But for half that time they lived intimately with a great social evil and the other half with its aftermath... Much of the South's intellectual energy went into a desperate effort to convince the world that its peculiar evil was actually a 'positive good,' but it failed even to convince itself. (1989:20f.)

'The experience of evil and the experience of tragedy,' he concluded, 'are parts of the Southern heritage that are as difficult to reconcile with the American legend of innocence and social felicity as the experience of poverty and defeat are to reconcile with the legends of abundance and success' (1989:21), making the South, as he put it, 'the poor, defeated, guilt-ridden member of a prosperous, victorious, and successful family.'

Lillian Smith, born in the South in same year as Faulkner, and like him interested in deeper psychological realities 'based on paradox or contradiction' (Foster 1990:669) rather than in surface appearances, remembered:

> Even its children knew that the South was in trouble. No one had to tell them; no words said aloud. To them, it was a vague thing weaving in and out of their play, like a ghost haunting an old graveyard or whispers after the household sleeps—fleeting mystery, vague menace to which each responded in his own way. Some learned to screen out all except the soft and the soothing; others denied even as they saw plainly, and heard. But all knew that under quiet words and warmth and laughter, under the slow ease and tender concern about small matters, there was a heavy burden on all of us and as heavy a refusal to confess it. (1978:25)

Making this observation more personal, she explained:

> We who were born in the South called this mesh of feeling and memory 'loyalty.' We thought of it sometimes as 'love.' We identified with the South's trouble as if we, individually, were responsible for all of it. We defended the sins and the sorrows of three hundred years as if each sin had been committed by us alone and each sorrow had cut across our heart. We were as hurt at criticism of our region as if our own name had been called aloud by the critic. We knew guilt without understanding it, and there is no tie that binds men closer to the past and each other than that. (1978:26)

W.J. Cash believed that in antebellum times already the South was 'a society beset by the specters of defeat, of shame, of guilt—a society driven by the need to bolster its morale, to nerve its arm against waxing odds, to justify itself in its own eyes and in those of the world' (1969:63). Because slavery was a necessary element in their society, Southerners simply had to reduce the blacks that worked for them to less than human beings. Two versions were, in fact, possible: black people were not quite grown-up, being too innocent and vulnerable to live a free and equal life, and thus needed white protection[176]; or alternatively, black people were not quite human, being too savage to live a free and equal life, and thus needed white control. The stories of *Absalom, Absalom!* generally fit this last pattern. Sutpen's slaves, even though Sutpen himself never needed to raise his voice at them according to General Compson (41), are generally called 'wild,' or 'somewhat tamed,' as if they were animals; a 'band of wild niggers like beasts half tamed to walk upright like men' (4f.), who do not fight 'like white men fight, with rules and weapons, but like negroes fight to hurt one another quick and bad' (30).

D.A. Hartman has argued that in addition to rationalizations such as: 'slavery protected the "honor" of the white women of the South' (1922:29), people used a number of other defense mechanisms, such as projection, to relieve their guilt. I have already mentioned the impetus this was for establishing southern higher education. As Hartman explained the defense meachanism of projection: 'The South defended itself from the idea of its own moral conditions by hunting out those of the North.' In George Fitzhugh's *Cannibals All!*, he points out, 'mention is made of "New York Free Love, and Oneida Incest, and Mormon Polygamy." The North was the land of "free love, free lands, free women and free churches"' (Fitzhugh 1875:376ff.; quoted in Hartman 1922:269f).

Yet, people could never really convince themselves that blacks were less than human beings. 'However much they tried, [they] could not persuade themselves that slavery was a positive good.' 'Many of them, as their unpublished records eloquently testify, knew that their critics were essentially right' (Stampp 1983:260).[177] Often knowing them intimately, having been nursed and brought up by them, and having had them as their first and best playmates,[178] they knew deepdown that black people were *people*, with the same human emotions that they themselves had. Smith, who knew this paradox from her own experience, wrote:

> I knew that my old nurse who had cared for me through long months of illness, who had given me refuge when a little sister took my place as the baby of the family, who soothed, fed me, delighted me with her stories and games, let me fall asleep on her deep warm breast, was not worthy of the passionate love I felt for her

She pointed to the result: 'I learned to use a soft voice to oil my words of superiority. I learned to cheapen with tears and sentimental talk of "my old mammy" one of the profound relationships of my life' (1978:28). The Southerner's 'lies and defenses and fabulous justifications' (1978:62), she concluded, did not keep them from feeling their

---

176 How much this situation needed to be continued is clear from laws that forbade the teaching of blacks. When T. Washington Jones of Washington, Mississippi, offered to teach 'children of color,' he made himself liable to a fine of $3,000, and the 'pupil of color' to a fine of $3,000, or ten days' imprisonment and thirty-nine lashes. (*Mississippi Republican*, vol VII, p.2, June 4, 1818; quoted in Jobe 1930:36).

177 As Stampp put it: 'all southern churches long ago had recognized the humanity of black people. However inferior in talents they might have been, they were acknowledged to be the sons and daughters of Adam, with immortal souls, equal to whites in the sight of God' (1983:261).

178 'It was not a rare sight in my generation,' Smith wrote, 'to see a black woman with a dark baby at one breast and a white one at the other, rocking them both in her wide lap, shushing them to sleep as she hummed her old songs. Still swinging them from side to side in her arms, she would lay them down on the same pallet underneath a shade tree and leave them there, little black little white together, sleeping in peace. These intimacies fill our memories and do strange things now to our segregated grown-up lives' (1978:130).

guilt; 'guilt was then and is today the biggest crop raised in Dixie' (1978:103).

Lillian Smith offered 'a psychological interpretation of southern racism that incorporated what later became some of the standard features of the guilt thesis' (Foster 1990:669).[179] She explicitly linked the guilt of the South to their ultimate defeat in the War between the States. As she put it, people 'felt... a need to suffer, and like guilty people everywhere, they had to find "enemies" to be punished by. The "dam-yankee" was the perfect psychological enemy' (1978:62).[180] In other words, the South simply *had* to lose the war because it was wrong.[181] Such 'modernist' views were not very influential among historians at the time, because not much evidence of guilt was documented. However, Foster argues, modernists 'rarely felt the need to offer definitive proofs' because they 'assumed surface realities were misleading.' Instead, they 'sought explanations based on paradox or contradiction' that lurk beneath surface realities (1990:669).

One can study such contradictions and paradoxes in the mind-styles of Faulkner's narrators. Miss Rosa Coldfield's story indeed seems to raise the question of guilt when it speaks of a 'fatality and curse on the South and on our family': 'a land primed for fatality and already cursed with it': 'the land and the time already cursed' (20f.). How-ever, to her the curse of the South is not the institution of slavery but the person of Thomas Sutpen. The way Sutpen acquired his position of wealth in her home-town, without conforming to any code of behavior associated with such a position, still fills her with rage after all these years. If Miss Rosa's text does not connect the curse of the South with the institution of slavery—she believes the war to have been an honor-able fight 'for the soil and traditions of the land' (19)—she nevertheless shows a certain defensiveness where slaves are concerned. When she contrasts her father's righteous-ness with Sutpen's brutality in order to explain to herself the enigma of her father's involvement with Sutpen, she implicitly raises the slavery question: 'what there could have been between a man like that and papa... a man who owned neither land nor slaves except two house servants whom he had freed as soon as he got them, bought them' (20). The manumission of slaves, Foster writes, is among the signs of un-conscious guilt mentioned in the literature (1990:688). The defensiveness shown in Miss Rosa's mind-style is another. Fred Hobson, however, has explained that in some areas in the South it was not uncommon 'to hate both slavery and the slave, to want no part of either.' As Fitzhugh put this in 1857: 'hatred to slavery is very generally

179 For an overview of subsequent arguments for and against this guilt thesis, see Foster 1990. It is not my intention here to defend the thesis, but to investigate whether Faulkner's characterizations show similarities with it.

180 Bell I. Wiley, also, wrote that the 'southern defeat in the Civil War' found its reason in part in 'a sense of guilt about slavery' (1956:102; quoted in Foster 1990:671). Woodward contended that the South 'writhed in the torments of its own conscience until it plunged into catastrophe to escape' (1989:21). 'Many Southerners,' Stampp argued, 'outwardly appeared to support the Confederate cause,' but 'had inward doubts about its validity': 'some, perhaps unconsciously, welcomed its defeat' (1983:247). Defeat offered white Southerners as its reward 'a way to rid themselves of the moral burden of slavery' (1983:260).

181 Reviewing the causes of the defeat proposed by other historians, Stampp argued: 'the failure of political leadership, the absurd lengths to which state rights was carried, the reluctance of Southerners to accept the discipline that war demanded, and the internal conflicts among the southern people—point to a Confederate weakness that matched in importance its physical handicaps. This was a weakness of morale' (1983:251). He concludes: 'I believe that many of them [Southerners] unconsciously felt that the fruits of defeat would be less bitter than those of success' (1983:269).

little more than hatred of negroes' (1857:297; quoted in Hobson 1983:48). Whatever the case may be, to Miss Rosa, Sutpen's black plantation workers are simply 'a herd of wild beasts' (14), and his driver 'that wild negro in his christian clothes' (24), who speaks 'without words, not needing words probably, in that tongue in which they slept in the mud' (25).

Miss Rosa's text becomes more clearly paradoxical, however, where it concerns Judith and Henry's half-sister Clytie. She considers Clytie's race *'older'* and *'purer'* than her own (171), yet considers Clytie's blood *'untamed'* and faithful only to *'its own savageness'* (195). In the crucial passage that describes how Clytie stops her from going upstairs where Judith is with Bon's body, Clytie's touch causes in Miss Rosa more than *'mere amazement and outrage at that black arresting and untimorous hand'* on her *'white woman's flesh,'* even if she calls out: *'Take your hand off me, nigger!'* (173). Miss Rosa is highly aware of difference—'black... hand': 'white... flesh'—but also of similarity. At the touch of the flesh, she is able, for a short time, to acknowledge the basic reality of a common biology. She sees *'the eggshell shibboleth of caste and color'* (173) fall, allowing her to reach briefly not a 'nigger,' but a woman like herself: two women, each segregated in her own way.[182] The repressed, lonesome, motherless young woman experiences this other woman's touch as a present of identity:

> Because it was not the name, the word, the fact that she had called me
> Rosa. As children she had called me that... That was not what she meant at
> all; in fact, during that instant while we stood face to face... she did me
> more grace and respect than anyone else I knew... 'Rosa?' I cried. 'To me?
> To my face?' Then she touched me
> (172f.)

'Grace,' a word belonging to the semantic field of the Cavalier myth, has transmigrated across the borders of gentility.

Mr. Compson's story raises the question of slavery in an imagined discussion between Charles Bon and Henry Sutpen, after Bon has taken Henry to New Orleans to see his 'octoroon' wife and son. Notice, incidentally, that Mr. Compson's text evokes the exception formed by New Orleans's racial stratification, which Thomas Sutpen was incapable of seeing. When Henry protests: 'But a bought woman. A whore' (142), Bon, in Mr. Compson's imagination, answers:

> Not whore. Dont say that... Not whores. And not whores because of us, the
> thousand. We—the thousand, the white men—made them, created and
> produced them; we even made the laws which declare that one eighth of a
> specified kind of blood shall outweigh seven eighths of another kind. I
> admit that. But that same white race would have made them slaves too,
> laborers, cooks, maybe even field hands, if it were not for this thousand,
> these few men like myself without principles or honor either, perhaps you
> will say. We cannot, perhaps we do not even want to, save all of them;
> perhaps the thousand we save are not one in a thousand. But we save that

---

182 Woman, Lillian Smith argued, 'smelled the death in the word *segregation*,' because she herself was segregated, 'always and forever [put] in her 'place''' (quoted in Hobson 1983:240; cf. Sides 1970, Scott 1974).

one. God may mark every sparrow, but we do not pretend to be God, you
see.
(142f.)

Under the guise of Bon's answer, Mr. Compson's text here conveys his ideas about the
fate of the female slave who is sold to 'any brute' who can afford her, 'not sold to him
for the night like a white prostitute, but body and soul for life to him who could have
used her with more impunity than he would dare to use an animal, heifer or mare, and
then discarded or sold or even murdered when worn out or when her keep and her
price no longer balanced' (144).

Why Mr. Compson would make up this elaborate version of Bon's answer is not
clear, but the story is not an accidental creation. Naturally, it touches Mr. Compson
personally as a white man and as a lawyer, and thus implicates him: 'we even made
the laws which declare that one eighth of a specified kind of blood shall outweigh
seven eighths of another kind. I admit that.' But if he feels, subconsciously, that his
race is guilty, this finds expression only through projection unto another man, one,
ironically, whose supposed blackness is the cause of his ultimate defeat. The mind-style
that Mr. Compson attributes to Bon clearly shows his own characteristic nihilism ('men
like myself without principles or honor') and defeatism ('we cannot, perhaps we do not
even want to, save all of them'). His text shows as well as an erotic fascination with
the 'colored' woman, linking her with 'strange and ancient curious pleasures of the
flesh... which her white sisters of a mushroom yesterday flee from in moral and outraged horror' (144).

Lillian Smith has explained how such erotic fascination finds its origin in
childhood. The small child that has learned 'to love both mother and nurse,' she
argues, is 'never certain which it loves better.' The 'colored mother' always fulfills its
needs more completely, yet somehow it knows that the 'white mother' has priority over
the 'colored mother,' that somehow it '"belongs" more to her.' It is the 'white mother'
who punishes, while the 'colored mother' is always available afterwards for comforting, 'easy, permissive, less afraid of simple earthy biological needs and manifestations'
(1978:131f.). As Smith put it:

> And now curious things happen. Strong bonds begin to grow as the most
> profound relationships of his life are formed, holding him to two women
> whose paths will take them far from each other. It is as if he were fastened
> to two umbilical cords which wrap themselves together in a terrifying
> tangle, and then suddenly, inexplicably, but with awful sureness, begin
> steadily to move, each in a different direction. Because white mother has
> always set up right and wrong, has with authority established the 'do' and
> the 'don't' of behavior, his conscience, as it grows in him, ties its
> allegiance to her and to the white culture and authority which she and his
> father represent. But to colored mother, persuasive in her relaxed attitude
> towards 'sin,' easy and warm in her physical ministrations, generous with
> her petting, he ties his pleasure feelings.
> (1978:132).

In William Alexander Percy's autobiography, for instance, the erotic fascination with
his 'divinely café-au-lait' mammy is obvious: 'I loved her devotedly and never had any
other nurse. Everything about her was sweet-smelling, of the right temperature, and

dozy... Chiefly I remember her bosom: it was soft and warm, an ideal place to cuddle one's head against. My earliest clear recollection is of a song she would sing me so cuddled-rather, not of the song itself, but of its effect on me. The words and the tune have gone, but not what they did to me' (1990:26).

Although Mr. Compson never becomes this personal, his mind-style is paradoxical and complex where women, both black and white, are concerned. Even if he raises the question of female slavery and admits to guilt, he is not concerned with prejudice against the black race, but with the fact that according to the law one drop of this 'inferior' blood can 'spoil' the whole human being. At the same time, however, he seems to consider this one drop the best part when he emphasizes the primacy, the dignity and the completeness of the African race and land. His story presents Bon's mulatto mistress as 'a female principle which existed, queenly and complete, in the hot equatorial groin of the world long before that white one of ours came down from trees and lost its hair and bleached out' (144). But, for all his fascination with the unknown mulatto woman, he 'simply' calls the mulatto he does know, Clytie, 'the grim coffee-colored woman who would come on bare feet to the door,' behaving 'with restrained savageness.'

In the story of Quentin there is no explicit sense of guilt over slavery, or over the treatment of blacks. Both he and Shreve uncritically adopt the derogatory phrases of the other speakers. Quentin presents his grandfather's conceptualization of Haiti in terms of 'violence,' 'injustice,' 'bloodshed,' 'greed,' cruelty,' 'oppression' and 'exploitation' (312f.), but the story does not include a discussion of the situation in Mississippi. As Quentin conveys it, his grandfather's story is paradoxical and contradictory, like the other stories. For instance, he believes on the one hand that the blacks on the Haiti plantation 'maybe' perceived Sutpen's arms and legs to be 'shaped like theirs and from which blood could be made to spurt and flow as it could from theirs' (317), showing themselves to be humans. On the other hand he also believes that 'maybe' they chased Sutpen's architect so they could 'cook and eat him' (320), showing themselves to be cannibals. Thus General Compson's conceptualizations, in Quentin's story, show the characteristic Southern confusion over the precise biological and social status of the black slave.

Quentin, in addition, presents his father's understanding of Mr. Coldfield's sense of guilt, and the latter's refusal to project this guilt onto Sutpen: 'it was his conscience he hated, not Sutpen;—his conscience and the land, the country which had created his conscience.' As the story goes, Mr. Coldfield 'hated that country so much that he was even glad when he saw it drifting closer and closer to a doomed and fatal war' (324); a war which, in Quentin's account of what his father told him, he saw as 'the price for having erected its economic edifice not on the rock of stern morality but on the shifting sands of opportunism and moral brigandage' (324f.). Here Faulkner came closest to having one of his characters explicitly subscribe to guilt. Mr. Coldfield, Quentin reports, would even have joined the Yankees if he could have, something that Shreve takes for granted: "Sure,' Shreve said. 'That's fine" (325).

There is compassion in the stories of Shreve and Quentin for individuals on account of the fate that awaits them because they are black or believed to be black. Firstly, Quentin elaborates on the story of his father, which presents the two Sutpen women, Judith and Clytie, trying to break the pattern of history by bringing Charles

Bon's only child, the mulatto Charles Etienne, to live at Sutpen's Hundred. Kuyk admires Judith and Clytie for taking 'the nameless stranger into the family,' who thereby come closer to completing Sutpen's design, without ever knowing it, than Sutpen himself ever did, even if they fail to save Charles Etienne because, as Kuyk puts it, they 'fail to find a way through the thickets of society's prejudices and their own' (1990:77). In Quentin's story Judith indeed asks the little mulatto boy to call her 'Aunt Judith' (261). But Quentin's text does not so much show admiration for the aunt as compassion for the reluctant child, who, as if it were a little animal, is 'cajoled' into 'the thicket' by a woman who does not dare to put out her hand to touch it, speaking to it instead in a voice 'soft and swooning, filled with that seduction, that celestial promise which is the female's weapon' (261). Once again, Quentin's own fear of seduction is clear.

Secondly, there is compassion with the fate of Charles Bon, who, according to the two friends, suffers because he is disowned by his father on account of his mixed race. The issue is linked to the war in a curious way, as Shreve gives Quentin's father credit for believing that Bon and Henry hoped the war would settle their dispute, so that they would not have to settle it themselves (427f.). Quentin does not protest this view; neither Bon and Henry, nor Quentin and Shreve, the narrator explains, were the first young men 'to believe (or at least apparently act on the assumption) that wars were sometimes created for the sole aim of settling youth's private difficulties and concerns.' This, finally, seems to include even the author, as his own 'war experiences' indicate.

6

Character, Personality, and Psychostylistics

In this study of characterization in Faulkner's major psychological novels—*The Sound and the Fury*, *As I Lay Dying*, *Light in August* and *Absalom, Absalom!*—the literary character is approached through the notion of personality. Personality is a construct that allows for a place of contact between the flesh-and-blood person that we encounter in the real world and the artistic creation that we encounter in the novel. To make operable the concept of personality, I have relied on the various psychoanalytic perspectives that problematize the complexity and layeredness of the mental functioning found in Faulkner's characters. Rather than searching for the 'truth' of a person's life experience, psychoanalysis seeks to provide a narrative account of it: a 'possible world,' one might say, that fulfills the individual's need for order. Thus personality can be seen as a pragmatic issue insofar as it represents the motivation for, or the energy behind, the creation of this world. The way Faulkner's characters create their worlds is determined by their individual needs and desires, as well as by the needs and desires of others, as these are represented by the family, society and history.

In Faulkner's novels, the different structural components of personality may be approached as 'voices': the voices of human nature, of history and of culture, of prior experience, and even of those whose judgment is anticipated; all of which tell the individual what to see and how to see it. Lucas Beauchamp, in *Intruder in the Dust*, for instance, cannot see himself as one of the common Negro slaves because of his blood kinship with the white patriarch. He refuses, therefore, '*to mean mister to anybody even when he says it*' (58). From his point of view, the white villagers are his inferiors rather than his superiors. Even though he is forced, by being black, to address them in the way prescribed for blacks towards whites, he does not entertain the matching mental representation, and he shows this through his ostentatious behavior, which cannot be ignored by the community and which almost costs him his life. Lucas's ostentatious behavior, in fact, shows a conflict between the voice of nature, which dictates his equality, the conflicting voices of his culture, which dictate his inferiority as well as his superiority, and the various expected or imagined voices of those he confronts with his behavior.

Faulkner's novels are really what the Russian critic and literary theorist Mikhail Bakhtin has called 'an orchestration of many voices.' Each of the characters presents himself as an echo-chamber of other voices: a muddle of unconscious voices, a reservoir of social speech. Normally, the individual is not consciously aware of these voices; they form the unconscious contributions of others in the back, so to speak, of the individual's mind. This is the case because the 'ego' works towards integrating and internalizing these voices, so that they are experienced as a personal voice. In times of heightened awareness or stress, however, the individual may acknowledge the presence of these voices and actually hear them. Faulkner's Joe Christmas in *Light in August* seems to feel as much when he, contemplating his future actions, hears around him 'a myriad sounds... voices, murmurs, whispers: of trees, darkness, earth; people: his own voice; other voices evocative of names and times and places' (115). Quentin Compson in *Absalom, Absalom!* feels 'his very body' to be 'an empty hall echoing with sonorous defeated names' (9).[183] Problems in relating such voices to the self point to the individual's developmental or emotional problems, and convey his difficulties in creating a world that he may call his own.

Personality and Mind-Style
The linguistic behavior of Faulkner's characters has provided a wealth of material for the study of what Fowler has called 'mind-style': the linguistic expression of the conceptualization of the world achieved by the individual, including the conceptualization of the individual himself in this world. Relying on theories of Fowler, Halliday, Taylor and others, I showed how concept formation takes place and how relations between concepts are laid down in language. To account for the pattern of stability and change in the individual's linguistic choices, I have argued, is to account for this individual's personality as a process. The narrow scope of first-person narration in *The Sound and the Fury* makes it a perfect text for such a study of personality. Any discussion about personality, however, involves categorization and labeling to some extent. From his text, Benjy Compson may well be labeled, or 'diagnosed' as mentally retarded with autistic tendencies; Quentin as schizoid[184]; and Jason as paranoic. Such classifications may serve certain purposes, but, one might object, they also leave out all that is unstable, complex, and specific: all that the novel is about.

It may be helpful to realize that personality classifications are essentially prototype categories, with fuzzy boundaries and more central and more marginal members. This is clear from the fact that hedges can be used with them. Hedges express the degree or kind of category membership of a concept; they can open up the categories to allow for complexity and specificity. We can say, for instance, that Benjy is mentally retarded with autistic tendencies *in that* he tends to echolalia. The hedge *in that* makes clear the reason why Benjy fits the category even though he does not possess certain essential qualities, or possesses other qualities that do not fit the category. One might object that personality categories devised for real human beings should not be used for literary characters. Hedges will prove illustrative here as well. Let us consider the hedge *strictly speaking* used in a negative context in the following way: '*Strictly speaking*, Benjy is *not* mentally retarded with autistic tendencies.' That this sentence is an acceptable one (while, for instance, 'strictly speaking, Benjy is not a horse' is not)

183 Compare Stephen Ross's 'phenomenal voice,' a voice disseminated through the discourse rather than 'merely derivative of depicted speakers and their speech acts' (1989:29). My approach to such voices is that, even if they entail the 'separation of voice from speaker' (1989:36), they are usually heard by a specific listener, and thus belong to this listener's conceptualization of reality.
184 Jay Martin has argued that Quentin is best classified as a male hysteric (personal communication).

illustrates that his position, if not situated precisely in the category 'mentally retarded with autistic tendencies,' is still sufficiently close to it. One may subsequently try to account for this observation.

My discussion of the mind-styles of the Compson brothers has simultaneously addressed both of the problems mentioned above. Firstly, to use the case of Benjy again as an example: which aspects of his text make it possible to classify Benjy as mentally retarded with autistic tendencies, and which do not? Secondly, which aspects of his text position him in the artistic twin-category of the mentally retarded with autistic tendencies? The first question involves an exploration of the fuzzy boundaries of the category. It presumes 'entering' the fictional world, by joining what Peter Rabinowitz has called the 'narrative audience' (1977:121ff.; cf. Phelan 1989:5f.), and what I have called 'stepping into the shoes of the internal addressee.' I have focused on aspects of Benjy's text such as his echolalia and his lack of a 'theory of mind,' which are considered essential attributes of the category. I have also shown that Benjy's text lacks certain aspects that are deemed essential, such as the unwillingness or inability to communicate in any form whatsoever. Rather, Benjy's desperate endeavors to communicate—'I tried to say but they went on'—produce some of the most moving passages of his text. The second question involves an exploration of the artistic duplication of categories. It entails 'stepping back from' the fictional world, and joining what Rabinowitz has called the 'authorial audience' (1977:121ff.; Phelan 1989:5f.). Thus I have explored the devices by means of which Faulkner creates the artistic equivalent of the attributes associated with the category, for instance the deviant punctuation (by which reporting sentences are separated from their quotations) that represents Benjy's communicative problems.

A third objection that could be made against the categorization approach of personality concerns its static quality. Personality is after all a process rather than a stable phenomenon, entity, or state. A discussion of personality, even if it involves categorization, should therefore always leave open the possibility of movement within the applicable category, from center to margins and vice versa, as well as movement from one applicable category to another. Focusing on this, I explored the temporal complexities of the texts of the three brothers. As far as Benjy Compson is concerned, his ability to return to his memories and actually relive them has allowed me to study his text as a long-term process, even if his narration concerns only one day, April seventh, 1928. Thus I have been able to show that when Benjy was younger, he had more advanced cognitive and affective abilities, and was able to perceive cause and effect relations, to summarize, and to perform introspection. After the disappearance of Caddy these advanced capabilities have disappeared.

Uncontrolled and intensely relived memories form a part of Quentin Compson's text as well. As in Benjy's case, these memories largely concern their beloved sister Caddy. In Quentin's case, however, the memories are not only beyond his control and very intense, but finally so distorted that they amount to an actual psychotic breakdown. I have shown how, after warding off this psychosis through rationalization for most of the day of his narration, June second, 1910, the tactile sensation of blood running from his nose brings on an uncontrollable 'memory' that merges Quentin's blood with that of the beloved sister. Faulkner's techniques here include the poetic lay-out of the passage, with multiple enjambment, and with run-on sentences of an uncharacteristic grammatical simplicity, to create the 'delusion peace' of psychosis. When Quentin tries to recover with a return to his rationalizations, this is doomed to fail. His memories now show the effects of ego fragmentation, crafted graphologically by the artist: 'i will never do that nobody knows what i know' (204).

Jason Compson's text contains such an excess of control that it would seem to preclude any intensely 'relived' returns to the past, basically making it a straightforward account of the day of his narration, April sixth, 1928. Because of its narrow temporal scope, then, it seems to convey mood rather than personality. However, the rigidity and one-dimensionality of his mind-style also strongly suggest the static personality of the paranoic. In order to study Jason's personality as a process, it was necessary to give a great deal of attention to the one relatively uncontrolled return to his past that can be found in the text. This is the scene of his father's funeral, when Jason begins 'to feel sort of funny' (232). Four consecutive progressives here, in a text that is otherwise utterly devoid of them, slow down the pace of Jason's furious self-assertion, and make him relive a moment of genuine feeling, shared with the despised sister Caddy.

Clearly, the important sister, Caddy, is located at the heart of each brother's mind-style, as she is for Faulkner himself, who wrote:

So I, who never had a sister and was fated to lose my daughter in infancy, set out to make myself a beautiful and tragic little girl.

For all her importance, however, she remains an absence. The approach through mind-style that I chose for *The Sound and the Fury* cannot capture her, as she has no narration of her own. She lives only in the conceptualizations of her brothers, who have already lost her as they narrate; who are, as Donald Kartiganer puts it, 'left with the memory of their sister, a word—"Caddy"—they arbitrarily use to name their despair' (1992:67).

Personality and the Family

The key female at the heart of the novel *As I Lay Dying* is certainly not in the same situation as Caddy Compson. Addie Bundren's one narrative section, in fact, not only provides material for the exploration of her own personality, but for the personalities of her children—Cash, Darl, Jewel, Dewey Dell and Vardaman—as well. Although mind-style, with its psychoanalytic implications, has remained my starting-point here, my exploration of personality in *As I Lay Dying* had to expand my mind-style approach of *The Sound and the Fury* to include the influence of the family—especially the central mother figure—on the personality of the individual. In *As I Lay Dying* I have been able to show directly how the personalities of all of the Bundren siblings were influenced by their mother's conceptualization of their existence: the needs, desires and discontents that she projected unto them. One need only look at the predicates with which Addie presents her initial reaction to them: 'I knew I had Cash'; 'I found I had Darl... I would not believe it'; 'I found that I had Jewel... I waked to remember to discover it'; 'I gave Anse Dewey Dell': 'Then I gave him Vardaman.'

The Freudian approach of the first chapter was supplemented here by post-freudian theories, especially those of Melanie Klein, with their emphasis on pre-Oedipal ego-development. Thematically, *As I Lay Dying* can be read as a collection of texts on mourning. Addie Bundren's children, each in a personal way, try to come to terms with the death of this powerful woman. Klein has stressed the importance of the child's first love object—the mother's breast—and its loss at the time of weaning. As she saw it, each subsequent loss that an individual suffers revitalizes the feelings and the developmental tasks associated with the period of weaning. Addie's text is explicitly violent where this developmental task is concerned. In her presentation, weaning is a very traumatic experience, in which even her husband is included: she 'refused' her breast to them 'after their time was up' (161).

Faulkner's technique in *As I Lay Dying* includes an aspect that was only marginal in *The Sound and the Fury*: the presentation of elements of one speaker's behavior by another speaker. This entails two separate manners of characterization that should be distinguished. For this purpose I have introduced the phrase *characterization from the outside*, as opposed to the *characterization from the inside* that mind-style represents. The material discussed here is not necessarily verbal, but includes a whole range of verbal, paraverbal and nonverbal behaviors. Paraverbal and nonverbal behavior, like verbal behavior, create meanings in that they 'say something' about the behaver. Memorable are, for instance, Jewel's erect posture as he 'sits' his horse, 'gazing straight ahead' (106) and the way he talks to his horse 'in a soothing murmur' (133); Vardaman's eyes that become round as he sees that his mother has died (45); Dewey Dell's leg 'coming long from beneath her tightening dress' as she mounts the wagon (91); and Cash's hands lying flat on the coffin that contains Addie, 'rocking her a little' (133). We must remember, however, that the way one character sees another is never completely reliable. In *As I Lay Dying* it often tells us more about the observer than about the observee.

Personality and Society

The question of the reliability of different presentations of a character's behavior, already raised in my discussion of *As I Lay Dying*, is a crucial issue in understanding Joe Christmas in *Light in August*. If a character, such as Joe Christmas, is given very little voice of his own, characterization from the outside, the reports that others make of his behavior, as well as the way they interpret his behavior and classify his personality, including the degree of freedom they allow this classification, acquire major importance. To approach this issue in a third-person narrative, I have had to distinguish two types, or levels, of 'narrative audiences': the 'intradiegetic level' of the characters and the 'extradiegetic level' of the narrator/narratee. In addition, I had to make the important distinction between *reliability* and *credibility*: between trustworthiness and being trusted. The task I set myself then was to account for the issues of reliability and credibility on both of the fictional levels mentioned above, and their important influence on the characterization of Joe Christmas. Neo-freudian theory (and in particular Horneyan) has provided a framework here.

Firstly, on the level of the characters I analyzed the accounts of all the major speakers in terms of the reliability and the credibility of their accounts as two separate issues. A large discrepancy between the two was often encountered, with credibility being high when reliability was in fact quite low, and pointing to the general level of prejudice present in the town of Jefferson. Speakers, in Jefferson, are credible to their fellows on account of a 'lopsided' version of 'truth,' which ignores biological reality (the truths that all people naturally share because of their similarity as a species; the truth, for instance, that Chick Mallison learns when he sees a black man cry) and distorts social reality (truths that are negotiated within a certain community or society) by denying half the population a voice. On the level of the narrator/narratee a completely different situation was found. Extradiegetic narrators very often have the task of disambiguating, summarizing, classifying and labeling the various behaviors conveyed or presented on the 'lower' level of the characters. The narrator of *Light in August*, however, is of a completely different kind, consistently abstaining from classifying and labeling. What is more, his accounts constantly problematize the classifications and labelings that the people of Jefferson make so easily. Although convention dictates that the narrator has more 'authentication authority' than a character (Doležel 1988:490), readers and professional critics alike have rarely paid due attention to the narrator's text, giving far too much weight to the accounts of the internal speakers, and readily labeling Joe Christmas—with the (white) people of Jefferson—as the murderer of Joanna Burden. My discussion has tried to address the question of why this is so.

Possible answers to this question can be found on the two fictional levels in the text. Firstly, on the level of the characters, one can see that Joe Christmas's desire to be named by others wages a constant battle against his fear of coming under the influence of others. Appearing white, he might have lived a peaceful life working at the mill, but instead he is driven to flaunt his undefinable otherness in front of his fellow workers, and, with them, in front of the reader, as part of the 'narrative audience.' The complexity in his personality keeps Christmas daring others to label him, but no suspicion about his racial status ever started until Joe Brown, the initial suspect of the murder, said the words that secured Christmas's fate: 'he's got niggerblood.' Secondly, on the level of the narrator/narratee, the accounts of the novel's major internal speaker, Byron Bunch (who presents the events leading up to Christmas's arrest), are initially invested with much authority because the narrator repeatedly uses an attributive verb that signals his consent: 'Byron Bunch *knew* this' (my emphasis). Social psychology has shown that if reliability is established early on, before an audience has been able to form its own conceptualizations, the effects may be very long-lasting (Sternthal, Phillips and Dholakia 1978:289). Here, obviously, the narrator's signals of consent have retained their influence far beyond this initial section of the text, making Bunch a credible speaker long after he has, in fact, become much too involved to be reliable, thus illustrating Donald Spence's argument that when motive becomes important, 'truth takes the back seat' (1982:95). Apart from these linguistic considerations, however, the narrator's elaborate accounts of Joe Christmas's past life may seem to provide a motive for killing Joanna Burden. Such readings can easily be deconstructed. Narrative accounts of anyone's background can provide all sorts of motives for all sorts of actions; and even if one were to take such a motive as established, it forms no proof in itself that Christmas is a murderer.

To move up, finally, to the 'authorial level,' the most difficult question of all remains unanswered: what did Faulkner intend with the text he created? The question, of course, is essentially unanswerable, and many would not even want to consider it. But I have often wondered: was Faulkner, in his later work *Intruder in the Dust*, forced to rewrite the story of the man who refuses to be classified, and who is consequently believed to be a murderer because this 'made the folks so mad'? Did he have to make the case more explicit there, by using his young narrator Chick Mallison to solve the mystery and thus save Lucas Beauchamp's life, because the prejudiced labeling process that he meant to put up for inspection in *Light in August* proved to entice the reader too easily, too fast and too much? Whether or not Christmas was the murderer of Joanna Burden, the people of Jefferson cannot know it from the evidence they have, and neither can the reader. After all is said and done, Christmas was lynched on the word of Joe Brown, the man who provided the label only to get himself acquitted. Lynchings performed simply because a man was black, or believed to be black, were of great concern to Faulkner, and they still happened in his hometown of Oxford, Mississippi long after he wrote the novels.

According to Lillian Smith, 'although 3,148 lynchings took place in the South from 1882 to 1946, no member of a lynch mob was given a death sentence or life imprisonment' (1978:201). One story of the 1940s tells of a black man from Oxford who was repeatedly sent to Memphis by a white woman to buy liquor for her. When the black man was seen at her window one day, the young woman, who was afraid that she would be accused of fraternizing with 'negroes,' told her uncle, the sheriff, that he had tried to climb into her window with the intention of raping her. The man, who was respected and trusted by many in Oxford, and hired by them as a sanitary repair man and admitted into their homes, was arrested, presumably tried, and sent to Parchman prison. But when his wife wanted to bring him some cigarettes there, she was told that he was somewhere where he would need no cigarettes. The man was never seen again; most likely he was never tried and never even reached Parchman penitentiary.[185]

Personality and History

I have touched, here, on the South's particular social situation during the first half of the twentieth century as it meets Faulkner's work. Although I did not ignore the Southern situation in my earlier chapters, it finally became the focal point of my discussion of *Light in August*. Moving beyond this situation to its historical context—the 'peculiar history of the South' (Cash 1969:viii)—I traced the direction that Faulkner set out for *Absalom, Absalom!* In this novel, various historical events are explicitly mentioned, especially at the beginning of the Civil War: the election of Lincoln, the fall of Fort Sumter, the secession of Mississippi;[186] the battle of Bull Run, and the formation of a special Confederate unit at the University of Mississippi, the 'University Grays.' Faulkner, however, was not in the first place interested in the War as a series of events, but rather in the conceptualizations of these events as history in the minds of his characters, including especially the motivations and emotions that these conceptualizations imply, as well as the possible conflicts that they hide; thus providing the link between personality and history that my discussion has focused on.

---

185 Personal information by Mrs. Lena Nelson of Oxford, Mississippi.

186 Duncan McCollum, a student at the University of Mississippi at Oxford, described January 9, 1861 as a very special day: 'Glorious day for Mississippi, seceded at 3 p.m. today. News came at sundown. Great demonstration at college and town illuminated. A salute fired. Boys parade a torchlight procession went to town and was joined by citizens. Several speeches. Fire balls on campus. Mrs. Lamar illuminated her dwelling. Immense excitement. Much music. Rain Turns cold. Mud deep. Buy pencil ten cents' (1986:24). Kenneth Stampp, however, argued that 'in fact, nearly all the public celebrations in the seceded states during the dismal winter of 1860-61 had about them a quality of forced gaiety.' 'Whatever was to be gained from independence,' he argued, 'Southerners knew that some priceless things would inevitably be lost. They could hate the Yankees, but that was not quite the same as hating the Union' (1983:257).

To Miss Rosa Coldfield, for instance, the defeat of the South is something that 'Heaven saw fit' because Thomas Sutpen, and men like him, had 'valor and strength' but no 'pity or honor' (19). She herself experienced this in a most intimate way. Thus the defeat of the South acquires, for Miss Rosa, the character of a personal revenge. How she would classify Sutpen—this demon—is expressed repeatedly, albeit negatively: he was no gentleman. But for all the decisiveness of her attributions and classifications, Miss Rosa's text, as I have been able to show, is full of paradox. Repetition and paradox are among the symptoms that point beyond conceptualizations of the world towards 'the problems of the human heart in conflict with itself.' Here I have focused especially on some of the myths brought together as 'the glorification of the Southern heritage' (Cash 1969:128), which function to subdue such conflicts through narratives of denial, undoing, projection and justification.

One of the tasks of the myth was, according to many students of Southern culture, to deal with the South's guilt over slavery, which could not but violate the prevalent American myth of innocence. Two different versions of the myth depicted blacks either as beasts or as children, neither of which was satisfactory. They could not take away the South's feelings of guilt. At best, they succeeded in pushing them below the level of consciousness. Lillian Smith has argued that such unconscious feelings of guilt, which according to her were the cause of the Southern defeat, influenced not only those people actually guilty of owning slaves, but also those who never did, and even those who had not even yet been born.

The issue as it figures in *Absalom, Absalom!* is worth exploring. Miss Rosa Coldfield speaks of a 'curse' on the South, and even on her family, but she does not consciously link this curse to the issue of slavery. Yet, she is defensive about the two slaves that her father once owned. Mr. Compson actually admits guilt when he has Charles Bon say: 'we even made the laws,' but that does not keep him from speaking of 'wild niggers' too. His text, as well as that of Miss Rosa, is riven by paradox, pointing to the level of conflict underneath.

In the texts of Quentin and Shreve, Faulkner has inscribed most clearly his position of at once insider and outsider with respect to the country about which he writes. Together, outsider and insider come to experience, through narrative, a real compassion with—and an understanding of—the plight of the man of mixed race who is denied his existence by his white father and brother. Yet the outsider ends his narration with a cynical conclusion made possible by distance:

> So it takes two niggers to get rid of one Sutpen, don't it?.. Which is all right, it's fine; it clears the whole ledger, you can tear all the pages out and burn them, except for one thing. And do you know what that is?... You've got one nigger left. One nigger Sutpen left.
> (470f.)

Quentin, who only recently identified with one fatherless black man, does not protest this cynical treatment of another. Maybe he cannot, because, in its cynicism, Shreve's remark sounds so much 'like Father.' His final statement encompasses, however, all the ambivalence of one who, to adapt the words of Darl Bundren, is forced to love but hates himself for having to do it:

> I dont hate it
> I dont hate it

I dont hate it
I dont. I dont! I dont hate it! I dont hate it!
(471)

What Quentin desperately needs to deny, to himself more than to Shreve, is his desperation over the sense of defeat in the South, in his father, and ultimately in his own story.

Absalom, Absalom! is the last of Faulkner's great psychological novels, in which 'the problems of the human heart in conflict with itself' form the major theme. Nowhere in his work can such a passionate clinging to both defeat *and* victory be found.

I hope I have demonstrated how the 'happy marriage' of mind-style and mainstream psychiatry and psychology that I have termed *psychostylistics* can lead to a new and more precise understanding of the literary character, its construction, its internal cohesion—or lack of it—and its reception. With its emphasis on conflict and paradox, the method is a valuable one, not only for the study of Faulkner's characters but also for all those novels that concentrate on voice, and in which the mental self and its stability are not taken for granted.

Epilogue:
Personality, Fiction, and the Author

And don't all my stories, true or false, tend towards
the same conclusion? Don't they all have the same
meaning? So what does it matter whether they are
true or false if, in both cases, they are significant
of what I have been and of what I am?
(Albert Camus)

In his essay 'Dangerous Inventions,' the Mississippi writer Lewis Nordan tells of a hunting trip he once took with his father on grounds that were reserved for the governor of the state. After their dog—'this yellow brain-damaged oversexed rabbit chaser that my father called Blue' (1992:4f.)—attacked one of the men in the governor's party, they are summoned to leave the grounds, to avoid having to 'spend a night in jail.' As Nordan expresses it, he and his father 'left the woods and fields in disgrace.' However, Nordan immediately adds here that his father obviously did not quite feel it this way, because, as he puts it: 'here is the punchline of the anecdote... even after this my father referred to the incident as "the day me and my boy went hunting with the governor"' (1992:5).[187] Nordan told the adventure so many times that it became, as he put it, 'a part of who I am, one of many deep important memories that have shaped my life' (1992:5). One can sense why this might be so from the text. The phrase 'me and my boy,' for instance, conveys the importance of the little boy for the father, and their togetherness in this adventure.

Surprisingly, then, Nordan immediately goes on to confess that nothing, 'not one word of the story' is true. He never went on a hunting trip with his father when he was young; they never owned a dog named Blue, although he owns a similar one now; he never saw the governor except once very briefly in school; and, finally, he never even knew his father, who died when he was eighteen months old. But even though this story about his father—and many others he told his friends—is untrue, Nordan continues to explain: 'it is in some senses more a true part of me than much of the stuff that actually did happen and that made little or no impression on me' (1992:5). Exploring why this would be so, Nordan links the need for such stories to the fact that he never knew what his father was like; that he never saw any of his father's personal belongings; that he never owned any photographs of him except for one in which his father's face was shaded by a hat; and that he heard virtually no anecdotes about him. In addition, the man who eventually became his stepfather was utterly unsatisfactory to him, so that his mind became fixed on a wish that his mother had married his father's brother Uncle Bud, a 'dashing and handsome physician' who served in Africa with General Patton.' Nordan describes this uncle as 'outrageous and imaginative and garrulous'; who else would have 'climbed into his magnolia tree with a brush and a

---

187 That the father might say this precisely because he *did* feel disgraced is not part of the son's story.

bucket of red paint' one Christmas, and 'painted all the leaves red so that the magnolia looked like a tree full of elephantine poinsettias' (1992:5). The truth of this story, however, also remains undecided. Explaining his urge to create such stories further, Nordan writes:

> In all my fictions, written and spoken, I have been doing one thing, and it was not to hurt others or to impress my friends, and it was only for myself. I have been inventing a father... Without a father I was intolerable to myself. Without a father I was not a person worthy of my own regard. For all my life it has been unacceptable to me that I could not have the father that death took from me, or if not him, then the father of my fantasy, the one I made up from selected detail from the life of my Uncle Bud. (1992:7)

Nordan's stories—the fictionality of which remained outside the reach of his own conscious awareness for a long time—bring to mind Freud's family romance, complicated here by the fact that the available father is not just imagined to be a substitute, but known to be one.

The need to invent realities, however, goes beyond the need for a satisfactory father (or mother). 'It is a central fact of human life,' the psychoanalyst and literary critic Jay Martin writes, 'that each person invents a reality in which to live. We do not discover reality, we construct it... We create our reality by the way we search for it and what we search for' (1988:26). Nordan's story emphasizes that through his creation of a world he created his own identity as well; this, in fact, was the very goal of his activities: 'I have been inventing the father I always wanted, imperfect and yet redeemable as well, like the father who makes the joke about going hunting with the governor. And the point is, I have been inventing a Buddy Nordan who had such a father' (1992:7). But even though these fictions seem to have been beneficial for the young Lewis, Nordan uses the title 'dangerous inventions' for his essay. In his conclusion he returns to the issue: 'here is what I wonder: What are the lies yet to be uncovered in me? What dangerous protective fictions silence the intimate heart so that the inventions may live instead?' (1992:7).

Martin raises the same issue in his discussion of people's identification with existing fictions in the form of novels, drama and film. As he argues, 'identification with fictions can become obsessive, monolithic, more or less permanent, unconditioned, and unqualified. People who experience themselves as empty may look to fictions to provide a fixed, predictable role... Those who feel weak and ineffectual may find in fictions grandiose representations of power... Those who feel diffuse, fragmented, and unstable may find rigid guidelines and premeditated shapes in fictions...' What these roles, representations, guidelines and shapes hide, however, is the 'reactive anger and depression that arose from early frustration and disappointment, when the budding self was left helpless and unformed—in search first of parents; and, when these failed, for other sources of new birth' (1988:24f.). Creating fictional images of himself was one of Faulkner's specialties, whether it be the English gentleman, the eccentric, or a mixture of the two. In Oxford he liked to play the English gentleman, but when he was in Toronto, where people were more English than the English, he was happy to be considered French. As he wrote to his mother: 'the people up here all think that I am French, from Montreal, for some reason' (Watson 1992:102). As Charles Nelson and

David Goforth, two 'neighbors,' wrote prior to the novelist's death, 'he has almost completely cut himself off from any normal trafficking with the town... Even if he let down his drawbridge he would still be an anomaly. His personal appearance, his dress, his purpose in life run counter to those predominant in Oxford... Yet he has an admirable—and undoubtedly successful—habit of blending in with his background when he wants to, through an artful series of carefully arranged movements' (1977:8). 'If William Faulkner had not chosen writing as his profession,' they suggest, 'he might have tried acting: he certainly shows talent in that area' (1977:24). Pretending to be 'a literary bumpkin, growing up isolated from the main currents of modern writing in a small southern town,' he told his publisher that he owned 'no books at all,' and inter- viewers that he never read Joyce, Freud 'or any other contemporary whose work seemed to have influenced his own' (Singal 1982:157).

Inhabitants of Oxford, Mississippi remember how he would check out books from the small drugstore lending library but would make others sign his name. As he said, he was going to be famous one day, and he knew that his signature would then be worth a lot of money. Therefore he was not about to give it away for free.[188] This last 'fiction,' of course, was one that he lived to make true. Other fictions were not so much predictive as they were protective. As Donald Kartiganer describes the writer's 'World War I adventures': 'Faulkner finally managed to get into the Canadian RAF but did not even learn to fly, let alone see action—which did not prevent him from sub- sequently inventing a rich war record of training-camp fiascoes and combat crashes resulting in near-fatal wounds' (1992:65). In a letter home to his mother, for instance, he wrote on November 22, 1918: 'This weather is awful. I came down the other day, so cold that I had to be lifted out of the machine, could scarcely stand' (1992:133). It is well-known that when he arrived back in Oxford he limped, supposedly from a war accident that necessitated a silver plate being put in his head. The limp gradually faded out over time, but could also suddenly reappear when needed.

Martin argues that with these wartime inventions Faulkner had to protect himself from feelings of emptiness and worthlessness. Faulkner himself clearly was not the only one to hold the opinion that he was worthless. As Kartiganer writes: 'Faulkner's own uncle—and he was not alone—publicly ridiculed him: "Billy just ain't worth a damn, and that's all there is to it... Never has been worth a damn and never will be. Not worth killing"' (1992:65). When his childhood sweetheart Estelle Oldham an- nounced her marriage, Faulkner's need to create a fictional personality for himself had once more become urgent. As Martin puts it: 'Estelle had married an officer? All right, Faulkner determined to become an officer' (1988:194).[189] Considering the seriousness and the duration of this invention, Martin argues, his feelings of emptiness must have been a reprise of earlier ones.

In this connection, Martin quotes Faulkner's brother John: 'for the first year of his life "Bill... had the colic every night. Mother said the only way she could ease him

---

188 Personal information by Charles Nelson of Oxford, Mississippi.
189 William Alexander Percy expressed a more general purpose: 'husky young Southerners... believed that if they failed to become officers the war would be lost and they might just as well have been born out of wedlock in New England' (1990:173). He wrote his mother from the front in France: 'One must be a soldier these days—there is no other part a man may play and be a man' (1990:201).

enough to stop his crying was to rock him in a straight chair, the kind you have in the kitchen."' The straight chair, used as if it were a rocking chair, obviously made so much noise that 'the neighbors said the Faulkners were the queerest people they ever knew; they spent all night in the kitchen chopping kindling on the floor' (1988:188f.; Faulkner 1963:10f.). Perhaps the baby enjoyed this noisy, bumpy rocking; perhaps the Faulkners did not own a real rocking chair, but Martin sees in this somewhat uncomfortable arrangement 'a suggestion of ambivalence about mothering on her part—a commitment to the duty of meeting the infant's needs, rather than softness or tenderness.' 'The image that emerges,' he argues, 'is of Maud as a reliable but not warm mother, an impression confirmed by later evidence. Faulkner's mother apparently fulfilled her obligations, but there seems little of the mutuality in feeding and playing necessary to nourish the infant's psyche at its source' (1988:189).

Whether or not this is so, Faulkner's attachment to his mother reveals certain neurotic qualities. His mother always played the central role in Faulkner's life; as Frederick Karl puts it, 'Maud never gave up on her sons... The situation, however, went beyond Freud's dictum that the son with his mother's love can go all the way. Maud gave love, but she expected deference and obedience in return. She tried to be the central woman in all her sons' lives' (1989:380). According to James Watson, she insisted that all her sons write her every week when they were away from home (1992:22). It was the oldest of the four brothers, William, who was closest to his mother, in physical appearance (he had her small posture,[191] her hooded eyes, and her thin lips[192]), in intellectual interest (she read Shakespeare, Balzac, Conrad and others), and emotionally as well. On absences from his hometown Oxford during his youth, Faulkner wrote home on average once every five days. The earliest existing letter, of 1912, carries the salutation: 'Dear Miss Lady,' and conveys a curious form of attachment: 'I was going to town the other day and saw a man and I started to yell "Hello Dad," when I saw his face. I havent seen any one that looks like you 'cause Lady, you're too pretty' (Watson 1992:40). Six years later, he wrote to her from New Haven: 'I couldn't live here at all but for your letters. I love you darling'; and 'I can... realize that home is greater that [sic] war, or lightning, or marriage, or any other unavoidable thing' (Watson 1992:53 and 12).[193]

In later letters from the RAF training camp in Toronto, Faulkner shows himself extremely demanding of his mother. In nearly every letter home he asks for, or acknowledges the receipt of, money, food and articles of clothing: 'the sweater, socks and cigs came yesterday, and Ive just gotten another package Havent opened it yet, but I have an idea its something to eat' (Watson 1992:97). Especially the soft articles of

191 Maud Falkner was always worried about William's posture. When he was thirteen and fourteen she made him wear a whalebone corset to straighten him; and when he was twenty-eight and living in New Orleans, he still felt obliged to write to his mother 'my shoulders are all right, moms... I expect I am straighter than I was at home' (Watson 1992:206).
192 This similarity in appearance with his mother earned Faulkner the nick-name 'snake-lips,' which his father gave him and which was at the same time a sneer towards his mother.
193 In his letters to his mother Faulkner does not often write about women that attracted him. One exception is his letter of April 20, 1925, when he writes about a Mrs. Gumble: 'she is the nicest one I have met. She is twenty four and has the most beautiful hair I ever saw. It is really gold—sometimes it looks yellow and sometimes it is red, like a gold coin. There is something about the shape of her forehead and eyes that reminds me of you' (Watson 1992:202).

clothing that his mother sent pleased him: 'I am in my tent... admiring the sweater which came today. Its the softest thing I ever had on'; 'I am sitting in the sun with my shirt open so every one can see my sweater'; 'Its still cold. Every so often I feel inside my shirt to touch my sweater, and laugh' (1992:87f.). About his mother's food he was extremely possessive: 'My tent is full of people now, and as I do not care for people, I'm waiting until they go to open my box... I refuse to give your cakes to every Tom and Dick in the camp here. This crowd hangs about like a crowd of vultures, waiting until some one to get a box from home. If I were not naturally rather unapproachable, they'd take it away from me' (Watson 1992:97).

Martin comments on one of Faulkner's early memories of spending the night with his aunt and cousins. As Faulkner remembered it, the experience left him with 'one of those spells of loneliness and nameless sorrow that children suffer, for what or because of what they do not know' (1988:189). Consequently, the two cousins had to take him home: 'Vannye... impersonal; quite aloof... holding the lamp' and 'Natalie... quick and dark. She was touching me. She must have carried me.' As Martin argues, the 'confusing contrast' between the two girls—one 'aloof,' the other 'touching'—may suggest 'the confused, fused, ambivalent attitudes he held towards mothering and, ultimately, his mother' (1988:190).

The image of Faulkner's mother 'rocking' him in a straight kitchen chair, meanwhile, brings to mind a scene in *As I Lay Dying*, where a fictional mother holds her favorite son on a pillow 'in the lamplight' (130), like the kitchen chair, not the best place for a baby to sleep. The neurotic need for a constant supply of food and soft clothing manufactured by mother in Faulkner's letters home brings to mind another scene, where the same fictional mother explains how she weaned her sons: 'I refused my breast to Cash and Darl after their time was up' (161). Finally, the 'homesickness-scene,' with the conflicting images of young women—suggesting the conflicting emotions invested in mother—cannot but remind one of the fictional mother in *The Sound and the Fury*, whose verbal behavior is endearing while her nonverbal behavior creates distance. It seems that Faulkner found himself as novelist by working through the emptiness and ambivalence that governed his early life. As Martin puts it: What Faulkner 'experienced and suffered long before he became an artist created the personality—the original, passionate, time-obsessed, ultimately hopeful life—that the adult re-transformed into fiction' (1988:199).

As he embarked on his great modernist novels, Singal has argued, 'writer and subject had begun to fuse... leaving him to wonder "if I had invented the (teeming) world to which I should give life or if it had invented me, giving me an illusion of greatness".'[193] He was, as Singal puts it, 'engaged in a fresh exploration of southern culture, but instead of cataloging the objective manifestations of that culture, his method was to probe deep inside his own mind... Once having reached his innermost psychological stratum, Faulkner's great achievement was to pour his subconscious freely onto paper, bringing to daylight all those problematic impulses and instincts... endemic to human nature as they took shape in the southern psyche' (1982:153f.).

---

193 Autobiographical fragment, n.d. [1930 or 1931], *William Faulkner Papers*, Yale University.

In his fictional persons, his fictional families, his fictional society of Jefferson, and his fictional history of the South, as well as in his fictional outsider, Faulkner projected different aspects of his family, his society, his history and himself, creating a testing ground for different ways of being in the world. He could create the fictional father who, as a result of his own feelings of defeat, fails his son. But he could also create the young Chick Mallison, who, like Lewis Nordan—and like Sigmund Freud—wished he had been his uncle's son.

Bibliography

Adamowski, T.H. (1971). 'Joe Christmas: The Tyranny of Childhood.' *Novel* 4:3, 240-251.

Adams, Richard P. (1968). *Faulkner: Myth and Motion*. Princeton: Princeton University Press.

Allen, Judson Boyce. (1954). *Rightness Beyond Morality: The Intelligible Form of* The Sound and the Fury. Doctoral Dissertation Vanderbilt University. Nashville, Tennessee.

Allport, Gordon Willard. (1979). *The Nature of Prejudice*. Reading, Mass.: Addison-Wesley.

Allport, Gordon Willard. (1968). 'The Historical Background of Modern Psychology.' In *The Handbook of Social Psychology* vol. I. G. Lindzey and E. Aronson, eds. Reading, Mass: Addison-Wesley.

Allport Gordon Willard and L.J. Postman. (1958). 'The Basic Psychology of Rumor.' In *Readings in Social Psychology*. E. Maccoby, T.M. Newcomb and E.L. Hartley, eds. New York: Holt, Rinehart and Winston, 54-65.

Alvarez, A. (1973). *The Savage God: A Study of Suicide*. New York: Bantam.

Apter, T.E. (1979). *Virginia Woolf: A Study of her Novels*. New York: New York University Press.

Arieti, Silvano. (1981). *Understanding and Helping the Schizophrenic*. Harmondsworth: Penguin.

Arnheim, Rudolf. (1954). *Art and Visual Perception: a Psychology of the Creative Eye*. Berkeley: The University of California Press.

Auster, Paul. (1988). 'City of Glass.' In *The New York Trilogy*. London: Faber and Faber.

Bailey, Ronald W. (1986). 'Access and Equity in Mississippi Higher Education.' In *Mississippi Mindscape: Historical and Literary Links Between People, Places and Traditions*. Jackson: Mississippi Committee for the Humanities.

Baillargeon, Renée; Elizabeth S. Spelke and Stanley Wasserman. (1985). 'Object Permanence in Five-month-old Infants.' *Cognition* 20, 191-208.

Bakhtin, Mikhail M. (1986). *Speech Genres & Other Late Essays*. V.W. McGee, trans., C. Emerson and M. Holquist, eds. Austin: The University of Texas Press.

Baneke, Joost J. (1993). 'Psychological Structures in Biblical Narrative and Psychoanalysis.' *Proceedings of the Ninth International Conference on Literature and Psychoanalysis 1992*. F. Pereira, ed. Lisbon: Instituto Superior de Psicologia Aplicada.

Baneke, Joost J. (1991). 'Persoonlijkheid of Fictie?' In *Persoonlijkheid en Personage: Over de Grenzen van Psychoanalyse en Literatuur*. J.J. Baneke and H. de Jong, eds. Amsterdam: Rodopi.

Bannister, D. and F. Fransella. (1986). *Inquiring Man: The Psychology of Personal Constructs*. London: Croom Helm.

Barker, John. (1982). *The Superhistorians: Makers of Our Past*. New York: Charles Scribner's Sons.

Baron-Cohen, Simon; Alan M. Leslie and Uta Frith. (1985). 'Does the Autistic Child have a "Theory of Mind"?' *Cognition* 21, 37-46.

Barrett, William G. (1951). 'Killers of the Dream.' *Psychoanalytic Quarterly* XX, 129-130.

Bateson, Gregory. (1972). *Steps to an Ecology of Mind*. New York: Ballantine Books.

Bellak, L. (1986). *The TAT, CAT and SAT in Clinical Use*. New York: Harcourt Brace Jovanovich.

Berkowitz, Leonard. (1980). *A Survey of Social Psychology*. New York: Holt, Rinehart and Winston.

Berkowitz, Leonard and D.A. Knurek. (1969). 'Label-Mediated Hostility Generalization.' *Journal of Personality and Social Psychology* 13, 200-206.

Berman, Jeffrey. (1987). *The Talking Cure: Literary Representations of Psychoanalysis*. New York: New York University Press.

Bernheim, Kayla F. and Richard R.J. Lewine. (1979). *Schizophrenia: Symptoms, Causes, Treatments*. New York: Norton.

Bernstein, Leonard. (1976). *The Unanswered Question: Six Talks at Harvard*. Cambridge, Mass.: Harvard University Press.

Blanchard, Margaret. (1969). 'The Rhetoric of Communication: Voice in *The Sound and the Fury*.' *American Literature* XLI:2, 555-565.

Bleikasten, André. (1987). '*Light in August*: The Closed Society and Its Subjects.' In *New Essays on* Light in August. M. Millgate, ed. Cambridge: Cambridge University Press.

Bleikasten, André. (1976). *The Most Splendid Failure: Faulkner's* The Sound and the Fury. Bloomington: Indiana University Press.

Bleikasten, André. (1973). *Faulkner's* As I Lay Dying. R. Little, trans. Bloomington: Indiana University Press.

Blos, Peter. (1941). *The Adolescent Personality: A Study of Individual Behavior*. New York: Appleton-Century-Crofts.

Blotner, Joseph. (1984). *Faulkner: A Biography*. New York: Random House.

Bockting, Ineke. (1995). 'Mammies, Milkbrothers and Milksisters in the Interface between Southern History and Literature.' In *Proceedings of the Eleventh International Conference on Literature and Psychoanalysis, 1994*. F. Pereira, ed. Lisbon: Instituto Superior de Psicologia Aplicada.

Bockting, Ineke. (1994). '*Light in August* and the Issue of Unreliability.' In *Literature and the New Interdisciplinarity: Poetics, Linguistics, History*. Roger Sell and Peter Verdonk, eds. Amsterdam: Rodopi.

Bockting, Ineke. (1994). 'The Figure of Parental Fusion in the Novels of William Faulkner.' In *Fathers and Mothers in Literature*. Henk Hillenaar and Walter Schönau, eds. Amsterdam: Rodopi.

Bockting, Ineke. (1994). 'Mind Style as an Interdisciplinary Approach to Characterization in Faulkner.' *Language and Literature* 3:3.

Bockting, Ineke. (1993). '(On)schuld in William Faulkner's *Absalom, Absalom!*' In *The Pursuit of Happiness en de Paradox van de Vrijheid*. Hans Bak, ed. Nijmegen: Universiteitsdrukkerij.

Bockting, Ineke. (1993). '"If He Were to Wake and Cry, I Would suckle Him, too": The Powerful Mother in Faulkner.' In *Proceedings of the Ninth International Conference on Literature and Psychoanalysis 1992*. F. Pereira, ed. Lisbon: Instituto Superior de Psicologia Aplicada.

Bockting, Ineke. (1990). 'The Impossible World of the "schizophrenic": William Faulkner's Quentin Compson' *Style* 24:3; reprinted in *Literary Character*. John V. Knapp, ed. Lanham, Maryland: University Press of America.

Bockting, Ineke. (in press). 'A Pragmatics of Personality: Characterization in the Novels of William Faulkner.' *Language and Style*.

Brehm, Jack W. and Arthur R. Cohen. (1962). *Explorations in Cognitive Dissonance*. New York: John Wiley & Sons.

Brenner, Hans D. and Wolfgang Böker, eds. (1989). *Schizophrenia as a Systems Disorder: The Relevance of Mediating Processes for Theory and Therapy*. Special Issue of *The British Journal of Psychiatry* 155:5.

Breuer, Rolf. (1980). 'Irony, Literature, and Schizophrenia.' *New Literary History* XII:1, 107-118.

Brodsky, L.D. and Robert W. Hamblin. (1983). *Faulkner: A Comprehensive Guide to the Brodsky Collection*. Jackson: The University Press of Mississippi.

Brooks, Cleanth. (1979). *William Faulkner: Towards Yoknapatawpha and Beyond*. New Haven: Yale University Press.

Brooks, Cleanth. (1964). *William Faulkner: The Yoknapatawpha Country*. New Haven: Yale University Press.

Brooks, Peter. (1987). 'The Idea of a Psychoanalytic Literary Criticism.' In *Discourse in Psychoanalysis and Literature*. S. Rimmon-Kenan, ed. London: Methuen.

Brown, William R. (1967). 'Faulkner's Paradox in Pathology and Salvation: *Sanctuary, Light in August, Requim for a Nun*.' *Texas Studies in Literature and Language*. IX:5, 429-449.

Bruner, Jerome. (1986). *Actual Minds, Possible Worlds*. Cambridge, Mass.: Harvard University Press.

Calvin, William H. (1986). *The River That Flows Uphill: A Journey from the Big Bang to the Big Brain*. San Francisco: Sierra Club.

Cantor, Nancy; Walter Mischel and Judith C. Schwartz. (1982). 'A Prototype Analysis of Psychological Situations.' *Cognitive Psychology* 14, 45-77.

Cash, Wilbur Joseph. (1969). *The Mind of the South*. New York: Vintage.

Cason, Clarence. (1935). *90° in the Shade*. Chapel Hill: The University of North Carolina Press.

Chafe, Wallace L. (1976). 'Givenness, Contrastiveness, Definiteness, Subjects and Topics.' *Subject & Topic.*

Chase, Richard. (1971). 'Faulkner's *Light in August.*' In *Twentieth-Century Interpretations of* Light in August: *A Collection of Critical Essays*. D. Minter, ed. Englewood Cliff, N.J.: Prentice-Hall.

Ciompi, Luc. (1989). 'The Dynamics of Complex Biological-Psychosocial Systems: Four Fundamental Psycho-Biological Mediators in the Long-term Evolution of Schizophrenia.' *The British Journal of Psychiatry* 155:5, 15-21.

Clayton, Bruce. (1992). 'No Ordinary History: W.J. Cash's *The Mind of the South.*' In *The Mind of the South Fifty Years Later*. Charles W. Eagles, ed. Jackson: University Press of Mississippi.

Clayton, Bruce. (1988). 'W.J. Cash and the Creative Impulse.' *Southern Review* XXIV.

Clayton, Bruce. (1981). *W.J. Cash: A Life*. Baton Rouge: Louisiana State University Press.

Cohn, Dorrit. (1983). *Transparent Minds: Narrative Modes for Presenting Consciousness in Fiction*. Princeton: Princeton University Press.

Coleman, Rosemary. (1988). 'Family Ties: Generating Narratives in *Absalom, Absalom!*' *Mississippi Quarterly* XLI:3, 421-431.

Collins, Carvel. (1982). 'The Other Competitors for the Cross: Joanna Burden and Gail Hightower.' In *William Faulkner's* Light in August: *A Critical Casebook*. F. Pitavy, ed. New York: Garland Publishing Inc.

Collins, Carvel. (1954). 'The Interior Monologues of *The Sound and the Fury.*' *English Institute Essays 1952*. New York: Columbia University Press.

Cools, A.R. (1975). 'An Integrated Theory of the Aetiology of Schizophrenia.' In *On the Origin of Schizophrenic Psychoses*. H.M. van Praag, ed. Amsterdam: De Erven Bohn.

Cullen, John B. and Floyd C. Watkins. (1954). *Old Times in the Faulkner Country*. Chapel Hill: The University of North Carolina Press.

Cunningham, Rodger. (1987). *Apples on the Flood: The Southern Mountain Experience*. Knoxville: The University of Tennessee Press.

Davidson, Gerald C. and John M. Neale. (1986). *Abnormal Psychology: An Experimental Clinical Approach*. New York: John Wiley & Sons.

Davis, David Brion. (1975). *The Problem of Slavery in the Age of Revolution 1770-1823*. Ithaca: Cornell University Press.

Davis, Thadious M. (1983). *Faulkner's 'Negro': Art and the Southern Context*. Baton Rouge: Louisiana State University Press.

De Levita, David Joël. (1965). *The Concept of Identity*. Doctoral Dissertation University of Utrecht. Utrecht, The Netherlands.

Dexter, Pete. (1989). *Paris Trout*. New York: Penguin.

Dilman, Ilham. (1984). 'Dostoyevsky: Psychology and the Novelist.' *Philosophy and Literature*. A. Phillips Griffiths, ed. Cambridge: Cambridge University Press.

Dodd, William E. (1921). *The Cotton Kingdom: A Chronicle of the Old South*. New Haven: Yale University Press.

Doležel, Lubomír. (1988). 'Mimesis and Possible Worlds.' *Poetics Today* 9:3, 475-496.

Drabble, Margaret. (1988). *The Radiant Way*. Harmondsworth: Penguin.

Duncan, Birt L. (1976). 'Differential Social Perception and Attribution of Intergroup Violence: Testing the Lower Limits of Stereotyping of Blacks.' *Journal of Personality and Social Psychology* 34:4, 590-598.

Duytschaever, Joris. (1990). 'Een Psychanalytische Benadering van Verhalend Proza: Het Motief van het Kind.' In *Literatuur in Psychoanalytisch Perspectief*. H. Hillenaar and W. Schönau, eds. Amsterdam: Rodopi.

Duvall, John N. (1987). 'Murder and the Communities: Ideology In and Around *Light in August*.' *Novel* 20:2, 101-122.

Ellsworth, Phoebe C. (1980). 'Regarding the Author as Patient.' *New Literary History* XII:1, 187-197.

Erikson, Erik H. (1959). 'Identity and the Life Cycle: Selected Papers.' *Psychological Issue* 1, 1-71.

Fadiman, Regina K. (1975). *Faulkner's* Light in August: *A Description and Interpretation of the Revisions*. Charlottesville: The University Press of Virginia.

Fant, Joseph L. and Robert Ashley, eds. (1964). *Faulkner at West Point*. New York: Random House.

Faulkner, John. (1963). *My Brother Bill: An Affectionate Reminiscence*. New York: Trident Press.

Faulkner, William. (1979). *Uncollected Stories of William Faulkner*. Joseph Blotner, ed. New York: Random House.

Faulkner, William. (1951 [1927]). *Mosquitoes*. New York: Boni & Liveright.

Faulkner, William. (1987 [1929]). *The Sound and the Fury*. New York: Vintage.

Faulkner, William. (1987 [1930]). *As I Lay Dying*. New York: Vintage.

Faulkner, William. (1987 [1932]). *Light in August*. New York: Vintage.

Faulkner, William. (1987 [1936]). *Absalom, Absalom!* New York: Vintage.

Faulkner, William. (1987 [1942]). *Go Down, Moses*. New York: Vintage.

Faulkner, William. (1972 [1948]). *Intruder in the Dust*. New York: Vintage.

Faulkner, William. (1975 [1950]). *Requiem for a Nun*. New York: Vintage.

Faulkner, William. (1965 [1959]). *The Mansion*. New York: Vintage.

Fehr, B. (1938). 'Substitutionary Narration and Description: A Chapter in Stylistics.' *English Studies* 20, 97-107.

Festinger, Leon A. (1957). *A Theory of Cognitive Dissonance*. Stanford: Stanford University Press.

Festinger, Leon A.; S. Schachter and K. Back. (1950). *Social Pressures in Informal Groups: A Study of Human Factors in Housing*. New York: Harper.

Fillmore, Charles J. (1981). 'Pragmatics and the Description of Discourse.' In *Radical Pragmatics*. P. Cole, ed. New York: Academic Press.

Fillmore, Charles J. (1971). *Santa Cruz Lectures on Deixis*. Berkeley: The University of California Press.

Fine, Reuben. (1987). *The Development of Freud's Thought*. Northvale, N.J.: Jason Aronson.

Fitzhugh, George. (1875). *Cannibals All!* Richmond: A. Morris.

Fivaz Depeursinge, Elizabeth. (1991). 'Documenting a Time-Bound, Circular View of Hierarchies: A Microanalysis of Parent-Infant Dyadic Interaction.' *Family Process*, 30:1.

Ford Jr., Lacy K. (1992). 'Commentary on James L. Roark's "Cash and Continuity in Southern History".' In *The Mind of the South Fifty Years Later*. Charles W. Eagles, ed. Jackson: University Press of Mississippi.

Forster, Edward Morgan. (1988). *Aspects of the Novel*. Harmondsworth: Penguin.

Foster, Gaines M. (1990). 'Guilt Over Slavery: A Historiographical Analysis.' *The Journal of Southern History* LVI:4, 665-694.

Foster, Gaines M. (1987). *Ghosts of the Confederacy: Defeat, the Lost Cause, and the Emergence of the New South*. New York: Oxford University Press.

Foucault, Michel. (1972). *The Archaeology of Knowledge & The Discourse on Language*. A.M. Sheridan Smith, trans. New York: Pantheon.

Fowler, Doreen. (1986). 'Joe Christmas and "Womanshenegroe".' In *Faulkner and Women; Faulkner and Yoknapatawpha, 1985*. D. Fowler and A.J. Abadie, eds. Jackson: The University Press of Mississippi.

Fowler, Roger. (1986). *Linguistic Criticism*. Oxford: Oxford University Press.

Fowler, Roger. (1977). *Linguistics and the Novel*. London: Methuen.

Frame, Janet. (1991). *Faces in the Water*. London: The Women's Press.

Frank, Lawrence K. (1938). 'Culture and Personality, A Round Table Discussion.' *The American Journal of Orthopsychiatry* VIII.

Freedman, William A. (1961-1962). 'The Technique of Isolation in *The Sound and The Fury*.' *Mississippi Quarterly* XV:1, 21-26.

Freud, Anna, ed. (1986). *The Essentials of Psycho-Analysis: Sigmund Freud*. J. Strachey, trans. London: The Hogarth Press.

Freud, Anna. (1937). *The Ego and the Mechanisms of Defence*. London: The Hogarth Press.

Freud, Sigmund. (1978). *The Standard Edition of the Complete Psychological Works of Sigmund Freud*. London: The Hogarth Press.
  (1900). 'The Interpretation of Dreams.' *Standard Edition* 4-5.
  (1905). 'Three Essays on the Theory of Sexuality.' *Standard Edition* 7.
  (1907). 'Delusions and Dreams in Jensen's "Gradiva".' *Standard Edition* 9.
  (1908). 'Creative Writers and Daydreaming.' *Standard Edition* 9.
  (1914). 'Remembering, Repeating and Working-Through.' *Standard Edition* 12.
  (1915). 'Repression.' *Standard Edition* 14.
  (1915). 'The Unconscious.' *Standard Edition* 14.
  (1917). 'Mourning and Melancholia.' *Standard Edition* 14.
  (1920). 'Beyond the Pleasure Principle.' *Standard Edition* 18.

(1923). 'The Ego and The Id.' *Standard Edition* 19.

(1932). 'New Introductory Lectures on Psycho-analysis.' *Standard Edition* 22.

Frye, Douglas and Chris Moore. (1991). *Children's Theories of Mind: Mental States and Social Understanding.* Hillsdale, N.J.: Lawrence Erlbaum.

Geismar, Maxwell. (1971). 'Sex and Women in *Light in August.*' In *Twentieth-Century Interpretations of* Light in August*: a Collection of Critical Essays.* D. Minter, ed. Englewood Cliffs, N.J.: Prentice-Hall.

Genette, Gérard. (1986). *Narrative Discourse.* J.E. Lewin, trans. Oxford: Basil Blackwell.

Gibbons, Kathryn Gibbs. (1962). 'Quentin's Shadow.' *Literature and Psychology* XII:1, 16-24.

Gidley, Mick. (1971). 'Another Psychologist, a Physiologist and William Faulkner.' *Ariel* 2:4, 78-86.

Giffin, Kim. (1967). 'The Contribution of Studies of Source Credibility to a Theory of Interpersonal Trust in the Communication Process.' *Psychological Bulletin* 68:2, 104-120.

Godden, Richard. (1980). 'Call Me Nigger!: Race and Speech in Faulkner's *Light in August.*' *Journal of American Studies* 14:2.

Goldsmith, John and Erich Woisetschlaeger. (1982). 'The Logic of the English Progressive.' *Linguistic Inquiry*, 13:1, 79-89.

Gordon, Lyndall. (1988). *Eliot's New Life.* Oxford: Oxford University Press.

Gray, Richard. (1989). *Writing the South: Ideas of an American Region.* Cambridge: Cambridge University Press.

Gwynn, Frederick L. and Joseph L. Blotner, eds. (1959). *Faulkner in the University: Class Conferences at the University of Virginia 1957-1958.* Charlottesville: The University of Virginia Press.

Haley, Jay. (1972). *Strategies of Psychotherapy.* New York: Grune & Stratton.

Halliday, M.A.K. (1971). 'Linguistic Function and Literary Style: An Inquiry into the Language of William Golding's *The Inheritors.*' In *Literary Style: A Symposium.* S. Chatman, ed. Oxford: Oxford University Press.

Hampson, Sarah E. (1982). *The Construction of Personality.* London: Routledge.

Hartman, D.A. (1922). 'The Psychological Point of View in History: Some Phases of the Slavery Struggle.' *Journal of Abnormal and Social Psychology* XVII, 261-273.

Harvey, William J. (1965). *Character and the Novel.* London: Chatto & Windus.

Henke, Suzette A. (1981). 'Virginia Woolf's Septimus Smith: An Analysis of "Paraphrenia" and the Schizophrenic Use of Language.' *Literature and Psychology* XXXI:4, 13-23.

Herrmann, L. (1975). 'On "in that".' *Proceedings of the Berkeley Linguistic Society* 1, 189-195.

Hillenaar, Henk. (1990). 'De Literaire Stijl en het Onbewuste.' In *Literatuur in Psychoanalytisch Perspectief.* H. Hillenaar and W. Schönau, eds. Amsterdam: Rodopi.

Hobson, Fred. (1983). *Tell About the South: The Southern Rage to Explain*. Baton Rouge: Louisiana State University Press.

Hoetink, H. (1973). *Slavery and Race Relations in the Americas: Comparative Notes on their Nature and Nexus*. New York: Harper & Row.

Hoffman, Lois Wladis. (1991). 'The Influence of the Family Environment on Personality: Accounting for Sibling Differences.' *Psychological Bulletin* 110:2, 187-203.

Hofstadter, Douglas R. (1980). *Gödel, Escher, Bach: An Eternal Golden Braid*. New York: Vintage.

Holland, Norman. N. (1975). 'Unity Identity Text Self' *PMLA* XC:5, 813-822.

Holman, Hugh. (1958). 'The Unity of Faulkner's *Light in August*.' *PMLA* LXXIII:1, 155-167.

Horney, Karen. (1956). 'The Search for Glory.' In *The Self: Explorations in Personal Growth*. C. E. Moustakas, ed. New York: Harper & Row.

Horney, Karen. (1950). *Neurosis and Human Growth*. New York: Norton.

Howe, Irving. (1962). *William Faulkner: A Critical Study*. New York: Vintage.

Howes D.H. and C.E. Osgood. (1954). 'On the Combination of Associative Probabilities in Linguistic Contexts.' *American Journal of Psychology* 67, 241-258.

Hull, Richard. (1992). 'Critique of Characterization: It Was in Not Knowing That He Loved Her.' *Style* 26:1, 33-49.

Hungerford, Harold. (1983). 'Past and Present in *Light in August*.' *American Literature* LV:2, 183-197.

Hurst, Mary Jane. (1987). 'Characterization and Language: A Case-Grammar Study of *As I Lay Dying*.' *Language and Style* 20:1, 71-87.

Hutcheon, Linda. (1990). *A Poetics of Postmodernism: History, Theory, Fiction*. London: Routledge.

Irwin, John T. (1980). *Doubling & Incest, Repetition & Revenge: A Speculative Reading of Faulkner*. Baltimore: The Johns Hopkins University Press.

Isbister, J.N. (1985). *Freud: An Introduction to his Life & Work*. Cambridge: Polity Press.

Jacoby, Russell. (1975). *Social Amnesia: A Critique of Contemporary Psychology from Adler to Laing*. Boston: Beacon Press.

James, Henry. (1983 [1903]). 'The Beast in the Jungle.' In *The Portable Henry James*. Morton Dauwen Zabel, ed., 327-383.

Jehlen, Myra. (1976). *Class and Character in Faulkner's South*. New York: Columbia University Press.

Jenkins, Lee. (1981). *Faulkner and Black-White Relations: A Psychoanalytic Approach*. New York: Columbia University Press.

Jobe, E.R. (1930). *Social History of Ante-Bellum Mississippi*. Doctoral Dissertation University of Mississippi, Oxford, Mississippi.

Jones, E.E. and V. A. Harris. (1967). 'The Attribution of Attitudes.' *Journal of Experimental Social Psychology* 3, 1-24

Joyce, James. (1985). 'A Painful Case.' In *Dubliners*. London: Granada.

Kaluza, Irena. (1967). *The Functioning of Sentence Structure in the Stream of Consciousness Technique of William Faulkner's* The Sound and the Fury: *a Study in Linguistic Stylistics*. Krakow: Nakladem Uniwersytetu Jagiellonskiego.

Kaplan, Bert, ed. (1964). *The Inner World of Mental Illness: A Series of First-Person Accounts of What It Was Like*. New York: Harper & Row.

Kaplan, Harold I. and Benjamin J. Sadock. (1988). *Synopsis of Psychiatry: Behavioral Sciences, Clinical Psychiatry*. Baltimore: Williams & Wilkins.

Karl, Frederick R. (1989). *William Faulkner: American Writer*. New York: Weidenfeld & Nicolson.

Kartiganer, Donald M. (1992). 'A Marriage of Speaking and Hearing.' *The Oxford American* 1:1, 63-70.

Kartiganer, Donald M. (1982). *'Light in August.'* In *William Faulkner's* Light in August: *A Critical Casebook*. F. Pitavy, ed. New York: Garland Publishing Inc.

Kartiganer, Donald M. (1979). *The Fragile Thread: The Meaning of Form in Faulkner's Novels*. Amherst: The University of Massachusetts Press.

Kassin, Saul M. and Reuben M. Baron (1985). 'Basic Determinants of Attribution and Social Perception.' In *Attribution: Basic Issues and Applications*. J.H. Harvey and G. Weary, eds. New York: Academic Press.

Kawin, Bruce F. (1977). *Faulkner and Film*. New York: Frederick Ungar.

Kawin, Bruce F. (1972). *Telling it Again and Again: Repetition in Literature and Film*. Ithaca: Cornell University Press.

Keen, Ernest. (1986). 'Paranoia and Cataclysmic Narrative.' In *Narrative Psychology: The Storied Nature of Human Conduct*. T.R. Sarbin, ed. New York: Praeger.

Kelley, Harold. (1980). 'Perceived Causal Structures.' In *Annual Review of Psychology* 31. M.R. Rosenzweig and L.M. Porter, eds. Palo Alto: Annual Review Inc.

Kelley, Harold and J.L. Michela (1980). 'Attribution Theory and Research.' In *Annual Review of Psychology* 31. M.R. Rosenzweig and L.M. Porter, eds. Palo Alto: Annual Review Inc.

Kernan, Keith T. (1990). 'Indications of Epistemology in the Discourse of Mentally Retarded Adults.' *Text* 10:3, 209-223.

Kinney, Arthur F. (1978). *Faulkner's Narrative Poetics: Style as Vision*. Amherst: The University of Massachusetts Press.

Klein, Melanie. (1975). *Envy and Gratitude and Other Works 1946-1963*. London: The Hogarth Press.

Knapp, John V. (1990). 'Self-Preservation and Self-Transformation: Interdiciplinary Approaches to Literary Character.' *Style* 24:3, 349-364.

Kristeva, Julia. (1986). 'Stabat Mater.' In *The Female Body in Western Culture: Contemporary Perspectives*, S.R. Suleiman, ed. Cambridge: Harvard University Press.

Kubie, Lawrence S. (1961). *Neurotic Distortion of the Creative Process*. New York: Noonday.

Kuyk, Dirk Jr. (1990). *Sutpen's Design: Interpreting Faulkner's* Absalom, Absalom! Charlottesville: The University Press of Virginia.

Labov, William. (1972). *Language in the Inner City: Studies in the Black English Vernacular*. Philadelphia: The University of Pennsylvania Press.

Lafeber, Chr. (1982). *Psychotische Kinderen*. Rotterdam: Lemniscaat.

Laffal, Julius. (1979). *A Source Document in Schizophrenia*. Hope Valley, Rhode Island: Gallery Press.

Laing, R.D. (1965). *The Divided Self: An Existential Study in Sanity and Madness*. Baltimore: Pelican.

Langer, Jonas. (1981). 'Logic in Infancy.' *Cognition* 10, 181-186.

Lanser, Susan Sniader. (1981). *The Narrative Act: Point of View in Prose Fiction*. Princeton: Princeton University Press.

Lasch, Christopher. (1978). *The Culture of Narcissism. American Life in an Age of Diminishing Expectations*. New York: Norton.

Leech, Geoffrey N. (1983). *Principles of Pragmatics*. London: Longman.

Leech, Geoffrey N. and Michael H. Short. (1985). *Style in Fiction*. London: Longman.

Leek, Frederike C. van der. (1992). 'Significant Syntax: The Case of Exceptional Passives.' *DWPELL* 27, 1-28.

Leek, Frederike C. van der. (1989). *Casting A Cold Eye On Generative Practice*. Doctoral Dissertation University of Amsterdam. Amsterdam, The Netherlands.

Leslie, Alan M. and Stephanie Keeble. (1987). 'Do six-month-old infants perceive causality?' *Cognition* 25, 265-288.

Lesser, Simon O. (1957). *Fiction and the Unconscious*. Boston: Beacon Press.

Levinson, Stephen C. (1983). *Pragmatics*. Cambridge: Cambridge University Press.

Lewis, Mary Agnes. (1967). 'Slavery and Personality: A Further Comment.' *American Quarterly* XIX:1, 114-121.

Lidz, T., S. Fleck, and A.R. Cornelison. (1965). *Schizophrenia and the Family*. New York: International Universities Press.

Lippman, Bert. (1971). 'Literature and Life.' *The Georgia Review* XXV: 2, 145-158.

London, Harvey. (1973). *Psychology of the Persuader*. Morristown, N.J.: General Learning Press.

Longley, John Lewis. (1963). *The Tragic Mask: A Study of Faulkner's Heroes*. Chapel Hill: The University of North Carolina Press.

Lyons, John. (1977) *Semantics*, vol 2. Cambridge: Cambridge University Press.

Martin, Jay. (1988). *Who Am I This Time?: Uncovering the Fictive Personality*. New York: Norton.

Martínez-Bonati, Félix. (1981). *Fictive Discourse and the Structures of Literature*. P.W. Silver, trans. Ithaca: Cornell University Press.

McCullers, Carson. (1987). *The Member of the Wedding*. Harmondsworth: Penguin.

McLaughlin, Sara. (1987). 'Faulkner's Faux Pas: Referring to Benjamin Compson as an Idiot.' *Literature and Psychology* 33:2, 34-40.

McPherson, James. (1988). *Battle Cry of Freedom: The Civil War Era*. New York: Oxford University Press.

Meats, Stephen E. (1982). 'The Chronology of *Light in August*.' In *William Faulkner's* Light in August: *A Critical Casebook*. F. Pitavy, ed. New York: Garland.

Meats, Stephen E. (1971). 'Who Killed Joanna Burden?' *Mississippi Quarterly* XXIV:3, 271-277.

Mellard, James M. (1970). 'Caliban as Prospero: Benjy and *The Sound and the Fury*.' *Novel* 3:3, 233-248.

Meriwether, James B., ed. (1967). *Essays, Speeches & Public Letters by William Faulkner*. London: Chatto & Windus.

Meriwether, James B. and Michael Millgate, eds. (1980). *Lion in the Garden: Interviews with William Faulkner, 1926-1962*. Lincoln: The University of Nebraska Press.

Millgate, Michael, ed. and intro. (1987). '"A Novel: Not an Anecdote": Faulkner's *Light in August*.' In *New Essays on* Light in August. Cambridge: Cambridge University Press.

Millgate, Michael. (1966). *The Achievement of William Faulkner*. New York: Random House.

Minsky, Marvin. (1988). *The Society of Mind*. New York: Simon & Schuster.

Minter, David L. (1981). *William Faulkner: His Life and Work*. Baltimore: The Johns Hopkins University Press.

Minter, David L. (1979). 'Faulkner, Childhood, and the Making of *The Sound and the Fury*.' *American Literature*, LI:3, 376-393.

Mississippi Committee for the Humanities. (1986). *Mississippi Mindscape: Historical and Literary Links Between People, Places and Traditions*. Jackson Mississippi.

Moak, Franklin E. (1986). *A History of the Alumni Association of the University of Mississippi 1852-1986*. Oxford: University of Mississippi.

Moore, Gene M. (1989). 'Focalization and Narrative Voice in *What Maisie Knew*.' *Language and Style* 22:1, 3-24.

Moore, Gene M. (1986). 'Chronotopes and Voices in *Under Western Eyes*' *Conradiana* XVIII: 1, 9-25.

Morea, Peter. (1990). *Personality: An Introduction to the Theories of Psychology*. Harmondsworth: Penguin.

Morrison, Sister Kirstin. (1982). 'Faulkner's Joe Christmas: Character through Voice.' In *William Faulkner's* Light in August: *A Critical Casebook*. F. Pitavy, ed. New York: Garland.

Murray, H.A. (1943). *Thematic Apperception Test Manual*. Cambridge: Harvard University Press.

Naipaul, V.S. (1989). *A Turn in the South*. New York: Alfred A. Knopf.

Nelson, Charles and David Goforth. (1977). *Our Neighbor, William Faulkner.* Chicago: Adams Press.

Nordan, Lewis. (1992). 'Dangerous Inventions.' *The Oxford American* 1: 1, 4-7.

Oakes, James. (1990). *Slavery and Freedom: An Interpretation of the Old South.* New York: Alfred A. Knopf.

Oates, Joyce Carol. (1983). '"At Least I Have Made a Woman of Her': Images of Women in Twentieth-Century Literature.' *The Georgia Review* XXXVII:1.

O'Brien, Michael. (1988). *Rethinking the South: Essays in Intellectual History.* Baltimore: The Johns Hopkins University Press.

Palliser, Charles. (1978). 'Fate and Madness: The Determinist Vision of Darl Bundren.' *American Literature* XLIX:4, 619-633.

Paris, Bernard J. (1991). 'A Horneyan Approach to Literature.' *The American Journal of Psychoanalysis* 51:3, 319-337.

Paris, Bernard J. (1974). *A Psychological Approach to Fiction: Studies in Thackeray, Stendhal, George Eliot, Dostoevsky, and Conrad.* Bloomington: Indiana University Press.

Peavy, Charles D. (1971). *Go Slow Now: Faulkner and the Race Question.* Eugene, Oregon: The University of Oregon.

Percy, Walker. (1966). *The Last Gentleman.* New York: Ivy Books.

Percy, Walker. (1956). 'Stoicism in the South.' *Commonweal*, July 6, 342-344.

Percy, William Alexander. (1990 [1941]). *Lanterns on the Levee: Recollections of a Planter's Son.* Baton Rouge: Louisiana State University Press.

Perry, Menakhem. (1979). 'Literary Dynamics: How the Order of a Text Creates its Meanings.' *Poetics Today* 1:1-2, 35-64 and 311-361.

Pervin, Lawrence A. (1984). *Personality.* New York: John Wiley & Sons.

Pettey, Homer. B. (1987). 'Reading and Raping in *Sanctuary.*' *The Faulkner Journal* III:1, 71-84.

Phelan, James. (1989). *Reading People, Reading Plots.* Chicago: The University of Chicago Press.

Pierce, Neil R. and Jerry Hagstrom. (1984). *The Book of America: Inside Fifty States Today.* New York: Warner.

Pirsig, Robert M. (1982). *Zen and the Art of Motorcycle Maintenance: An Inquiry into Values.* New York: Bantam.

Pitavy, François L. (1982). 'A Stylistic Approach to *Light in August.*' In *William Faulkner's* Light in August: *A Critical Casebook.* F. Pitavy, ed. New York: Garland.

Pitavy, François L. (1982). 'Voice and Voices in *Light in August.*' In *William Faulkner's* Light in August: *A Critical Casebook.* F. Pitavy, ed. New York: Garland.

Pitavy, François L. (1970). 'The Landscape in *Light in August.*' *Mississippi Quarterly* XXIII:3, 265-272.

Pladott, Dinnah. (1985). 'William Faulkner: The Tragic Enigma.' *The Journal of Narrative Technique* 15:2, 97-119.

Plath, Sylvia. (1981). *The Bell Jar.* New York: Bantam.

Pole J.R. (1979). 'Slavery, Race, and the Debate on Personality.' In *Paths to the American Past.* Oxford: Oxford University Press.

Poyatos, Fernando. (1983). *New Perspectives in Nonverbal Communication: Studies in Cultural Anthropology, Social Psychology, Linguistics, Literature, and Semiotics.* New York: Pergamon Press.

Praag, H.M. van, ed. (1975). *On the Origin of Schizophrenic Psychoses.* Amsterdam: De Erven Bohm.

Rabinowitz, Peter J. (1981). 'Assertion and Assumption: Fictional Patterns and the External World.' *PMLA* XCVI:3, 408-419.

Rabinowitz, Peter J. (1977). 'Truth in Fiction: A Reexamination of Audiences.' *Critical Inquiry* 4:121-141.

Ragan, David Paul. (1986). '"That Tragedy is Second-Hand": Quentin, Henry, and the Ending of *Absalom, Absalom!*' *Mississippi Quarterly* XXXIX:3, 337-350.

Ree, F. van. (1975). *Schizoforme Syndromen & Psycholinguistiek. Krankzinnigheid en Taalonmacht.* Assen: van Gorkum.

Reed, John Shelton. (1992). '*The Mind of the South* and Southern Distinctiveness.' In *The Mind of the South Fifty Years Later.* Charles W. Eagles, ed. Jackson: University Press of Mississippi.

Research Committee of the Group for the Advancement of Psychiatry. (1984). *Research and the Complex Causality of the Schizophrenias.* New York: Brummer/Mazel.

Rimmon-Kenan, Shlomith. (1987). *Narrative Fiction: Contemporary Poetics.* London: Methuen.

Rimmon-Kenan, Shlomith. (1987). 'Narration as Repetition: the Case of Günter Grass's *Cat and Mouse.*' In *Discourse in Psychoanalysis and Literature.* S. Rimmon-Kenan, ed. London: Methuen.

Rimmon-Kenan, Shlomith. (1978). 'From Reproduction to Production: The Status of Narration in Faulkner's *Absalom, Absalom!*' *Dégres* 6:16, 1-19.

Robbins, Deborah. (1981). 'The Desperate Eloquence of *Absalom, Absalom!*' *Mississippi Quarterly* XXXIV:3, 315-324.

Robert, Marthe. (1980). *Origins of the Novel.* S. Rabinovitch, trans. Brighton: The Harvester Press.

Rose, Gilbert J. (1986). *The Power of Form: A Psychoanalytic Approach to Aesthetic Form.* Madison, Conn: International Universities Press.

Rosenbaum, Bent and Harly Sonne. (1986). *The Language of Psychosis.* New York: New York University Press.

Ross, Stephen M. (1989). *Fiction's Inexhaustible Voice: Speech & Writing in Faulkner.* Athens: The University of Georgia Press.

Ruitenbeck, Hendrik. (1973). *Freud as We Knew Him.* Detroit: Wayne State University Press.

Ruppersburg, Hugh Michael. (1983). *Voice and Eye in Faulkner's Fiction.* Athens: The University of Georgia Press.

Ruppersburg, Hugh Michael. (1978). *Narrative Mode in the Novels of William Faulkner.* Doctoral Dissertation University of South Carolina.

Sacks, Oliver. (1986). *The Man Who Mistook his Wife for a Hat*. London: Pan Books.

Salinger, J.D. (1984). *The Catcher in the Rye*. Harmondsworth: Penguin.

Salinger, J.D. (1981). *Nine Stories*. New York: Bantam.

Salinger, J.D. (1980). *Franny and Zooey*. Harmondsworth: Penguin.

Sansing, David and Michael P. Dean. (1986). 'The Politics of Place.' In *Mississippi Mindscape: Historical and Literary Links Between People, Places and Traditions*. Jackson: Mississippi Committee for the Humanities.

Schafer, Roy. (1980). 'Action and Narration in Psychoanalysis.' *New Literary History* XII:1, 61-85.

Schafer, Roy. (1979). 'The Appreciative Analytic Attitude and the Construction of Multiple Histories.' *Psychoanalysis and Contemporary Thought* 2, 3-24.

Schoenberg, Estella. (1977). *Old Tales and Talking: Quentin Compson in William Faulkner's* Absalom, Absalom! *and Related Works*. Jackson: The University Press of Mississippi.

Scott, Anne Firor. (1974). 'Women's Perspective on the Patriarchy in the 1850s.' *Journal of American History* LXI, 52-64.

Sechehaye, Marguerite. (1951). *Autobiography of a Schizophrenic Girl*. New York: Grune & Stratton.

Shakespeare, William. (1963). *Hamlet*. London: Collins.

Shaw, Valerie. (1986). *The Short Story: A Critical Introduction*. London: Longman.

Sides, Sudie Duncan. (1970). 'Southern Women and Slavery. Part I.' *History Today* XX, 54-60.

Singal, Daniel Joseph. (1982). *The War Within: From Victorian to Modernist Thought in the South 1919-1945*. Chapel Hill: The University of North Carolina Press.

Slatoff, Walter J. (1961). *Quest for Failure: A Study of William Faulkner*. Ithaca: Cornell University Press.

Small, Leonard. (1980). *Neuropsychodiagnosis in Psychotherapy*. New York: Brunner/Mazel.

Smith, Lillian. (1978). *Killers of the Dream*. New York: Norton.

Smith, Lillian. (1972). 'Man born of Woman.' In *From the Mountain: Selections from* Pseudopodia, *the* North Georgia Review, *and* South Today. H. White and R.S. Suggs Jr., eds. Memphis: Memphis State University Press.

Smith Churchland, Patricia. (1986). *Neurophilosophy: Towards a Unified Science of the Mind/Brain*. Cambridge, Mass.: The MIT Press.

Snead, James A. (1987). '*Light in August* and the Rhetorics of Racial Division.' In *Faulkner and Race: Faulkner and Yoknapatawpha, 1986*. D. Fowler and A.J. Abadie, eds. Jackson: The University Press of Mississippi.

Snead, James A. (1986). *Figures of Division: William Faulkner's Major Novels*. New York: Methuen.

Snell, Susan. (1991). *Phil Stone of Oxford: A Vicarious Life*. Athens: The University of Georgia Press.

Spence, Donald P. (1987). 'Narrative Recursion.' In *Discourse and Psychoanalysis in Literature*. S. Rimmon-Kenan, ed. London: Methuen.

Spence, Donald. (1986). 'Narrative Smoothing and Clinical Wisdom.' In *Narrative Psychology: The Storied Nature of Human Conduct*. T.R. Sarbin, ed. New York: Praeger.

Spence, Donald P. (1982). *Narrative Truth and Historical Truth: Meaning and Interpretation in Psychoanalysis*. New York: Norton.

Sperber, Dan and Deirdre Wilson. (1986). *Relevance, Communication and Cognition*. Oxford: Basil Blackwell.

Stampp, Kenneth M. (1983). *The Imperiled Union: Essays on the Background of the Civil War*. Oxford: Oxford University Press.

Sternthal, B.; L.W. Phillips and R. Dholakia. (1978). 'The Persuasive Effect of Source Credibility: A Situational Analysis.' *Public Opinion Quarterly* 42, 285-314.

Taylor, John. R. (1989). *Linguistic Categorization: Prototypes in Linguistic Theory*. Oxford: Clarendon Press.

Toolan, Michael J. (1990). *The Stylistics of Fiction: A Literary-Linguistic Approach*. London: Routledge.

Tustin, Frances. (1986). *Autistic Barriers in Neurotic Patients*. London: Karnac Books.

Tversky, Barbara and Kathleen Hemenway. (1983). 'Categories of Environmental Scenes.' *Cognitive Psychology* 15, 121-149.

Verdonk, Peter, ed. (1993). *Literary Stylistic Criticism of Twentieth-Century Poetry: From text to Context*. London: Routledge.

Verdonk, Peter. (1988). *How Can We Know the Dancer from the Dance?* Doctoral Dissertation University of Amsterdam. Amsterdam, The Netherlands.

Vickery, Olga W. (1971). 'The Shadow and the Mirror: *Light in August*.' In *Twentieth- Century Interpretations of* Light in August*: A Collection of Critical Essays*. D. Minter, ed. Englewood Cliffs, N.J.: Prentice-Hall.

Vickery, Olga W. (1959). *The Novels of William Faulkner: A Critical Interpretation*. Baton Rouge: Louisiana State University Press.

Vickery, Olga W. (1954). '*The Sound and the Fury*: A Study in Perspective.' *PMLA* LXIX:5, 1017-1037.

Volpe, Edmond L. (1964). *A Reader's Guide to William Faulkner*. London: Thames and Hudson.

Waggoner, Hyatt H. (1966). *William Faulkner: From Jefferson to the World*. Lexington: The University of Kentucky Press.

Wagner, Linda Welshimer. (1971). 'Faulkner's Fiction: Studies in Organic Form.' *The Journal of Narrative Technique* 1:1.

Watson, James G., ed. (1992). *Thinking of Home: William Faulkner's Letters to His Mother and Father 1918-1925*. New York: Norton.

Werth, Paul. (1984). *Focus, Coherence and Emphasis*. Beckenham: Croom Helm.

Werth, Paul. (1981). 'Tense, Modality, and Possible Worlds.' *Rapport d'Activités de l'Institut de Phonétique* 16: 17-30.

Wicklund, Robert A. and Jack W. Brehm. (1976). *Perspectives on Cognitive Dissonance*. New York: Wiley.

Widdowson, Henry. (1993). 'Person to Person: Relationships in the Poetry of Tony Harrison.' *Literary Stylistic Criticism of Twentieth-century Poetry: From text to Context*. P. Verdonk, ed. London: Routledge.

Wiley, Bell I. (1956). *The Road to Appomattox*. Memphis: Memphis State University Press.

Woods, John. (1974). *The Logic of Fiction*. The Hague: Mouton.

Woodward, C. Vann. (1989). *The Burden of Southern History*. Baton Rouge: Louisiana State University Press.

Woodward, C. Vann. (1969). 'W.J. Cash Remembered.' *The New York Review of Books*, December 4, 28-34.

Woodward, C. Vann. (1941). 'Review of *The Mind of the South*.' *Journal of Southern History* VIII, 400-402.

Woolf, Virginia. (1984 [1925]). *Mrs Dalloway*. London: Granada.

Worchel, Stephen and Joel Cooper. (1979). *Understanding Social Psychology*. Homewood, Ill.: Dorsey Press.

Wyatt-Brown, Bertram. (1988). 'The Evolution of Heroes' Honor in the Southern Literary Tradition.' In *The Evolution of Southern Culture*. N.V. Bartley, ed. Athens: The University of Georgia Press.

Index

on Quentin Compson *75,76,222, 248*
on racism *131*
on reliability *178*
on Shrevlin McCannon *229*
on the emptiness of words *102*
on the freedom of the character *12-13*
on the freedom to hope and believe *91*
on the 'realness' of the character *12*
on the universality of human emotions *14,23-24,91,276*
on Thomas Sutpen *212*
Fehr, B. *162*
Festinger, Leon A. *151,170*
Fillmore, Charles J. *31*
Fitzhugh, George *260,261-262*
Fivaz Depeursinge, Elizabeth *19*
Ford Jr., Lacy K. *252*
Forster, Edward Morgan *12*
Fort Sumter *274*
Foster, Gaines M. *259,261*
Foucault, Michel *150,152*
Fowler, Doreen *185*
Fowler, Roger *23,26,27,28,29,36, 46,47,51,91,149,269*
Frame, Janet *41*
Frames and scripts *37-40*
and alien norms *154*
and ambiguity *38*
and behavior *37*
and culture *37-38*
and default options *37*
and filling gaps *38*
and literature *37-40*
and mind-style *63,67*
and personality *40,59*
and prototype categories *37, 269-270*
and reality *37,38,40*
and retrospective transformation; backward action *39,48*
and rumors *169*

and stories; fictions *39-40*
as guiding norm *40*
as set of hypotheses *38*
baby frame *44-49*
changing of *39,44*
deathbed frame *97*
depression frame *63*
mental illness frame *67*
paranoia frame *82*
reframing; extending of the frame *39,48*
the danger of *170,196-197*
Frank, Lawrence K. *26*
Franny and Zooey 110
Freedman, William A. *87,92*
Freud, Anna *16,69*
Freud, Sigmund *12,14,15,16,17,18, 20,69,71,102,113,131,154,271, 283*
and literature *15*
and Faulkner *14-15,280*
Frontier life *252,254*
Frye, Douglas *47*
Fusion of the parents *18,72*

Gaps in the text *88,90,192-196*
Geismar, Maxwell *147*
Genette, Gérard *146,153,155,156*
Gibbons, Kathryn Gibbs *63*
Gidley, Mick *14*
Giffin, Kim *148,153*
Go Down Moses 24
Godden, Richard *174,175*
Goforth, David *280*
Goldsmith, John *36*
Gordon, Lyndall *12,69*
Gossip *168,169-170,177*
and frame knowledge *169*
Gray, Richard *191,198*
Guilt *18,77,87,103,104,118,130,153, 184,186,249,259-260,261,264,275*
and defense mechanisms *86-87,260*
and mind-style *261*
and the Southern defeat *261,275*
guilt thesis *261*

and defense mechanisms *71*
and the deictic system *70-71,116*
and double bind *21,69,151*
and fragmentation *70-71*
and honesty; sincerity *152*
and irony *72*
and language; thinking *70-71*
and laughter *66,67,69,72,115-116,*
236
and memory *71*
and metonymic substitution *71*
and poetry *72*
and reality; reality testing
68-69,71-72,115
and regression *71*
and silence *69*
and social interaction *71*
and synaesthesia *70*
as a communication disorder *20-21,*
69-70
as label *269*
biological predisposition *68-69*
etiology of *20,67-69*
pain of *69*
precipitating events *68*
splitting in *66,67,68,115-116,218,*
234,236
susceptible individuals *68-69*
syndrome *67-68*
symptoms *67-68,72,115*
Schoenberg, Estella *220,222,224,235,*
236,241
Scott, Anne Firor *262*
Sechehaye, Marguerite *70*
Self; I
and proper name *29,96*
and other; family, society,
history *8,22*
and text *8*
and the need for stories *278-279*
assigning roles to *29,46-47,*
62-63,80,98-99,105,106,117,
122-123,138,182-183,230-231,239
boundaries of *60,72,116*

(fear of) disintegration of *110,*
142
splitting of *34,45,66,106,107,*
109,115,218,234,236
Shakespeare, William *110,281*
Shaw, Valerie *147*
Short, Michael H. *44,48,50*
Sides, Sudie Duncan *262*
Sin *103-104,184,186*
Singal, Daniel Joseph *63,193,252,255,*
280,282
Slatoff, Walter J. *216*
Slavery; slaves *251-252,259-265,268,*
275
Small, Leonard *43-44,50*
Small-clause *32-35,44-45,51-52,*
128-129,197,213,231,234,236-237
Smith Churchland, Patricia *42,50*
Smith, Lillian *255,256,258,260,261,*
262,263,274,275
Smith, Septimus (character in *Mrs*
Dalloway) *152,153-154*
Snead, James A. *195*
Snell, Susan *14,124*
Sonne, Harly *50,69,70,71,115*
Spence, Donald P. *21,153,157,273*
Sperber, Dan *28*
Split brain patients *42*
St. Elmo *74*
Stampp, Kenneth M. *260,261,274*
Sternthal, B. *150,273*
Stone, Phil *14,124*
Suicide *21,75,76,78,86,98,222,223,*
248,256
Sumners, Bessie *10,249*
Synaesthesia *51*
and mental retardation *51*
and neurosis *187*
and schizophrenia *70*
and the small-clause *51-52,*
128-129

Taboo on Criticism *256*
Taylor, John. R. *27,28,29,44,45,54,*
55,269